SCIENCE AND PSYCHICAL PHENOMENA

SCIENCE AND PSYCHICAL PHENOMENA

BY

G. N. M. TYRRELL

133.07
T98

HARPER & BROTHERS
PUBLISHERS
NEW YORK AND LONDON

' Man is not born to solve the problem of the Universe, but to find out where the problem begins and then to restrain himself within the limits of the comprehensible.'

Goethe

PREFACE

PROBABLY no subject is more misunderstood than Psychical Research. By the general public it is supposed, vaguely, to have something to do with Spiritualism, if, indeed, it is not merely an alternative name for Spiritualism; and those who work in it are associated with crankiness and an amiable gullibility. The true importance of the subject, its seriousness and strictly scientific basis, are realized only by a few.

The object of the present book is to correct this impression and to substitute for it an accurate idea of what Psychical Research is, by offering to the reader an outline of what has been accomplished by strictly scientific method. In sketching this outline, I have not stopped short at a recital of the bare evidence, for, although a basis of fact is the first essential, facts alone are dull reading, and, also, no subject is adequately dealt with unless the *meaning* of the facts is taken into account. A good deal of space has therefore been devoted to theory and to the significance of the phenomena.

Since there is no subject on which opinions (even those of experts) differ so widely, none of the facts of Psychical Research have yet met with general acceptance. It is impossible, therefore, to adopt the impersonal method of treatment which can be accorded to an established science. Everything is a matter of opinion; and so it seemed best to write in the first person, freely criticizing from one's own point of view and expressing one's own opinions. This violates the injunction given to school-room essayists never to speak in the first person; but in the present instance it is hoped that the reader may find it more interesting.

In a book which undertakes to cover a large amount of ground in a small compass, the presentation of evidence is a difficult matter, since evidence, to be of any real value, must be presented at length and in detail. The pieces of evidence here quoted have, perforce, been abridged in most cases and should be regarded as samples, indicating to the reader the different classes for which they stand. The student of the subject is referred in all cases to the original reports. The greater part of the evidence has been taken from the records of the English Society for Psychical Research, since this body, owing to the length of time over which its work extends, and the high standard of evidence which it has always maintained, still constitutes the main source of reliable evidence. But this is not to say that good evidence does not exist elsewhere.

Although the standing of this Society and the quality of its work have been repeatedly stressed, the present volume is in no sense a publication written on its behalf or under its auspices, but is entirely an independent work for which I alone am responsible. And it must be made clear that none of the authors quoted are to be regarded as in any way responsible for theories or deductions which may have the appearance of being drawn from these quotations.

The highly speculative character of some of the following chapters may well invite criticism ; but criticism becomes by custom the native air of the psychical researcher, and if thereby thought is provoked and attention drawn to the importance of the subject, the most drastic criticism is welcome.

My thanks are due to the Council of the Society for Psychical Research for permission to quote from the Society's private *Journal*, as well as to those personally concerned in the quotations. Also to Dr. C. D. Broad, for permission to quote from a Paper read by him to the Aristotelian Society and Mind Association, and to Dr. H. H. Price for permission to quote from the discussion. Further, I am indebted to my wife for assistance in many ways, and for the preparation of the Index.

G.N.M.T.

March, 1938.

CONTENTS

PART IV

THE MEDIUMISTIC TRANCE

PART V

THEORETICAL ASPECT OF THE MEDIUMISTIC TRANCE

INTRODUCTION

TO write on the subject of Psychical Research is to write on a subject which a large number of people have already pigeon-holed in their minds and labelled as dealing with mediums, ghosts, spooks and spoof. Tags are tenacious things : it is difficult to remove them, and yet, until this is done, no reader who possesses such a tag is in a position to listen to a description of what psychical research is about. It is to be hoped that, if the reader's preconceived idea is not so strong as to prevent him from entering upon the subject, the label in course of reading may wear off.

Psychical research, properly so-called, is, in fact, a branch of Psychology—that is to say, it is an inquiry into the lesser-known faculties of the human mind ; and, if it lacks the murky sensationalism of Spiritualism and the Occult, it more than makes up for this loss by definiteness and by the deep significance which attaches to the results its sober methods of research have obtained. It may be regarded as a branch of psychology in this sense, that it has thrust out a spear-head into the unknown between normal psychology on the one hand, whose business it is to deal with the mind in relation to the affairs of ordinary life, and abnormal psychology, on the other, which deals with the mind in derangement and disease. Between these two lies a field of intense interest, wherein appear *unusual*, but not *abnormal*, states of consciousness, manifesting faculties of cognition and other phenomena, which do not appear in ordinary life, but which enable us to obtain a glimpse into the deepest recesses of human individuality.

Psychical Research lies at the meeting-point of three great

departments of human thought, Science, Philosophy, and Religion ; and the matter it deals with has a vital interest for all three ; but the centrality of its position and the importance of its matter are very far from being generally appreciated. It may be easier to see this if we reflect on the crucial character of knowledge about human personality and of how that personality lies at the core of most of the major problems with which society is faced. However impersonal and objective the outset of any inquiry may have been, in the end it has led back to man. Inquisitiveness first turned man's attention *outwards* to explore the natural world, and out of that inquisitiveness science was born. Curiosity about distant parts of the world led in the same way to geographical discovery, and both these outward-feeling movements marked the awakening of consciousness at the time of the Renaissance. But maturer experience stepped in to reinterpret the movement, and to show that if one goes on investigating long enough, the external world loses the pristine purity of its objectivity and independence. Philosophy, following the road of reason and analysis, discovered how large a contribution we ourselves make towards the sense-picture of the things about us ; while physical science has come to realize the relativity of its discoveries to the observer. So the outward movement swung full circle and is now pointing again to the pivotal character of its originator—man. We now see that all human problems, from those of religion at one end of the scale to those of economics at the other, are, at root, *psychological* problems. All the pathways of discovery lead, in the end, back to man. That is why the work of psychical research is so important. It is the only science which penetrates deep enough into human personality to shed a light on those urgent problems, which so far have oppressed and eluded us. But that is not all. At the same time, very significant side-lights are thrown on the nature of the external world through the strange faculty which psychical research has brought to light—

a faculty which appears to make contact with events without any visible means, and not only with contemporary events, but with future events as well.

No one whose interest is in the large and important things of life—who wishes to know what manner of being he is, what kind of world he lives in, how far the discoveries of science are to be accepted as final truth, where religion stands in the scheme of things and what reaction these other facts have on it, can afford to neglect psychical research. Humanity, in the modern world, is outgrowing its knowledge on just these points, and for lack of this knowledge is relapsing into materialism and violence. It is like the stars, which ' blindly run,' with no outlook beyond mechanism ; but it has reached the point of development at which it deserves the dignity of enlightenment, and alone of all the sciences psychical research appears to be in a position to provide it. From what other source is this enlightenment to come ? A science which is dependent on the senses cannot provide it, for the gold of enlightenment must come from beyond the purview of the senses. Perhaps it will be said that this is the province of religion. But where is the religion of inward experience ? May it not reasonably be doubted whether religion in the West has not dropped the essential gold in pursuit of worldly ascendency, or else has merged itself with philanthropic humanism ?

A famous psychologist once, speaking of Psychical Research, said : ' Unless Psychical Research—that is to say, inquiry according to the strictest principles of empirical science—can discover facts incompatible with materialism, materialism will continue to spread. No other power can stop it ; revealed religion and metaphysical philosophy are equally helpless before the advancing tide. And if that tide continues to rise and to advance as it is doing now, all the signs point to the view that it will be a destroying tide, that it will sweep away all the hard-won gains of humanity, all the moral traditions built up by the efforts of countless generations for the increase of truth, justice, and charity.' [1]

One of the strangest features in the thought of the present time is the widespread acceptance of that conjunction of irreconcilables, the belief that humanity matters as a collective whole, while the individual is intrinsically devoid of importance and merely exists as a unit to serve the interest of the community—as if the community had some invisible and supernatural existence of its own apart from the lives of the individuals who constitute it. It is precisely at this point that the study of Psychical Research acts as a corrective, by showing that the centre of importance lies in the individual and not in the mass.

Much of the scientific work in this subject has been done by the English Society for Psychical Research, a body founded in 1882 by a group of Cambridge men, who were determined to sift the mass of occult phenomena by rigorous scientific method and thorough criticism and to find out what, if anything, of truth it contained. They carried on their campaign in the teeth of a characteristically nineteenth-century opposition, and the Society they founded has since maintained the same high standard of work under a cross-fire of criticism, one camp accusing it of credulously dabbling in ' spooks,' while the opposite camp accuses it of a determined will to disprove the supernormal ! After fifty-five years of steady work, its *Proceedings* and *Journal* have grown into a veritable mine of carefully ascertained information. Yet comparatively few people care to read this information or take any interest in its work. The tag labelling psychical phenomena ' spooks and spoof ' is strong enough to prevent the majority of people from making a discriminating investigation for themselves. And so the work of a body which is scientific to the core (probably no other group of investigators has ever worked under so much

[1] W. McDougall, *Religion and the Sciences of Life*, p. 59.

scathing criticism or learnt to such good effect the use of care and caution) and whose presidents have been without exception men of distinction in science, literature or philosophy, is disregarded by all but a handful of far-seeing individuals. Nor has the work of psychical research been without its practical applications to immediate issues. Much of the knowledge brought to the study of neuroses after the War came through members of this Society; and numberless people have received from it the comfort of information based on solid fact when in the distress of bereavement.

Other bodies, of course, also carry on the work of psychical research on scientific lines, as, for example, the Boston Society for Psychic Research in America, and the Institut Métapsychique in France, besides individual undertakings. A welcome sign of the times is the tendency in certain cases for the subject to find a place in the psychological departments of universities. This has been notably the case in the Duke University, North Carolina, where Professor J. B. Rhine has introduced the subject into the laboratory and has carried out a series of noteworthy tests. (See Chapter VII.) Laboratory experiments, carried out on similar lines by the present writer, have also yielded results of remarkable interest. (See Chapter VIII.)

The first aspect of the subject to be dealt with will, however, be evidence of a spontaneously occurring kind.

Part I

SPONTANEOUS EXTRA-SENSORY
PERCEPTION

'Why we should dispute matter of fact because we cannot solve things of which we have no certain or demonstrative notions seems strange to me.'

Daniel Defoe : 'The Apparition of Mrs. Veal'

Chapter I

THE NATURE OF SPONTANEOUS EVIDENCE

THE CEMENT OF COMMUNITIES.—The present age, with its brightly lit stage of world-affairs, knit closely together by the inventions of science, tends to concentrate our attention on collective events and to destroy the leisure and peace of mind necessary for contemplating the problems of the individual. Although social problems are the more vociferous and urgent, individual problems are the deeper ; and, indeed, it is upon the nature and destiny of the individual that all else depends. Group-mankind, whether in the form of state or nation or as a world-whole, has no super-existence of its own. It is, and must remain, a group of loosely-knit individuals whose character and importance is solely dependent on that of the units who constitute it. But we are carried away. The fear of war ; revolts against the existing order in many parts of the world ; the appeal to youth, stirring it to a passion for nationalism in one place and for materialistic humanism in another, fixes our attention on states and communities, so that we forget how slender are the links which bind human individuals into these collective wholes, and in what abysmal depths of isolation the springs of thought and action are hidden.

Group-humanity bears a marked similarity with the non-living world by which it is surrounded, in that it manifests a similar inertia and conservatism and indifference to circumstances. It is resistant to change and lacking in spontaneity to such an extent as to become a fit subject for the attention of the statistician, who is able to predict much about its future behaviour. As individuals, for example, we all know that more care and consideration would eliminate most of the accidents

3

on the road ; and the public is continually being adjured to observe this necessary care. Yet the number of road-accidents during forthcoming weeks is predictable within narrow limits. Individually we all know that if mankind does not destroy its armaments, its armaments will destroy it. Yet it shows no change of character, though conservatism in the face of the danger means suicide. The machinery for peace is disregarded ; conferences are allowed to fail ; collective humanity behaves like a *thing*. It is not supra-human ; it is infra-human. It is in the individual that the centre of interest lies ; it is the individual which is the source of new reactions and new possibilities. Yet we disregard the individual. Instead of devoting our energies to exploring and understanding it we throw all our interest into the inept adventures of human groups.

It is astonishing to reflect on the inchoate character of the unity which a human group-aggregate possesses, and on the imperfection of the means by which its individual constituents make contact with one another. We know each other only by the use of five imperfect senses, which, in order to link mind with mind, are obliged to make use of roundabout channels through the external world. If one individual, A, wishes to communicate with another, B, the process is as follows. A, by movements of his body, brings about changes of some kind in the outer world, which B observes through his organs of sense, usually through those of sight or hearing. A may have spoken words or written them on paper or may have merely made certain gestures or changed his facial expression. B receives these as sights or sounds, which are really *codes* representing meanings according to a quite arbitrary system. But, because B is acquainted with this system, he is able to retranslate the code into the meanings which A intended to convey. Thus, all communications between minds are carried on, either by means of spoken or written words, which are highly sophisticated codes, or by means of gestures, which are simpler codes with universally understood meanings. All codes, in order that they may be transmitted, must be converted into alterations of something in the external world—it may be into peculiarly modified streams of sound-energy as in speech or telephony, or in alterations of physical objects as in writing and printing, or into any changes, in fact, which can suitably affect the senses of the recipient.

Upon these clumsy and roundabout code-systems, pregnant with opportunities for misunderstanding, the working of the social machine depends : so that it is, perhaps, not so surprising after all if human society continues to present, from age to age, the same symptoms of internal chaos, ' To understand is to sympathize.' People brought into really close contact with one another seldom fail to pull together ; but we do not sympathize because we do not understand ; and we do not understand because the inadequacy of our means of communication forces us to remain at arm's length from one another. The diplomatist who remarked that language is given us to conceal our thoughts, was making a cynical but apt comment on the inadequacy of the cement which binds human society together. Nothing would seem more necessary, if civilization is to continue, than a cement which would give more fundamental solidarity to corporate life. I do not suggest that any such cement exists in a form to be of use to the practical sociologist ; but it is of great interest to inquire whether there is any evidence that it exists at all.

In the present chapter, we shall have to consider this question. Do these five inadequate senses really exhaust the possibilities of communication between mind and mind ? There has always been a vague belief in some more direct mode of intercourse—a belief stretching back into a remote antiquity. A typical instance occurs in the Old Testament, where we find recorded the chagrin of the king of Syria at the mysterious leakage of his military secrets to his enemy, the king of Israel. ' Will ye not show me which of us is for the king of Israel ? ' ' None, my lord, O king : but Elisha the prophet that is in Israel telleth the king of Israel the words that thou speakest in thy bed-chamber.' [1] And perhaps the reaction of the king of Syria is still typical of that of the practical man of to-day. Traitors, he thought, were more

[1] 2 Kings, vi. 12.

likely than telepathy ; yet he had enough belief in the unknown to try to capture the alleged seer and put him out of harm's way.

Telepathy and psychical phenomena in general have always figured in folk-lore and legend and round them formed that distrusted block of phenomena known as the ' occult.' Only within quite recent times, since the coming of the study of the mind, has the subject been considered as in any way a possible one for scientific inquiry.

Definition of Terms.—Before attempting to describe what rigorous scientific method has won from this nebulous region, it will be necessary to define the terms to be used in the forthcoming chapters.

Extra-Sensory Perception.—I will begin with this as a term of very general scope used to cover all cases in which knowledge of things or events is acquired by a person, in whatever manner, without the use of the ordinary channels of sense-perception, of logical inference or of memory. Extra-sensory perception will be divided into two main heads : (i) Spontaneous and (ii) Experimental. The term is due to Dr. J. B. Rhine, Associate Professor of Psychology at Duke University, North Carolina, but he confines its use mainly to the second or experimental group of phenomena, whereas we shall use it here to denote both groups.

The Subliminal Self.—About the year 1900, when writing his classical work entitled *Human Personality and its Survival of Bodily Death*, Frederick Myers coined the term ' the Subliminal Self ' or self beneath the conscious threshold. He believed that the normal, conscious mind had a variable threshold (*limen*) and that beyond or beneath it (*sub*) there existed a wider region of the self, which could have intercourse with the normal or conscious portion through or across the threshold. Psychologists, largely owing to the work of Freud, also recognize an extra-conscious portion of the self, which they have called (perhaps not very fortunately) the ' Unconscious.' Myers' Subliminal and the psychologists' Unconscious overlap to a considerable extent, but the Unconscious was the product of the medical line of approach and largely supplied the needs of pathology, whereas the Subliminal was a much wider conception, including both the organizations of the subconscious and the manifestations of the supraconscious, as found in genius, states of ecstasy and the phenomena of psychical research. It should be noted that the term ' Unconscious ' is not, apparently, intended to make any statement as to the consciousness or unconsciousness of the portion of human personality to which it is applied but only to differentiate it from the normal consciousness. The ' Unconscious ' might, therefore, be co-conscious with the conscious !

Supernormal.—This term was applied to processes or events, etc., of an unrecognized kind, which are met with in psychical research, in preference to the older term ' supernatural,' since there is no reason to suppose that such processes, etc., are other than natural. A more recent version of the term is ' Paranormal.' It is difficult to define the word with precision since the line between Normal and Supernormal is by no means rigid. In the long run, it is doubtful whether Supernormal means anything more than Unusual.

Telepathy.—Myers, in 1882, defined Telepathy as ' the communication of impressions of any kind from one mind to another, independently of the recognized channels of sense.' [1]

Agent.—The person who transmits an impression telepathically to another, whether intentionally or not, is called the Agent.

Percipient.—The person who receives the telepathic impressions of another, whether intentionally or not, is called the Percipient.

Telaesthesia.—This term will be applied, without prejudice as to whether it exists or not, to the kind of telepathy in which the activities of Agent and Percipient are combined in one person. Thus, if A reaches out and helps himself to the contents of B's mind, without the knowledge or assistance of B, the process will be called Telaesthesia. The word is not used in this sense by all writers.

Subject.—The term ' Subject ' will be applied generally to

[1] *Human Personality*, vol. i. p. xxii.

any person who has a supernormal experience, or who is subjected to any kind of supernormal test or experiment.

Automatist.—Cases in which the movements of the body are controlled by the Subliminal instead of by the Supraliminal or normal self, are often called automatic movements or ' automatisms.' This term is especially applied to writing which is done without conscious control, and those who do this writing are called ' Automatists.'

Clairvoyance.—If a person becomes aware of some event or circumstance in the external world, of which no one else is cognizant (as, for example, of a card in a shuffled pack), the faculty involved will be called ' Clairvoyance.' It is not to be inferred from this that anything analagous to ' seeing ' necessarily enters into the process.

Precognition.—If knowledge is acquired of an event which has not yet happened, but which later happens as foretold ; and if this knowledge could not have been obtained by logical inference from present facts, and could not result from an intention to fulfil the prediction, and is of too precise or detailed a character for its fulfilment to be attributed to chance, then the case is said to be one of Precognition. Precognition thus means the *direct* perception of events which have not yet happened.

Retrocognition.—If knowledge is shown of an event which has happened in the past and which is unknown to any living person at the time when it is described, and has never come within the experience of the percipient and is beyond the range of fulfilment by chance, the knowledge is said to have been obtained by Retrocognition. Retrocognition is thus *direct* perception of events which are past. (The term is sometimes used in a different sense to indicate cases of revived memory.)

Hallucination.—If a person experiences sense-imagery which does not correspond with any physical fact in a way directly consistent with normal perception, he is said to experience a Hallucination. Hallucinations may be veridical in the sense that they may correspond with external events in an indirect manner.

The Nature of Spontaneous Evidence.—The investigation of

psychical phenomena which occur spontaneously does not lie strictly within the field of science. Since the evidence depends on the testimony of witnesses, of written records and of attendant circumstances, the methods employed are partly those of the historian and partly those of the law-courts. Professor Henri Bergson said : ' I am led to believe in telepathy in the same way that I believe, for example, in the defeat of the Invincible Armada.' [1] But, human testimony being notoriously fallible, it is essential, when collecting spontaneous evidence, to cross-examine the witnesses and to obtain corroboration wherever possible from independent witnesses and extraneous sources. All documents must be carefully examined and compared. There is also the question of the likelihood that a coincidence, apparently due to a causal connexion, may in reality be due to chance. Clearly the cases collected will vary a good deal in the matter of evidential quality. It may be taken as a general rule that only first hand evidence, corroborated by other witnesses, should be accepted ; but a good deal will depend on the character, intelligence, and reputation for accuracy of the principal witness.

The Society for Psychical Research has made it a rule never to publish evidence unless it has passed the test of close scrutiny on the above lines ; therefore its *Proceedings* and *Journal* contain a larger collection of well-evidenced cases than is to be found elsewhere ; and it is from this source that most of the examples quoted below have been taken.

How to Secure Good Evidence.—Hundreds of good cases have been lost because the percipients have not thought it worth while to take steps to make their experiences evidential at the time, or to report them at once to experts on the subject. A striking dream or other experience, if left unrecorded at the moment, because the experient feels that it would be foolish to make a fuss about it, soon fades from the memory and loses its evidential value. When a dream or impression is verified by subsequent events, it is only rarely that it has been written down beforehand. Frequently the percipient contents himself with telling his experience to one or more of his friends with-

[1] *Proc. S.P.R.*, vol. xxxi. p. 462.

out writing it down.   Even some of these cases may be good
evidence, provided the experience has been told to witnesses
before its fulfilment, and provided that the witnesses give their
testimony while it is still fresh in their memories.

In order to make a dream or waking impression as evidential
as possible, it should be written down as fully as possible at
once, the date, time, and all relevant details being inserted, and
the account shown to friends for their corroborative evidence
and signatures.   In the case of a dream, one should rouse
oneself sufficiently at the first moment of waking to jot down
the principal items, though only in a few brief words.   It is
not merely that dreams fade rapidly from the memory on
waking ; the full light of waking consciousness soon tends to
rationalize the dream and to work it into a sophisticated form.
Brief points jotted down at the time will serve to recall more
later.   A good plan is to write the account on a letter-card
addressed to oneself (or to an intimate friend) so as to obtain
independent evidence of the date from the post-office stamp,
which, on a letter-card, is stamped on the document itself.

Either the present writer or the Research Officer of the
Society for Psychical Research, 31 Tavistock Square, London,
W.C.1, will always be glad to receive well-attested cases for
record and publication in the Society's *Journal*.   Pseudonyms
may be used if desired, provided that the real names and
addresses of those concerned are known to the Society's
officers.   More cases of this kind are badly needed.   Although
the number of cases on record is large, the ideally perfect case
is very rare, and it is important to secure as many of these
as possible.

Two Theories of Evidence.—There are two schools of thought
which differ on one important point with regard to evidence.
One school believes in what has been called the ' faggot '
theory—that is to say, the theory that imperfect cases, when
added together, become cumulative in their evidence.   The
other school denies that, if cases are imperfect, the total
evidence can be made stronger by numbers.   Where there is a
flaw in each case, it says, there is always a possible alternative
explanation, and therefore numbers do not strengthen the

probability of the explanation we wish to test. Proof, it says, depends on the perfect case. But the perfect case is as rare as an unbroken pot in an archæologist's find.

Probably there is right on both sides in this argument. The important point is the *kind* of flaw which the cases present. If, for example, it had to be decided whether the movement of a table at a séance for physical phenomena were due to some unknown force or due to a fraudulent trick on the part of the medium ; and if in each case when the table moved a clear loophole had been left open for fraud, then each case might reasonably be explained as fraudulent, and the fact of a large number of cases would not increase the evidence in favour of an unknown force. The ' faggot ' principle would not hold in this case. But if, on the other hand, the cases were of dream-fulfilments and each case taken alone might just possibly have been fulfilled by chance, then the larger the number of cases the less likelihood would there be of chance explaining them all. The ' faggot ' principle would hold. If a number of cases are imperfect in various ways, yet all point in the direction of a single explanation, it is reasonable to regard their evidence as cumulative. In ordinary life, we estimate various degrees of probability, using the principle that probability is cumulative, and the results justify our assumption. We shall probably not go far wrong if we allow common sense to decide between the two principles in psychical research.

There is, unfortunately, a certain type of criticism of an unconstructive kind, which finds in these two principles an ' escape mechanism.' Confronted with a number of imperfect cases, it says : Numbers carry no weight if every case is imperfect ; to carry conviction we need the perfect case. When confronted with the perfect case, it takes the opposite view, saying : Of course a single case proves nothing ; if you want us to believe in these phenomena, you must give us numbers !

Before passing to actual examples of spontaneous evidence, I will quote the result of an early attempt to test the distribution of the extra-sensory faculty among the population at large.

Distribution of Spontaneous Extra-Sensory Faculty.—In 1889 a committee of the Society for Psychical Research undertook a ' Census of Hallucinations ' [1] in order to ascertain what proportion of persons experienced sensory hallucinations, and to inquire into the details of those reported. They appointed 410 collectors and the question they circulated was : ' Have you ever, when believing yourself to be completely awake, had a vivid impression of seeing or being touched by a living being or inanimate object or of hearing a voice ; which impression, so far as you could discover, was not due to any external, physical cause ? ' This was designed to exclude dreams and the hallucinations of delirium and insanity. In all, 17,000 persons were questioned and 1684 answered in the affirmative —that is to say, 9·9 per cent. When the hallucinations were graded according to the time which had elapsed between the occurrence of the vision and the date when the census question was answered, it was found that the number decreased rapidly as the date of occurrence became more remote, thus indicating that this kind of experience tends to be forgotten. It was decided that the number of visual hallucinations reported must be multiplied by four to allow for those obviously forgotten.

Many cases were concerned with death. Based on the figure of the then death-rate in England and Wales, of 19·15 per thousand, it was estimated that the probability that any one person taken at random will die on a given day was 1 in 19,000 : in other words, out of every 19,000 apparitions of living persons there should be one death-coincidence by chance, supposing that there is no causal connexion between the apparition and the death. Actually they found 440 in 19,000. By ' coincidence ' was meant an apparition occurring within twelve hours of the death of the person seen.

Thus, the inquiry indicated that vivid impressions of the type likely to provide material for an investigation into psychical phenomena do occur to about 10 per cent. of the normal population ; and, further, that the number of coincident death-apparitions thus occurring was very considerably greater than the number which would be expected to occur by pure chance. The inquiry proceeded ; and in the next chapter

[1] *Proc. S.P.R.* vol. x. pp. 25–422.

some instances will be given of collected cases of spontaneous telepathy.

Number of Spontaneous Cases Collected by the Society for Psychical Research.—With regard to the volume of spontaneous evidence which the cases given in Chapters II, III, and IV represent, the Society for Psychical Research has, since it began its work in 1882, collected and published in its *Journal* 1309 cases of Telepathy, and 306 cases of Clairvoyance and Precognition. A number of spontaneous cases have also been published in its *Proceedings*, which are not included in these totals, and there are among these 130 cases of Precognition. These, of course, were all cases which had been thoroughly examined and checked, and the evidential standard found good enough for publication. There are, in addition, hundreds of cases in the files, whose evidential standard was not considered good enough for publication.

Chapter II

EXAMPLES OF SPONTANEOUS EVIDENCE :
TELEPATHY

SUBDIVISIONS OF THE SPONTANEOUS PHENOMENA.—Spontaneous extra-sensory perception falls under four headings, namely, Telepathy, Clairvoyance, Precognition and Retrocognition—terms which have been already defined. A fairly large proportion of the cases have to do with death, and often take the form of apparent communications from a dead person, so that the *prima facie* explanation of them is that they are due to the intervention of discarnate spirits. This explanation will not be considered now, but will be discussed in the final summing up of the evidence. For the present, all these cases will be classed as examples of extra-sensory perception. It may be noted that, even if the theory of discarnate spirits were adopted, it would be necessary to invoke telepathy from the dead in the first class of evidence. In the second class, there would still be clairvoyance, but on the part of the deceased, who would, in addition, have to pass on their knowledge by telepathy to the living. And in the third and fourth classes the problems of pre- and retro-cognition would remain unaltered, even if it were the discarnate spirits who possessed these faculties.

Telepathic Cases. Case 1.—To begin with a case of simple, spontaneous telepathy.[1] Miss Margaret Jones, the percipient, wrote as follows :

' I have to go into details to explain the circumstances ; I was on night duty (as a professional nurse) which explains why I was asleep in the day-time. One evening, May 19, 1931, I was startled out of my sleep by a voice, which called out my name distinctly,

[1] *Journal S.P.R.*, vol. xxviii. p. 253.

" Margaret, Margaret." I felt positive that some one had been in my room by my bed and rushed out again. I was never called by my Christian name at the hospital ; however, I did not pay much attention to that as I was asleep. I thought it must have been the maid calling the night nurses, and she had not switched my light on. I got out of bed and looked down the corridor. I did not hear or see anybody. I looked at my clock ; *it was* 5.30 *p.m.* This was quite early, as we were not called until 7.30 p.m. I sat up in bed thinking over the strangeness of the situation. However, I dropped off to sleep again.

' At breakfast that night I told some of my colleagues about my strange experience and they just joked about it. I went on duty at 10.30 p.m. The night sister came to me, called me to one side, and asked me did I know any one living at ——. I said " Yes, my sister lives there." " Well, nurse," she said, " I am afraid there is bad news for you." She handed me a telegram which said : " Darling Peggy passed away at 5.30 p.m." The telegram had been opened by Sister, as there were five Nurse Joneses in that particular hospital. Peggy was my little niece, aged eight years. We were great friends. She was taken suddenly ill and an immediate operation was performed, but she lived only a few hours. When I met my sister I told her what I had experienced, and she told me that the child called out, " Margaret," and she remarked to her husband, " Is she calling herself or Auntie Margaret ? " It is a strange fact that the stated time of the child's death on the wire was 5.30 p.m., just about the time that I was disturbed from my sleep. I did not know the child was ill ; it was very sudden. I cannot describe my feelings as I read the telegram, which reminded me of my strange experience at 5.30 p.m.'

The following corroborative statement was sent by the child's mother :

' This is to certify that my husband and I were present at the death of my little daughter on May 19, 1931. It is true that she called out, " Margaret," and that at the time I remarked to my husband, " Is she calling out her own name or Auntie's ? " And that two days afterwards I learnt from my sister that she had been disturbed from her sleep by a voice calling out, " Margaret " (twice), and that the same evening she received a telegram from us informing her of the death of our child.'

One of Miss Jones's colleagues to whom, as stated above, she mentioned her experience at the time, has also sent a corroborative statement as follows :

' This is to certify I was present in May 1931 when Margaret Jones related her dream with reference to her niece calling.'

One may dismiss the theory that this was a case of purposeless fraud, in which the sister, the other nurse, and the parents of the dead child were all in collusion with Nurse Jones. And as there seems to be little scope for misreporting, the only reasonable explanation, apart from telepathy, is chance.

Fulfilment of Dreams and Spontaneous Impressions by Chance.—It will be convenient here, before going on to cite further cases, to consider the question of chance-fulfilment in rather more detail. Thousands of dreams, it may be said, are dreamed every night and amongst them all there must be some remarkable cases of fulfilment by chance-coincidence. The occasional coincidences are remembered, and the failures are forgotten. As Bacon said : ' Men mark when they hit ; never when they miss.' The freaks of chance occurring amongst millions of unfulfilled dreams are mistaken for instances of supernormal faculty. This is the explanation which many readers will doubtless be inclined to give of such apparently telepathic dreams as the above. Indeed, the argument shows that there is a great need for some definite means of measuring the probability of fulfilment of dreams by chance. We want to know just *how* likely it is that an apparent case of telepathy could have been brought about by chance. But anything like measurement in such cases is obviously extremely difficult.

There are, however, two points about veridical dreams and impressions which it is essential to bear in mind. (i) Many of them are complex, consisting not merely of one event, but of a number of distinct details. (ii) A large proportion of them, if looked into closely, will be found to be marked by a very vivid character or powerful effect which they have on the percipient, such as ordinary dreams do not have. In fact, it is questionable whether some of these night-visions should be classed as dreams at all.

(i) The first point was illustrated in Bergson's Presidential

Address to the Society for Psychical Research, already referred to. Professor Bergson recounted how a celebrated French doctor once told a story in his hearing of a lady who had dreamed of the scene on the battlefield in which her husband was actually killed—' vision précise, de tous points conforme a la realite ' (an exact picture, in accord with the facts in every detail). She took this for a telepathic dream ; but the doctor reminded his audience that many women dream that their husbands are dead or dying when, in fact, they are perfectly well. These non-fulfilled dreams, he said, are soon forgotten ; but the occasional case in which the dream happens to coincide by chance with reality is remembered. Afterwards, a young girl came to Professor Bergson and said that she felt that the doctor's reasoning was wrong, but she could not see where the flaw lay. The flaw, however, was there. The doctor had confused an intimation of the *fact* of death with a vision of a *concrete scene* in which the death occurred. It was not merely that the lady had dreamed that her husband had died at the moment when he actually did ; there were details in the dream-picture of persons, etc., who were actually present in the scene. Now, if a prediction contains a number of items, all of which are fulfilled, the probability that the complex whole will come true by chance is very much less than the probability that a single item will do so.

If one is dealing with a series of *independent* events, such as throws of a die, the probability that a series of predictions will be fulfilled by chance is the *product* of the separate probabilities of each event being so fulfilled. One cannot say that the items of a dream are necessarily independent events. One can only say that the odds against a complex dream being fulfilled by chance are very much greater than the odds against a dream consisting of one single item being so fulfilled.

(ii) The second argument runs as follows : A few ordinary dreams or ordinary waking impressions or imaginative experiences, among the vast number which occur, are bound to come true by chance. The coincidences may sometimes be startling, but there is no reason to suppose that those which do come true are ' supernormal ' or differ in any way from those

2

which do not. They are falsely credited with being supernormal merely because they are the few lucky hits amongst an immense number of failures. Thus, the argument implies that if chance be the explanation of veridical dreams and impressions, any traits which are characteristic of veridical cases must be equally characteristic of ordinary or non-veridical cases. If this is not so—if veridical dreams and impressions have anything peculiar about them which is different from the rest— then they form a separate class and cannot be included with non-veridical cases for statistical purposes. If, in such a case, we were to include them in the same class with ordinary cases for the estimation of chance, we should get a nonsensical result. We must therefore examine our veridical evidence to find out whether it is in any way different from the ordinary mass of dreams and impressions.

It is clear that, if we were to mix together two categories of things which in their nature are separate and were to treat them as one class for a statistical calculation, we should get a result which was meaningless. Suppose, for example, that it were desired to find the average height of a group of people by measuring the height of each individual and then dividing the sum of the heights by the number of individuals in the group. And suppose further that the measurers neglected to notice that some of the people when measured were sitting down while others were standing up, the average height when worked out would tell us nothing at all. That is precisely what we should be doing if we mixed two classes of dream-cases together which were in reality separate, and estimated the likelihood of their fulfilment by chance.

In Case 1, above quoted, Nurse Jones was impelled by the impressiveness of her dream to get out of bed, to look down the corridor, and to note the time. If her dream of hearing her niece's voice were a chance-coincidence, then it must be the common characteristic of most dreams that they make us get out of bed and do these things. But clearly most dreams do not have this effect, so that the evidence points to the case being not an ordinary dream. Reading at random four cases (not quoted here) which happened to be included in the same group of evidence from which Case 1 was taken, we find in the first : ' I awoke perspiring and immediately told my wife of my dream.' The next is a collective vision simultaneously seen by the husband and wife, while even the baby, it is stated, ' gave a slight shout ! ' In the next : ' The sequence of events detailed in the last two paragraphs was extraordinarily vivid and clear . . . the whole thing made a great impression on me.' Finally : ' I awakened suddenly as if some one had touched me.' I do not think one can say that any of these are the nightly experiences of every dreamer.

Another point which has to do with chance-fulfilment of dreams was brought forward by Professor E. R. Dodds in a letter to the *Journal S.P.R.* [1] Ordinary dreams, he argues, are not infinite in their variety, but on Freudian principles tend to divide themselves into recognised symbolical groups. ' Thousands of dreamers use the same symbols to express essentially similar situations,' he says. In particular he criticises the case of a lady who dreamed that she was being chased by a monkey and who, on going for a walk next morning, actually *was* chased by one.[2] This, says Professor Dodds, was a piece of Freudian symbolism, expressing fear of sexual assault, which is exceedingly common, he alleges, in dreams of women. The argument is that if dreams run on limited and stereotyped lines, the likelihood of chance-fulfilment will be increased. There certainly are some cases to which this Freudian argument might conceivably apply. There is, for example, the dream of a bishop's wife, who dreamed that a pig had strayed into her dining-room and who, on going into the room after reading family prayers, found that the pig was actually there.[3] Whether this, too, has a sexual significance, or is any kind of stereotyped symbol, I do not know ; but we are not told of any particularly vivid or impressive feature in this dream, so it might be included for chance estimation with dreams in general.

Professor Dodds suggests that the whole class of death-

----

[1] *Journal S.P.R.*, vol. xxviii. p. 204.
[2] *Proc. S.P.R.*, vol. xi. p. 488.
[3] Ibid. p. 487.

predictions is weakened as evidence for precognition because of the now recognized existence of the ' repressed death-wish,' which increases the number of cases in which people will dream of the death of their relations. But if we examine them, we find that the great majority of veridical dreams about death (as indeed of veridical dreams and impressions in general) are marked off from other dreams by one of the following characteristics—either by the powerful effect that they have on the percipient at the time, or else by being recurrent or collective.

I have read carefully 100 cases of veridical dreams or impressions and have found that 82 of them possess one or other of these characteristics. But I suggest that the reader who is inclined to attribute veridical dreams to chance should read through a collection of well authenticated cases, such as that given by Mr. H. F. Saltmarsh in his paper of *Cases of Apparent Precognition*,[1] and should form his own judgment on this point. I think he will find very few of them of which he can say candidly : ' This is just the kind of dream I dream every night.' And this is what we must be able to say of any veridical dream which is to be put into the same class with ordinary dreams for the purposes of chance-calculation.

It must be admitted, however, that the line dividing normal from supernormal dreams is not sharply drawn. There are certain dreams which are apparently veridical without being unusually impressive ; and certain others which are unusually impressive without being veridical. Professor C. D. Broad has mentioned a case of the latter. On or about April 6, 1937, he dreamed that news was being shouted in the streets that the King had died at the time of the Coronation. He was sufficiently impressed and shocked by the dream to get out of bed and make a note of it.[2] Fortunately, as everyone knows, the dream was not fulfilled. But, that it does not do to disregard impressive dreams because such cases exist, the following illustration shows. One night a lady, who is personally known to me, dreamed again and again that a friend of hers, C, was

---

[1] *Proc. S.P.R.*, vol. xlii. pp. 94–8.
[2] *Journal S.P.R.*, vol. xxx. p. 82.

in great distress. She knew in her dream that C was completely incapacitated and that she was going about doing business for C ' with a feeling of pressure and urgency.' In the morning she resisted a strong impulse to go to C, because a certain Mrs. X, an acquaintance of hers, had given many warnings about friends being ill or in trouble which had always proved untrue. In the evening, however, she was sent for to go to C, who had collapsed with a heart-attack and who died soon after removal to a nursing home. Then all the business of the funeral arrangements, etc., devolved upon the percipient, which, she said, ' produced exactly the travelling about and the feeling of great urgency and pressure that I had experienced in the dreams.' C's death was brought about by over-exertion after the heart-attack and, had the urgency of the dream been attended to, her life might have been saved.

The next case illustrates that class of telepathy in which the visual image of a living agent is perceived by the percipient. The case was sent in by Sir Oliver Lodge, to whom the original report and the corroborative statement were addressed. The names and addresses of those concerned are known to the Society for Psychical Research, but pseudonyms are given here. The following letter was received by Sir Oliver Lodge early in November 1922 :

Case 2 :

' I know you will forgive a letter from me as I think you will find it interesting from a psychic standpoint. I have had (without having studied psychology to any extent) two very definite instances of materialization, I believe it is called.

' One occasion in Vancouver three years ago. My mother was ill and I was tending her in our little flat till we came home to England, and shortly before leaving, a friend asked me to go to the theatre with her for the last time. Having settled my mother for the night, I was ready to go, and my mother said, " Now Marjorie, do *not* come in to me when you come home to-night unless I *call* you," and I said I would not go in.

' At 11.30 p.m. my friend, Miss M——, said before we parted, " Do come in and have some refreshment, cake, cocoa or something." I said, " No, thank you, I think I must go straight home, as mother might wake up and be anxious if she found I was not in." But Miss M—— persisted in asking me, and I thought, I suppose, very intensely as to how mother was, and if I could stay out later, and I ended by going, as I thought I should require something to eat, and if I got it at home I might make a noise and disturb mother, as our flat was very small. I stayed out about an hour more and went quietly to bed on my return.

' Imagine my amazement when the next morning the first thing my mother asked me was : " Marjorie, why did you come in to me last night when I asked you not to ? " Of course I told her I had not thought of going in to her, as that had been arranged. She said she saw me come in, bend over her as I had often done—without speaking. She saw the light from the landing behind me—and when I went out—and she went off to sleep again.

'E. MARJORIE STANLEY.'

In reply to a letter from Sir Oliver Lodge asking for corroborative evidence from the mother, Mrs. Stanley wrote as follows :

' My daughter has asked me to corroborate the experience she has had which I will now relate : We were at the time living in Vancouver ; I was not in good health, and she did not like leaving me, and for some time had not spent an evening out. However, this evening she went out, at about eight o'clock, leaving me in bed, and I particularly told her not to come into my room when she came back. I soon fell asleep, a dreamless sleep. After two hours, I should think, I woke to find my daughter stooping over me. There was no light in the room, but there appeared to be in the passage, which showed me my daughter's figure plainly as the door appeared open. Then it all disappeared and I was asleep again. In the morning I asked my daughter why she had come into my room as I had asked her *not* to, and was much amazed to hear she had not been.

'E. STANLEY.'

The covering letter from Miss Stanley with which this was enclosed, bears the date December 4, 1922.[1]

Miss Stanley had another similar experience, which is described in the same place, but is omitted here.

Cases such as this have an important bearing on the way in

[1] *Journal S.P.R.*, vol. xxi. p. 292.

which telepathy works. Notice that the percipient's experience bears no direct relation to what is consciously in the mind of the agent at the time—that is to say, it is in no sense a case of thought transference from one conscious mind to another. Miss Stanley was thinking intensely about her mother's health, but not of herself as standing in her mother's bedroom. The telepathic communication seems to take place entirely below the level of consciousness, and to reach the percipient's mind in the form of sense-imagery which the percipient *must have created*.

Sense-Imagery.—It may be noticed that all the senses can enter into these telepathically created sense-pictures. In Case 1 the auditory sense was invoked. In Case 2 it is the visual sense. In one case, not quoted here,[1] it is the sense of touch : the percipient was awakened by a kiss on the forehead and then saw the apparition. In another,[2] the percipient had a vivid dream about a bottle of violet scent, the odour of which seemed to her to fill the house, and even to persist after she was awake. And in the early days of experiments in thought-transference, successful experiments were carried out with tastes.[3]

In a case such as that of Miss Stanley's, it is natural to ask the question : ' Was she *really there* when her mother saw her ? ' Of course her body was elsewhere ; but was she there mentally ? Does the question : ' Was she there mentally ? ' mean anything, however ? Can a mind be *anywhere* in space ? It is clear, I think, that there is no possible criterion of a mind's position in space. What Mrs. Stanley ' saw,' as she lay in bed— her daughter's form bending over her and the light shining in from the passage (which was actually dark)—was a telepathic message unconsciously sent by her daughter and occurring as a transaction between the subliminal portions or phases of the two minds, but translated finally into terms which could appeal to the conscious part of Mrs. Stanley's mind, namely, into a complete picture created out of visual sense-imagery.

[1] *Journal S.P.R.*, vol. xxvi. p. 133.
[2] Ibid. vol. xxi. p. 294.
[3] E. Gurney, *Phantasms of the Living*, p. 44.

Another case to which I shall give no number, since, for personal reasons, I am unable to quote it, but which I shall refer to as the ' pillow ' case, shows this point about imagery, perhaps, more clearly. A lady woke early one morning and saw what appeared to be half a sheet of note-paper lying on her pillow with the words written on it : ' Elsie (pseudonym) was dying last night.' There was only one person to which the message could refer and it turned out that she had, in fact, died during that night.

This shows very clearly the method employed by the subliminal self to bring to the notice of the conscious mind information which it has telepathically acquired. The telepathy in these cases apparently takes place in two stages : (i) the acquisition of the knowledge by the subconscious part of the mind, (ii) the passing on of the knowledge from the subconscious to the conscious mind by the *creation* of a visual hallucination which represents it.

Case 3.[1]—The next case is of a curious kind. The percipient during, at any rate, the first part of his experience, felt as though he were *identified* with one of the actors in the drama. Mr. Dudley F. Walker, of 18 Shepherd's Hill, Stoughton, near Guildford, dreamed on the night of June 27, 1928, that he was the witness of a railway accident. Describing his dream, he says :

' I was in an overhead signal-box, extending over a railway-line I had never seen before. It was night, and I saw approaching what I knew was an excursion train, full of people, returning from some big function. I knew it was my duty to signal this train through, which I did, but at the same time I had a feeling that the train was doomed. (I have nothing to do with railway work.)

' In my dream I seemed to hover in the air, and follow the express as it slowed to round a loop line. As it approached a station I saw, to my horror, another small train on the same line. Although they seemed both travelling slowly, they met with terrible impact. I saw the express and its coaches pitch and twist in the air, and the noise was terrible. Afterwards, I walked beside the wreckage in the dim light of dawn, viewing with a feeling of terror the huge

[1] *Journal S.P.R.*, vol. xxiv. p. 379.

overturned engine and smashed coaches, I was now amid an indescribable scene of horror, with dead and injured people, and rescue
workers everywhere.

' Most of the bodies lying by the side of the track were those of
woman and girls. As I passed with some unknown person leading
me, I saw one man's body in a ghastly state, lifted out and laid on
the side of an overturned coach.

' I distinctly heard a doctor say : " Poor chap, he's dead."
Some other voice said : " I believe I saw his eyelids move." Then
the doctor said : " It is only your nerves ; he has been dead some
time."

' I was quite upset on getting up, and felt too unwell to eat any
breakfast. All day at business I have been thinking about this
dream.

' On coming home, you can imagine my feelings when I beheld
the placards announcing the accident.'

Mr. Walker gave a detailed account of his dream to his
mother (who thereupon repeated it to her daughter). He also
told it to the Managing Director of his business, in both cases
before the news of the disaster was known. He also entered a
short note of it in his diary as soon as he arrived at the office
in the morning. An associate of the Society for Psychical
Research, who saw these documents and questioned the
percipient, discovered that the latter knew nothing of railway
management, knew no one at Darlington, and had never
before dreamed of a railway disaster. There seems indeed to
be no assignable reason why he should have been singled out
for this telepathic experience.

The *Northern Echo*, of Thursday, June 28, 1928, printed
the following account of the accident :

' A terrible accident occurred just before midnight last night
outside Darlington Bank Top Station.

' A Newcastle-Scarborough excursion returning to Newcastle,
collided at about 11.20 with an express goods train for London
from the North. The excursion train was full of trippers.

' It was learned at three this morning that at least eight people
were killed and about thirty injured. The eight bodies are those of
a man, six women, and one little girl. . . .

' The trains crashed with great force. Two coaches of the excursion train were telescoped and the engine of one of the trains was completely derailed and lay broadside on to the track.

' There were distressing scenes. . . . One gruesome sight was that of a man's body lying on top of one of the carriages. . . .'

There was also a brief account in the *Daily Mail*.

The percipient said that he was ' perfectly convinced that this is no ordinary dream ' ; that he was too upset by it to eat any breakfast that morning, and that he thought about it all day at business : also he was so struck by it that he immediately told it to others and entered it in his diary. So the point brought out before, that veridical dreams are marked off into a different class from others by something striking, compelling or vivid in their character, is well illustrated in this case. Clearly, if we are to estimate the probability of this dream being a coincidence which happened by chance to coincide with the real accident, on the basis that it is a lucky hit amongst the class of ordinary dreams, we shall have to maintain that there is nothing unusual about it—that is to say, we shall have to maintain that ordinary dreams affect thousands of people every night in the same way that this dream affected Mr. Walker. And they certainly do not. If they did, the business of going to sleep would be so hectic that doctors would be mainly engaged in curing us from the effects of our nights' rests !

Case 4.—The next case is a long one and has been greatly abridged. Mr. D., a Glasgow manufacturer, had befriended and taken into his employment, when almost starving, a youth named Robert Mackenzie, and the youth, in consequence, had become passionately attached to his employer. In 1862, Mr. D. settled in London and some eight or ten years later had a vivid dream, ' with no vagueness as in common dreams,' he says. He dreamed on a Tuesday morning, just before 8 a.m., that, as he was engaged in business with some one unknown, Robert Mackenzie appeared, thrusting himself forward with some importunity, and saying that he had not done a thing of which he was accused, and that he wished his

employer to know it and to forgive him.   Asked what it was
of which he was accused, Mackenzie said, ' Ye'll sune ken,'
in the most fervid tones, and at that Mr. D. awoke.   Shortly
afterwards his wife burst into the room, holding a letter in her
hand, and said, ' Oh, James, here's a terrible end to the work-
man's ball.   Robert Mackenzie has committed suicide ! '   To
this Mr. D. replied that he knew he had not, for Mackenzie
himself had just been there to tell him so.   In the dream, Mr.
D. had noticed, without being able to account for it, that
Mackenzie's face was ' of an indescribable bluish-pale colour,
and on his forehead appeared spots which seemed like blots of
sweat.   A letter soon arrived from the Manager in Glasgow
saying that on Saturday night, after the ball, Mackenzie had
drunk a glass of *aqua fortis* and had died in great agony.   It
was at first believed that he had committed suicide, but it
afterwards appeared that he had gulped down the *aqua fortis*
in mistake for whisky.

Here two veridical points were conveyed by the dream
(i) that Mackenzie was accused of doing something he had not
done, and (ii) the appearance of his face, which corresponded
with symptoms of acid-poisoning.   In considering chance as
an explanation we have again to notice the outstanding nature
of the experience as it impressed the percipient, ' not vague as
in common dreams,' says the narrator :   also there was ' no
blurring of outline or rapid passages from one thing disconnectedly to another.' [1]

If this was a case of telepathy, since Mackenzie died on
Sunday night and the dream occurred at 8 a.m. on Tuesday,
the emergence of the telepathic impulse must have been delayed
for over two days.   Mr. Gurney interviewed the narrator, and
said that his ' professional reputation was of the highest order.'

Case 5.—In this case the telepathic explanation becomes
more complex and roundabout, the *prima facie* explanation
of discarnate intervention being very strong.   The facts of the
case had already been sifted by members of the legal profession
in a contested law-suit, before a Canadian member of the

[1] *Proc. S.P.R.*, vol. iii. pp. 95–8.

S.P.R. instructed a lawyer to investigate the case on his own behalf, and the lawyer's full report was forwarded to the Society for Psychical Research in England, together with all documents and the sworn statements of two of the parties concerned.

James L. Chaffin, a farmer in Davie County, North Carolina, had four sons, John, James, Marshall, and Abner. On November 16, 1905, he made a will leaving his farm to his third son, Marshall, and leaving his widow and his three other sons unprovided for.   On January 16, 1919, being dissatisfied with this will, he made another as follows :

' After reading the 27th chapter of Genesis, I, James L. Chaffin, do make my last will and testament, and here it is.   I want, after giving my body a decent burial, my little property to be equally divided between my four children, if they are living at my death, both personal and real estate divided equal if not living, give share to their children.   And if she is living, you must all take care of your mammy.   Now this is my last will and testament.   Witness my hand and seal.

' JAMES L. CHAFFIN,
' This January 16, 1919.'

This will, though unattested, would be held legal in North Carolina, if proved to be in the testator's handwriting.

Having written the will, the testator placed it between two pages of a family Bible, folding the pages over so as to make a sort of pocket enclosing the will and choosing that part of the 27th chapter of Genesis which tells how Jacob supplanted Esau.

For some inscrutable reason, the testator did not mention the existence of this second will to any one, but, instead, wrote on a roll of paper, ' read the 27th chapter of Genesis in my daddie's old Bible,' and stitched up the paper in the inside pocket of one of his overcoats.

On September 7, 1921, the testator died as the result of a fall, and his third son, Marshall, obtained probate of the first will, which the mother and other brothers did not contest, knowing of no reason for doing so.

In June 1925 the second son, James, according to his own statement, began to have very vivid dreams. His father appeared at his bedside, and towards the end of June he appeared wearing a black overcoat, which the son recognized. Finally the apparition spoke. Pulling back its coat it said, ' You will find my will in my overcoat pocket.' Then it disappeared. The overcoat was sought for and found at the house of the eldest son, John, who lived twenty miles away, and the roll of paper was found stitched up in the pocket. In the presence of witnesses, who were Mr. T. Blackwelder and his daughter, as well as James Chaffin's daughter and the testator's widow, the Bible was found and opened, and the second will discovered to be in it. A law-suit about the second will was thereupon started, and in course of time came up for hearing in the following December. Meanwhile, the father's apparition again appeared to James and, to quote James's words, said, ' " Where is my old will ? " and showed considerable temper.'

Mr. Blackwelder writes as a witness his own attestation of these events. The son, Marshall, had died a year after his father, and, during the hearing of the case, the parties came to an amicable agreement about the new will, and the law-suit was abandoned. This new will was accepted by the Superior Court of Davie County, and the old will rescinded in December 1925, a copy of this judgment being enclosed with the evidence. Ten witnesses were prepared to give evidence that the second will was in the testator's handwriting, and the widow and the son seem to have admitted it as soon as they saw it. At any rate, they withdrew their opposition. So it seems incredible that the second will could have been a ' fake.'

The lawyer employed by the reporter of the case cross-examined the Chaffin family and tried to induce them to admit that there might have been a subconscious knowledge of the will hidden in the old Bible, but they said, ' Nay ; such an explanation is impossible. We never heard of the existence of the will till the visitation from my father's spirit.' He also says that he was much impressed by their appearance as ' honest, honourable country people.'

To explain this as a case of telepathy, one must note that

the telepathic impulse, if received by James, the son, from his father before the latter's death, must have lain dormant for three years and nine months before externalizing itself. This makes a telepathic explanation scarcely plausible. Perhaps the case is more likely to have been clairvoyant, James being the subject, and the dreams being the dramatic form which the clairvoyant message took in revealing itself to the percipient's conscious mind.

At any rate, setting aside the obvious view that the information came from the deceased father, the case illustrates a certain blending which often seems to occur of telepathy with clairvoyance. Mrs. Henry Sidgwick, in an article *On the Evidence for Clairvoyance*,[1] draws attention to the same thing when she says : ' It sometimes happens that B seems to see the scene of A's death as it actually occurred, with details which we can hardly suppose to have originated in the mind of B by accident, or to be due to previous knowledge or association, and which are unlikely to have been consciously in the mind of A.' Here there would be a kind of mingling of clairvoyance with telepathy, which again supports the view that the two are in some way very closely connected. Knowledge of B's death, telepathically received, combined with details clairvoyantly perceived, as if the two faculties were scarcely independent.

These few cases are merely examples of a large number, which the reader who is seriously interested is advised to study for himself.

We will now go on to consider some cases in which the conditions were such as to make it necessary to suppose that clairvoyance was operating alone.

[1] *Proc. S.P.R.*, vol. vii. p. 30.

Chapter III

EXAMPLES OF SPONTANEOUS EVIDENCE :
CLAIRVOYANCE

CLAIRVOYANT CASES. *Case* 6.—The following case was received by Mr. Saltmarsh as the result of an article on *Precognition* which he published in the *Spectator* of December 13, 1935 : [1]

' Letter from Mr. X (whose name and address is known to the Society), dated 1936, January 20 :

' " I send you herewith an account of an occurrence which took place in July last.

' " One afternoon my wife and I took a run into the country, with the intention of having a picnic and the expectation of a little fishing for myself.

' " On arrival at the place I left my wife near the bridge which crosses the stream and went off fishing. The stream runs through a wood, hardly a mile long, but very dense in parts and thick with undergrowth. There are no proper paths, as it is very little frequented, being far away from any village. On returning about two hours later, happening to put my hand in my pocket, I found a hole and that a small key which locked a drawer where I kept certain papers was missing. When and where the key had fallen I could not say. If here in the wood, there was no use looking for it. It would be worse than looking for a needle in a haystack. So the matter dropped.

' " Next morning my wife said she had had a dream. In her dream she was in the wood, sitting on a fallen tree trunk, and near a mossy stone she saw the key.

' " So impressed was she with the reality of the dream that in spite of my dissuasion she went there again that day, went through the wood, guided as it were by some force, until she saw the tree of her dream. Then she sat down on it for a few minutes, and then

[1] *Journal S.P.R.*, vol. xxix. p. 272.

saw the key beside the stone exactly as she had dreamt. I was greatly impressed when she came home in the evening with the key. She had not gone through the wood previously and had no knowledge where I had gone.

' " I may say that my wife has told me before of like happenings, but this one I can verify as being absolutely true."

' Mrs. X writes : " This is to confirm that all my husband has written regarding the loss of his key, together with my dream and the finding of the key, is quite correct." '

Here there is no question of some latent memory having been revived in the dream, since the percipient had never been in the wood before. Nor is a chance explanation plausible. The dream-vision included the mossy stone and the particular tree in addition to the spot in the wood where the key lay, and these three particulars could not possibly have been hit off together by chance. Telepathy as an explanation would be roundabout. One would have to suppose that Mr. X knew *subconsciously* where the key had been dropped, and passed on this knowledge, together with a subconscious memory of the surroundings, telepathically to his wife, who visualized it in her dreams. It sounds rather unplausible and looks more like direct clairvoyant perception of the scene.

Note that the feature of compelling emphasis, which is usually present in veridical dreams, is a feature of this dream also. Mrs. X felt a compulsion to go back to the wood, which was strong enough to overcome her husband's attempts to dissuade her.

Case 7.—A case of interest in connexion with clairvoyance may be mentioned next, although, from its nature, no corroboration of the percipient's statement is possible. The Editor of the *Journal S.P.R.* says, however : [1]

' We have no doubt whatever that to the best of his knowledge the writer has given an accurate account of what occurred." (Abstracting from this account, the writer says that he had been reading instances of people having seen hallucinatory clock-faces which showed the correct time.) ' Next morning,' he continues,

[1] *Journal S.P.R.*, vol. xxi. p. 54.

' after a long, hot climb on a Scotch mountain, I had lain down on the heather and gone to sleep ; some time later, perhaps an hour or an hour and a half, I awoke into a very drowsy state, and, before I had opened my eyes or moved in any way, the thought " . . . What's the time . . . ? " came vaguely into my mind, linked with the feeling that though close in spirit with my luncheon I was far removed from it physically. Following immediately came a per-fectly clear visualization of the face of my own watch, the hands being at " just short of twelve minutes to one."

' So absolutely life-like was it, indeed, that I had noted the time, exactly and at leisure, before I realized that my watch was still in my waistcoat pocket, that I had not yet opened my eyes, and that I was, in fact, supposed to be still half asleep.'

After describing how he gradually awoke and was dazzled by the sunshine, the writer says : ' Out came my watch : the minute-hand was just perceptibly past where it had been.' He means just past where he had seen it in his dream. This is probably a case of clairvoyance, although it might possibly have been one of subliminal calculation of time, reckoned from when last the percipient had looked at his watch.

Case 8.—This case belongs strictly under the heading of the mediumistic trance, but as it is susceptible of explanation as clairvoyance, it is more conveniently treated here. At a sitting with the medium, Mrs. Thompson, the sitter being Mrs. Verrall, it was stated that Mrs. A's mother ' had put things in a book of receipts, and that in particular there was a recipe for pomade, which she called ' pomatum.' The existence of the recipe-book was known only to Mrs. A, and no one knew of any recipe for pomade. Although there was what appeared to be a complete index, no mention of a recipe for pomade appeared in it. The book was written in from both ends ; at last, after a long search, the recipe for pomade was found. The comment is made that ' it was not very easy to find, even for those who had leisure to search.' The recipe-book had been left in a house to which Mrs. Thompson had never had access, and it appears that no living person knew of the existence of the recipe for pomade, which was known only to the deceased

3

communicator, Mrs. A's mother, who had compiled the book.[1]

Case 9.—A very interesting case, which serves the double purpose of illustrating the faculty of clairvoyance as well as that of object-reading, is given by Dr. Eugène Osty in his book, *Supernormal Faculties of Man.*[2] Dr. Osty's work will be mentioned again : he is well known in this country as a careful and able French investigator, and as director of the *Institut Métapsychique International.* He says :

' On March 18, 1914, M. Louis Mirault, manager of the estates of Baron Jaubert, living in the Château de Givry, near Cours-les-Barres (Cher), wrote to me to inquire whether it might be possible to trace an old man who had disappeared since March 2, and of whom no trace could be found, despite long and active search.

' I accepted, and M. Mirault brought me a neck-wrapper belonging to the old man taken from a wardrobe. In order not to complicate the experiment I asked him to tell me nothing about the old man's disappearance, but only to give me an exact description of him, so that I might be able to recognize any details that the sensitive might give. . . . He only told me that the man was eighty-two years of age and walked with a stoop. Nothing more.

' I was up to that time ignorant of the old man's existence. Concerning the estate of Baron Jaubert, which covers about 2750 acres of woods, I knew no more than can be seen from the road to the château.

' These were the conditions under which, on Monday, March 23, I placed the neck-wrapper in the hands of Mme Morel, in deep hypnosis, in Paris. She had never been to the department of Cher.

' " Look," I said, " for the person whose neckerchief I place in your hand." Mme Morel first described a person whom I recognized as myself, then that of another man who seemed to be M. Mirault, then that of a woman whom I thought might be the daughter-in-law of the old man, and lastly, that of the old man himself. Here are her words, *verbatim*.

' " I see a man lying at full length, his eyes are closed, as if sleeping, but he does not breathe . . . he is dead. . . . He is not

[1] *Proc. S.P.R.*, vol. xvii. p. 181.
[2] pp. 104–9.

in bed but on the ground . . . the ground is damp, very damp . . . flat ground, uncultivated. . . . There is water not far off . . . a large tree . . . some very big thing quite near . . . something very bushy—a wood."

' " Follow that man on the day he went there. Look for the way he went."

' " I see a country house. . . . He leaves that . . . he walks. . . . He is ill, his breathing is difficult . . . and his brain is confused. . . . He leaves the path . . . goes into a thicket, a wood . . . he sees much water near by . . . he falls on the damp ground . . . then after a little time he breathes no more. It is not far from the house to the place where he is lying. . . . Follow the path from the house towards the water. There are two paths from the house, one goes up and the other down towards the water. The latter is the one to take ; he went that way."

' " Describe the place where he is lying and give a description so as to find the place."

' " I see blocks of stone . . . very large trees . . . and water. . . . I see the body . . . it is lying on the wet ground. . . . He is bald, has a long nose . . . a little white hair above his ears and at the back of his head . . . wearing a long coat . . . soft shirt . . . hands closed. . . . I see one finger which has been hurt . . . very old and wrinkled . . . pendant lips. . . . Forehead much furrowed, very high and open. . . . He is lying on his right side, one leg bent under him."

' " Why did he fall there ? "

' " He threw himself down . . . confused ideas. . . . He fled from his house ; a troubled brain. . . . He had a notion of dying . . . he wished to die and lay down on the ground . . . it was then damp, but the rains have made it much wetter." '

Those searching were surprised at the exact description given of the old man, but they knew of no stones, and large trees were plentiful in the neighbourhood : there were several ponds, which had been dragged. All they knew was that the man was Etienne Lerasle, aged eighty-two, who had left his son's house on March 2 for his daily walk, and had not returned. The villagers had searched ; and on March 5, eighty men had been set to search by the Mayor, but without success.

In the course of two further sittings, Mme Morel repeated

the former details and added a description of the path which the old man had followed from his house, which was sufficiently accurate for the path to be identified.   Five men searched in the direction indicated, and one of them presently came across the ' stone ' which the sensitive had mentioned, and farther on found the body.   But the ' stone ' was really a huge tree-trunk, out of the ground, which looked like a moss-covered rock.   The ground was flat and there was a pool near by, and large trees as described.   The dress and appearance were as the sensitive had said.   The distance was about three-fifths of a mile from the house, which corresponded with the description ' not far.'

Looking at this case as an example of clairvoyance, we notice that the description of the old man could have been obtained telepathically from the minds of the villagers who knew him ; but the details of the position and appearance of the body and its surroundings, as well as of the path which he had taken, must be regarded as having been obtained clairvoyantly. With regard to the suggestion that Mme Morel's description may have been a piece of clever guesswork, at any rate it enabled the searchers to find the body, which they had been looking for in vain for a month.   This remarkable sensitive, who has worked habitually with Dr. Osty for a long time, had not been accustomed to the atmosphere of spiritualism, in which so many mediums develop.   Had she been so, it is quite probable that the information would have taken the form of messages proceeding from the deceased Lerasle.   As it was, it came as an impersonal description of the events.

We shall return presently to one strange feature of this case, namely, the rôle played by the old man's neckerchief.   For the present, the point to notice is that all the four cases quoted in this chapter contain incidents which exclude the explanation of telepathy from the mind of any one living, or at any rate, as in Case 6, render such an explanation extremely roundabout and far-fetched.   They all point to the existence of a faculty which can get in touch directly with events themselves, and this faculty we have called Clairvoyance.   The spontaneous cases giving evidence of clairvoyance are not nearly so numerous as those which we class as telepathy ; but it is not to be inferred from this that clairvoyance is necessarily rarer than telepathy, but only that the circumstances are usually such as to make both modes of cognition possible.

Clairvoyance, if we admit the evidence for it, is a fact of a very startling and far-reaching kind, remote from anything which occurs in common experience, and, if it exists, it must be a fact of major importance for human knowledge.   But a still more startling fact, if it be true, is Precognition, the knowledge of events before they happen.   In the next chapter, we will examine a few examples of this extraordinary faculty.

Chapter IV

EXAMPLES OF SPONTANEOUS EVIDENCE :
PRECOGNITION

PRECOGNITION.—In one sense of the word, ' Precognition ' is common enough. The aim of science, it is often said, is to enable us to predict and to perform actions which we know will bring about certain results. Astronomers, also, predict such events as eclipses ; statisticians predict what will happen to the population fifty years hence, or what the number of accidents will be on the roads next week. These latter predictions, however, are not exact ; they are only true within limits, being statistical inferences drawn from a knowledge of present facts. They do not in any literal sense peer into the *future*, for, in principle, they do not differ from the geologist's deductions about the state of the earth in the *past*, or the ordinary person's inferences about what is happening elsewhere in the *present*.

There is also another form of prediction, which is based on intention. Jones may predict that he will be in his office at ten o'clock as he sets out with the *intention* of catching the 9.15. Railway time-tables are books of prophecy of this kind, based on human intention, and more or less accurately verified by events.

But precognition, in the sense in which we are using the term, is something very different from this. It means, or appears to mean, *direct prehension* of events which have not yet occurred. Some people would deny the possibility of this kind of precognition out of hand, maintaining that it is a logical impossibility. They would say that future events cannot be apprehended *now* because they do not yet exist. But let us resist the impulse to jump to conclusions and examine the proposition more closely.

We have first to note that cases may arise which look like precognition at first sight, but which may, in reality, have other explanations. If we take the activity of the subconscious mind into account, there are the following possibilities : (i) A person who makes a prediction may have subconsciously observed certain facts and drawn certain conclusions without being aware of it. All this may rise to consciousness in the form of a prediction and the prediction may be fulfilled because his subconscious inferences were sound. (ii) A person may have formed a subconscious intention to do a certain thing and may have subconsciously initiated a train of events likely to bring this thing about, and subconscious knowledge of this may rise to consciousness in the form of a prediction. (iii) After a person has made a prediction from some cause or other, the fact of having made it may induce in him a subconscious desire to fulfil it, and he may unconsciously bring the fulfilment about. (iv) Some human being unknown to the subject may have either drawn a correct inference about some future event, or may have formed an intention of bringing about some event, and this may be telepathically and subconsciously transferred to the subject, who may externalize it in the form of a prediction about the event. Some events, of course, are beyond the power of the subject to influence. In order to be genuine instances of foreknowledge, cases of precognition must be inexplicable under any of the above headings ; and in considering the evidence, these possibilities should be borne in mind.

Let us now consider some examples. First, a very simple case.

Precognitive Cases.   Case 10.[1]—The young lady from whom we have the next case does not wish her name to be printed.

August 31, 1884.

' About a year ago, as nearly as I can remember, I had a remarkably vivid dream—that I went to Richmond Park (from London) with my sisters, and that upon a seat I found a brooch, which I gave to the maid. I mentioned this dream to the maid as she was doing

---

[1] Taken from a paper, 'On the Evidence for Premonitions,' by Mrs. Henry Sidgwick (*Proc.*, vol. v. pp. 345–6).

my hair next morning, also to one of my sisters. I did not at the time of the dream know that we were going to Richmond on the following afternoon.

' However, we did so, and as I was walking towards a bench with one of my sisters, we saw upon it a large, common black brooch. My sister claimed it, as being the elder, but in a few days she gave it to me, and I gave it to the maid.

' I may add that I dream a great deal, and sometimes prophetically. For instance, I dreamed one night last week that I received a letter from one of my cousins. In the morning I told my sister, who went downstairs and found on the table this particular letter, which I had no especial reason for expecting on that morning.

Her sister says in corroboration :

' " This is to certify that I remember that my sister told me that she dreamed she had found a brooch in Richmond Park on the morning after the dream, and before its fulfilment." '

This dream cannot be explained as telepathy from the loser of the brooch, as the precipient did not know at the time that she was going to Richmond Park ; or as a fulfilment of a subconscious intention to go there, since her going depended on the arrangements of her sisters.

In the next case, although from the nature of the incident there could be no witness of the percipient's subjective experience beforehand, the police were witnesses of the results of the accident. The case is reported in the *Journal S.P.R.* as follows :

Case 11 :

' We have received the following narrative through the Countess of Balfour, to whom the circumstances were described by Mr. Eames, of whom she was a patient, within a fortnight of the occurrence. He afterwards very kindly wrote out this account, incorporating in it the answers to some questions we asked.

' " *Narrative Statement of Mr. E. G. Eames*

' " On Saturday, May 24, 1930, I was driving as usual from St. Albans to London, along a road I knew exceedingly well, for I had traversed it hundreds and hundreds of times. My car is a fast one, I drive fastly, for I am always in a hurry, and on this particular morning I had some five operations to perform in London before lunch.

' " But a preceding car had for long prevented me from accelerating to a really quick speed. It was a Jowett car, being driven carefully and quietly by a typical family man, in a typical leisurely manner. The father, mother, and kiddie all enjoying the run, one assumes.

' " In the ordinary way I should have passed by, as I pass by hundreds of similar tourists and forgotten them—miles back. But on this occasion I absolutely could not pass. It was not the car that prevented me. On the contrary, it would have been easy to have got by, and I wanted to get by, but something insinuated into my subconscious brain that an accident was going to occur. It was definitely a force quite apart from, shall I say, earthly impressions. It was in no ways concerned with the driving of the man in front. Actually, he was driving very well. It certainly wasn't nerves, it was a very real presentiment that a crash was going to occur and a warning not to approach too near. For five miles then I hesitated behind this slow-going old car, blaming my foolishness, but very much aware all the time of a holding back. Soon, however, I was to be very grateful indeed for this intimation, for when we reached a point in Watling Street between Radlet and St. Albans the looked-for accident occurred.

' " A lorry preceded the Jowett which was immediately in front of me. The three of us slowly making our ways to London. On the opposite side of the road, a saloon car had stopped. Suddenly the door of the stationary car opened, the huge lorry, obliterating the entire view of the road could not quite get by. Without warning he stopped abruptly. The poor little Jowett went on. Turned out, found his road completely blocked in every direction, braked violently, skidded, and crashed first into the back part of the lorry and then into a brick wall.

' " And for five miles I had known very distinctly that it was going to happen. So very much so that during that time I had felt very inclined to go up and mention my presentiment to the driver of the little family car.

' " All that remains to say is that being immediately behind I must in the ordinary way have been smashed up too, but had kept just far enough back to be able to come to a standstill immediately beside the wrecked car.

' " I attended to the little child, who was badly cut, and rushed both he and his mother to the Orthopædic Hospital at Stanmore where I left him in the hands of the surgeons.

' " A local police-officer reviewing all the details of the accident later, after measurements, etc., had been confirmed, was quite unable to understand at all how I had managed myself to avoid being injured or at least concerned in the smash, and when I rather reticently explained that I gathered something was going to happen, and this in spite of the care of the driver, he, knowing my usual speed, one assumes, said, ' It *must* have been a blooming strong *presentiment* for you to have waited behind.' Which, quite frankly, I feel you will agree, was that.

' " This is the third time in my life that I have felt these strong compelling forces or influences warning me of danger, and always I have been afterwards very deeply grateful that I have been fore-warned." ' [1]

One may agree with the policeman that the strength and urgency of a subliminal message could scarcely be put to a severer test than that of keeping a fast-driving motorist behind a slow car for five miles ! In nearly every case this forcible feature makes its appearance and marks off the veridical case from the non-veridical one.

The next case is remarkable in that the percipient was a Quaker, and as such not only opposed to racing and betting, but unlikely to embellish his account or to make inaccurate statements.

Case 12.—Dream of the Result of a Race.[2]

Mr. John H. Williams, a Cornish Quaker, of Willcott, Woodwarde Road, Dulwich, sent in the following account of a dream which he experienced on the morning of Derby Day, May 31, 1933. Mr. Williams, an octogenarian, was taking his breakfast in bed. He says :

' I am an ardent opponent of betting and gambling, was not thinking of the Derby, am not interested in racing, and did not

[1] *Journal S.P.R.*, vol. xxvi. p. 117.
[2] Ibid. vol. xxviii. p. 216.

know the names of any of the horses in the race which was to be run at about 2 p.m.

'I fell asleep at 8.20 and at 8.35 was aroused from a dream in which I heard a detailed account of the race as by radio, and the names of the first four winners—Hyperion, King Salmon, and two others which I failed to remember (not being acquainted with the names) and was suddenly cut off by the knock at my door with breakfast.

'I had dreamed of listening-in on 'phones from a rather ancient crystal receiver and hearing the whole of the race from the start to "around Tattenham Corner," and, in excited tones, how Hyperion gained the lead and won, when I was disturbed.

'I knew the crystal set was out of order, but was so impressed with the seeming reality of the account that I resolved to put the set right and listen at 2 p.m. This I did, and when the race was proceeding, heard the identical expressions and names as in the dream !

'Can this be explained ?

'In confirmation of the above, to remove any natural doubt by readers of this, it may be well to mention that the same morning at eleven o'clock, having to make a short journey by 'bus, I met a neighbour in it to whom I related my morning's experience and asked him to note the result of the race. I also told it to another person in Peckham, to whom I went on business matters at 11.20 a.m.

'The neighbour referred to was also heard to relate in a restaurant, long before the race, what I had told him at 11 a.m.

'The two persons to whom I spoke in the morning hereby certify to the fact by their signatures, viz. :

(Signed) C. A. YOUNG, 71 Court Lane, Dulwich.
                  Retired Civil Servant.
          W. E. ROWLAND DOUGHTY, 7 Camomile
                  Street, E.C.3.   Certified Accountant.
          JOHN H. WILLIAMS (also a Cornish Quaker).
30 *November* 1933.

Mr. Saltmarsh wrote to the two witnesses and Mr. Doughty replied as follows (March 2, 1934) :

'With great pleasure I accede to your request for permission to publish my signature certifying that Mr. John H. Williams related the story of his dream to me.

' On the morning of Derby Day I was working at the address of a client in Rye Lane, Peckham, when an elderly gentleman called and agreed to wait for the return of my client who had just gone out. He sat down in the office with me and we chatted together when the subject of betting came under discussion and the credulity of those who bet in signs and omens. In the course of conversation Mr. Williams told me that he had had a dream, to which backers of horses would attach much significance. . . . " During the interval of my first awakening and getting up, I fell asleep again," said Mr. Williams, " and dreamed that I was listening-in to a wireless account of the Derby : the progress of the race was described by the announcer, and at last I heard him say " Hyperion has won." ' '

' My client returned during the morning, and when Mr. Williams had gone I repeated to him the story Mr. Williams had told me, and ascertained the name and profession of his caller.'

Mr. Young replied as follows (March 3, 1934) :

' I am quite willing that you should publish my name as verifying the narrative of Mr. Williams's dream.

' The main facts are incontestable. On the morning of last Derby Day I boarded a 'bus for about fifteen minutes' run, and Mr. Williams, whom I knew as a casual acquaintance, got on the same 'bus. We settled down to a chat. The time being about 11.30 or a little earlier.

' Mr. Williams then related to me the incident he has described. As I have the elderly man's failing of not being quite certain of remembering all the remarks that passed, I will give what I am certain of. After commenting on the usual topic, the weather, Mr. Williams said I had a curious thing happen to me this morning. . . . I had my breakfast in bed and then dropped off to sleep, and I heard quite clearly the result of the Derby come through on the wireless and the shouts of " Hyperion first " or " Hyperion wins " (I cannot be certain which and I don't remember whether he told me he also heard the other placed horses).

' As Mr. Williams is the last person in the world to suggest an interest in racing, I observed to him that he must have unconsciously read the names of the Derby horses in the morning paper, but he assured me that he had not then seen the daily paper.

' I was so impressed and interested by his dream that I mentioned it to several persons—a clerk in my local bank, a bank manager I met at a monthly lunch at a " Settlement " at 12.30, and this last relation was heard by other visitors at that luncheon.

' I may perhaps add that the first time I saw Mr. Williams afterwards, he told me that the wireless announcement, which he had the curiosity to listen to, was exactly as he had heard it in his dream.'

The only point of difference in the evidence is that both Mr. Young and Mr. Doughty spoke only of one horse being mentioned by Mr. Williams to them, and confirmed this in subsequent letters. But Mr. Williams, interviewed by the Research Officer of the S.P.R. (who regarded him as an excellent witness), was quite clear that he dreamed definitely of the first four horses of the race. Despite this discrepancy, the case is a good one.

With regard to the theory that the explanation might be chance-coincidence, one has to remember, as is so often the case, that it is not merely a matter of the probability of guessing the first two horses, but that the percipient says that he ' heard the identical expressions and names as in the dream ' when he listened to the wireless announcer.

Case 13.[1]—The next case is abridged from a long account of a remarkable veridical dream and its sequel which occurred many years ago, but which at the time was well attested. The case is rare, for not only did the same dream recur three times at long intervals, but the fulfilment took place no less than six years after the first intimation of it. The percipient, Lady Q, writes :

' My father died when I was a child ; my mother married again, and I went to live with an uncle, who became like a father to me. In the spring of 1882 I dreamt that my sister and I were sitting in my uncle's drawing-room. In my dream it was a brilliant spring day, and from the window we saw quantities of flowers in the garden, many more than were in fact to be seen from that window. But over the garden there lay a thin covering of snow. I knew in my dream that my uncle had been found dead by the side of a certain bridle-path about three miles from the house—a field-road where

[1] *Proc. S.P.R.*, vol. xi. p. 577.

I had often ridden with him, and along which he often rode when going to fish in a neighbouring lake. I knew that his horse was standing by him, and that he was wearing a dark homespun suit of cloth made from the wool of a herd of black sheep which he kept. I knew that his body was being brought home in a waggon with two horses, with hay at the bottom, and that we were waiting for his body to arrive. Then in my dream the waggon came to the door ; and two men well known to me—one a gardener, the other the kennel huntsman—helped to carry the body up the stairs, which were rather narrow. My uncle was a very tall and heavy man, and in my dream I saw the men carrying him with difficulty, and his left hand hanging down and striking against the banisters as the men mounted the stairs. This detail gave me in my dream an unreasonable horror. I could not help painfully thinking, " Oh, why did they not prevent his hand from being bruised in this way ? "

' In the sadness and horror of this sight I awoke, and I slept no more that night. I had determined not to tell my uncle of the dream ; but in the morning I looked so changed and ill that I could not escape his affectionate questioning. . . .'

We may note in this last detail the powerful effect of the dream on the dreamer.

Lady Q goes on to say how she made her uncle promise not to go that way unaccompanied after that : ' Two years passed by, and the thought of the dream was becoming less frequent, when I dreamt it again with all its details the same as before, and again with the same profoundly disturbing effect.'

Finally : ' In the May of 1888 I was in London expecting my baby. On the night before I was taken ill, I dreamt the same dream again, but with this variation. . . .' Lady Q in this dream knew she was in London ; and, after the scene of bringing home the body, a gentleman dressed in black, whose face she could not see, stood by her bedside and told her that her uncle was dead. A few days later her stepfather, dressed in black, came and stood by her bedside, and she recognized the figure in the dream and said : ' The Colonel is dead—I know all about it—I have dreamt it often.'

Lady Q's uncle had felt faint and slipped from his horse in the very place she had dreamed of, and had died of heart-disease. ' The same two men,' she continues, ' whom I had seen in my dream as helping to carry the body, had, in fact, done so, and my nurse admitted that the left hand knocked against the banisters. The body, she says, had been brought back as she described and he was wearing the same homespun suit she had seen in her dreams.

The multitudes of flowers and the snow did not figure in the actual scene ; but they carried a significance for the percipient which makes it fairly clear that they were introduced into the dream as being symbolical of death.

The account is signed by both Lord and Lady Q, and is stated by them to be true in every particular. Lady Q's stepfather also attests what happened when he informed Lady Q in London of her uncle's death. It is also stated that an unauthorized version of the main points was compiled shortly after the event. It is very unlikely that the percipient should be mistaken about a recurrent dream of this nature ; and extremely unlikely that all the details should be fulfilled by chance.

If it be accepted, it is striking on account of the length of time (six years) which elapsed between the first dream and its final fulfilment. It also raises the question of free-will in an acute form. If we suppose that human, voluntary action breaks into a rigid causal sequence in some way, which would otherwise render every future event ' fixed,' in the sense of being implicit in present conditions, would not a single free action of the part of the uncle during these six years have prevented the fulfilment of the dream, or at least altered it in some of its details ?

In a few cases, which are of exceptional interest, the course of events foretold by the precipient are partly, but not wholly, fulfilled. It looks in these cases as if any one with knowledge of the prediction itself can use that knowledge to turn the course of events. The following is an abridged account of one of these cases.

Frederick Myers, in reporting this case, says that Lady Z, the experient, who recounts the case, was personally known to him.

Case 14 :

' We were living in about 188–, in Hertford Street, Mayfair. One day I determined that on the morrow I would drive to Woolwich in our brougham, taking my little child and nurse, to spend the day with a relation.   During the night I had a painfully clear dream in vision of the brougham turning up one of the streets north of Piccadilly ;   and then of myself standing on the pavement and holding my child, our old coachman falling on his head on the road—his hat smashed in.   This so much discomposed me that when in the morning I sent for the coachman to give him his orders, I almost hoped that some obstacle to the drive might arise, so that I might have an excuse for going by train.   The coachman was an old and valued servant.   I asked him if he would have the carriage ready to drive to Woolwich at ten.   He was not given to making difficulties ;   but he hesitated, and when I suggested eleven instead, he said that he would prefer that hour.   He gave no reason for his hesitation and said that the horse was quite well.   I told him almost eagerly that I could quite well go by train ;   but he said that all was right.

' We went to Woolwich and spent the day.   All went well until we reached Piccadilly on the return journey.   Then I saw that other coachmen were looking at us ;   and looking through the glass front of the brougham I saw that the coachman was leaning back in his seat, as though the horses were pulling violently, of which, however, I felt no sign.   We turned up Down Street.   He retained his attitude.   My dream flashed back upon me.   I called to him to stop, jumped out, caught hold of my child, and called to a policeman to catch the coachman.   Just as he did so the coachman swayed and fell off the box.   If I had been in the least less prompt, he would have fallen just as I saw him in my dream.   I found afterwards that the poor man had been suffering from a serious attack of diarrhœa on the previous day, and had gradually fainted from exhaustion during the drive home.   He was absolutely sober ; and his only mistake had been in thinking that he was strong enough to undertake the long drive.   In this case my premonitory dream differed from the reality in two points.   In my dream we approached Down Street from the west ;   in reality we came from the east.   In my dream the coachman actually fell on his head ;   the crushing of his hat on the road being the most vivid point of the dream.   In reality this was just averted by the prompt action which my anxious memory of the dream inspired.[1]

(Signed)   '[LADY Z.]'

The coming to Down Street from the opposite direction, as well as the saving of the coachman's fall, suggests, not so much a preperception of the physical occurrence itself, as a constructed picture based on a more or less fluid nexus of possibilities.

Case 15.—Although not strictly belonging to the class of spontaneous cases, a small and apparently precognitive incident, which occurred in the automatic scripts of Dame Edith Lyttelton, may suitably be referred to here. In the course of a long series of automatic writings the following occurred : On February 20, 1914, Mrs. Lyttelton wrote the name ' Lusitania,' and in the immediate context the words, ' foam and fire—mest [*sic*] the funnel,' thus showing conclusively that the ship *Lusitania* was being referred to. The principal reason, says Mr. J. G. Piddington, in reporting on these writings, against regarding the coincidence as accidental, is that, ' " Lusitania " occurs twice in a series of scripts which for various reasons appear to contain a good many predictions of the Great War, in which the sinking of the *Lusitania* was an event of outstanding importance.'

The *Lusitania*, it may be remembered, was sunk on May 7, 1915—that is, some fifteen months after the above script was written.

The Main Body of the Spontaneous Evidence for Precognition.—For further information concerning precognitive evidence of the spontaneous kind, the reader is referred to the report on the subject by Mr. H. F. Saltmarsh, which has been already mentioned, and which contains a careful survey of the cases collected by the Society for Psychical Research during more than fifty years. In this report, the evidence for each case is examined and the cases graded according to evidential value. Although all have been previously scrutinized before acceptance, the writer rejects the weakest and is still left

[1] *Proc. S.P.R.*, vol. xi. p. 497.

4

with 183 cases, which constitute, as he says, ' a mass of evidence far too weighty to be set aside.' These cases are recommended to the reader as well worthy of study ; also some remarkably interesting cases recorded by Eugène Osty,[1] and several cases in the *Revue Métapsychique*.

At the end of what may be called his expert examination of the evidence, Mr. Saltmarsh writes : ' After prolonged study I have no hesitation in affirming that precognitions do occur. In doing so I have the support of many authorities in psychical research.   Should the reader feel any doubt remaining, I would refer him to Professor Chas. Richet's excellent little book, *L'Avenir et la Prémonition*.' [2]

Retrocognition.—We now come to the curious alleged faculty of retrocognition.   Certainly, if one admits precognition it would be unreasonable to boggle over retrocognition. A faculty which can range forwards in time may surely also range backwards.   But a little reflection will show that evidence for retrocognition, if it exists, will be far harder to obtain. Almost every past event which can be verified is either in some one's memory or is recorded in some document or exists in a hidden object of some sort, so that, if we admit telepathy and clairvoyance, they almost always form an alternative explanation of cases of apparent retrocognition.   It is not surprising, therefore, that the evidence for genuine retrocognition is small.

One well-known case of apparent retrocognition is contained in the series of incidents reported by Miss Anne Moberley and Miss E. F. Jourdain in their book entitled *An Adventure.* They described how, sometimes together and sometimes alone, on various occasions during the years 1901, 1902, 1904, and 1908, they seemed to be walking in the Gardens of Versailles as they were in the time of Marie Antoinette, in or about the year 1789.

Retrocognitive Case.—The case which I shall quote here is,

---

[1] *Supernormal Faculties in Man.   (La Connaissance Supranormale.)*
[2] A book entitled *Some Cases of Prediction*, by Dame Edith Lyttelton (Bell, 2s. 6d.), contains some interesting and hitherto unpublished cases of Precognition.

however, one reported by Miss A. Goodrich Freer, taken
from among her many interesting experiences.[1] She was
a lady of a robust and by no means neurotic type of
mind, personally known to Frederick Myers, who writes of
her : ' I have been intimately acquainted with Miss A. and
her family for some years, and have personally witnessed
many of these phenomena.'[2] The case is related by Lady
Radnor, who was present with the percipient in Salisbury
Cathedral when it occurred.

Case 16 :

' On February 23, 1890, Miss A. and I were in the " Cage "
[or Hungerford Chapel] and she told me she saw a grand ceremonial
taking place. There appeared to be a tall chair which obstructed
the view down the choir, and gradually the place appeared filled
with clericals and others dressed in their best attire. Then she
saw a tall big man, slowly walking up, dressed in red and with white
lace over it, something that hung round his neck and down to his
feet of gold and embroidery, and a broad sort of mitre (but not
peaked) more like a biretta, of beautiful embroidery.
' Then there were three or four dressed very much like him,
gorgeously dressed, and lots of little boys about in red and white
and lace—holding candles, books, etc. The whole place was very
full of people, and it was evidently a great occasion. After the
principal figure had knelt in front of the chair—looking to the
west for some little time—he stood up, and ten little boys lifted up
the chair, and carried it higher up and placed it in front of the altar,
still facing west. Then the principal figure walked up two steps and
faced the east. (The whole of the arrangements of the altar, etc., as
Miss A. saw them, are quite different from what they are now.)
[It is here meant that Miss A.'s description was correct for that past
date ; as Lord Radnor explicitly told me was the case.] He had
nothing on his head now. He knelt some little time, and then the
most gorgeously dressed of the other figures placed something like
a mitre on his head and retired, and the principal figure walked up
to the chair, and sat down on it facing the congregation. Miss A.
said she saw him later dead in a coffin, with the Winchester Cross

[1] See *Essays in Psychical Research*, by Miss X, London, 1899.
[2] *Human Personality*, vol. i. p. 590.

over him. She says he was tall, big, clean-shaven, a little curling hair, and blue-grey eyes.

' Miss A. asked what she was seeing, and the answer came by raps.

' (*A.*) The induction of Briant Uppa.

' Then Miss A. said : " There can't be such a name ; it must be wrong."

' She tried again, and got :

' (*A.*) You are wrong. It is Duppa, not Uppa. Brian Duppa. (*Q.*) Who was Brian Duppa ? (*A.*) Chister. (*Q.*) What was he ? (*A.*) Bishop here. (*Q.*) When ? or what was his date ? (*A.*) 44–16. His researches would help you. Manuscripts should lay in Winchester.

' On returning home, we were talking after tea, and I casually took up Britton's *History of Wiltshire*, and said to Miss A., laughing : " Now I will look for your bishop. . . ." The pages where the bishops' names were were uncut, sides and top. I cut them, and to our delight we found on p. 149 :

' " Brian Duppa or De Uphaugh, D.D. . . . tutor to Prince Charles . . . translated to the See of Chichester (Chister ?) . . . Bishop of 1641 . . . (deposed soon after by Parliament) . . . preferred soon after the Restoration to the See of Winchester." He was at Carisbrooke with Charles I, and is supposed to have assisted him in the writing of the *Eikon Basilike*, which book Miss A. had been looking at in my boudoir a few days previously, but which contains no mention of him nor his name.' [1]

It is, of course, possible to suppose that Miss Goodrich Freer had read all these details and had completely forgotten about them afterwards, but it does not seem likely, especially as this is not an isolated case of hers. There is one small point about the psychology of emergence which is worth noticing, namely, the way in which the date 1644 is given. We shall find other instances of this curious inversion later.

Object-Reading or ' Psychometry.'—Another strange phenomenon, which psychical research has disclosed, is the power possessed by some sensitives of obtaining present, past, or future facts about a person's life, as well as about their traits of character and personal appearance, by touching some object

[1] *Human Personality*, vol. i. p. 592.

which they have possessed or touched. There seems to be some evidence that the holding of an object which belongs, or has belonged, to a person in some way helps the trance-medium to get into touch with the person. We read, for example, in the careful report which Mrs. Henry Sidgwick wrote on Mrs. Piper's trance, of how an object, or ' influence,' was put into the medium's hand. ' One's first impression,' she says, ' naturally is that all this must be nonsense, but the evidence on the whole seems to show that some effect is produced by influences, though probably not in the way controls say and perhaps think.' [1] But the most striking examples appear to come from French sensitives and have been the subject of prolonged study by Dr. Eugène Osty, the able medical man above referred to, who gave up his practice in order to carry out the study of psychical phenomena on strictly scientific lines, while organizing the Institut Métapsychique in Paris to assist him in this work.

Mme Morel, one of the best sensitives with whom Dr. Osty worked, was particularly successful in the art of character-reading through objects, and a large number of interesting examples will be found in his book already referred to. Owing to the exigencies of space, the only case which can be quoted here is Case 9, which must serve the double purpose of illustrating Clairvoyance and Object-reading.

The theoretical significance of object-reading is great, and the following points summarized from Dr. Osty's work on it must here be noticed.

(i) It is found that if an object, which has belonged to a particular person, is handed to the sensitive, Mme Morel, she describes not necessarily the person to whom it belongs, but any one who happens to have touched it. Sometimes Dr. Osty himself is described, or the person who has brought the object. When asked to describe the person to whom the object belongs, she will sometimes do so, and sometimes describe yet another person who has touched it.[2] (ii) A single contact between the sensitive and the object is often sufficient. Once

[1] *Proc. S.P.R.*, vol. xxviii. p. 306.
[2] Eugène Osty, *Supernormal Faculties in Man*, p. 190.

the train of information has been started, the object can be destroyed without affecting the supply of information, which continues afterwards. Even though fresh events may have happened to the possessor of the object after its destruction, these events will be described.[1] (iii) With some sensitives the object is not necessary at all ; similar information is given without it.[1] (iv) Correct information about persons who have touched the object is not limited to their present or to their past, but includes their future as well.[2]

It is pretty clear, therefore, that the function of the object is not that of *conveying* information which has been in some way stamped upon it. Its function must be to act as a link for putting the sensitive *en rapport* with the subject. One may note here that in Case 9, the neckerchief belonging to the old man, which was brought to Mme Morel, was taken from his wardrobe *after* his departure and had not accompanied him on his last, fatal walk ; yet this did not prevent the sensitive from following the events which happened to him after he had left the neckerchief behind. It seems that one must regard the sensitive's achievement as in some way telepathic ; but it must be a kind of acquisitive telepathy, which we have here decided to call ' telaesthesia.' It seems able to ransack a subject's mind and the ransacking is not confined to the mind as it is at present.

Object-reading would appear to be evidence, therefore, for the faculty of telaesthesia. We shall return to this question when dealing with the mediumistic trance. But there is one more lesson to be drawn from it, namely, that a close connexion must exist between telepathy and clairvoyance. *Somehow* the presence of the physical object assists the operation of this telæsthetic form of telepathy. But the relation between a physical object and the extra-sensory faculty is just the puzzle set by clairvoyance. If only we knew *how* the object affected the telaesthesia we should have made a great step towards understanding clairvoyance. But that is just what we do not know. All we can say is that it points strongly towards the

[1] Eugène Osty, *Supernormal Faculties in Man*, p. 191.
[2] Ibid. chap. iv.

view that there must be a vast amount of *something behind* the physical object as it appears to our senses.   In fact, the sense-presentation of the physical world must be the thinnest and most conventionalized of abstractions if we accept the evidence for clairvoyance and object-reading.

The close link between telepathy and clairvoyance comes into view again in the evidence supplied by the ' Book-tests,' which we shall deal with presently ; and yet again in the Experimental work, which we shall now deal with in Part II.

Psychical research is often criticized as not being an experimental science.   It is said that it depends for its evidence on the word of doubtful witnesses, and that until it enters the laboratory and produces its results to order under test conditions, it cannot expect to be taken much notice of.

Possibly the critics who make this judgment would be surprised if they knew how much experimental evidence there is.   For some inscrutable reason, people criticize psychical research without troubling to look at the evidence, which they often seem to consider irrelevant.   There is, in fact, much more experimental evidence than can be dealt with in the present volume, even in briefest summary.   Some attempt, however, will be made in the next four chapters to place an epitome of it before the reader by giving, first, a cursory account of the historical lines of approach, and afterwards a review of more recent work in greater detail.

Part II

EXPERIMENTAL EXTRA-SENSORY
PERCEPTION

'There is hardly any form of telepathy that cannot be imitated by conjurers and other professional entertainers.'

Wells and Huxley : ' The Science of Life '

Chapter V

THE HISTORY OF THE SUBJECT

HISTORICAL SUMMARY.—Like the spontaneous aspect of extra-sensory perception, the experimental aspect also reveals the faculty under the three divisions of Telepathy, Clairvoyance, and Precognition. The fourth, and more doubtful, division, Retrocognition, has not yet, so far as I am aware, entered the experimental field.

Most of the early experimental work was carried out under conditions which allowed of the operation of telepathy and clairvoyance simultaneously. The first necessity was, of course, to establish the existence of the extra-sensory faculty before distinguishing between its modes. The subject entered on its experimental phase with the discovery of Mesmerism in the eighteenth century, the rationalizing tendency of thought at that time tending to interpret psychical phenomena in terms of ' forces ' or physical ' influences ' emanating from the operator and affecting the subject, so that the basis for scientific experiment began to be laid. Esdaile, Presidency Surgeon in Calcutta, and other competent men vouched for the existence of the faculty, although their experiments no doubt lacked the scientific accuracy we should demand to-day. But Edmund Gurney, writing of these early times, says : ' We cannot but account it strange that such items of testimony as these men supplied should have been neglected, even by those who were most repelled by the ignorance and fanaticism which infected a large amount of the mesmeric literature.' [1] But, perhaps, in the light of the attitude taken up by men of science to-day towards far stronger evidence, it was not so strange after all.

[1] *Phantasms of the Living*, p. 10.

In 1881–2 [1] experiments were made with the Creery family by a group of investigators which included Professor Barrett, Mr. and Mrs. Sidgwick, Professor Balfour Stewart, and Professor Alfred Hopkinson, in which playing-cards, words and numbers were used, the Creery children proving to be especially good subjects. In 497 trials there were 95 first-guess successes, the most probable number of chance-successes being 27. The odds against this result being due to chance worked out at several billions to one.

In 1883–5 [2] a long series of experiments in thought-transference was carried out by Mr. Malcolm Guthrie, J.P., of Liverpool, and were recorded by Mr. James Birchall, hon. secretary of the Liverpool Literary and Philosophical Society. These included the transference of drawings and tastes as well as other experiments, and, on the whole, a very fair amount of success was obtained.

In 1885 [3] Professor Pierre Janet on several occasions successfully induced hypnosis in his subject, ' Léonie,' when she was at a distance, thus showing the existence of telepathic *rapport*.

In 1888–90 [4] some experiments of a rather different kind were carried out by Dr. Alfred Backman, of Kalmar in Sweden, who regarded them as evidence of clairvoyance rather than of telepathy. His method consisted in telling his hypnotized subject to ' go to ' certain places mentally, and to observe what was happening there. One of his best subjects was Anna Samuelsson, a girl of fourteen, who seems to have had some remarkable successes. For example, on June 20, 1888, in the presence of four officers of the Reserve Royal Regiment at Kalmar, all of whom sign the report as witnesses, Anna reported, when hypnotized, what the under-quarter-master was doing in his office at a distance, adding unexpected details about things in the room, all of which proved to be correct. A number of these experiments was carried out with

---

[1] *Phantasms of the Living*, pp. 16 ff. (abridged edition).
[2] Ibid. pp. 28 ff.
[3] *Revue Philosophique*, vol. xviii. Dec. 1884.
[4] *Proc. S.P.R.*, vol. vii. pp. 199–220.

different subjects, who saw telepathically or clairvoyantly more than could be attributed to chance.

In 1892 [1] Dr. A Blair Thaw, of New York, conducted a series of telepathic experiments carefully recorded, with his wife as percipient, in the presence of a witness (Mrs. Dow). There was no contact between agent and percipient during the experiments. The percipient's eyes were bandaged, and the object kept outside what would have been the field of vision had there been no bandage. Silence was maintained. To quote one short experiment : ' Object, a Cabinet Photo of " X " brought by agent from upstairs before sitting. Percipient says : *Something square. A picture. A picture of a brass bed.* Agent says : *Wrong. Photograph of " X."* ' (Experiment took two or three minutes.)

Of thirteen objects, six were correctly named, and in five of the remaining seven, the answers indicated that the percipient was on the right track. Two were failures. Experiments with colours and numbers also showed some success. The manner of reporting these experiments shows that they were carefully carried out.

In 1889 [2] a long series of very carefully conducted experiments was carried out by Professor and Mrs. Henry Sidgwick and Mr. G. A. Smith, in which the subjects were under hypnosis. Colours and numbers were chiefly used, and the conditions were varied. The experimenters were particularly on the look-out for possible hyperaesthesia of the normal senses on the part of the subjects, and in some of the experiments, placed them in separate rooms. The results are elaborately tabulated and described. They show striking positive results and deserve careful attention.

In 1890 [3] this series of experiments was continued by Mrs. Henry Sidgwick and Miss Alice Johnson, occasionally assisted by Dr. A. T. Myers and others. Again the experiments are lengthy and tabulated with much detail, the able experimenters showing themselves alive to every possibility. In

---

[1] *Proc. S.P.R.*, vol. viii. pp. 422–35.
[2] Ibid. vol. vi. pp. 128–70.
[3] Ibid. vol. viii. pp. 536–96.

order to judge of them and estimate their evidential strength, it is necessary to read carefully all the details and conditions under which they were carried out. The investigators soberly remark at the conclusion of their experiments : ' We think that they add materially to the already accumulated evidence for the fact of telepathy or communication between mind and mind, otherwise than through the ordinary channels of sense.'

One interesting thing is that in these latter experiments practically no success was obtained when the agent and percipient were in separate rooms. At first sight this suggests that some loophole for normal or hyperaesthetic perception might have been overlooked. But, on the other hand, in the first series significant success in separate rooms had been observed, and also, modern investigation has revealed the power exerted by any slight inhibitory suggestion of increased difficulty, even although the conscious mind does not accept it. Mrs. Sidgwick remarks : ' We may refer to the danger . . . of drawing conclusions from negative experiments. We have encountered instances of this on two lines of experiment . . . in both of which conditions apparently fatal to success at one time were subsequently found to present no insuperable difficulty.' This, in my own view, is characteristic of extra-sensory perception.

Between 1890 and 1895 [1] Mrs. Verrall carried out a series of experiments with playing-cards, in which her daughter, who was then a child, sometimes took part. Some of these experiments were designed, not to test the extra-sensory faculty, but to try the art of detecting cards by the sense of touch. Mrs. Verrall, who was a critical investigator, and also a sensitive, was able to supply information about the subjective side of the experiments. When her daughter was acting as percipient, Mrs. Verrall often knew beforehand what the former was going to guess ; she then began noting her impression *before* each guess, and found that it was confirmed by the result. She says : ' It is difficult for me to describe what is the nature of the impression I receive, which leads me to

[1] *Proc. S.P.R.*, vol. xi. pp. 174-95.

believe that the percipient has been successful. All who have tried to convey an idea by thought-transference must be familiar with the sensation that after a special effort the thought has been actually projected into space leaving one fatigued and conscious of a loss. But in this case that I am trying to describe, the effort made seems to meet with a response, the force exerted, instead of departing, returns, and the momentary fatigue is followed by so vivid an impression of recovery of power that it amounts to a pleasurable physical sensation. Difficult as it is to describe, the sensation is unmistakable, and—what is more important—seems rarely to be misleading.' These card-experiments were analysed by a statistician, Mr. C. P. Sanger, F.S.S., with the result that some other cause than chance was shown to have been operative in certain of the series.

In 1905 [1] two ladies, Miss Clarissa Miles and Miss Hermione Ramsden, both members of the Society for Psychical Research, carried out a series of experiments on qualitative lines ; and in 1907 they extended the series. Miss Miles lived in London, and Miss Ramsden at Gerrard's Cross, about twenty miles from London. They consulted Professor William Barrett as to how they should carry out and record their experiments, and in their report they say :

' Miss Miles noted at the time of each experiment, in a book kept for the purpose, the idea or image which she wished to convey, while Miss Ramsden wrote down each day the impressions that had come into her mind and sent the record to Miss Miles before knowing what she had attempted on her side. Miss Miles then pasted this record into her book opposite her own notes, and in some cases added a further note explanatory of her circumstances at the time, to which it will be seen that Miss Ramsden's impressions often corresponded. Whenever it was possible, Miss Miles obtained confirmatory evidence from other persons as to the circumstances that had not been noted at the time, and the corroboration of these persons was written in her book and is printed below. All the original records of these experiments were submitted to the Editor.'

[1] *Proc. S.P.R.*, vol. xxi. pp. 60–93.

The following—the gist of Experiment VII—is quoted here as an example :

'(a) October 27th. SPECTACLES. C.M.
 (b) Friday, October 27th. 7 p.m.
                        " Spectacles."

' This was the only idea that came to me after waiting a long time. I thought of " sense-perception," but that only confirms the above. My mind was such a complete blank that I fell asleep and dreamed a foolish dream (but not about you). At 7.25 I woke with a start.—H.R.'

In this case the exact idea of which the agent was thinking was caught by the percipient. But sometimes, though the main idea was received, it was changed in the manner of presentation. Thus, on one occasion Miss Miles chose as her subject a sunset scene over Brompton Oratory, which she was able to watch from her window. Miss Ramsden saw the sun with rays, and a picture which became the Crucifixion. There were, on the Oratory, three upright pinnacles, the centre one of which was actually a figure, and these apparently acted as *points de répere* for the three figures of the Crucifixion. It is characteristic of the telepathic impulse when emerging to feel its way along by means of the nearest chain of association. For example, in one experiment Miss Miles thought of SPHINX. Miss Ramsden got Lusac (the publisher) and then Luxor in Egypt. In another, Miss Miles wished the percipient to see the Bishop of Bristol, whom she had visited unknown to her. Miss Ramsden got ' latme,' Bishop Latimer, Archbishop. The whole series is an interesting one. The question of chance cannot be mathematically dealt with in qualitative cases, but the Editor, in summing up, says : ' After studying all the records . . . it appears to us that, while some of the co-incidences of thought between the two experimenters are probably accidental, the total amount of correspondence is more than can be thus accounted for, and points distinctly to the action of telepathy between them.'

Many students, after reading this series, will probably think that this judgment is well on the conservative side. If we admit telepathy here, it will be noticed that agent and percipient were twenty miles apart in the earlier group of experiments, while latterly Miss Ramsden moved to Kingussie, in Scotland, and the distance was then something like 400 miles.

This bird's-eye view of a portion of the earlier work gives only a superficial impression of it. It will be noticed that it is in all cases the work of responsible and well-educated people, alive to the possibilities of deception and error. The reader is again urged to make its acquaintance at closer quarters, and in particular, to form his own judgment as to the strength of the evidence and the adequacy of the precautions taken.

MORE RECENT WORK

Long-Distance Telepathy. — The following instance of telepathy over a long distance is inserted here because it is *experimental*. Mr. Hereward Carrington, an American worker in psychical research, says in his book : [1]

' I have in mind specially one remarkable (but hitherto unpublished) experiment with Mrs. Piper.[2] A certain lady of my acquaintance—an old Piper sitter—had tried to convey a certain word to " Rector " telepathically, to be given by automatic writing through the trance. Several attempts failed. Finally, one day, the lady in question wrote out the word on a blackboard and sat looking at it for about half an hour. The word was given the next day through Mrs. Piper. The blackboard was in the lady's own house, distant some 800 miles from Mrs. Piper in Boston.'

The Upton Sinclair Experiments.[3]—A series of experiments in direct telepathy, largely by the use of drawings, was carried out in 1928–29 by the American author, Upton Sinclair and his wife. Space will not permit of a description of these experiments ; they confirm the earlier work done on the same lines and provide strong evidence for telepathy. Mr. John F. Thomas says of them : ' In total, the Sinclairs made 290

---

[1] *Problems of Psychical Research* (English edition), p. 371.
[2] A celebrated American medium.
[3] See *Mental Radio*, London 1930.

experiments, of which 23 per cent. were judged by Mr. Sinclair as successful, 53 per cent. as partially successful, and 24 per cent. as failures. Dr. Prince agrees with Mr. Sinclair's general estimate of the results, and also gives his conclusions as follows :

'After years of experience in solving hundreds of human riddles—cases of conscious and unconscious deception, delusion, and illusion—and with a due regard for my reputation for caution and perspicacity, I here register my conviction that Mrs. Sinclair has amply demonstrated the phenomena known as telepathy.'[1] Dr. Walter Franklin Prince was a psychologist and worker in psychical research of high repute and very great experience.

Dr. Gilbert Murray's Experiments.—Between 1910 and 1915[2] Dr. Murray carried out a series of carefully recorded experiments in telepathy, in which his daughter, Mrs. Arnold Toynbee, usually acted as agent. He thus describes the method : 'I go out of the room and of course out of earshot. Some one in the room, generally my eldest daughter, thinks of a scene or an incident, or anything she likes, and says it aloud. It is written down and I am called. I come in, usually take my daughter's hand, and then if I have luck, describe in detail what she thought of. The least disturbance of our customary method, change of time or place, presence of strangers, controversy, and especially noise, is apt to make things go wrong. I become myself somewhat over-sensitive and irritable, though not, I believe, to a noticeable degree.' There were usually half a dozen or so people present, who remained silent, but Dr. Murray sometimes asked questions, which were recorded by the note-taker. A total of 505 experiments were reported, of which 33·1 per cent. were successes, 27·9 per cent. partial successes, and 39 per cent. failures. Later, Dr. Murray reported a further series of 295 experiments extending up to 1924, which divided up into 36 per cent. successes, 23·3 per cent. partial successes, and 40·7 per cent. failures, though 16 of these failures *might* have been counted as partial successes. Roughly, one may say that the three classes claim one third

[1] *Beyond Normal Cognition*, pp. 203–4.
[2] See *Proc. S.P.R.*, vol. xxix. pp. 46–110 and vol. xxxiv. pp. 212–74.

each. There can, however, be no question of chance being the explanation of the successes, as the correspondences are far too detailed. For example, Case 57, on September 20, 1910, was :

' *Subject*—Mrs. Arnold Toynbee (agent) : F—— washing a blouse in a wash-hand basin.'

Professor Murray : ' This is F—— arranging flowers in a basin.' (" Not quite right.") ' Then she's washing clothes.'

Contact was not essential to success. Out of eleven cases with no contact, nine were successful.

Dr. Murray could not normally have heard the suggested topics. The only explanation which suggests itself as a possible alternative to telepathy in these experiments is auditory hyperaesthesia.

In favour of the hyperaesthic explanation we have—(i) Dr. Murray always knew when some one else had chosen (and spoken) the subject. Had he subconsciously heard the change of voice ? (ii) In 10 cases the subject was written down *only* and was not spoken : they were all failures. (iii) In 17 cases mistakes occurred which suggest mishearing, e.g. ' hall ' is said instead of ' horse,' and ' Mrs. Carr ' instead of ' Mrs. Carlyle.' (iv) Dr. Murray said that he rather disliked doing the experiments, and added : ' I think this probably means that I get into a state of slight hyperaesthesia, and am particularly sensitive to every kind of impression. Noises, for instance, become intolerable.' This suggests hyper-sensitivity to sounds.

On the other hand, there were 45 cases in which the *idea* of the subject was caught, whereas names were not, and this suggests telepathy. Dr. Murray himself regarded the cases as telepathic.

We will now consider the efforts which have been made to discover whether telepathy exists as a mass-faculty, slightly possessed by all mankind.

Chapter VI

THE METHOD OF COLLECTIVE EXPERIMENT

MASS-EXPERIMENTS.—We come now to a group of experiments in which the collective principle was adopted, the idea being to get as many people as possible to try an experiment on set lines, and to then analyse the results by statistical methods so as to discover whether the mass-product showed signs of being significantly greater than chance could account for.

Evidence for Clairvoyance in Card-Guessing.—In 1924[1] Miss Ina Jephson, a scientific investigator and Member of Council of the Society for Psychical Research, thinking that a good many ' undifferentiated ' experiments, hitherto put down to telepathy, might in reality be due to clairvoyance, determined to experiment with playing-cards under conditions which should admit of pure clairvoyance only. The use of cards presents the obvious advantages for telepathic and clairvoyant experiments of rapidity and ease of control, while the element of chance can be accurately calculated. In this latter problem Miss Jephson received assistance from Professor R. A. Fisher.

She practised with cards for some months and was surprised at her own success. One day she told a doctor of her acquaintance that she imagined she knew what a playing-card was without looking at it. He gave her, she says, a piercing diagnostic glance, and said that he knew of a quiet little place in Cornwall where he sometimes sent his patients. Would she like the address ? This little side-light reminds one that the mental attitude of different people towards psychical research forms in itself a very instructive psychological study, which no student of the subject can afford to ignore.

The complete analysis of scoring with playing-cards is very

[1] *Proc. S.P.R.*, vol. xxxviii. pp. 223–68.

complicated ; there are, in fact, nine grades of guessing in all, (i) value and suit, (ii) value and colour, (iii) value only, (iv) suit and rank, (v) suit only, (vi) colour and rank, (vii) colour only, (viii) rank only, (ix) nothing right ; and each of these has to have a different score-value assigned to it. For this reason something simpler than playing-cards is preferable.

Miss Jephson extended the scope of her experiments to include 300 subjects, to whom she sent directions for carrying them out. They were to draw one card face downwards from the shuffled pack, guess it, enter the guess on the score-sheet, turn it up and enter the real card beside the guess. After five guesses the completed score-sheets were to be returned to Miss Jephson.

In all, 240 subjects sent in a total of 6,000 trials. The average score per guess for pure chance was 11·14 : the actual average score per guess sent in was 13·03, so that the results of the experiment, when tested for significance, were definitely above chance.

The method depended, of course, on the integrity of the subjects, who were spread over six different countries ; but the fact that all tended to score highest in the Value-and-Suit class is some evidence that there was no dishonesty.

One curious result was that there seemed to be a distinct tendency for the first trial to be the best, and Miss Jephson was inclined to attribute this to an element of fatigue which soon set in ; but it seems to be rather a general experience for a person who tries an experiment of this sort to do best the first time, and it may be, that the frame of mind on first approach is psychologically helpful, but that this afterwards tends to be destroyed by too much effort or expectancy.

This excellent piece of work by Miss Jephson may be said to have initiated a series of collective experiments, and the method was amplified and improved in the next series.

A Series of Experiments in Clairvoyance Conducted at a Distance.[1]—This series was conducted jointly by Miss Jephson, Mr. S. G. Soal, and Mr. Theodore Besterman. The series included (i) the main experiment, consisting of 6,361 guesses,

[1] *Proc. S.P.R.*, vol. xxxix. pp. 375–414.

(ii) 200 guesses made by the eight best subjects of the previous series, (iii) 2,031 guesses made by 95 members of the Boston S.P.R., (iv) 784 guesses by 157 subjects conducted by Professor Gardner Murphy of Columbia University, (v) 120 guesses by 24 students of University College, London, conducted by Professor J. C. Flügel. The total amounted to 9,496 guesses by 567 subjects.

In order to avoid the necessity for putting any trust in the integrity of the subjects, it was decided to send the cards to them in sealed envelopes. Elaborate precautions were taken ; the cards exactly fitted the envelopes. The envelopes were blue, of strong, coarse paper ' which cannot be rendered transparent by strong light, X-rays, water, alcohol, ether, or the like.' A strip of figured paper was fastened all round the envelope, since the figuring on such paper runs if wetted. The envelopes were stuck down with strong adhesive by the officials of Mudie's Library. Dark blue tissue paper was gummed over the flap of each envelope, since this shows the slightest trace of moisture and cannot be removed without leaving traces. The Society's relief stamp was impressed on the envelope marking the card inside. The envelopes, filled with the cards face downwards, were sent away for sealing : no one knew what any envelope contained, thus rendering telepathy impossible. Each subject had twenty-five envelopes, which he returned with his completed score-sheet, and a statistical analysis of the results was made by Mr. S. G. Soal, who is a professional mathematician. The final result was negative.

The other experiments included in this group showed no better success.

Mass Experiments : Broadcasting an Experiment in Telepathy.—On February 16, 1927, a further experiment was carried out by the Society for Psychical Research in undifferentiated telepathy and clairvoyance, notification of each experiment being sent to all the percipients by signals broadcast by the B.B.C.[1] Eight agents were isolated in the rooms of

[1] V. J. Woolley, ' The Broadcasting Experiment in Mass-Telepathy ' (*Proc. S.P.R.*, vol. xxxviii. p. 1).

the S.P.R., away from telephones, from the beginning of the experiment until the letter-boxes had been cleared the next morning, percipients being asked to post their results immediately the experiment was over. Thus the possibility of normal communication between the agents and the percipients during the ' danger ' period was prevented. Five objects were selected by Dr. Woolley for the experiments, two of which were playing-cards of unusual design, having coloured pips on a black ground. Sir Oliver Lodge, at the microphone of the B.B.C., announced the time of each experiment, while the agents at the rooms of the S.P.R. concentrated their attention on each object for three minutes at a time. Sir Oliver himself did not know what the objects were, except that Nos. 1 and 4 were unusual types of playing-cards, and that No. 2 was a picture. These facts he announced. The experiment lasted from 11.15 till 11.35 p.m.

24,659 results were received, but there was no clear indication of telepathy. Dr. Woolley says : ' There is certainly nothing which can be taken as a proof or even as a strong argument, but there does seem an indication of a supernormal faculty on the part of a few of those who took part, though their successes are swamped by the very large mass of failures on the part of others.'

A similar experiment had been tried by Professor Gardner Murphy of Columbia University on March 3, 1924, in which wireless was also used, but there also the result is described as being ' highly inconclusive.'

Experiments in Supernormal Perception at a Distance.— Under this heading, Mr. S. G. Soal conducted another mass-experiment,[1] incorporating the 127 subjects who had showed some individual signs of success in the previous experiment. Synchronization was achieved, not by broadcast signals, but by sitting at prearranged times. These experiments were carried out in 1927–28, and were on the same lines as the above. Precautions were taken to prevent leakage of information from agents to percipients by normal means, and agents and percipients were for the most part unknown to one another.

[1] *Proc. S.P.R.*, vol. xl. pp. 165–362.

The investigator, with praiseworthy industry, issued a closely worded report of 197 pages, into the details of which there is here no space to enter. The result was entirely negative. The author notes the striking contrast between the abundant evidence for extra-sensory perception produced by trance-mediums, such as Mrs. Piper and Mrs. Leonard, and his own abortive experiment, and concludes, perhaps with a touch of naïveté : ' . . . it may be that the conditions of the present experiment are not those under which supernormal knowledge makes its appearance.'

Mass-experiments, of course, proceed on the assumption that the extra-sensory faculty is a *fixed* characteristic of the subject's which is simply there to be found, like a physical characteristic, such as having red hair, or being double-jointed. It supposes that you have only to set a sort of test-paper and, if the faculty is possessed by any individual, it is bound to show itself. Work with individual subjects, however, tends to show that there are two factors in the problem, (i) that a few individuals possess the extra-sensory faculty much more markedly than others, (ii) that in order to get the faculty to work on any specific occasion, even with a good subject, the psychological resistances normally tending to prevent its expression must be allayed. Mass-experiments ignore this second factor and therefore usually fail.

Precognitive Dream-Experiments Suggested by a Theory of Mr. J. W. Dunne.—In a book entitled *An Experiment with Time*, which itself contains several examples of precognitive dreams, Mr. J. W. Dunne, put forward the theory that dreams concerning future events are about as common as dreams of past events, but that we are not aware of this because our minds have a natural tendency to reject the idea of precognition, and we do not recognize the fulfilments when they come to pass.

In 1932 the Society for Psychical Research carried out a series of experiments, to some extent with Mr. Dunne's co-operation, in order to test the truth of this theory, though it appears that Mr. Dunne was not satisfied that the results constituted a conclusive test of it.

The experiments were divided into three series :

1. Twenty volunteer subjects, all members of the S.P.R., were circularized with instructions as to how to record and report their dreams. They were to record them at once ; to amplify them by adding separate notes in the morning ; to dispatch records to headquarters before reading the paper or doing anything else ; and to note any subsequent events which seemed to be fulfilments of their dreams, obtaining independent corroboration where possible.

The results showed that 14 subjects sent in no precognitive dreams, while the remaining 6 subjects sent in 7, which represented 2·6 per cent. of the total. One of these, on analysis, proved to be non-precognitive. In four cases, Mr. Besterman says, ' the amount of coincidence is so slight that it would be improper to assume the presence of any element of precognition,' while of the two remaining cases he says that neither is of more than moderate value.

2. Mr. Dunne suggested that the subjects might have been too old, on the principle that the older a person was, the more his dreams would be concerned with the past and the less with the future. The experiment was therefore repeated with 22 Oxford undergraduates as subjects, under the same rules, Professor H. H. Price collecting and forwarding the records. There was some irregularity in recording owing to the approach of examinations, but 148 records were sent in. Ten of the subjects claimed no success, but the remaining 12 sent in 33 dreams, claiming them to be precognitive. These, however, seemed to show some over-optimism, for 21 had to be ruled out as of no value, while 10 were ' poor or indifferent,' and 2 were good, though neither was conclusive. ' Thus,' says Mr. Besterman, ' out of 148 dreams of the Oxford group, we have a total of 12 apparent precognitions (just over 8 per cent.), including 2 good ones, but no " conclusive " instance.'

3. Mr. Dunne himself sent in 17 records of his own, 5 of which he regarded as precognitive. ' Of these five cases,' says Mr. Besterman, ' it will probably be agreed that number five must be rejected as showing no evidence of precognition,

and that the remaining four cases offer fair or moderate *prima facie* cases for precognition.'

If we take the three experiments together, they include 430 records of dreams sent in by 43 subjects, and the final summary says : ' These 43 subjects, then, put forward 45 events in their dreams as being possibly precognitive, or an average of just one apiece. Of these 45 cases, I regard 18 as having a *prima facie* case, of which two have a good case. I do not regard any of these 18 cases as capable of being regarded as conclusive instances of precognition.'

It is dangerous to attach any great weight to negative evidence, especially in psychical research ; but it looks as if Mr. Dunne's impression of the frequency and universality of precognitive dreams may have been based on a peculiarly favourable period in his own experience.

The Gröningen Experiment.—A striking experiment in telepathy was carried out by the psychological staff of the University of Gröningen, in Holland, and was reported by Dr. Brugmans to the International Congress of Psychical Research in 1921. There were several agents in this case, who occupied an upper room where they were provided with two bags, one containing letters and the other figures. A letter was drawn from one bag and a figure from the other, at random, and all the agents concentrated their attention on these. Seated in a room below was the percipient, with curtains in front of him, and outside the curtains was a board marked out in squares, a series of letters running along one edge and a series of figures along the edge at right angles. Pointing to any square would therefore indicate a letter and a figure by cross-reference. This board was rendered visible to the experimenters in the room above by means of a double-glazed aperture in the floor immediately above it. At each experiment, the percipient would thrust out his hand from behind the curtains and point to one of the squares. The most probable number of successes by pure chance in any given number of trials could be calculated and the actual results compared with this. Care was taken in addition to test the sound-proofness of the floor, and the possibility of the percipient's obtaining any information by normal means. The number of experiments carried out was 187, for which the most probable number of chance-successes was $4\frac{1}{2}$. The actual number of successes obtained was 60, showing that some faculty of selecting besides chance must have been in operation. This, of course, was an experiment of the 'undifferentiated' type, which might have been due either to telepathy or clairvoyance.

The Ossowiecki Experiment.[1]—M. Stefan Ossowiecki, a Polish gentleman, known as a successful amateur clairvoyant, has collaborated in successful experiments with Dr. Osty, Director of the Institut Métapsychique of Paris, and has been visited by members of the English Society for Psychical Research. Mr. Theodore Besterman, as Research Officer of the S.P.R., visited Warsaw in the spring of 1933, and obtained a promise from M. Ossowiecki that he would attempt to read the contents of a sealed envelope sent to him from London. Accordingly, on May 17, 1933, Mr. Besterman sent a carefully prepared, sealed packet, which, however, aroused the suspicions of the letter-censorship, and was opened by the postal authorities in Poland before delivery. Another packet was then prepared by Mr. Besterman and sent to M. Gravier, President of the Polskie Towarzystwo Badań Psychicznych, through a Madame Wodzinska, since Mr. Besterman did not know M. Gravier's address. This was on July 14, 1933.

The mode of preparation of the sealed packet, carried out by Mr. Besterman in his office at the rooms of the Society for Psychical Research in London, was as follows. He took a sheet of paper measuring 93 mm. by 107 mm., and ruled with lines, from a loose-leafed note-book, and drew on it a rough sketch of an ink-bottle, writing in capital letters the words SWAN INK, one on each side of the bottle. Under the word SWAN, which was on the left of the bottle, he drew a blue line, and under the word INK on the other side he drew a red line. Then he folded the paper twice at right angles, one of the folds running right through the word SWAN.[2]

---

[1] See *Proc. S.P.R.*, vol. xli. p. 345.
[2] There is a photographic reproduction in the Report.

'This,' says Mr. Besterman, 'was placed in a reddish-orange "Ensign" light-tight envelope (that is not transparent to white light), measuring 94 mm. by 119 mm. This envelope was in turn enclosed in a black "Ensign" light-tight envelope, measuring 106 mm. by 130 mm. This black envelope was finally enclosed in a large Manilla envelope doubled in two, and thus measuring 114 mm. by 152 mm. Each of these envelopes was closed in a special way and bore private and invisible marks. The outer doubled envelope was, in addition, sealed with surgical tape arranged in a special way and signed by me. This packet was then further enclosed in a stout outer envelope and sent to Mme Wodzinska, who remitted it direct to M. Gravier. Both he and Mme Wodzinska sent signed statements registering their parts in the affair, which are reproduced in the report.'

At the first sitting on August 8, 1933, in M. Gravier's presence, everything being noted in French, M. Ossowiecki said that there were four envelopes, one inside the other, and that they contained a picture from an English illustrated paper. This was true as regards the envelopes, but might have been inferred from the earlier packet, which, presumably, he had received open. In the second sitting of August 9, M. Ossowiecki corrected his statement, saying that it was not an illustration but a drawing, and giving the colours of the envelopes. He went on to say of the drawing :

'It represents something like a goblet closed with a cork, and there is something written, not on the goblet, but around it. I see a W—I see a capital I—I also see an S, and something red and something blue. That makes me confuse it with the letters.'

At the end of September, Lord Charles Hope, accompanied by Miss Alice Reutiner and Mr. John Evelyn, all members of the Society for Psychical Research, went to Warsaw and joined M. Gravier. But M. Ossowiecki then said that he did not care to go on with the experiment unless, at the conclusion, the envelope was opened in his presence. This raised a difficulty, because it had been intended to bring the sealed packet back intact. However, under the circumstances, it was decided that, after the experiment was over, the above three English representatives should take the responsibility of opening it. Lord Charles Hope had guarded it since his arrival. He wrote : ' Soon after M. Gravier's arrival at M. Ossowiecki's flat, he handed the envelope to me, and I kept it in my pocket. I watched the envelope the whole time during the experiment, and myself opened it at the finish of M. Ossowiecki's " reading " of the contents.'

During the whole course of the experiment, M. Gravier made a record in French of what was said and done by M. Ossowiecki, and a literal translation of this is given in the report.

It is a curious fact that M. Ossowiecki's ' readings ' did not take the form which suggested that he was actually reading the contents of the packet. Instead, he went backwards in time and described the scene in Mr. Besterman's office when the packet was being prepared, giving, in fact, certain details about Mr. Besterman's surroundings and the time of the day when the packet was sealed, and so forth, which could not possibly have been obtained from anything in the packet itself. He then took a pencil and drew an approximation to a bottle with a line on either side of it, adding ' something written and something red.' Next, he drew an unmistakable bottle with the letters SWA on the left and the letters IN on the right. Finally, he made a complete drawing of a bottle in the middle of the paper, and the word SWAN on the left and INK on the right, both in capital letters. Some distance below the word SWAN (not immediately underneath it as in the original), he drew a line with his pencil, which he said was *red*. Actually, in the original, SWAN was underlined in *blue*, and the word INK on the other side of the bottle was underlined in red. But for this mistake, the reproduction was perfect, the shape of the bottle being exact.

The experiment concluded, Lord Charles Hope opened the envelopes, taking great care to leave the seals and special fastenings intact for later examination. The account of all the proceedings was then signed by Lord Charles Hope, by Mr. John Evelyn, by Prince J. Woroniecki, and by seven others who were present. The markings and sealings of the envelopes were evidently the points of main importance, and Mr. Besterman says of them :

' On October 3, 1933, Lord Charles Hope handed to me, in London, the original of the above account, M. Ossowiecki's drawings, and the opened envelopes. I minutely examined the envelopes and found that, with the exception of considerable wear and tear on the outer envelope, they were all intact. The private marks which I had made and which would have been inevitably disturbed on any attempt to open the envelopes, were all in order. [These marks were known to three other officials of the Society only.] I have no hesitation in saying that none of the three envelopes was opened. I am also satisfied that no effort was made, an effort which would not in any case have been successful (because, among other reasons, of the special folding of the paper), to render the contents transparent by chemical means. The same is true of X-ray and similar methods. It will thus be seen that M. Ossowiecki's clairvoyant reading (as it may for convenience be called, though other supernormal theories are not excluded) was almost completely successful.'

Mr. Besterman adds :

' A point of theoretical interest is this : the subject of the test was deliberately of such a kind (e.g. " Swan ") as to be capable of being symbolically " perceived " ; also the drawing was so disposed that the folding of the paper completely destroyed the form of the bottle and of one word, leaving the other intact. None of these things affected M. Ossowiecki's " reading," which is almost an enlarged facsimile, except that in his second drawing there are lines that might be taken to indicate the folding.'

No one except Mr. Besterman knew what the packet contained, and he was in England. Chance and fraud seem to be equally out of the question in this case, and the supernormal explanation remains as the only tenable one. Although classed here under the heading of experimental clairvoyance, it might possibly be a case of telepathy of a kind, M. Ossowiecki getting the information from Mr. Besterman's mind. This would not be strictly telepathy, but what we have defined as telaesthesia, the percipient playing an active rôle and filching information from the mind of another. The distance from

London to Warsaw is of the order of 900 miles, so that, unless it was a case of immediate clairvoyance of the packet, it supplies another instance of the extra-sensory faculty working over a long distance. It might also have been a case of retrocognition. It is in any case an extraordinarily clear piece of evidence for the existence of supernormal faculty.

Incidentally, it teaches another kind of lesson. The device of leaving a sealed letter, the contents of which the writer hopes to divulge after his death through the agency of a medium, could not alone be accepted as proof of such identity, since the medium might be able to read the contents of the letter directly. There is also other evidence for clairvoyance which supports this.

We will now turn to two cases in which the test of the extra-sensory faculty has been brought into the laboratory and submitted to examination under a laboratory technique, not, however, with the use of a mass-method, but with individual subjects.

Chapter VII

LABORATORY WORK

PROFESSOR J. B. RHINE'S EXPERIMENTS.—We come now to a very remarkable piece of work, carried out by Dr. J. B. Rhine, Associate Professor of Psychology in Duke University, Durham, North Carolina, and published by him in 1934 in a book [1] giving an account of the work accomplished by him since 1930. This work was sponsored by Professor William M'Dougall, who occupies the Chair of Psychology in that University, and who writes in his foreword to Dr. Rhine's book :

' The work reported in this volume is the first-fruit of the policy of naturalization of " psychical research " within the universities. It goes far to justify that policy ; to show, first, that a university may provide conditions that will greatly facilitate and promote this most difficult branch of science ; secondly, that the university may benefit from such liberal extension of its field of studies. . . . The manifest sincerity and integrity,' he continues, ' of Dr. Rhine's personality, his striking combination of humane sympathy with the most single-minded devotion to truth have induced in his collaborators a serene confidence in the worthwhileness of the effort, and have set a tone which, to the best of my judgment, pervades the group and contributes an important, perhaps an indispensible condition, of the striking successes here reported.'

Of this ' indispensible condition ' more will be said later. Before coming to grips with his subject, Dr. Rhine outlines its historical background, and is struck, as surely every one must be struck, by the fact that a long line of investigators have discovered extra-sensory perception over and over again. ' This will, I predict, be one of the more amazing facts for the

---

[1] *Extra-Sensory Perception*, by J. B. Rhine. (There is an English as well as an American edition.)

future historian of science,' says Dr. Rhine. 'After reading Bruck and Warcollier, and Coover and Estabrooks, and Sinclair, as well as the more numerous and more varied series that preceded, still the student who would work in the field to-day must set out first to prove it all over again ! '

The Method.—Dr. Rhine's method was to use cards, thus reducing the question of chance-expectation to a matter of exact calculation. The cards bore five simple diagrams, a Circle, a Rectangle, a Cross, a triple group of Wavy Lines (' Waves '), and a Star—diagrams suggested by a psychologist, Dr. Zener, as being simple, yet clearly distinguishable ; hence these cards are often called ' Zener Cards.' The designs were lightly stamped in ink on blanks with a playing-card finish.

Experimental Conditions.—It is not altogether easy, from Dr. Rhine's book, to state exactly the conditions under which each experiment was made, but the following description of the conditions of experiment with his principal subject, Hubert E. Pearce, may be taken as applying generally to the major work, except where otherwise stated. He says :

' The working conditions were these : observer and subject sat opposite each other at a table, on which lay about a dozen packs of the Zener cards and a record book. One of the packs would be handed to Pearce and he allowed to shuffle it. (He felt it gave more real " contact.") Then it was laid down and was cut by the observer. Following this Pearce would, as a rule, pick up the pack, lift off the top card, keeping both the pack and the removed card face down and, after calling it, he would lay the card on the table, still face down. The observer would record the call. Either after five calls or after twenty-five calls—and we used both conditions generally about equally—the called cards would be turned over and checked off against the calls recorded in the book. The observer saw each card and checked each one personally, though the subject was asked to help in checking by laying off the cards as checked. There is no legerdemain by which an alert observer can be repeatedly deceived at this simple task in his own laboratory. (And, of course, we are not dealing even with amateur magicians.) For the next run another pack of cards would be taken up.' [1]

[1] *Extra-Sensory Perception*, pp. 73–4. (American edition.)

Dr. Rhine's work has been criticized on the double ground that, (i) except in the ' down through ' experiments, in which the pack remained untouched until the end of the experiment, the conditions were not such as to make it absolutely certain that his subjects got no subconscious hints from possible slight marks or peculiarities on the backs of the cards, and (ii) that the experimental conditions were not adequately reported. Without maintaining that these criticisms are groundless, I would point out one other thing—we must bear in mind that the chief cause of the criticisms has been the large number of Dr. Rhine's subjects who were successful. This certainly is a surprising fact ; but the essential point is that the surprise seems to be based mainly on an *a priori* conception of what extra-sensory perception is, namely, that it is a *fixed* characteristic possessed by certain individuals and not possessed by others, so that if one comes across any one who does possess it, a simple test with cards is bound to reveal the fact. Hence, if Dr. Rhine finds that so many per cent. of his subjects score, that means, on this theory, that the same percentage of people will score anywhere.

I think these assumptions are fallacious. It is probably one of the ill effects of the mass-method of experiment, in which investigator and subject never meet, that it has tended to blind certain investigators to the true nature of the extra-sensory problem. Work with the individual subject reveals that the main task lies in the removal of inhibitions, or, in other words, in inducing the faculty to work. It is not enough to find sensitives who *possess* the faculty ; it is also necessary to get the extra-sensory material *externalized*, by creating sub-liminal confidence and allaying the natural inhibitions, which always tend to block its path. This cannot be done by posting forms to subjects whom the experimenter has never seen. It needs personal influence.

It seems to me that the following passage in a review by Professor Thouless of Rhine's work illustrates this point : ' Most important of all is the fact that his methods are so simple, and his results so clear, that his experiments can easily be repeated, and it will be possible without difficulty for other experimentalists to convince themselves whether Rhine's conclusions are valid or whether they are due to some flaw in his experimental methods.' [1] My own experience is that one cannot repeat any experiment of this kind with certainty five minutes later.

The internal, psychological state of the subject, as it affects the working of the faculty, appears to flicker like a shadow in the firelight. And, in addition to this, in an atmosphere of enthusiasm, confidence, friendliness and positive encouragement, the extra-sensory faculty will produce results which will be looked for in vain in chilly or repressive surroundings ; and personal and social influences, which are too subtle to be defined, make all the difference between success and failure. I think it would be impossible to ' repeat ' Dr. Rhine's experiments without introducing a factor equivalent to the personal influence of Dr. Rhine himself. To repeat any experiment, one must reproduce *all* the essential conditions, and not merely the conditions which one assumes on *a priori* grounds *ought* to be relevant. Some people do not wish to admit that features exist in these experiments which differentiate them entirely from experiments in physics. They wish to take account only of the *external* conditions, and point to this procedure as being the only ' scientific ' course, because the external conditions are so arranged as to eliminate all possible sources of leakage. Of course it is necessary to eliminate possible sources of leakage, but there is nothing scientific in experimenting under conditions which prevent the phenomenon one wishes to observe from occurring, or in carrying over into psychology methods which have nothing to recommend them except that they have been successful in physics. This is to dictate to nature the conditions under which one will accept results instead of trying to find out the conditions under which one is likely to get them.

The assumption made by what I may call the ' fixed faculty ' theory is that, given so many subjects, and so many similar packs of cards, all the conditions for reproducing a former set of experiments are provided. It assumes that it is

[1] *Proc. S.P.R.*, vol. xliii. p. 24.

only the external conditions which are important—a state of affairs we have grown used to in the physical sciences. But there surely should be no need to stress the obvious platitude that psychology is not physics.

The Factor of Chance in the Experiments.—Before giving a summary of Dr. Rhine's results, it will be as well to explain briefly on what principle the chance-factor has been dealt with in estimating their significance. Mathematical probability is expressed as a fraction. Thus, in tossing a coin, the common phrase that ' odds are even ' would be expressed by saying that the probability of heads or tails turning up is $\frac{1}{2}$. If the odds are 99 to 1 against pure chance having produced a result, this is expressed by saying that the probability that chance would have produced it is $\frac{1}{100}$ or 0·01, and so on. When we reach figures expressing very large odds, such, for example, as a probability of $\frac{1}{1000000}$ it is not usually written out as a decimal (0·000001), but, for brevity and convenience, as a power of 10. Thus, $\frac{1}{1000000} = 0\cdot000001 = 10^{-6}$, the negative index denoting that the power of 10 is in the denominator of the fraction.

A pack of cards, properly shuffled, may be regarded as being ' frozen ' in a random order. In the case of Zener packs, there is a certain deviation from strict randomness, which we shall mention later. Ignoring this, suppose that the subject guesses that the fourth card from the top of the pack is a Circle, that card is *equally likely* to bear any one of the five diagrams. So is any other card : equal likelihood applies all through the pack, no matter whether each card is removed as it is guessed or not, provided no card is looked at until the end. One is dealing then with independent events. The probability that any card will bear any particular diagram is $\frac{1}{5}$. But the probability that the subject will guess any particular card on any particular occasion is not necessarily $\frac{1}{5}$. Apart from any causal relation, people have preferences for certain numbers, diagrams, etc., and favour them at the expense of others.

If the respective probabilities of the subject's guessing each of the five diagrams, Circle, Rectangle, Cross, Waves,

Star, are p_1, p_2, p_3, p_4, p_5, the probability by pure chance of a success, say, with a Circle, is the *product* of the probabilities of the separate events occurring, namely, $\frac{1}{5}$ p_1. That is the probability that there will be a success with one particular diagram, namely, a Circle. But the probability of a success with *any* diagram is given by the *sum* of the probabilities of successes with each particular diagram—that is, the probability of a success by pure chance at any trial is $\frac{1}{5}$ ($p_1 + p_2 + p_3 + p_4 + p_5$). But the sum of the ' p's,' however they may differ amongst themselves, is always unity. Hence, the probability of a success by chance on any occasion is $\frac{1}{5}$. We see from this that habits or preferences on the part of the subject make no difference to the chance-result, so long as the pack of cards is shuffled in a truly random order. Granted this condition, if chance alone is acting, the *mean expectation* is that $\frac{1}{5}$ (or 20 per cent.) of the total number of trials will be successes. If the actual number of successes obtained is *significantly* greater or less than 20 per cent. of the trials, we may be sure that some other cause besides pure chance is operating.

The next question is, What do we mean by ' significantly ' greater or less ? We shall not get exactly 20 per cent. successes in every experiment, even if only chance is acting. Sometimes we shall get more, and sometimes less. Chance *expectation* of $\frac{1}{5}$ means that the longer we go on the nearer will the successes approach to the 20 per cent. value. We *may* get any number of successes in any experiment ; all we can say is that the farther the successes depart from 20 per cent. the more unlikely they are to be due to chance. The mathematics of probability enables us to say *how* likely or unlikely pure chance is to give any particular result. To use this, we have to proceed as follows. Given the number of Trials and the number of Successes, we first work out the Deviation—that is, the excess or defect of successes from 20 per cent. We next calculate a quantity called the Standard Deviation or Standard Error (σ). We divide the Deviation by the Standard Error, which gives us a quantity (X). Here we come to the convention which decides the degree of unlikelihood of chance as an explanation, beyond which we shall agree to count our results as *significant*

—that is, beyond that point we shall say that there is definite evidence of some other factor besides chance. In ordinary scientific work, this point is taken when $X=2$: but it may be stated at once that the results to be dealt with in this and the following chapter are so far beyond the point of significance that the exact point is immaterial in this particular connexion.

Let us take an imaginary example, in which 2,255 Trials have yielded 539 Successes.

T = number of Trials.

S = number of Successes.

% = the Successes as a percentage of the Number of Trials.

D = the Deviation (pos. or neg.) of the Successes from the mean chance expectation of $\frac{1}{5}$.

σ = the Standard Deviation or Error, $= \sqrt{pqT}$.

p = the Probability of Success in each Trial.

q = the Probability of Failure in each Trial.

$X = \dfrac{D}{\sigma}$

P = Probability that the final result is due to Chance.

$p = \frac{1}{5}$ and $q = \frac{4}{5}$, so that $pq = \frac{4}{25} = 0\cdot 16$.

T.	S.	%	D.	X.	P.
2,255	539	23·9	+88	4·63	10^{-5} to 10^{-6}.

Now, the mean expectation of successes due to pure chance would be $\frac{1}{5}$ of 2,255—that is, 451. Subtracting this from 539 gives a positive Deviation of 88. The Standard Error $= \sqrt{0\cdot 16 \times 2,255} = 18\cdot 96$ (approx.) $X = \dfrac{D}{\sigma} = \dfrac{88}{18\cdot 96} = 4\cdot 63$.

Tables given in books on the mathematics of probability [1] correlate values of X with their corresponding probabilities, and from these we can find out what we want to know. (Strictly these values should be halved, when, as in this case, positive and negative deviations are both significant. But with large values of X, this becomes unimportant.)

The odds against chance lie between a hundred thousand to one and a million to one. It does not much matter where it

[1] See R. A. Fisher, *Statistical Methods for Research Workers.*

lies between, or whether we halve it or not. We can say with confidence that something besides pure chance is at work here. Note that the percentage rate of scoring (23·9) is not very high : but, because of the large number of trials, the +3·9 per cent. tells heavily in the long run.

Dr. Rhine's Results.—Dr. Rhine defines the objects of his research into extra-sensory perception as twofold ; firstly, ' to answer, if possible, by mathematically indisputable evidence the question of its occurrence and its range ' ; secondly, ' to further its understanding by the discovery of its relationships to other mental processes, and to the essential physiological and physical conditions.' [1] At first he tried guessing games with children, guessing with sealed envelopes and other methods. After more than 5,000 trials, he discovered an undergraduate named Linzmayer who had the power of scoring with cards consistently above chance. Soon afterwards, two more, Stuart and Pearce, were found, who could do the same. The work grew, and the results reported in the book were obtained with eight major subjects, all of whom were students or ex-students of Duke University, while one was a graduate assistant in the Department of Psychology. Latterly, the number of his subjects has been greatly increased.

Much of the earlier and historical work, which had been called ' telepathy,' had been done under conditions permitting of either telepathy or clairvoyance, or both. Dr. Rhine determined to differentiate between the two conditions, and many of his experiments permitted only of pure clairvoyance. After the pack of cards had been so shuffled that no one knew the order, he kept all cards face downwards until the end of the experiment, thus making telepathy impossible. Where both conditions were required, the experimenter looked at each card as it was drawn from the pack ; and where pure telepathy alone was desired, a mental method was used with no cards at all, the agent thinking each time of one of the diagrams and recording his thought after each trial was over.

Linzmayer's Results.—The first subject was A. J. Linzmayer. Two sets of trials were made for the purpose of comparing

[1] *Extra-Sensory Perception*, p. 46.

the undifferentiated with the purely clairvoyant condition, 360 trials of the first and 240 of the second, making 600 in all. Linzmayer kept up the same very high average rate of scoring in both, 49·5 per cent., the cutting out of the possibility of telepathy seeming to make no difference. The odds against chance were billions to one.

On five occasions Dr. Rhine tried the experiment of urging Linzmayer to go on working at the cards after he was tired and anxious to get away. The result was that the score first dropped to chance expectation and then went *below* it, thus showing the extra-sensory faculty *negatively* applied.

As time went on, Linzmayer's rate of scoring began to decline, until, at the end of two years, it was very little above chance. In all, he totalled 4,505 trials, and his average rate of scoring over the entire range was 33·6 per cent., the odds against chance reaching a figure which might almost be called super-astronomical !

This gradual rate of decline certainly seems to be evidence that a genuine faculty was at work. Anything in the nature of trickery or skill should attain increasing success with practice.

Stuart's Results.—Dr. Rhine says of Charles E. Stuart, the next subject, who was a graduate assistant in the Department : ' Through the years I have known him, one of the ablest students within my acquaintance. His experiments were, I believe, very carefully conducted. He always impresses me as being very cautious and responsible. I think no one of our Departmental group would have the least hesitation in taking his report of his own unwitnessed experiments in E.S.P.' He started in 1931 a series of 7,500 trials. ' In this procedure,' says Rhine, ' Stuart held the cards behind him, cut the pack there at the start, and held each card by the corner between finger and thumb, recording each call when made, and checking up after every five calls (and then reshuffling).' These trials were done under the condition of pure clairvoyance, and the average rate of scoring was 24·2 per cent. Even so, the odds against chance for the series are again billions to one.

Like Linzmayer, his scoring afterwards began to decline.

In 1902 he did 2,100 more trials, also under the clairvoyant condition. The average rate of scoring this time was 27·2 per cent. and the odds against chance overwhelming.

He tried at one time the interesting experiment of calling each card twice, one call intended to be right and the other wrong. He found that the calls intended to be wrong were about as much *below* chance-expectation as the calls intended to be right were above it.

Pearce's Results.—Hubert E. Pearce was a student preparing for the Methodist ministry. Dr. Rhine says : ' All of Pearce's work has been carefully witnessed ; but I wish to state in addition that I have the fullest confidence in his honesty, although in this work the question of honesty arises in the mind of every one, preacher or no.'

Pearce scarcely scored above chance for the first 100 trials, but afterwards picked up. He then did 10,300 trials under the condition of pure clairvoyance at an average rate of scoring of 36·4 per cent. In some of these trials he did not look at the backs of the cards at all ; in some he did not touch the pack, and in some the pack remained face downwards on the table untouched until the end of the experiment. This is what Rhine calls the ' down through ' condition. Each condition separately showed significant odds against chance.

Under the ' down through ' condition (and pure clairvoyance) Pearce did 1,625 trials at an average rate of scoring of 29·6 per cent., again with colossal odds against chance.

It is recorded that a professional magician was invited to watch Pearce at work and to try to score under the same conditions ; but that he failed to score above chance and said that he did not see how Pearce did it.

Effect of Special Conditions.—Dr. Rhine observed certain interesting things about the conditions affecting Pearce's scoring : (i) The presence of visitors tended to send the score down at first, but after a time it recovered. (ii) The effect of any new condition was to send the score down for a time. (iii) The effect of sodium amytal, a dissociative drug, was to lower his rate of scoring almost to chance value : the same happened with Linzmayer. Caffeine, an integrative drug, raised his rate of scoring to 40 per cent. over 450 trials.

Pure telepathy was tried. The conditions were these. The agent thought of the images of cards one by one but had no actual cards with him. Each time he thought of a card he pressed a key, which gave electrically an audible tap, which the percipient could hear. The agent mentally selected his card-images in batches of five at a time, trying to get them in a random order. Guesses and cards thought of were afterwards compared.

Two long series of experiments were tried (*a*) under the condition of pure clairvoyance, and (*b*) under the condition of pure telepathy. The rate of scoring in (*a*) was 28·4 per cent., and in (*b*) 28·8 per cent., both fairly high rates of scoring and nearly the same. Chance, as usual, was entirely out of the question.

Pearce was also successful under the clairvoyant condition between different buildings of the University, at ranges of 100 and 250 yards. Some telepathic experiments over a distance were also successful.

Other Subjects.—Experiments with five other major subjects are reported, Miss Owenby and Mr. G. Zirkle, assistants in the Department of Psychology, and Miss F. M. Turner, Miss J. Bailey and Mr. T. C. Cooper, undergraduates. The same general results were obtained with them as with the others, including 6,125 trials under the ' down through ' condition at an average rate of scoring of 28·4 per cent. The same drugs were tried with similar results.

General Observations.—Three general conclusions remain to be mentioned. (i) Rates of scoring with all percipients were found to be subject to continuous and erratic variation. This appears to be a general characteristic of the extra-sensory faculty. Also, it argues in favour of the genuineness of the results, since fraud or a mistake in the estimate of the probability of chance-success would give a much more constant rate of scoring. (ii) Taking all the results ' by and large,' the average rate of scoring seems to hover about the point of 30 per cent., where 20 per cent. is the average chance expectation. It may be that this figure represents a rough psychological constant for the extra-sensory faculty. (iii) It is possible that the scoring

is done in short bursts when the percipient's state of consciousness departs a little from the normal. Dr. Rhine says : ' Miss
Bailey practically goes into light trance with eyes closed. Pearce
seems to me to approximate light trance after he works steadily
for some time. In fact, his eyes almost close and the pupils
turn somewhat upward. Cooper, Zircle, and Miss Turner
close their eyes when they do not have to keep them open.
This was not required of them. Both Linzmayer and Pearce
like to look off with a " far away look," much of the time.' In
this mental state may lie the secret of scoring.

The reader should examine the curves summing up the
results at the end of Dr. Rhine's book.

Finally, one may refer again to Professor M'Dougall's
remark that the ' tone ' pervading his group of workers, which
was set by Dr. Rhine, may be an ' indispensible condition ' for
success. I think it is. All Dr. Rhine's subjects were certainly
under his personal influence, had a high regard for him, lived
in a buoyant atmosphere and were affected by his enthusiasm.
If my own experience counts for anything, these circumstances
are likely to have had more influence on the results than anything else. They are essential for removing the natural
inhibitions with which the faculty is hampered.

In the next chapter some experiments will be described,
which were carried out by myself on similar lines to those
above detailed.

Chapter VIII

FURTHER LABORATORY WORK

THE TYRRELL EXPERIMENTS.—This account of my own work had better open with some description of the only subject who has worked with me under the conditions of continued personal contact, of which we have just been speaking, as distinct from the condition of brief and occasional collaboration, which I may call ' casual ' experiment. The subject, Miss Gertrude Johnson, has been intimately known to me and to my family for a number of years. Our experiments began in 1921, when Miss Johnson, then a young girl, carried out some experiments during a long visit. That she possessed the extra-sensory faculty in a marked degree was obvious, since it showed in all the affairs of daily life. We carried out some experiments with playing-cards.[1] The pack was shuffled by myself at the back of the room, the cards face downwards. I then placed the pack face downwards on the table in front of me, while Miss Johnson (to whom I will in future refer as G. J.), sitting beside me, would give the denominations (but not the suits) of the first six or eight cards in the pack. This she did successfully on seven occasions, but not without great nervous strain. Chance, of course, could not possibly account for this. I noted at the time that the difficulty seemed to be to bring the supernormal knowledge of the cards into correlation with the motor-mechanism of speech. The knowledge seemed to be somewhere in the mind, but not related to brain-mechanism in the same way as with normally acquired ideas.

G. J., as I can attest from the result of many years' friendship, shows no signs of instability as a result of her faculty. It is, with her, a ' normal ' power of perception ; it could only

[1] See Report in *Journal S.P.R.*, vol. xx. p. 294.

be called ' abnormal ' in the sense that it does not easily run in double harness with the normal faculties ; the tendency is for the two to alternate rather than to co-exist, the accompanying states of consciousness being rather different. There is always a difficulty in externalizing the extra-sensory type of knowledge, which lies in some department of the mind, on the fringe of normal consciousness. G. J.'s integrity is quite unquestionable, and her attitude towards psychical phenomena in general one of robust common sense tinged with healthy scepticism.

Opportunity to resume experiments of the kind mentioned above did not recur until 1934, when it occurred to me that G. J. had a flair for finding lost objects, and always did it when not consciously looking for them. Why not convert this finding instinct, I thought, into an experiment on quantitative lines ?

The Pointer Apparatus.[1]—Accordingly, I placed in a row five small boxes, with sloping and overhanging lids facing the subject, and fitted a large screen over the whole, in such a way that the subject, sitting on one side of a narrow table, was completely hidden from myself on the other side. The boxes were left open on my side of the screen and were carefully padded inside and lined with soft flannel. I provided myself with a polished wooden pointer, and placed the end in one box after another, choosing the boxes at random, and saying the word ' In ' each time I did so, while G. J., on the other side of the screen, tried to ' find ' the pointer by opening the box it was in. It was a kind of game of hide and seek. I found that by placing a light behind the subject, I could check the whole operation by the light which came through each box as it was opened. I could also see that only one box was opened at a time ; hence, I could score the results as I went along, marking each trial as a success or failure. The experiment was very simple and quick ; in fact, I found I could not go fast enough to please the subject, who wanted a trial every second. Supposing that these pointer-hidings could be taken as independent events, the probability of success by pure chance alone was, of

[1] See *Journal S.P.R.*, vol. xxix. p. 52.

course, $\frac{1}{5}$ and the probability of failure $\frac{4}{5}$ at each trial, as with the Zener cards.

The question whether or not it was possible for the subject to hear the pointer being put into the box was, of course, very important ; but it was thoroughly tested. Several people tried by putting their ears close against the boxes on the other side (a position in which the subject could not work the experiment) to hear it, but all failed to locate it, though a few said that occasionally they could just hear something. Of course the *location* of a sound is much more difficult than its *detection*.

Results with Pointer Apparatus.—Between October 20, 1934, and February 20, 1935, the following results were obtained with G. J. as subject and myself as operator.

One Operator and One Subject.

Trials.	Successes, Actual.	Successes, Chance-Expected.	Odds against Result being Chance.
30,000	9,364 = 30·2%	6,000	Billions to one.

Chance, as an explanation, was quite clearly out of the question from the start, the method of estimating chance - probabilities being the same as that given in Chapter VII.

In the above experiments, I was myself the operator ; but further experiments were carried out in which six others acted as operators, the results being as follows. G. J. was the subject throughout.

Six Operators and One Subject.

Trials.	Successes, Actual.	Successes, Chance-Expected.	Odds against Result being Chance.
8,500	2,126 = 25·0%	1,700	Billions to one.

The results were significantly above chance, not only as regards the total, but with each of five out of six operators independently.

In a third series of experiments, I acted as operator

with 29 different subjects (excluding G. J.), with these results :

One Operator and 29 Subjects.

Trials.	Successes, Actual.	Successes, Chance-Expected.	Odds against Result being Chance.
37,100	7,756 = 20·9%	7,420	10^{-5} or a hundred thousand to one.

Here we see that the rate of scoring of these 29 subjects is scarcely over the chance-expected rate of scoring of 20 per cent. It is very slightly over, and this is due mainly to one subject, who scored distinctly above chance. Even this slight excess above the chance rate of scoring raises the odds against chance for the whole score to a hundred thousand to one on account of the very large number of trials.

The results, therefore, provide us with the following facts :

With myself as operator, G. J.'s rate of scoring was about 30 per cent.

With others as operators, G. J.'s rate of scoring was about 25 per cent.

With myself as operator and other subjects, the rate of scoring was about 21 per cent. I use the round figures for clearness.

There are certain conclusions to be drawn from these figures. First, with myself as operator and a random sample of people acting as subjects, the rate of scoring is very close to the chance-expected value of 20 per cent. This makes it look very much as if G. J.'s high scoring with me is due to some special relation, normal or supernormal, between herself and me. Suppose it is due to a normal relation, such as a co-incidence of preferences for certain boxes, there must be a similarity between her preferences and mine. But we find that G. J. scored well above chance with each of five other people taken at random and acting as operators (myself being absent). True, the rate of scoring was not so high as with me, but it was amply significant. Therefore, there must be, on the theory of coincident preferences, coincidences between G. J.'s number-preferences and theirs. There is a strange fact here.

I had experimented with 29 subjects and had found only one who scored in a way at all comparable with G. J. Only 1 in 29, that is to say, whose number-preferences must, on this theory, have been similar to my own. But G. J. scored with 6 out of the first 7 operators she experimented with. And a more remarkable fact is this : 3 of these (I will call them A, B, and C) were also among the 29 subjects for whom I acted as operator, and they all failed to score. (C also failed to score with G. J., and is therefore eliminated.) If, therefore, coincidence of number-habits accounted for G. J.'s scoring, we must say : (i) that G. J.'s number-habits and mine are similar, because she scored when I was operator, (ii) that G. J.'s number-habits were similar to A's and B's, because she scored when they were operators. Hence it follows that A's and B's habits are similar to mine. But A and B failed to score with me when I was operator. Why ? This tells strongly against the theory that scoring is due to similarity of number-habits with this apparatus. It suggests that G. J. was scoring on account of a faculty which she possesses individually, and not on account of a similarity between some characteristic of hers and the operator's. The irregularity of her scoring points to the same thing. Why should a similarity of number-habits exist between two people on some days and not on others ? Apart from a telepathic faculty, I can only think of one possibility in the present case, and that is auditory hyperaesthesia. It was shown conclusively that it was not possible to tell in which box the pointer was by normal hearing, but if G. J.'s hearing were preternaturally acute, it might be suggested that that accounted for it. I do not think this is a very plausible theory, partly because there is no independent evidence that G. J. possesses abnormal hearing, but also because it is by no means clear the auditory hyperaesthesia, if it existed, would help in the matter of *locating* sounds as distinct from *detecting* them. The sense of direction in hearing is never very exact, and I doubt very much whether in acute audition it is improved.

The question of what effect coincidences of number-habits or preferences would be likely to have on rates of scoring will be dealt with shortly, when the newer form of apparatus is described.

It may, perhaps, be mentioned, that the signal for opening the boxes was sometimes given by a tap instead of by saying the word ' In,' but this made no difference to the results, showing that the operator's tone of voice had nothing to do with it.

These experiments were witnessed by Dr. Broad, the Hon. Mrs. Alfred Lyttelton, Mr. Gerald Heard, Mr. Kenneth Richmond, and several others, some of whom also acted as subjects.

It is, I think, of some importance to notice that G. J., the successful subject, had been working under conditions of personal contact with myself and had, therefore, a sense of complete freedom, and was not tied down to particular times of experiment. The other subjects were working under what I should call ' casual ' conditions, coming for an experiment for half an hour or so from time to time, by appointment ; and with them very little happened. Now this ' casual ' condition, although not quite the same as the condition of the mass-experiments, which conspicuously failed, seems to me to be sufficiently like it to come under the same condemnation. It is very likely not suitable for dispersing the screen of natural inhibitions.

An Electrical Apparatus.[1]—It was not easy to see how the results with the Pointer Apparatus could have been obtained except by means of a faculty of extra-sensory perception on the part of G. J. At the same time, the apparatus was clearly capable of improvement, and I resolved to make a new one which should embody the following features :

(1) Means should be provided for selecting the boxes to be opened in a mechanically-determined, random order. (2) It should be possible for the operator to be in ignorance of which box he was dealing with. This would enable him to eliminate telepathy and test pure clairvoyance, and would also eliminate all possibility of his conveying any information to the subject by unconscious whispering, etc. (3) The results should be

[1] See *Proc. S.P.R.*, vol. xliv. p. 99.

automatically recorded. (4) The whole arrangement should be proof against possible fraud or misuse (not that there was ever the faintest suggestion that such was used, but in psychical research nothing must depend on the good faith of one's subjects).

Accordingly, I used five small boxes as before, but instead of using the pointer, I fitted each with a small electric pea-lamp and provided five silent keys for lighting the lamps. The idea was now that the lamps should be lit one at a time instead of thrusting the pointer into the boxes, and the subject should try to open the box with the lighted lamp in it. To render the boxes light-tight, the lids were revetted, faced with fine red velvet and held down by springs. Also, the lamps were kept rather dull.

(1) *The Mechanical Selector.*—The next thing was to instal a mechanical arrangement for selecting and lighting the lamps. Though described first, this part of the apparatus was actually the last item to be finished. It consisted of a rotating arm, continually passing over five contacts, and was stopped by chance on one of the contacts by the pressing of a key. On whatever contact it happened to stop, the corresponding lamp was lit in one of the boxes. Actually, twenty-five contacts, irregularly grouped in fives, were employed, and the mechanical difficulties to be overcome were by no means simple. But in the end a satisfactory and reliable selector was made, which, on being tested and subjected to mathematical analysis, was found to be free from bias. This arrangement, therefore, gave an indefinite and truly random series of selections from five numbers.

(2) *The Commutator.*—While the experimental work on the selector was going on, five keys, placed in a row, were used to light the five lamps. In order to render them silent, they were provided with mercury contacts. The wires running from these keys to the lamps were taken through the Commutator, whose part it was to mix up or transpose the wires in various orders. The Commutator could be set without opening its box by merely pressing a button. Then the operator, not knowing the order of connexions between keys and lamps, did not know, when pressing any key, which lamp he was lighting.

This, of course, eliminated the possibility of telepathy. But it did more than that. It also broke up any possible co-incidences of number-preferences. This, I think, will be clear if we visualize the five keys in a row, 1, 2, 3, 4, 5, joined to the five lamps, 1, 2, 3, 4, 5, in a one to one order, the first key lighting the first lamp and so on. Suppose that both operator and subject have a strong preference for the middle number, No. 3. This will cause some increase in the number of successes due to chance ; but if the keys be connected to the lamps in any other order, it will cause a decrease. The subject will now be opening box 3 an undue number of times, and the operator will be pressing key 3 an undue number of times ; but he will be lighting lamp 2 (or some other) in doing so. The same will be true of sequence-preferences, as, for example, if both had a habit of using the order 1, 2, 3. The commutator would break up this order for the operator in various ways. It is only necessary to reset the Commutator for each experiment in order to eliminate the effects of such possible number-habits. It is, of course, only *coincidences* of number-habits which can raise the score. Non-coincident number-habits, if they exist, tend to lower it.

Repetition Intervals.—A short digression is necessary here in order to deal with a point which arises in connexion with randomness of distribution. It was mentioned in Chapter VII (p. 84) that a certain deviation from strict randomness occurs with packs of Zener cards, which would be mentioned later. The deviation arises in this way. However a pack of 25 Zener cards is shuffled, there is always the condition imposed that there must be five cards of each kind in the pack ; but this is a condition which would seldom occur in a truly random arrangement. If, for example, a pack of 25 were drawn from a well-shuffled pool of three or four hundred, the pack would usually contain more than five cards of one kind, and less than five of another. This means that the genuinely random spacing between repetitions is more irregular than the spacing in the actual shuffled packs, the *maximum* intervals between repetitions being greater in the former case than in the latter. This deviation from pure chance arrangement is of theoretical rather than of practical interest. It could not account for Dr. Rhine's results, but it is mentioned here because the same thing was found to apply when a human operator selects the order of five boxes or keys. He is not so erratic as chance would be in the matter of *repetitions*. It must be understood that this peculiarity is something quite apart from the number-habits and preferences which we have been considering, and is of far less importance. The Commutator eliminates number-habits, whether of the preference or sequence type, by breaking them up and redistributing them. It does not alter these repetition intervals ; but that does not matter because they do not affect the score and can only be made to do so in one particular way. This way is as follows : If the percipient were to select one box and keep on opening it again and again, until a success were scored, and were then to go on to another box and repeat the process, and so on, this would increase the number of successes scored by chance because of the absence of the long maximum intervals between repetitions which mechanical randomness would provide. That G. J. never used this method I am able to testify, and not on her word alone. There is conclusive evidence of it. For she scored above chance while an observer took down the sequence of boxes she opened,[1] and the record shows that she was not using the peculiar method above. Further, when I was acting as operator with the Pointer Apparatus, and was choosing the order of the boxes, 26 out of the 29 subjects scored at the expected-chance rate of 20 per cent. And with the Zener cards 21 subjects did the same. Clearly, then, apart from the use of this special method, which we know was not then being used, this peculiarity of randomness does not affect the score.

Since, however, this curious peculiarity about randomness was not discovered until the experiments were well in progress, many of the results were obtained while the operator was selecting the order of lighting of the lamps in the boxes, and it is formally necessary to inform the reader of this. G. J., the percipient, always opened the boxes in the order in which she

[1] See *Proc. S.P.R.*, vol. xliv. p. 167.

was moved to do so, and the peculiar idea of keeping on with one at a time never occurred to her. Many features in the results testify to the fact that the scoring was not due to any constant error in the estimation of the chance-expectation of success. For one thing, the score fell whenever any new feature was introduced, and rose again as soon as the new feature became familiar. It fell to chance whenever the subject was tired or unwell ; it rose suddenly if she was elated. The records showed that the scoring was done in groups or batches which could not be obtained by the above method. But in any case, the whole matter was clinched when this peculiarity in randomness became known by substituting for the operator's choice of order an order determined by the tested mechanical selector, with which the method of opening one box continuously gave only a chance score. That G. J. had not been using this artificial and fake method of scoring was then made plain, for she continued to score with the mechanically selected numbers. The results obtained with them are given on p. 107, and it will be seen that they are enormously above anything that chance could have produced. The possible effect of number-habits had been removed by the Commutator. The operator did not know what lamps he was lighting, and therefore could not give any information to the subject, either consciously or otherwise. The light-tightness of the boxes had been previously dealt with. The keys were silent, and in any case could have told nothing. The order of lighting of the lamps was mechanically determined. The speed of working was from 60 to 70 trials a minute, far too fast for any peeping into boxes, even had this not been guarded against by automatic devices, and had the subject not been an old and trusted friend. The apparatus was tested as we went along. I am quite unable to think of any explanation of these results other than extra-sensory perception, nor has any critic been able to suggest one. To return now from this digression to the description of the apparatus.

(3) *The Automatic Recorder.*—This consisted of a strip of moving paper, driven by clock-work, over which were two ink-wheels, side by side. Every time a box was opened by the

raising of the lid, a contact closed, causing one of the ink-wheels to mark the tape. Every time a box was opened which contained a lighted lamp, both the ink-wheels marked the tape. This was arranged for by a series of contacts and double relays. Thus a single mark on the tape recorded a failure, and a double mark a success, and the mode of grouping of the successes was left for inspection.

(4) *The Safety Devices.*—There were only two ways in which such an apparatus could conceivably be misused. It might be said that the subject, if not controlled by a witness, could open the boxes a little way and look in before making a trial. Actually, we worked at the rate of seventy trials a minute, since speed seemed to be helpful, and this would have made any manipulations of this kind impossible ; but the contacts were so set that the slightest upward motion of the lid worked the recorder and the trial was recorded before the lid was sufficiently far open to allow the subject to see in. The other possibility was that the subject might open more than one box, or all the boxes, at a time. This was guarded against by a device which cut out the success-recorder when more than one box-lid was opened.

No words at all were spoken by the operator during experiments, and the subject was well hidden from him by a large screen, and latterly sat at a different table, when both tables were provided with screens. But during most of the experiments nothing could have been observed by the subject which would have been of the least use in scoring, even if there had been no screens.

A Delay-Action Device and the question of Light-Leakage.— The advantage of using mechanical and electrical devices, such as this apparatus embodies, is that it enables quick and silent changes to be made from one condition to another without the subject's normal knowledge. For example, I had at first thought of subjecting the boxes to photographic tests in the dark in order to prove whether the lids were light-tight. But it occurred to me that this might be unnecessary. Instead, I introduced a relay into the lighting circuit of the lamps, which had the effect that, when a key was pressed by the operator, it

selected the circuit of a particular lamp, but the relay placed a
gap in the circuit so that the lamp did not light. As soon as
any box-lid was raised, however, this worked the relay and lit
the selected lamp. Thus, the operator selected a lamp,
without knowing which, and the subject unconsciously lit it.
By means of a switch on my own table, I could throw this
arrangement in or out of action at will, and so could compare
the results with and without it. All I had to do was to put it
into action suddenly without telling the subject and see what
happened. I did so, and found that she continued to score as
before. Clearly, then, she could not have been helped to score
by any leakage of light or warmth or radiation of any kind from
the lamp, or she would have failed as soon as the delay-action
was used. This objection was therefore cleared away at one
blow. And, since the arrangement acted so quickly that the
lamp was found alight in the box when it was opened, whether
the delay-action was in use or not, the subject knew nothing
and went on scoring as usual. These are the comparative
results :

With and Without Delay-Action.

Trials.	Successes, Actual.	Successes, Chance-Expected.	Odds against Result being Chance.
(Lamp lit beforehand.)			
845	242 = 28·6%	169	A thousand millions to one.
(Lamp lit by Delay-Action.)			
855	224 = 26·2%	171	A million to one.

Clairvoyance.—It was early found that when the possibility
of telepathy was removed by the use of the Commutator, the
scoring continued just the same ; thus, most of the results
obtained must presumably be attributed to clairvoyance. One
would imagine that the subject must be clairvoyantly perceiving
the lighted lamp in the box. But the results above quoted
throw some doubt upon this. How, with the Delay-Action,
can the subject select the box which *will* contain a lighted lamp
just after she begins to open it ? She has not much to go upon,
it would seem. A particular key has been pressed by the

operator behind a screen. Suppose that she becomes clairvoyantly aware of this, it will be no help. He does not know
which lamp corresponds with the key pressed, and in the
normal way no one could know without tracing out the complicated connexions in the closed Commutator box. It would
have to be supposed that the subject's clairvoyant power does
this in a very small fraction of a second, and decides which box
to open ; but this does not sound very convincing, for the
following reason.

It has been said that the normal rate of working was about
seventy trials a minute. In practice, one inevitably worked in
a rhythm, I, as operator, pressing one of the five silent keys
with my right hand, and simultaneously the key which gave
the signal to the subject to open a box with the left. As G. J.
lifted a box-lid, and set off the recorder, I always noticed that
the click of the recorder, the tap of the signal-sounder, and my
pressing of the lamp-key occurred together. There was no
perceptible time-interval at all between my pressing the key
and lighting the lamp, and the recording of the trial, so that
G. J.'s hand must usually have begun to move towards the box
she was going to open before the lamp was lit. It looked very
much as if the delay-action trials quoted above must have
been precognitive.

Slow Trials.—Since, at our usual rate of working, the time
during which a lamp was alight in a box before a box was
opened was extremely brief, I tried, in certain experiments,
lighting the lamp from half to three-quarters of a second before
giving the signal for opening a box. It is very difficult to
compare results obtained under different conditions, because
the scoring keeps on fluctuating even while the external
conditions remain the same. The score obtained in one block
of a hundred trials is scarcely ever repeated in the next hundred.
So I arranged a change-over switch, worked silently with the
foot, by means of which I could change the condition in the
middle of a run, without any apparent pause, and so get fifty
trials done under each condition. This was the nearest
approximation I could get to a comparison of external conditions. It cannot always be used. For example, the change

from rapid to slow working is one which the subject was bound to know about. The slow experiments gave scarcely as good results as the fast ones. Length of ' exposure ' of the lamp was obviously not a necessary condition.

Precognition.—It was evidently possible to test the suggestion that a precognitive faculty might be at work. It was only necessary to get the subject to open the box before the key was pressed or selected in order to make the trials precognitive. I accordingly gave the signal to open the box with my left hand before I pressed a key with my right. And here the automatic recorder came in useful as a check. In any success which was really precognitive, the trial-line on the tape would be bound to overlap the success-line, extending backwards a little way behind it, since the trial-line began when the box opened, and the success-line when the lamp lit up. It was therefore shown whether all the successes really were precognitive.

Precognitive Results.

Trials.	Successes, Actual.	Successes, Chance-Expected.	Odds against Result being Chance.
2,255	539 = 23·9%	451	Many millions to one.

Finally, since this mode of testing precognition could not be used without the subject's knowledge, another automatic device was installed in conjunction with the mechanical selector. It was arranged that the subject should work the entire apparatus herself. The Selector was set running, and by a system of relays, the act of opening any box stopped it and lit the lamp corresponding with the contact it happened to stop on. To succeed with this, of course, involved precognition. This arrangement could be switched on by the use of the foot-switch. I found that if G. J. knew or guessed that it was in use she frequently failed with it ; but that if she did not know it was in use she succeeded with it.

It was not at all easy to keep G. J. in ignorance of the arrangement which was being used. She seemed to know telepathically, and would often tell me what arrangement I was using when

I was trying to hide it from her. So long as she did not know or guess, it did not seem to make the slightest difference to her scoring what the conditions of the experiment were.

It is, indeed, one of the most extraordinary things that it did not appear to matter, so far as scoring was concerned, whether the lamp was lit before the box was opened or afterwards. If precognitive scoring had been an impossibility, opening the boxes before the lamps were lit would always have prevented the result from being significantly above chance. The same would have been true if the subject had been guided by light-leakage, heat, or any other radiation from the lighted lamps, and it would not have been difficult to establish this by repeatedly throwing in the delay-action device during periods of good scoring. But that was certainly not the case. On days of good results, successes could be attained with any arrangement, whether precognitive or not, and on bad days, there was failure with all arrangements alike.

Results with Mechanically Selected Numbers.—Many experiments were done with numbers taken from the Mechanical Selector, written down beforehand, and then passed through the keys and Commutator. With these, of course, there was not even the formal objection that the repetition intervals differed somewhat from those of a purely random selection, although, as we have seen, this could not have affected the actual results as they were obtained. It has to be clearly understood that what we are concerned with are the *coincidences* occurring between two series of selections, and, so long as *one* series is truly random, it does not matter how much the other differs from randomness, the probability of success by chance will remain the same. In the following results the operator's selected series had been taken from the Mechanical Selector, which was known to give a purely random selection, and passed through the Commutator. The expectation of success by chance was, therefore, as previously, 20 per cent. ; telepathy was eliminated by the Commutator, as also was any possibility of information being unconsciously conveyed to the subject by the operator. He could not convey what he did not know.   The average rate of scoring was certainly lower than on some previous occasions, but this tells us little.   It merely means that the series included more blank days, since, of course, all the results were included, good and bad alike.   We must not conclude that the low rate of scoring is necessarily caused by the external conditions of experiment.

Results with Mechanically Selected Numbers.

Trials.	Successes, Actually Scored.	Successes, Expected by Chance.	Probability of Result being Chance.
7,809	1,841 = 23.5%	1,562	10^{-14} or a hundred billions to one.

As has been said before, no one has suggested any alternative explanation for these results, other than that of extra-sensory perception.

General Observations.—It may be suggested that the apparatus was, perhaps, not reliable, and recorded incorrectly. It was, as a matter of fact, examined and approved by a very prominent scientific experimentalist.   Also, I made a practice of testing it before each experiment, and, when good results were obtained, immediately afterwards as well.   Faults of using, such as that of the operator and subject getting out of step, made it possible to lose successes but not to gain extra ones.[1]

Nor are we confined entirely to the figures in judging whether or not an extra-sensory faculty was at work.   There are qualitative indications as well.   One of the most instructive things is the variability of the faculty and its constant failures. It is pretty clear that if there had been some mistake about the chance-expectation of success, and it had for some reason been put too low, then, if chance were actually giving the results, they would be at least fairly constant.   Also, the subjects who were tested on the machine, and did score at the rate of 20 per cent., would have been scoring subnormally and significantly.   They would not fail completely on certain days, and rise suddenly

[1] A synchronizing lamp was used for keeping in step, which showed the operator when a box-lid was open.

on others ; nor would the failures coincide with days of illness or depression on the part of the subject, as was actually observed.   G. J., the one person who has scored highly on the machine, has also given proof of possessing an extra-sensory faculty in countless ways in daily life.   Each new condition, when first introduced, sent the rate of scoring down, but it afterwards rose again.   The presence of visitors sent the score down at first, but there was a subsequent recovery.   This is exactly what Rhine found with his subjects.   All this points to the cause of scoring as something variable within the subject.

Grouping.—The tape records, in cases where the score has been well above the chance-expected 20 per cent., are very instructive.   They show that the increased score is due to short bursts of successes superimposed here and there on the chance-successes.   There may be groups of from six to ten consecutive successes in one or two places in an otherwise chance record of a hundred trials.   G. J. is quite definitely aware, during the periods when these groups occur, of almost losing consciousness of her surroundings.   She says that a peculiar, and rather exalted feeling comes over her, making her feel that it is almost impossible to fail, and so long as this lasts, the successes follow one another in an almost unbroken chain ; but it is never maintained for more than a few seconds at a time.   One sees here a kind of mental dissociation (it may be not unlike that which often accompanies automatic writing) which lets the extra-sensory faculty overcome its customary inhibitions for a moment or two.   Compare the dreamy states in which Rhine's subjects worked.

It is very easy to ask what are the conditions under which these favourable moments are likely to occur, but the question is not at all easy to answer.   I can only say in the most general terms that the main condition seems to me to be that of mental and physical well-being ; the faculty goes with health and happiness, and an absence of any conditions tending to self-consciousness.   If I were asked, from my observations of G. J., to state in a word the condition most essential for success, I should say *joie de vivre*.

There is a certain class of critic who maintains that extra-sensory perception will only become credible when it has been rendered productable in the laboratory with the ease and certainty of physical phenomena—as it were, by the turning on of a tap. They are suspicious of the extra-sensory faculty because it cannot be verified with the ease and certainty of a physical experiment. If this faculty exists, they say, why cannot it be made to work at will ? Why cannot the sensitive tell us the value of the turned-down card, or what is enclosed in the sealed envelope, every time these are presented to him ? The answer has, I think, been sufficiently indicated. It is because normal perception tends to oust the supernormal and keep the field to itself. In order that the deep mental stratum which has the supernormal knowledge may use the normal motor mechanisms to get this knowledge externalized, there must be some very delicate liaison work between the two types of consciousness involved, which is hard to establish and easy to derange. No doubt, when *all* the conditions are right, extra-sensory perception *always* occurs. But some of the conditions are psychological, very delicate, and largely unknown. Much depends on atmosphere ; and, after all, extra-sensory perception is not the only thing which is dependent on atmosphere. Humour, for example, is markedly susceptable to it. Try the same experiment with a humorist that the above type of critic wishes to try with the sensitive. Say to him : You said some very witty things at dinner last night. To-night I have got some people coming to hear you make some more jokes and take them down ! Note the result. The very fact that an experiment is being tried tends to inhibit a faculty which depends on spontaneity. Because the subject-matter of physics is dependable and certain, this type of critic insists that psychological phenomena *ought* to be the same. There is no reason for this, except a mental inertia, which refuses to change its habits of thought ; but the attitude is extremely common.

This brings us to the end of our review of the experimental evidence. Before discussing further evidence of a different kind, it will be well to pause, and review certain points of theory.[1]

[1] Among further examples of experimental work on extra-sensory perception, the reader is referred to Prof. Charles Richet on ' Clairvoyance,' *Proc. S.P.R.*, vol. v. pp. 77–116, and vol. vi. pp. 66–83 ; Estabrooks, *Bulletin* 5, Feb. 1927, Boston S.P.R. ; Coover, *Experiments in Psychic Research*, Stanford Junior University Publications ; Warcollier, *La Télépathie*, Paris, 1921 ; Hans Bender, *Zum Problem der Aussersinnlichen Wahrnehmung*, Leipzig, 1936.

Part III

SIGNIFICANCE OF THE EVIDENCE

' And here we wander in illusions ;
Some blessed power deliver us from hence.'
' The Comedy of Errors '

Chapter IX

THE THEORETICAL ASPECT OF EXTRA-SENSORY PERCEPTION

UNITARY CHARACTER OF THE EXTRA-SENSORY FACULTY.—This would seem to be an opportune point at which to turn from the consideration of the actual evidence to a discussion of its significance. The spontaneous cases which have been quoted are, of course, no more than samples to indicate the nature of different classes of evidence ; and, although the experimental work cited covers a larger proportion of its respective field, the reader is reminded that all the evidence given above has had to be drastically condensed owing to considerations of space, and he is urged to consult the fuller reports indicated by the references.

The question which now faces us is this : How big a thing is this extra-sensory faculty ? Is it a pigmy or a colossus ? In 1920, Professor William M'Dougall said : ' I believe that telepathy is very nearly established for all time among the facts recognized by Science, mainly by the work of this Society. If, and when, that result shall have been achieved, its importance for Science and Philosophy will far outweigh the sum of the achievements of all the psychological laboratories of the universities of two continents.'[1] Was he exaggerating the importance of a mere psychological curiosity, so far overlooked by science ? Or was he pointing to a discovery destined to be of far-reaching importance for mankind ?

When we look back at the cases which have been cited, we are struck by the extraordinary indifference which the extra-sensory faculty manifests to what appear to be radical changes in the conditions. In the ' pillow ' case the percipient reads a

---

[1] Presidential Address to the S.P.R., *Proc.* vol. xxxi. p. 109.

8

message on a hallucinatory piece of notepaper ; this case is telepathic.   In Case 10, the percipient reads the time on a hallucinatory watch-face ; this case is clairvoyant ; but the mode of presentation of the knowledge is in both cases the same, namely, by a visual picture, which has in some way been provided.

In Case 10, Nurse Jones hears the voice of her niece just as the latter is speaking at the moment.   In Case 15, Mr. Williams hears the voice of the wireless announcer just as it *will* sound to him some hours later.   The mode of presentation of these apparently vastly different phenomena is precisely the same.

In Case 2, Marjorie Stanley appears as if in the flesh standing beside her mother's bed at exactly the moment when she is thinking of her intensely.   In Case 17, the stepfather of Lady Z appears as if in the flesh standing by her bedside in precisely the same way that he was *going* to appear a few days later.

There are many cases in which the subject is warned by visual hallucinations of *present* danger.   In Case 14, a man is warned in exactly the same way of a *future* danger, namely, that there is going to be an accident five miles farther along the road.   There is nothing in any of these cases to indicate any difference in the *modus operandi* of the telepathic, clairvoyant, and precognitive modes of extra-sensory perception.   If difference there be, then that difference lies in a deeper stratum of the self and underlies the process of presentation to the conscious mind.

All this points to the final stage of presentation as being a separate process—an internal and unconscious action on the part of the percipient himself, performed in a kind of psychological artist's studio, in which various kinds of messages are actualized in the form of created groups of sense-imagery, and in this form thrust upon the conscious attention.

The experimental branch of extra-sensory perception shows the same indifference to the time-factor and to the divisions between the telepathic, clairvoyant, and precognitive modes of the faculty as do the spontaneous cases.   If we experiment under conditions which allow the telepathic and clairvoyant faculties to operate together, and then remove the possibility of telepathy, we find that this makes no difference to the rate of scoring. Or we can switch over suddenly and unostentatiously from the condition permitting clairvoyance to the condition necessitating precognition ; or, from the condition permitting telepathy to the condition necessitating precognition, without causing any discernible alteration in the course of the experiment. On the other hand, slight changes in the psychical or emotional tone of the subject, or expectation, extraneously or self-induced, cause profound changes in all the results.

These facts point to a curious indifference on the part of the extra-sensory faculty to changes which we, as observers in the physical world, regard as of fundamental importance.

Other workers in the subject have remarked the same thing. Mrs. Henry Sidgwick, in a paper on ' An Examination of Book-Tests,'[1] says :

' I think the present records suggest a thing which may be worth keeping in mind in future experiments, namely, that telepathy and clairvoyance are probably in some way closely connected. Telepathic clairvoyance—perception of external things not known to any one present but known to some one somewhere—probably merges into pure clairvoyance, while the line between more ordinary telepathy and telepathic clairvoyance is not a well-marked one. I think it is likely that the processes not only merge into each other, but that they may sometimes operate simultaneously.'

Professor Charles Richet, when describing experiments in clairvoyance, says :

' Cette télépathie n'est qu'un cas particulier d'un fait bien plus général—la faculté de connaissance des somnambules.' (This telepathy is only a particular case of a much more general fact—the faculty of trance-knowledge.)

And Myers in *Human Personality* says that the distinction between telepathy and clairvoyance ' cannot be made fundamental.'

This solidarity on the part of what one would imagine to

[1] *Proc. S.P.R.*, vol. xxxi. p. 377.

be three entirely distinct modes of perception points to the faculty as being something very remote from ordinary experience. To what extent is such a faculty, including, as it apparently does, the startling power of apprehending future events, to be regarded as antecedently improbable ? And how will its antecedent probability or improbability affect our attitude towards the evidence ? To this point of crucial importance we must now direct our attention.

Is the Evidence for Extra-Sensory Perception a priori *Incredible?* In a valuable address given to the Society for Psychical Research,[1] Professor C. D. Broad said :

' Of course each of us is influenced to some extent by psychological causes, which are logically irrelevant, when he accepts or rejects an alleged fact or a suggested theory on the strength of evidence submitted to him. But an important logical principle is involved too. The degree of belief which it is reasonable to attach to an alleged fact or a proposed theory depends jointly on two factors, namely, (*a*) its antecedent probability or improbability, and (*b*) the trustworthiness of the evidence and the extent to which it seems to exclude all alternatives except the one suggested.'

And further :

' Now antecedent probability depends very largely on analogy or coherence of the suggested proposition with what is already known or reasonably believed about the subject-matter with which it is concerned.'

We are thus plunged at once into a difficulty of a very profound nature. What degree of analogy or coherence would it be reasonable to expect between anything so new and strange as extra-sensory perception and the phenomena with which we are familiar ? Dr. Broad searches for an analogy between clairvoyance and normal modes of perception, and, failing to find any, faces us with the following curious dilemma :

' Have those who believe that clairvoyance occurs,' he asks, ' and deny that it is analogous to any form of sense-perception, any

[1] 'Normal Cognition, Clairvoyance, and Telepathy,' Presidential Address, May 1, 1935, *Proc. S.P.R.*, vol. xliii. p. 398.

positive notion of its psychological nature or its *modus operandi* ?
If they have, it is most desirable that they should expound it.   If
they have not, they are just postulating what Locke would have
called " a something I know not what."   Since their postulate will
then have no discernable analogy or connexion with anything that is
already known and admitted to be a fact, it will be impossible to
assign a degree of antecedent probability or improbability to it.
In that case we shall be unable to come to any rationally justified
degree of belief or disbelief when they produce their empirical
evidence, however impressive it may be.' [1]

The difficulty is very real.   And I believe that it exercises
a decisive influence on the attitude of the educated public
towards psychical phenomena in general.

Two opposing principles come into conflict—the empirical
and the rational.   What should we do in the extreme case in
which we had overwhelming empirical evidence in favour of a
certain proposition, which at the same time involved a logical
contradiction ?   Von Helmholtz is reported to have said :
' Neither the testimony of all the Fellows of the Royal Society,
nor even the evidence of my own senses could lead me to
believe in the transmission of thought from one person to
another independently of the recognized channels of sensation.
It is clearly impossible. . . .'   That represents the extreme view
of the anti-empiricist.   Galileo, armed with his telescope,
arguing with the ecclesiastics, and pointing to the satellites of
Jupiter, represents the empiricist appealing to fact against
misgrounded but still logical reason.   Our difficulty is that we
have solid empirical evidence for the existence of extra-
sensory perception, but what we can discover about it will not
fit into the scheme of the universe as we understand it.   It
remains for us to inquire whether this difficulty is insuperable.

If telepathy and clairvoyance showed signs of behaving in a
way analogous with the modes of perception which we know,
then the ground of analogy and coherence with the known,
for which we are seeking, would be found.   Taking telepathy
first, let us inquire whether a physical theory of it is acceptable.

---

[1] ' Normal Cognition, Clairvoyance, and Telepathy,' Presidential Address,
May 1, 1935, *Proc. S.P.R.*, vol. xliii. p. 414.

Is Telepathy a Physical Mode of Intercommunication ?—Any physical explanation of telepathy would demand that some kind of physical radiant energy must emanate from the brain of the agent A and proceed through space to the brain of the percipient B, and there set up a thought similar to that which A had when the radiation started. All kinds of radiant energy known to science obey the inverse square law when travelling in a uniform medium, unless means have been taken to concentrate them into a beam. So that telepathic energy, if it is physical, must, as a general rule at least, fall off with the square of the distance from the agent. There are many instances of telepathy between people in different countries, or at great distances apart. There is, for example, the telepathic experiment with Mrs. Piper carried out over a distance of 800 miles, mentioned before.[1] It is certain that any transmitter of physical energy which could affect a percipient 800 miles away would have an immensely greater effect on a percipient at close quarters, say, in the same room. Indeed, the influence would be so strong at a range of six inches as to be absolutely certain in its effect, and telepathy would have been established long ago as a fact in nature. Probably the power would be so strong at short ranges as to be highly dangerous. But there is no experimental evidence tending to show that distance makes any difference to telepathy.

Transmission of physical radiation also necessitates the use of a transmitter and a receiver, and it is not conceivable that such highly complex instruments as would be necessary, and instruments of so much power, could have escaped the notice of anatomists if they had existed anywhere within the human body or brain.

Also, this physical energy would produce physical effects in the media through which it passed, if the latter absorbed it, and these effects would have been noticed by the delicate instruments used by physicists. If, on the other hand, the energy were so penetrating that nothing absorbed it, then it would have no effect on the brain of the percipient. It could scarcely be maintained that all brains

[1] p. 65.

were transparent to it except the brain of the one individual for whom the message happened to possess an interest!

There is, however, a more serious objection still to the physical theory of telepathy. It is that ideas cannot be conveyed from one mind to another by any physical means without first being translated into a code, then transmitted, and finally retranslated from the code back into ideas. Language is a *code* for conveying ideas through a physical medium. In speaking, words become a modified train of sound-waves in the air which travel to the listener, who decodes the sounds into ideas through his knowledge of the code-system. Or the word may be encoded in the form of printed or written marks on paper; or of electro-magnetic radiation which travels with the speed of light to the wireless receiver, there to be retranslated, first into sound by the instrument, and then into ideas by the listener. If telepathy is a physical process, the ideas transmitted must certainly be encoded in some way or other in order to be sent out as modulations of a stream of physical energy, and this coding must be done by the unconscious part of the agent's mind. Are words spelt out in the Morse code as in telegraphy? Telepathy seems to work a good deal quicker than this, unless there is concealed in the recesses of the brain a Wheatstone automatic transmitter which anatomists have carelessly overlooked! Or perhaps it is a microphone with amplifying valves made of brain-cells into which the ' unconscious ' speaks in a physical voice which is pitched so high as to be beyond the compass of the human ear! There is no need surely to labour the obvious point that a physical theory of telepathy is completely untenable. Yet it is as well to lay some stress on this, since there is a widely popular tendency to regard telepathy as a manifestation of physical radiation of some sort. Witness a book by the American writer, Upton Sinclair, which is entitled *The Mental Radio*. Probably this view is due to the general familiarity with radio-telephony; and it is very likely on this account that the public is more ready to accept telepathy as a fact than the other modes of extra-sensory perception, since the fancied analogy with wireless offers a pseudo-explanation of it.

Other Possible Modes of Telepathic Action.—But, if we set aside the theory of a physically transmitted telepathy as incompatible with the facts, there are other possible modes of telepathy which must also be considered. These, however, would have to be classed as ‘ supernormal ’ theories. We conceive a person’s mind and brain to interact with one another. What if a similar action can go on when the mind and the brain belong to two different people ? In all, we should have to consider three cases. (i) There may be an extension of the mode by which A’s brain normally affects A’s own mind, so that now A’s brain directly affects B’s mind, irrespective of the distance between A’s and B’s bodies. This we can call the ‘ brain-to-mind ’ theory. (ii) There may be an extension of the mode by which A’s mind normally affects A’s brain so that now A’s mind directly affects B’s brain. This we may call the ‘ mind-to-brain ’ theory. (iii) A’s mind might directly affect B’s mind without the use of any material intermediary. This we may call the ‘ mind-to-mind ’ theory.

Now, we do know that there is apparent interaction between A’s mind and A’s own brain, and it might be said that it is quite conceivable that the interaction might sometimes occur directly between A’s mind and B’s brain, or between A’s brain and B’s mind. The difficulty is that we have not the least idea why A’s mind should, in this case, affect B’s brain (or A’s brain affect B’s mind) in particular rather than any one of several million others. We are left without any sign of causal guidance. Case (iii) is even worse in this respect. Now let us turn to Clairvoyance.

Is a Physical Explanation of Clairvoyance Possible ?—In clairvoyance we are dealing with the perception of a physical event, or a physical object without the use of the normal senses. Let us suppose that we have discovered, as the result of experiments such as have been quoted, that a percipient is able to perceive clairvoyantly the character of cards in a shuffled pack, which lies face downwards on the table, the order of the cards being unknown to any one. Suppose that the card perceived contains a black circle on a white ground, and that it is situated near the middle of the pack. If physical radiation of some sort is conveying the information to the percipient, the same general considerations as to the effect of distance, and the penetrability of obstacles, apply as in the case of telepathy. And there is again the absence of any known receiving organ. The radiation must pass through the other cards in the pack, and through the percipient's skull in order to reach the brain. Why do these obstacles not absorb it on the way ? If it is because the radiation is so penetrating, why does it not pass through the brain of the percipient also without producing any effect ?

How does the percipient perceive the qualitative difference between the black circle and the white ground ? This must be because the differences in surface-quality of the card, which cause the reflection or absorption respectively of white light, react in a similar way with regard to the kind of radiation which is used in clairvoyance. This is remarkable. Different kinds of radiation usually behave differently with regard to reflecting and refracting media ; for example, short wireless waves are refracted through a prism, not of glass but of pitch. We should not expect this penetrating radiation, which has escaped the detection of physicists, to behave so similarly to light.

All the other cards in the pack must be sending out the same kind of radiation from the different designs which they contain, as is the particular card perceived, and what would reach the percipient would be a jumble from all the cards. How does he differentiate the particular card he wishes to describe ?

In what way does he know that the design on the card is a circle ? In visual perception, the rays of light, having been brought to a focus by the eye, form an image of the perceived object on the retina, and it is on this that the visual perception of shape depends. There must be some organ which can collect and focus the energy used in clairvoyance and form a similar image, and there must be nervous mechanism corresponding to the retina and optic nerve which transmits it to the appropriate part of the brain ; but nothing of all this has been discovered by anatomists !

Physical radiation always travels in straight lines. If radiation is coming from the pack, it would only be necessary to place it so that the plane of the cards was in the line joining the percipient's brain to the pack, in order to make clairvoyant perception impossible. Indeed, clairvoyance would always be impossible unless the cards were inside a certain cone having the receiver in the brain for apex. It should not, therefore, be difficult to locate the position of the receiver in the percipient's brain or body, by moving the pack of cards into various positions. Needless to say, there is no sign of any of these conditions being fulfilled.

There is also another difficulty of a psychological kind. The clairvoyant radiation, whatever it is, has brought to the percipient experience of a *visual* ' sensum,' which is black and circular. But the immediate experience of the clairvoyant which the special clairvoyant radiation brings, is not visual. How does the percipient *know* that the differentiations of the clairvoyant sensa correspond to the peculiar differentiations of the visual sensa ? The problem is similar to that of a man born blind, who has for the first time received his sight. He would not know that his visual experiences corresponded in any way with his tactual experiences. For example, we say that a polished table *looks* smooth and *feels* smooth. But such a man would not connect these two experiences in the least with one another. He would have to learn to connect them. How, then, would the clairvoyant connect his immediate clairvoyant experiences with his visual experiences, so as to be able to say, on receiving the former : ' The tenth card from the top is a black circle ' ? Dr. Broad suggests that the clairvoyant may from infancy have grown accustomed to correlating the two sense-fields, the clairvoyant and the visual, unconsciously, albeit the clairvoyant field is in the unconscious and the visual field is in the conscious. This does not surely sound very convincing. As he says : ' It seems at first sight most unplausible to postulate in the clairvoyant's mind a whole special group of sensations of which he is totally unaware, and then to postulate that they are intimately correlated with his ordinary visual sensations, and eventually become associated with the latter.'[1] But, as he remarks, a similar thing is suggested by orthodox psychologists, who explain the vision of solidity by unconscious sensations of accommodation and convergence.

But clairvoyance is not so simple a thing as the conveyance of the visual impression of an object to the percipient's conscious mind. Sometimes it initiates an involuntary motor action, and sometimes it produces a strong urge to do something. In all this we are confronted by a lack of obvious causes.

The Causal Difficulty.—To sum up the causal difficulty, the world, as the mind conceives it, consists of causally related sequences of events ; so that when an event is *directly pre-hended* by the mind, as distinct from being *logically inferred* by the mind, that event itself must enter into the causal ancestry which leads to its own apprehension. In the case of normal sense-perception it is demonstrably the case that this occurs. If the physical event is a flash of light, we can trace the chain of physical and physiological causes and effects which lead from the occurrence of the flash to the brain-disturbance which goes hand in hand with the visual experience or sensation of light. This latter is a mental event giving us knowledge that the flash has occurred. Similarly, if the physical event is the contact of our hand with a solid object, a chain of physical and physiological processes precedes our experience of the sensation of solidity. If the physical event is the ringing of a bell, there is another causal chain leading from the physical disturbance of the metal to our experience of the sound. In all these cases we can trace a connexion between the physical events and our knowledge of them. But in the case of extra-sensory perception, the event cognized and the event constituted by the cognition do not appear to be causally connected.

We have examined clairvoyance to see whether any physical process, more or less analagous with that of vision, could be traced in order to account for it ; but we found the difficulties

---

[1] 'Normal Cognition, Clairvoyance, and Telepathy,' Presidential Address, May 1 1935, *Proc. S.P.R.*, vol. xliii. pp. 412-3.

in the way of such an explanation too great. We examined telepathy to see if a physical explanation could be held to account for that, but found as great difficulties as in the case of clairvoyance. Besides the physical explanation, we glanced at three other theories of a supernormal type, but found there an equal difficulty in the absence of any apparent cause for its selectivity. Extra-sensory perception has every appearance of breaking away from the scheme of the world as we at present understand it, and of refusing to fall into line with the causal scheme. Two conflicting factors stand face to face—the empirical evidence on the one hand, and the lack of antecedent probability on the other. The empirical evidence cannot be got rid of by vaguely suggesting explanations which will not bear scrutiny when examined scientifically and in detail. It is useless to talk about chance or fraud or credulity in an airy and general way, unless it can be shown *in detail* that each case can be more reasonably explained by these causes than by a supernormal explanation. Until that is done, the evidence stands and must be admitted. On the other hand, unless a physical explanation for extra-sensory perception can be accepted, where are we to find that ground of analogy and coherence with the present body of knowledge which is necessary if we are to assign to it any certain degree of antecedent probability ? On this fundamental point, the whole of the evidence for extra-sensory perception would seem to break away from our present outlook on the nature of things.

But if telepathy and clairvoyance refuse to be assimilated into the general scientific outlook, there is worse to come. What are we to say about Precognition ?

The Puzzle of Time.—It is with the greatest diffidence that I venture to make a few remarks about the theoretical aspect of Time and Precognition. Let me hasten to say that I make no claim whatever to understand it. But I should like first of all to point out the enormous importance for science which the repercussion of Precognition may quite possibly have on our conception of the nature of Time. The interpretation of the whole scientific scheme hangs largely on our conception of the nature of Time. This is seen very clearly in the domain of biology, which is bound up with the theory of Organic Evolution. The extent to which we regard Evolution as an *explanatory* term in biology depends on the meaning we attach to the idea of Time. What has to be explained in the biological sciences is not merely something which happened long ago when life first originated on the earth, or when living beings grew to consciousness. It has also to explain what has happened at every moment, and what is happening *now*, in every living thing. A noted biologist has said : ' Consciousness arises anew in every human being. Its first origin on the earth presents no less mystery than its last.' [1] The dawn of consciousness in each individual presents precisely the same problem as the dawn of consciousness in the race. And it is the same with every other characteristic of organic beings. The problem is : What happens when *anything* new appears ? On the answer to this question depends the whole interpretation of biological science and any meaning we may be able to attach to such words as Evolution and Emergence. How does the new, or emergent, property come to be ? The same author speaks of Emergence as follows :

' Particularly hostile to scientific progress,' he says, ' are the extremer forms of emergence. According to these, a material system of a certain degree of complexity suddenly exhibits qualitatively new properties such as life and mind, which cannot be explained by those of the constituents of the system. There is clearly an element of truth in this view. We can only discern a little mind in a dog, and at present none in an oyster or an oak. Nevertheless, science is committed to the attempt to unify human experience by explaining the complex in terms of the simple. This may be a vain endeavour, but I do not at present see any evidence of its vanity.

' I will give an example of its success in the realm of physics. J. J. Thomson and Rutherford showed that the hydrogen atom could be separated into two components, the electron and the proton, which behaved in many situations like very small spherical electric charges attracting one another according to Coulomb's law. But the hydrogen atom has very complex qualities. It emits a series of characteristic radiations whose frequencies are related by

[1] J. B. S. Haldane, *Possible Worlds*, p. 44.

definite laws like those of a piano. This is the simplest example of emergence, or holism, the properties of the whole being far more complex than those of the parts. It held up the progress of theoretical physics for a generation. Then de Broglie (1930) produced wave-mechanics. To explain these facts, he said, we must attribute to the electron certain undulatory properties. These properties were soon after experimentally verified by G. P. Thomson (1930) and others. The electron and the proton were seen to be more complex than they at first appeared, though by no means so complex as the hydrogen atom.

' I regard this as a model for scientific explanation. If we ever explain life and mind in terms of atoms, I think we shall have to attribute to the atoms the same nature as that of minds or constituents of minds such as sensations.' [1]

The question is whether this ' model for scientific explanation ' really *explains* anything at all. The puzzle that the hydrogen atom exhibited emergent undulatory properties, which nothing in its constituents could account for, was solved by discovering that the constituents contained, after all, identically the same kind of properties as the atom. The puzzle that living and thinking beings, who appear to be constituted by atoms which possess neither life nor mind, are radically unlike their constituents, is to be solved by attributing to the atoms mind-like properties. The facts which the emergentists point to as *new* are thus explained by putting the characteristics of the resultant into the constituents, and assuming that there is no problem if it becomes only a matter of growth in degree, and not of change in kind. Of course, this makes ' emergence ' a good deal easier ; but might one respectfully suggest that if the rabbit is put into the hat in sight of the audience, the applause, when it is taken out again on the conjurer's table, cannot be expected to be so hearty ? The problem is not how to explain the appearance of the *startlingly* new : it is how to explain the appearance of *anything* new. Whatever meaning there may be in the terms ' Evolution ' and ' Emergence,' depends on the meaning we attach to the terms ' Novelty ' and ' Change.' It is precisely here that the

[1] J. B. S. Haldane, *The Causes of Evolution*, pp. 157–8.

crux lies, for, when we come to ask : What *is* novelty and what *is* change ? we get no answer at all. Scientific explanation is bankrupt ; so is philosophy. All it can do is to record the *experience* that the new appears to flash into existence out of nothingness. It *was not* : it *is* ; and that is all that can be said about it. Dr. F. C. S. Schiller seems to me to be entirely justified when he says :

'It is true that nothing ever arises out of absolutely nothing. There is always something out of which it grows, but that does not explain it wholly. It does not account for the *new* in it. It is only so far as it is still the old, or the old over again, that it is accounted for by what it grew out of. In so far as it is new, it remains un-accountable, unpredictable, uncontrolled, undetermined, free. *That* factor in it, therefore, *has* arisen out of nothing, and Novelty as such *means*, Creation out of nothing ! ' [1]

And he adds the pertinent corollory that novelties ' play havoc with a very widespread notion of causation.'

We do not in the least understand what we mean by the process of Becoming ; and Becoming is the most essential characteristic of Time. Like so many other things which *seem* to be intelligible, and indeed obvious, in common life, Time breaks up on analysis into a series of insoluble problems, of which the bombshell of Precognition is only the last and most spectacular. The evidence for Precognition brings home to us with a shock what has really been the truth all along, namely, that Time is inherently unintelligible : but our minds have been so ' doctored ' in the interests of biological necessity (and not with regard to Time alone, but with regard to all the fundamentals of the world of sense-perception), as to make us as blind to the most glaring defects and inconsistencies, as Titania was to the Ass's head. It is in this blindness that the scientific interpretation of the world has been built up, and no suspicion of it dawns upon us until we meet with something which comes from outside the charmed circle of the senses— something ' extra-sensory.' Then, for the first time, the completeness of the antinomy begins to dawn upon us. We

[1] F. C. S. Schiller, *Must Philosophers Disagree ?*, p. 231.

have been working in terms of a myth, and a myth with set limitations. Science, based on sense-perception, is exploring in a limited circle, like a goat tethered to a stake, perfectly free to explore the universe—until the tether tightens.

The Theoretical Aspect of Precognition.[1]—Precognition, more than any other alleged fact, seems to be at variance with all we know. The main difficulty is the apparent lack of any cause linking the event foreseen with the act of foreseeing it. As has been previously pointed out, the same difficulty is met with in Clairvoyance and a kindred difficulty in Telepathy. In the case of Precognition it is more obvious and startling, but in truth the difficulty pervades extra-sensory perception as a whole.

Dr. Broad pointed out in the paper referred to below that three main difficulties or objections exist in the way of accepting precognition. These he set forth with philosophical accuracy and precision, but in the present brief and cursory survey of the subject, I shall refer to them in far looser language, more adapted to the general reader. The three difficulties are these : (1) How, without inferring it, can we *know* of an event which does not exist because it is still in the future ? (2) How can we have knowledge of an event when there is no causal connexion between the event and our knowledge ? (3) Precognition appears to be incompatible with free will.

1. In precognition we are dealing with immediate (not inferred) knowledge of events, which are separated from us by a gap in time. There is an analogy between this situation and that presented by memory, in which also we have awareness of an event across a gap in time. How can we have immediate knowledge of an event which does exist because it is now in the past ? The answer is that, in memory, we do not *prehend* the past event itself. What we immediately prehend is a present image representative of the event. This is clear, because

---

[1] In what follows I am allowed by the kindness of Dr. C. D. Broad, to quote from a paper on Precognition entitled ' Philosophical Implications of Foreknowledge,' published in Supplementary Volume xvi. of the *Proceedings of the Aristotelian Society*, and read by him to the Aristotelian Society and Mind Association in July 1937.

memory often turns out to have been delusive. We prehend the present image and uncritically accept (not by inference) the proposition that there was an event in our past experience corresponding with it, which proposition may be either true or false. Analagously, in the case of precognition, it is a present image which we prehend—not a future event. The present image is not always ostensibly precognitive, even if it is in fact so. For instance, a person may have a complex dream of events which subsequently come to pass : but at the time of the dream he may regard these events as present and not as future. Neither memory nor precognition are, then, *prehensive* ; and it will be seen in Chapter X that sense-perception cannot be prehensive either, although it purports to be. Thus the first difficulty, how can we *know* a non-existent event, disappears on analysis. Neither in memory nor in precognition do we become directly aware of an event which is distant in time, but only of its present representative.

2. The Causal difficulty is much more serious. Since a future event cannot leave causal trains in the past, no causal descendant of an event which has been precognized can exist in the percipient when he makes the precognition.

Now, there is one peculiarity about memories ; anything which we can remember must have lain within our *own* personal experience. We are not in the least surprised if a person shows knowledge of a past event which once formed part of his experience, despite the fact that the event does not now exist, and is separated from his present knowledge of it by a gap in time. But we are very surprised if he shows knowledge (apart from inference) of a past event which never entered in any way into his personal experience. An instance of such a case was given in Chapter IV (Case 16), and we have called it Retrocognition. Now, precognitions may refer either to events which will, when they occur, fall within the experience of the percipient, or to events which will fall outside his experience, but in either case we are equally as surprised by them as we are by a case of retrocognition, and equally at a loss to explain them. When faced by evidence for precognition, we incline to adopt, if it is at all possible, one of the theories

9

mentioned in Chapter IV (p. 39)—that is to say, that these predictions arise from subconscious inferences about events or subconscious intentions to bring them about ; or the fact of having made a prediction may induce a subconscious desire to fulfil it ; or telepathic information may have been unconsciously received from some person who is in a position to make a forecast about the event or is in a position to bring it about. As applied to the actual evidence, these theories are not, as a rule, at all easy to believe in. But there is one other suggestion which has been put forward by Dr. Broad in the paper above referred to. It is, he says, ' a perfectly fantastic suggestion,' and he puts it forward, fully realizing, of course, the difficulties and objections which it contains, and with the warning that it may well prove to be nonsense. But, he says : ' (i) So far as I can see, it is the one and only way in which the prehensive analysis of ostensible foreseeing, which we rejected long ago, could possibly be made intelligible and rehabilitated. And (ii) even if we continue to reject the prehensive analysis, the suggestion would enable us to deal with the causal difficulty in a way which we have hitherto shunned as impossible.'

The suggestion is that there might be a second dimension of Time which, normally, we know nothing about, lying, so to speak, at right angles to our familiar dimension.

To quote Dr. Broad :

' If there is only one temporal dimension, any two events of finite duration are either separated by a temporal gap or are adjoined, so that the end of one exactly coincides with the beginning of the other or they wholly or partially overlap. But if there be a second temporal dimension, events which are separated by a temporal gap in one dimension may be adjoined without any gap in the other, just as two points in the earth's surface which differ in longitude may be identical in latitude. Now, traces are postulated in order to reconcile with a certain principle, which seems self-evident to most people, the existence of causal connexions of events which are temporally separated in the one familiar temporal dimension. If this is the only temporal dimension, there is no other way to reconcile the facts with the principle. But if there is a second temporal dimension, with which we are not acquainted in ordinary life, we can suppose that events which are separated by a temporal gap in the familiar time-dimension and yet are causally connected, are adjoined in the second and unfamiliar time-dimension.'

Our axiom about causality would have to be modified as follows :

' We might have to say that x cannot be a causal ancestor of y unless x is before y in *at least one* temporal dimension ; but that x can be a causal factor of y, provided it is before y in *one* temporal dimension, even if it be after y in the other temporal dimension.'

One may imagine our familiar time as being represented by a line going from West to East, and the second dimension of time by a line going from South to North.   Thus, to quote an illustration given by Dr. Price during the discussion on this paper, Mother Shipton, who lived in the sixteenth century, is said to have foretold the invention of motor-cars.   This would be explained, on the two-dimensional time theory, by saying that, although in our familiar dimension of time, the invention of motor-cars occurred more than two centuries after Mother Shipton's prediction, yet, in the second and unknown dimension of time, it occurred just before the prediction.

In the course of the discussion on the paper, Dr. H. H. Price brought out the great difficulties to which a two-dimensional theory of time leads, particularly if Precognition is regarded as being analogous to memory.   Mother Shipton, predicting the invention of motor-cars, more than two hundred years before the event in *our* dimension of time, was doing something analogous to *remembering* the invention of motor-cars, which took place quite recently for her in the *other* dimension of time ;   and as memory is explained by traces left by the event (probably at least in part physical traces affecting the brain), we have to admit that we may be physically affected by events which have not yet happened in *our* dimension of time.   Perhaps we are going to be run over and killed by a motor-car twenty years hence in Time 1, but we were run over and killed by it yesterday in Time 2, which we normally know nothing about.   Still, the effects of our death injuries should be upon our body *now* ; and we should be dead in one time but not in the other. And we are confronted with another difficulty. The theory only deals satisfactorily with *one* of the characteristics of Time, namely, that of temporal order, in which events are arranged in a series of *earlier* and *later*. It does not deal with the second characteristic of Time, namely, the characteristic of *becoming*. Dr. Price says :

' We ordinarily conceive of the Universe growing longer and longer in time as new events continually " become," and get added on to those which have become already. Now it is in regard to this notion of becoming that difficulties seem to arise. What can be meant by saying that the Universe grows longer in two distinct and independent ways ? It cannot be like a sheet of water which spreads both Northwards and Eastwards ; for these two spreadings occur in *the same* time-dimension though in different spatial dimensions. Nor must we say that it grows longer in two ways *at once* ; for this again would bring us back to a single time-dimension. We may put the point another way (for it is a particularly muddling one) by saying that we are committed to the curious notion of a *Double Now*. The word " now " will no longer be unambiguous in its application. What is " now " in one respect may be " past " or " not yet " in another respect ; or, I suppose, it may be " now " in both respects. It may be said that this is not so intolerable, for something like it occurs in the theory of Relativity. But there is something worse. I think we are also committed to the even more curious notion of *Partial Becoming*. Suppose that I precognize an event which is to occur next Saturday. In one respect this event has not yet come into being : it is still future, and does not yet exist. But in another respect it is past, and so *has* come into being. It is, so to speak, half real ; it has *partially become* but not wholly. When next Saturday arrives, but not before, it will receive its second instalment of being, and will then be completely real. Yet will it ? For those two halves of its being are, so to speak, out of step. For when it begins to be in the West-to-East dimension, it will already be long past in the South-to-North dimension.'

But he makes a further and interesting suggestion, drawn from a consideration of the evidence, that perhaps precognition is confined entirely to the mental sphere.

A very remarkable feature in some of the cases is that the prediction is only partially fulfilled, and has the appearance of having been altered from what it would or might have been. A typical case of this kind was cited in Chapter IV (Case 16), in which the percipient had dreamed beforehand that her coachman would fall and strike his head on the pavement at a certain spot in the street, but, owing to her prompt action, based on her memory of her dream, she called to some one to catch him as he was falling, so that he did not strike his head on the pavement, and thus the latter part of the prediction was altered.   This suggests that the percipient may not have prehended the actual future event itself, but rather her own future mental state about the event—that is to say, her own belief about what was going to happen, and her belief may have been partly wrong.

In certain cases, when the fulfilment of the event will fall within the seer's own experience, we must postulate a causal relation between the seer's own mental state at the future time of the fulfilment of the event, and the seer's own present precognitive belief or knowledge about the future event. Dr. Broad has pointed out that this relation should be termed ' immanent purely psychical causation.' Although the difficulty of a causal relation which acts backwards in time still remains, it is now transferred entirely to the mental sphere, and this may possibly be thought to ease the situation. Further, this explanation can be extended to cover clairvoyance, thus doing away with the necessity for postulating supernormal cognition of events in the external world altogether. For, when a percipient becomes supernormally cognizant of a contemporary event in the external world, as of a card in a shuffled pack, we may say that what he really cognizes is not the card itself but the future mental state of the person who will verify what the card is ; and that, since every clairvoyantly cognized event must be normally known to some one at some time, if it is to be verified, clairvoyance as well as precognition can be kept within the mental world.   I think it might be possible to test this point experimentally by arranging that the clairvoyantly cognized events are never known to any one individually, but only the sum total of successes and failures.

This view would not remove the causal difficulty, but would confine it to the mental sphere.

The View that Time is only Mental.—Dr. Price alludes to a theory of time sometimes held. He says that people who speak of the unreality of time really mean that all events, whether of the physical or psychical order, are connected by relations of *earlier* and *later*, but that only psychical events are subject to *becoming*. Thus becoming would be a property of the mental but not of the physical world. Physical ' events ' would be, not truly events at all, but just existents of some sort arranged in a static order of their own, and their happening, or apparent becoming, would be due to the fact that the mind had come across them. A physical event could be earlier than another physical event and later than a third ; but none of these events could be referred to as being *present*, *past* or *future*, and of none of them could it be said that they have become, are becoming, or will become. What is present, past or future, on this theory, is not the physical event but the *cognition* of it. Thus physical events just *are*, in some sense or other, whereas psychical events come to be and cease to be. The two kinds of events, psychical and physical, are quite different from one another, having only this in common, that both kinds are ordered in a series of earlier-and-later. This view raises a great puzzle with regard to the nature of psycho-physical interaction.

Dr. Broad comments on it :

' I am inclined to think that the notion of earlier and later is inextricably interwoven with the notions of becoming and of past-ness, presentness, and futurity ; so that the suggestion that there might be a series of terms to which the latter did not apply, but which were nevertheless ordered by the relation of earlier and later, is really unintelligible.'

3. The Fatalistic objection to precognition presents us with two alternatives, neither of which we are inclined to accept. When a precognition has been fulfilled, which was

dependent upon a voluntary decision taken *after* the pre-cognitive announcement was made, we must suppose, either (i) that the voluntary action, which seemed to bring about the event foretold, had, in reality, nothing to do with it, or (ii) if it did, the voluntary action itself must have been completely determined. Nothing seems to help us over this difficulty.

It now remains to mention briefly two other theories of precognition.

Mr. J. W. Dunne's Theory of Time.—Mr. J. W. Dunne, in his book, *An Experiment with Time*, introduces a multi-dimensional scheme in an attempt to explain precognition ; and he has further developed this scheme in later publications. But, as Professor Broad has shown, these unlimited dimensions are unnecessary, and unless I have misunderstood Mr. Dunne's argument, they resolve themselves into space-dimensions, and the true problem of time—the problem of becoming, or the passage of events from future through present to past, is not explained by them but is still left on the author's hands at the end.

The Theory of the Greater Specious Present.—Mr. H. F. Saltmarsh, who is an expert in the evidence for precognition, has put forward an interesting theory of this phenomenon in the report, which has already been cited.[1] He bases his theory on the conception, accepted in psychology, that the ' present moment ' in which we perceive and act, is not a mere point-instant, but occupies a definite period of duration. The kind of present moment regarded in mathematics as a dimension-less point-instant, is, Mr. Saltmarsh insists, an abstraction from reality made in the interests of mathematical thought. Within the specious present there is no present, past or future, but there is a gradation with respect to clearness of appre-hension of that which lies within its compass, maximum clearness corresponding with the centre of the specious present and a gradual reduction in clearness taking place towards its extremities.

Now, so far as the normal, conscious mind is concerned,

---

[1] ' Report on Cases of Apparent Precognition,' *Proc. S.P.R.*, vol. xlii. p. 49 ff.

the specious present can only cover a short interval of time, but Mr. Saltmarsh suggests that beneath the threshold of consciousness, the span which it includes may be much greater. ' I suggest,' he says, ' that the specious present of the subliminal mind is of longer duration than that of the supraliminal, so that some events which are in the present of the subliminal would appear to be either past or future from the point of view of the supraliminal.' Such events would be physical events in the external world and these Mr. Saltmarsh would regard as ' existing ' in some non-temporal sense, having an inherent *order*, which gives them the characteristic of earlier-and-later, but not as themselves passing from futurity to become actual in the present and then go into the past.

One may perhaps think of this kind of specious present as it belongs to normal consciousness as the top of a rock which rises above the surface of the sea but has a much greater spread under the water. So the specious present of the subconscious self would extend over a much greater range. The specious presents succeeding one another would overlap beneath the ' water-line.'

If, now, at noon an event is precognized by some one which will occur later in the day, say at 6 p.m., the striking of noon by the clock occupies a specious present, which, for the normal self, is quite distinct from the specious present which will contain, also for the normal self, the experience of the actual event when 6 o'clock arrives. But, beneath the threshold of consciousness, it is to be supposed that these two specious presents overlap, and that intimation of that which is contained within the later one is somehow transmitted through the common portion into the earlier one and thence arises into conscious knowledge. Hence the conscious mind knows of the event before it occurs.

It will be seen that this theory explains precognition by denying it. Future events fall within the extended ' now ' of the subliminal consciousness, and Time is a reality only for the supraliminal mind.

This, however, is not the whole of the theory. Mr. Saltmarsh introduces a certain degree of plasticity into the world of temporally located events, conceiving it as to some extent alterable by human free will. To this extent it would appear to be subject to a true time of its own—not the same time as that in which mental events, such as enduring acts of perception, are occurring in the supraliminal mind. He likens the world to a bundle of approximately parallel wires seen through a slot, which moves in the direction of their length. All the wires are rigidly ' frozen ' in the past, the region over which the slit has passed, and some are frozen in the future, the region which the slit has not yet reached. Some, however, can be moved through the slot by the human percipient and actor, and the movement extends throughout the whole of their future length. Precognition is possible only with regard to future sections of the immovable wires. Free-will acts alter the movable wires and thus, to some extent, the whole of the future. It is not easy to understand how, on this theory, any long-range prediction comes to be fulfilled in detail.

In the next chapter we shall see that difficulties are not inherent in supernormal types of perception alone. They crop up to an embarrassing extent also in the analysis of normal sense-perception.

Chapter X

THE PROBLEMS OF SENSE-PERCEPTION

NORMAL SENSE-PERCEPTION IN ITS RELATION TO EXTRA-SENSORY PERCEPTION.—It is unfortunate that, if one aspires to go at all beyond a bare record of the evidence for extra-sensory perception, it is scarcely possible to avoid some consideration of normal sense-perception in connexion with it. This is unfortunate for the psychical researcher, because normal perception is a preserve of the professional philosopher, into which the layman strays at his peril. The only excuse which such a one has to offer for doing so is that the branches of his subject are so various that, if he is to deal with them all, he must be something of a Jack-of-all-trades, and that, in order to make progress in this queer subject, he must trespass in various people's gardens, even if the result is that he is summarily turned out. It may be that the person who pursues psychical research is, *ipso facto*, of the kind who rushes in ' where angels fear to tread ' !

At any rate, the extraordinary wealth of sense-imagery which characterizes the different states of consciousness with which the subject deals, compels one to reflect on the nature of the sense-imagery which we experience in normal life. I propose therefore to touch upon certain points in normal sense-perception which appear to be relevant to these states. In doing so, I shall quote certain passages from Professor H. H. Price's intensely interesting work on sense-perception ;[1] but I wish to make it absolutely clear that any conclusions reached or inferences drawn from these quotations are entirely my own, and are not to be attributed to the author of that work.

In venturing into this subject, I shall probably fall into all

[1] *Perception,* by H. H. Price. (Methuen, 1932.)

the inconsistencies and inaccuracies to which the layman is prone, but if, after I have muddled through, I shall have succeeded in sowing certain ideas in the mind of the reader, there to germinate, I shall be content. The view suggested (in my belief) by the facts of psychical research, will not here be put forward in philosophical detail but in the non-philosophical guise of a general impression.

First, with regard to the visual sense, let us consider the illustration which Dr. Price gives at the beginning of his book ; let us suppose that we are looking at a tomato. We recognize at a single glance a tomato as a red, spherical, softish fruit, juicy and edible, and occupying a certain position in space at a distance from us. Memory plays a part in this, of course, but we may call the act comprised in this glance an act of *perception*.[1] The act and the experience together are complex and analyzable, and include far more than the data which are immediately given to sense. To quote the author on this point :

' When I see a tomato there is much that I can doubt. I can doubt that it is a tomato that I am seeing, and not a cleverly painted piece of wax. I can doubt whether there is any material thing there at all. Perhaps what I took for a tomato is really a reflection ; perhaps I am even the victim of some hallucination. One thing, however, I cannot doubt : that there exists a red patch of a round and somewhat bulgy shape standing out from a background of other colour-patches and having a certain visual depth, and that this whole field of colour is directly present to my consciousness. What the red patch is, whether a substance or a state of a substance or an event, whether it is physical or psychical or neither, are questions that we may doubt about but that something is red and round then and there I cannot doubt. Whether the something persists even for a moment before and after it is present to my consciousness, whether other minds can be conscious of it as well as I, may be doubted. But that it now *exists*, and that *I* am conscious of it—by me at least who am conscious of it this cannot possibly be doubted." [2]

[1] Dr. Price does not use this word in the same context in which it is used below.

[2] *Perception*, p. 3.

With the other senses it is the same.

' Analagously, when I am in the situation called " touching something," " hearing it," and " smelling it," etc., in each case there is something which at that moment indubitably exists—a pressure or prement patch, a noise, a smell ; and that something is directly present to my consciousness.' Also Footnote [2] on page 139.

Now, these are the immediate data of perception. Dr. Price calls them *sense-data*. (Dr. Broad calls them *sensa* ; B. Russell in a slightly different sense speaks of *sensibilia*.) They are directly *given* to consciousness ; and the act of intuitively apprehending them is called the act of *sensing*. Sensing is, therefore, quite different from perception ; it is much simpler and is immune from all possibility of error or illusion.[1]   One may, for example, be looking at a wax-work figure and mistakenly believe it to be a man ; but the outline filled with colour which one *senses* is there, whether one is mistaken about what it belongs to or not.   About that there can be no mistake.   It is there or it is not there.

How the complete act of perception is arrived at ; by what jump we pass from the simple sensing of the round, red patch—the immediate datum—to the awareness of a physical tomato, existing in space, cannot be gone into here.   It may be remarked, however, that it is an *intuitive* jump of some sort, and not a logical inference.

The complete act of perception, when made, attributes the sense-data to the objects perceived, in the sense that they form integral elements in the constitution of such objects.   For example, the red, round, bulgy patch, which is immediately sensed when we see a tomato, is unhesitatingly accepted by us as being a literal constituent of the surface of the tomato.   We accept, without doubting, the *feeling* which forces itself upon us that this red, round patch exists out there in space and is quite independent of ourselves.   Yet a little reflection shows that sense-data such as this red patch must depend for their *existence* at least partly on ourselves.   Unless we are looking

---

[1] As to whether this analysis of sensing possesses the finality which it appears to, I should wish to reserve judgement.

in the right direction, for instance, or standing in the right place, have our eyes open and so forth, and have our eyes, nerves, and brain all functioning normally, these sense-data will *not exist* ; the feeling of their complete independence of ourselves is therefore spurious. Suppose we say that the tomato is red whether any one is looking at it or not, what does this mean ? Is a tomato red in the dark ? If so, how would you distinguish, in the dark, between a red tomato and a green one ? The redness of the tomato is evidently inseparable from the observer. It is a *sensation*. If it has an immediate object, that object is a *sense-datum* and not a tomato. Is it not true, then, that when we say that a tomato *is* red, we mean that it *causes* us to have a peculiar visual experience, which we unconsciously project on to the tomato ? If, when we look at the tomato, and have the sensation of redness, this is really *cognition* of something, and not merely having a feeling of a particular kind—feeling, so to speak, ' redly '—then it is a red *sense-datum* of which we are immediately aware, not a red tomato. And that sense-datum is not *part* of the tomato in the sense in which we commonly think it is—that is to say, it is not an independent constituent of the tomato. It is at least partly dependent for its existence upon ourselves. Whether, that being granted, it forms a literal constituent of a physical tomato as well is a question which can by no means be settled off-hand. What is true of certain visual sense-data is also true of certain tactual sense-data ; also of auditory, olfactory, and gustatory sense-data. Nor are we saved from this difficulty by distinguishing between the primary and secondary qualities of things.

The Privacy of Sense-Data.—The next point to observe is that these sense-data are not common property. Each observer's sense-data are private to himself. If a dozen observers look at a tomato from a dozen points of view, each senses a different sense-datum—different in shape and size, and possibly different in colour, for one observer may be colour blind, etc. There are, indeed, an infinite number of sense-data ' belonging ' to the tomato ; for it may be viewed from an infinite number of points of view. In what sense do they all ' belong ' to it ? If there are physical objects, which are neutral and public in their character, the sense-data, which we always assume to be integral constituents of them, are not so in reality. They are the private property of individual observers. In what sense, then, are there public and neutral objects in the world around us ? The answer to this question is no simple one ; and when we arrive at it, the physical object which is public to all, has become a very queer and unfamiliar thing indeed : it is just a locus of causal properties.

Another thing we have to reflect on is that sense-perception is subject to many illusions. If our sense of perception tells us that the red, round patch we sense when we look at a tomato *is*, in fact, the very surface of that tomato, what are we to say about reflections and distortions of various kinds ? When we see a tomato reflected in a mirror, the red, round patch we sense is there just as when we look at it direct, but now it cannot form part of the actual surface of any tomato. Or the distorted and discoloured object we see if we look at a tomato through an irregular piece of coloured glass—in what sense does the datum we sense now ' belong ' to the tomato ? Or the thirsty travellers in the desert who press on towards an oasis, which vanishes before they reach it because it is only a mirage ? Some sense-data there evidently are which ' belong ' to physical objects only in a remote and distant way ; these cannot, in the ordinary sense, help to *constitute* such objects ; yet these differ in no respect from those sense-data which we commonly believe do help to constitute physical objects.

Again, instances often occur in which sense-data of purely subjective origin blend with complete ease with the sense-data of normal perception, and are indistinguishable from them. An approaching omnibus sometimes appears in the distance to bear the number one is expecting, but on nearer approach the number changes to another, which is the one it actually bears. Traffic lights are seen to *move* up and down when they change colour. Actually, one goes out and another appears, but they are quite distinctly seen to move. This moving sense-datum must be contributed by the observer, and is illusory ; yet it is quite indistinguishable from that part of the picture which gives the correct positions and colours of the lights. Objects near at hand stand out in relief when looked at, the degree of stereoscopy lessening as the object is removed farther and farther from the observer. But the maximum distance of stereoscopy depends, amongst other things, upon the degree of *familiarity* which the observer has with the object. Hence the element of depth or relief in vision must, at least to some extent, be *supplied* by the percipient. It is a commonplace that expectation can cause physical objects to assume shapes different from those which they actually possess. To a nervous person, a bush in the dusk may look like a burglar. The chimney of a cottage seen through a fog once moved rhythmically in my own field of view, because I believed that there was a man hammering on the roof. The moment I realized that the man was hammering elsewhere, the object became a rigid chimney. I had *supplied* the moving sense-datum. When we reflect that all our sense-data are private and that we create some of them in response to entirely internal and mental causes, and that these created data can enter into ordinary perception on an equality with those which we believe to exist out in the world independently of ourselves, we can scarcely refrain from entertaining the suspicion that *all* our sense-data may arise in the same way and may all be our own creations. Their connexion with what we believe to be an ' outer ' world must then be a deep mystery.

Hallucinations.—There exist sense-data which have no connexion with physical objects at all, which we call ' hallucinatory.' These are experienced in dreams and delirium, after taking certain drugs, and very fully by subjects in a state of hypnosis. It is sometimes said that in these cases there is nothing corresponding to the full act of perception, and that all the experient does is to *sense* visual or other data. But this does not seem to be the case. There can be little doubt that hypnotic subjects are capable of ' perceiving ' persons and objects in just as complete a sense as that in which they are perceived in normal perception, although such persons and objects may be non-existent. A verbal difficulty arises over

the use of the word ' perception ' here for the sensuous appre-
hension of that which is not real. How can one ' perceive '
an object which does not exist ? But in order to save complication, the word to ' perceive ' is here used to include experiences
of the same kind as those constituting normal perception,
whether veridical or not.

An example of such an experience was recorded by Mrs.
Verrall when experimenting in the guessing of playing-cards
by feeling their faces with her thumbs.[1] She found that the
art of reading cards by feeling the number of pips was one
which could be learnt by practice ; and when the tactile impression of the card had been secured, the visual impression
of it immediately followed. But, she says : ' I may note a
curious instance of an illusory mental impression as to how
the guess was made. I am a very good visualiser, and as soon
as I think of a card, see a mental picture of it. On the third
night, namely, after a hundred guesses, I found that I was
mentally reversing these processes, and had it not been for
my experiences of the two preceding evenings, should have
said, not that I *felt* but that I *saw* the cards.' *Tactual* processes, then, can give immediate rise to *visual* sense-data ;
and tactual sense-data can be delayed while visual sense-data
occupy their proper place in the process of perception.

All these facts go to show that the sense-imagery that we
ordinarily regard as being somehow out in the world in normal
processes of seeing, hearing, etc., and as helping to constitute
physical objects, is all the time being created by psychological
machinery within our own personalities. These very same
data, out of which so obviously surrounding objects are built
(as we commonly think) can blend indistinguishably with
sense-data for which the percipient *must* be wholly responsible.
The conclusion indicated strongly by these facts is that we
actually *create all* our sense-data, in which case the truth
about the physical world may be very far indeed from that
which the perceptual faculties and common sense assign to it.

We cannot, then, come to the everyday world and use it as
a touchstone of truth with which to compare the new and

[1] *Proc. S.P.R.*, vol. xi. p. 176.

strange phenomena we meet with in psychical research. The everyday world is itself under deep suspicion of being other than it seems, and—important above all things to notice—it is shot through and through with relativity. The sense-data which we commonly take to be bricks in this outer construction—to form its surfaces and its qualities, are constructs of our own making. True, the external world is not a subjective illusion ; it is jointly produced by ourselves and *some* reality independent of us, whose intrinsic character we do not know, but which we find presented to us in a symbolical form, suited to the special needs and exigencies of our life.

Another, and very interesting, phenomenon points out how completely normal sense-perception can be simulated and reproduced by psychological efforts made within the self.

Eidetic Imagery.—This curious and interesting phenomenon —now sufficiently advanced to have received in psychology the name of ' Eidetics '—provides an instance of a quasi-perception lying on the borders of both normal sense-perception and memory. About 60 per cent. of children between the ages of ten and fifteen are said to possess this faculty, which atrophies in adult life, although traces of it may persist in some cases. Psychological experiment has distinguished the Eidetic Image from the Memory Image on the one hand, and from the After Image on the other. The method of experiment consists simply in presenting to the child a coloured picture on a grey ground for a period of about thirty-five seconds. The child is then told to report what he saw.

' All investigators agree in ascribing to the Eidetic Image a certain " perceptual " character. That is to say, the content of the Eidetic Image is " in a literal and true sense seen . . . " ; the attention of the observer is directed *outwards* . . . ; and there is a noticeable tension and pressure felt in the visual organ " incomparably stronger than that which attends the Memory Image," and often " stronger than that which attends ordinary accommodation for near objects. . . . " '

This attribute of external localization affords an unmistakable distinction between the Memory Image and the

10

Eidetic Image, but does not in itself serve to distinguish adequately between the Eidetic Image and the After Image.[1]

The following are a few of the characteristics of this faculty as summarized by the author of the above, which serve to differentiate it from the Memory Image :

It possesses a pseudo-perceptual character, i.e. is definitely localized in visual space even though recognizable as a subjective phenomenon : it is generally superior to the Memory Image in clearness and richness of detail ; it is more accurate in its reproduction of detail ; is more brilliant and accurate in colouration ; tends more to cohere with its ground ; is subject to voluntary recall after a considerable lapse of time, etc. But, like Memory Images, it depends upon interest ; can be altered by an act of will ; and is influenced by preceding images.

Where the Memory Image is deficient, the Eidetic Image can often supply the missing detail ; but a preceding Memory Image may prejudice the accuracy of the Eidetic Image. Unlike the Memory Image, there may be some rivalry between the details of the Eidetic Image and those of its physical background. It possesses ' depth.' We read : ' It is important to note that the Eidetic Image of a three-dimensional object is almost never devoid of bodily character, and that of the Eidetic Image of a two-dimensional object (e.g. a picture), especially among clear-cut cases of eidetic ability, frequently appears in marked relief. . . .'[2] This shows clearly that in Eidetic Imagery we are dealing with ' perception ' and not with mere sensing. The images are, however, ' frequently reversed, turned upside down, or displaced from right to left.'

Jaensch[3] has developed a theory that Eidetic Imagery is the genetic source of both memory and perception ; but the latter seems, in fact, to be very early differentiated in the child, and to be co-existent with the Eidetic faculty. Eidetic Imagery may well supply a particular need of childhood, for, in adult

---

[1] ' Eidetic Imagery,' by Gordon W. Allport, *British Journal of Psychology*, vol. xv. p. 102.

[2] Ibid. p. 106.

[3] E. R. Jaensch, *Eidetic Imagery*. (London, 1930.)

life, when modes of reaction have been created by habit and channels of association are many, the comparatively weak signal of the memory image may be sufficient to initiate response to a situation, whereas in the child who is learning to become familiar with the presentations of sense-perception, the memory image of them is not a sufficient stimulus. It needs to have situations prolonged, as it were, for continued inspection, so that the sense-image which is past is recreated in exact and vivid detail for it, thus giving rise to the Eidetic image. It is quite likely that, if the power of creating eidetic imagery were prolonged into adult life, it would come into harmful competition with normal activities.

This curious phenomenon shows with what completeness sense-imagery can be created by the percipient, even in normal states of consciousness. We must now consider briefly another important point about ordinary sense-perception, namely, its claim to be *prehensive*.

Sense-perception does not put us in Immediate Touch with Physical Objects.—When we perceive an object, we intuitively accept the suggestion, which is a part of the perceptual process itself, that we are directly *prehending* the perceived object. Yet this cannot be, in fact, the case. One argument alone is sufficient to show this. There is always a lapse of time between the moment when the physical stimulus occurs in the external world and the moment when the corresponding sensation is experienced. This time may be very short, but it is always there. If we touch an object, for instance, a certain time always elapses during which the pressure on the skin initiates nervous impulses which travel at a measurable, and by no means excessive speed, to the brain. If we look at an object, in addition to this physiologically imposed interval, there is the time taken for the light to travel from the object to the eye. Owing to the enormous velocity of light, this interval in most ordinary cases is extremely short. But not always ; we see the sun, for example, not as it is but as it was something like eight or more minutes ago. When we look at a star, we see the star as it was, perhaps, fifty thousand years ago. It may have undergone a radical change in the interval ; but we see it nevertheless as it *was* and not as it *is* : despite this fact, the suggestion accompanying the sight is that we are looking at something which *exists now* in the actual present. The whistle of a distant train comes to us after the puff of steam has cleared away, and the act of whistling is over. What we apprehend in sense-perception is always the *past* ; never the *present*. But, when we think about it, is it not only the present which exists and is *actual* ? How, then, do we come to apprehend with our senses that which no longer exists ? There must be, from this point of view alone, something specious and illusory about normal sense-perception, for undoubtedly our senses tell us quite a different story, namely, that we directly *prehend* what now exists. The fact is that, so long as the appropriate stimulations were applied to our minds or our brains, or to both, we should ' perceive ' an external world just the same, no matter whether it existed or not. Let us think of some cinema of the future, so perfected as to give us perfect illusions of all our senses, and to place us, to all appearances, visibly and tangibly, among the actors of the piece in three dimensions of space. Already we hear them speaking, so that we should then have the illusion of being actually in their world ; yet all would be done by the aid of apparatus such as projectors, loud-speakers, and the like. There is something remotely analogous to this in sense-perception.

Science, Sense-perception, and the Physical World.—It is natural to suggest that, if the nature of the physical world is in question, we should turn to the science of physics for information. And, further, that if the nature of sense-perception is in question, we should turn jointly to the sciences of Physics and Physiology. Have not experts in both these departments of knowledge studied these subjects with the aid of powerful instruments and discovered a great deal about them ? Certainly they have, but always subject to one limitation—a limitation which is unfortunately crucial. They have verified all their experiments by means of that very sense-perception whose nature we are now questioning. The situation amounts to this : Our senses reveal to us, at least roughly, the nature of what purports to be an external world. But what we want to know is : Are our senses telling us the truth ? Physicists proceed to explore the external world with refined instruments, by measuring, calculating, inferring ; but every experiment and calculation has to be brought back to the senses for verification. Consequently, whatever may vitiate the dicta of the senses in the first instance vitiates the whole body of physics. Then the physiologists and anatomists say : If you are doubtful about the nature of sense-perception, we will find out about it for you. They use *their* particular instruments, they measure nervous impulses, they examine the organs of sense, they dissect the brain, and so forth, and they give their version of how perception takes place. But they, too, have referred all their researches to the verdict of their own senses ; so that we are still where we were when we started. Asking the physical scientists about the ultimate nature of the world or of perception, or asking the biological scientists about the ultimate nature of life, is like trying to lift oneself up by one's own braces. As Dr. Price says : ' Empirical science can never be more trustworthy than perception, upon which it is based ; and it can hardly fail to be less so, since among its non-perceptual premises there can hardly fail to be some which are neither self-evident nor demonstrable.' [1]

Here, then, we are placed in a quandary. The orthodox sciences, taken together, have drawn a picture of the world which, so far as it goes, is fairly coherent and self-consistent. I think one may say that this picture is most satisfactory where the physical sciences are concerned ; not quite so satisfactory where the biological sciences are concerned, and still less satisfactory where the mental sciences are concerned. But still, so long as one is tactful enough not to ask searching questions, it is a very impressive picture. But all the sciences have based their pictures on the testimony of the normal senses ; and now we are beginning to obtain a glimpse of the world, fragmentary though it be, not from the point of view of the normal senses, but through supernormal or extra-sensory channels of perception ; and we are startled to find

[1] H. H. Price, *Perception*, p. 1.

that it does not agree in the least with the sense-picture. The difference is not superficial either, and does not look as if it were even one of degree ; it seems to be a difference in kind. Coherence with the sense-picture, either as presented by the senses in the raw, or as sophisticated by science, is practically nil. Fundamentals such as space and time seem to be ignored in the extra-sensory picture—a thing which makes nonsense of the normal sense-picture. What does it mean and what are we to do about it ? We are, so to speak, committed to the sense-picture. For one thing, Nature has instilled into us, with the power of a super-hypnotist, the conviction that the world about us is *there* in the most literal sense, and against this psychological compulsion, philosophical analysis, and psychical facts will, for the most part, appeal in vain. For another thing, we have invested our capital in the sense-scheme —scientific theories, systems of philosophy, and even religious institutions are built upon it : professional reputations are bound up with it ; the vested interests of churches are built into it. Above all, common sense is solidly behind it. And then psychical facts appear on the scene and threaten the whole structure with demolition. What is to be done ? Obviously, to thrust the psychical evidence away—to belittle it, to misrepresent it and to ridicule it. This suggests itself as the first move—and this is what is actually being done, as I shall show by quoting a concrete example. What would be the alternative if this were not done ? Every fact and indication in psychical inquiry, surely, points the same way : we should have to acknowledge that the world of the normal senses, and the entire scientific structure built upon it, is a particular and highly specialized form of *appearance* of a reality of whose intrinsic nature we know nothing—a form of appearance exactly correlated with the complex structure of our person- alities, serving our practical ends and controlled by psycho- logical mechanism which is interwoven with the substance of our personality itself. That our modes of reaction with this independent world are similarly unknown to us in their intrinsic nature, being refracted to us through the senses.

It seems to me that the progress of modern physics adds

its quota to the evidence pointing in this direction. In the course of its progress from the raw world of the senses from which it started, it has revealed not one world, but many. What are these worlds, or what is this constantly changing world, which physics keeps on discovering, if it is not a changing world of appearance ? Is it not significant that such a distinguished physicist as Max Planck should write :

'But besides the world of sense and the real world, there is also a third world which must be carefully distinguished from these : this is the world of Physics. It differs from the two others because it is a deliberate hypothesis put forward by a finite human mind; and as such it is subject to change and to a kind of evolution.' [1]

The progress of Physics is not an *additive* change, such as might be made by taking the picture of the world as the senses present it and merely filling in more detail. The telescope develops the view of the heavens in this additive way by filling in stars which cannot be seen by the naked eye. But the progress of physics is not like that, but is more like a changing panorama of scenery shown on a cinematograph film—one view keeps dissolving into the next until the whole scene is altered. Perhaps it is more like the continual change of aspect which one gets by walking round a house. But it is not getting any nearer to revealing the fundamental character of the physical universe ; it is merely exhibiting it from a series of different points of view.

The philosophical analysis of perception leaves us with the knowledge that we do not know the intrinsic character of physical objects and are not likely to know them. To quote again from Dr. Price's work :

'But although physical objects must have some intrinsic qualities or other, we have no means of knowing the specific nature of these qualities. Nor can any conceivable advance in natural science bring us a step nearer to this. Science can only show that the causal characteristics of a complex object, e.g. a stick of cordite, are dependent on the causal characteristics of its minute parts, and

[1] *The Universe in the Light of Modern Physics*, pp. 9–10.

upon their spatial relations to each other. It cannot tell us anything about the intrinsic qualities of the minute parts, nor does it attempt to do so.' [1]

I do not wish to carry this discussion too far afield, or to prolong it unnecessarily ; but it must be pointed out in a few words that the world of thought betrays just the same character of artificial specialization and adaptation to human personality as does the world of sense-perception.   It also is dependent on the peculiar construction of the human being.   Intellectual processes, which appear convincing and consistent until closely examined, reveal, when narrowly looked into, disjunctions which the mind glosses over in the processes of ordinary thought.   Thought, in fact, is made to serve the purposes of life and to *appear* convincing, much as the world of the senses is made to *appear* indubitably real.   Those acquainted with the works of F. H. Bradley will know his acute analyses of thought-situations.   I cannot devote space to this aspect of the subject, but will content myself with a single quotation from C. A. Campbell :

' I have argued that the path which the intellect takes and must take to avoid self-contradiction . . . is not a path which can lead to Reality.   Inherent in the very nature of the process is a reference beyond itself which raises fresh problems on the basis of temporary solutions.   So far as I can see one conclusion is unescapable. Reality in its true character must be pronounced disparate from each and every thought-product.   And the term " disparate " must be taken in its fullest significance.   I do not mean that there is here merely a difference of degree, such as might leave it possible for us to say that certain thought-products reveal more adequately than others, although none with perfect adequacy, the character of ultimate Reality.   I mean that there is a fundamental difference in kind, such as renders thought-products and Reality strictly incommensurable.' [2]

To sum up, I am pointing out in the most general terms that the scientific examination of psychical phenomena has

[1] H. H. Price, *Perception*, p. 294.
[2] *Scepticism and Construction*, pp. 19–20.

created an extraordinary situation by introducing a body of well attested fact which will not cohere with the general body of existing knowledge. And I am suggesting that the only hope of resolving this situation lies in admitting as a broad and general principle, that the world we live in—the world of ordinary sense-perception, and of scientific discovery, as also of common thought—is a kind of oasis in the heart of reality— an ' island world ' of appearance—in which an infinite universe is brought to focus as a world of constructed myth, and as such becomes a possible world for the finite mind to understand and to interact with. In fact, we live in a world which is more a product of biological necessity than it is a simple reality. In the next chapter we shall look at the attitude of scientists towards psychical phenomena, and shall see what light the above point of view has to shed on the situation.

Chapter XI

THE PREVAILING ATTITUDE TOWARDS
PSYCHICAL PHENOMENA

ANTECEDENT PROBABILITY FROM A NEW STANDPOINT.—Let us return to the question of the antecedent probability of extra-sensory perception and look at it in the light of the view which we have just been considering. If the world of normal sense-perception is regarded, in the most thoroughgoing sense, as a world of appearance, does it not ease the situation? An appearance in the nature of a constructed, representative picture, limited in its scope, might surely leave much outside it which need not be coherent with it, once we admit that the picture is, to a large extent, sophisticated and factitious. If we reject this point of view on account of its difficulties (which are doubtless many), continuing to demand a coherence which, manifestly, is not there, while psychical evidence continues to accumulate, I cannot see in what respect our attitude will differ from that of the person who, contemplating an enormous stuffed fish in a glass case, said : ' The man who caught that fish is a liar ! ' There would seem to be no room for compromise. The only policy would be that of von Helmholtz, namely, to call the supernormal impossible, and to deny the evidence for it out of hand. An American scientist, Joseph Jastrow, perhaps put the position even more uncompromisingly when he said : ' It is in loyalty to the spirit of science that I must deplore the animus of psychical research. . . . The trial is on. It is either psychology alive and metapsychics dead, or *vice versa*.' [1]

It may, perhaps, be said that in speaking of a world of reality which differs in character from the world presented by the normal senses (the noumenal behind the phenomenal) we are postulating a ' something we know not what,' and using words which have no meaning. But I am not sure that this is not the right way to explore. If a strange situation demands a

[1] *The Case for and against Psychical Belief.*

new hypothesis, why should we not postulate a ' something we know not what ' ? Is not this precisely framing a working hypothesis ? When the early experimenters in electricity and magnetism found that the wire joining the terminals of their battery became hot and deflected a compass-needle brought near, they said that an electric current was flowing in the wire. They did not know what an electric current was ; we do not altogether know to-day ; but what began as an empty phrase gradually accumulated meaning. As it is, gulfs of ignorance are hidden beneath most everyday names and phrases. It is only familiarity which creates in us the illusion that we understand things when we give them names.

The Present Attitude of the Educated Public towards Psychical Phenomena.—That the main fact which dictates the aloofness characteristic of the attitude of the educated and scientific public towards psychical phenomena is the incompatibility of the latter with their pre-accepted world-outlook, is shown clearly by their method of treating it. Some change has undoubtedly been brought about in the attitude of intelligent people towards the subject by the increase in reliable evidence which has taken place during the past few decades. Fifty years ago, psychical phenomena were roundly denied : to-day, they are not so much denied as ignored—rather studiously and anxiously ignored—after being accorded a brief, verbal recognition. Scientific writers mention them under constraint, and then pass on hurriedly, often after confiding to the reader the information (not at all superfluous) that they regard them with an open mind ! But they do not treat them with accuracy or candour. They seek, rather, to throw a smoke-screen over them under cover of which they hope to escape from the necessity of dealing with them.

The attitude characteristic of last century is illustrated by the following extract from a lecture delivered by Lord Kelvin in 1883 :[1]

' Now I have hinted at a possible seventh sense,' he says, ' a magnetic sense, and though out of the line I propose to follow, and although time is precious, and does not permit much of digression,

[1] *Popular Lectures and Addresses* (Nature Series), vol. i. p. 265.

I wish to remove the idea that I am in any way suggesting anything towards that wretched superstition of animal magnetism, and table-turning, and spiritualism, and mesmerism, and clairvoyance, and spirit-rapping of which we have heard so much.   There is no seventh sense of the mystic kind.   Clairvoyance and the like are the result of bad observation chiefly, somewhat mixed up, however, with the effects of wilful imposture, acting on an innocent, trusting mind.'

This dogmatic denial of ' clairvoyance and the like ' is not the line taken to-day.   The present policy is to whittle away as much of the evidence as possible, in the hope that the remainder will prove amenable to a physical explanation. Nevertheless, there are a very few exceptional men of science who face the issue with frankness and admit the evidence to be what it is.   An example of one of these is to be found in the report of the meeting of the British Association in 1927, the following being taken from the *Times* summary published on September 6, 1927.   Dr. T. W. Mitchell, in the course of a paper read to the Psychology Section, said :

' Telepathy or some mode of acquiring knowledge which for the present we might call supernormal must be admitted, for if we refused to accept telepathy we stood helpless in face of well-attested phenomena which we could not account for and could not deny.'

' Dr. C. T. S. Myers, who presided, said he would not like it to go forth that all psychologists had definitely made up their minds about telepathy.   Many of them neither denied nor accepted it, and he was one of these.   He felt that the evidence was not yet strong enough to decide whether telepathy existed or not.   He was maintaining an open mind.'

Not many are willing to risk their reputations by being as candid as Dr. Mitchell.   In a popular work on biology, entitled *The Science of Life*, written jointly by Messrs. H. G. Wells, Julian Huxley, and G. P. Wells,[1] there is a chapter on ' Borderland Science '[2] (that is to say, on Psychical Phenomena), which

[1] The criticism here made of Messrs. Wells' and Huxley's account of psychical phenomena is not to be taken as being personally directed against these distinguished authors.   The case is considered at some length because it is typical of a widespread attitude, and because of the light which it throws on this attitude.

[2] Book VIII, Chapter IX.

well illustrates the attitude of the average man of science towards psychical matters to-day. The authors omit reference to practically all the serious evidence, such as that summarized in the present volume. They quote, without the exactness necessary for scientific treatment, incidents from pseudo-evidence which lies outside the scientific boundary, making it appear as if this were the kind of evidence on which the whole subject rests. ' Aunt Sallies ' from this quarter are set up to be shied at, and are duly bowled over, until the desired effect is worked up in the reader's mind, and he is innoculated with the idea that all this psychical stuff is rubbish ! True, the authors reserve a loophole by saying of telepathy : ' There is no justification for an intolerant rejection of the idea ' ; but the chapter as a whole overwhelms this by a series of clever insinuations and innuendoes tending in the opposite direction. The reader of this chapter is left with no idea at all of what are the true facts of the case. Precognition, for example, is made to appear as if it rested on a few precognitive dreams published by Mr. J. W. Dunne. It is hinted that telepathic evidence may be explicable by chance because ' . . . there remains a vast proportion of failure in telepathic endeavours. The public is too apt to hear only of the telepathic successes,' though not, it seems, through ' scientific ' accounts such as this ! It is suggested (all in vague innuendo) that the evidence for telepathy may be accounted for by the desire of witnesses to make a good story. It is remarked how strange it is that, if telepathy exists, it does not manifest itself at bridge clubs and chess tournaments, where people meet together inspired by a common idea. It is suggested that, if telepathy does exist, it must have something to do with the ever-popular ' mental radio.' The authors speak of the ' opacity of the normal human skull to " thought-waves " ' ; and they go on to state that ' there is hardly any form of telepathy that cannot be imitated by conjurers and other professional entertainers,' and that, ' there is an undefinable element of untrustworthiness in most of the witnesses, and possibly in all ' !

What psychic bandage, one wonders, covering the eyes of these writers, allows them to make statements which hard facts so surely refute ? When one thinks of the distinguished men and women who have vouched for this and that piece of psychical evidence, and of the hundreds of members of the public who have attested to their experiences, and whose testimony, after cross-examination, has been accepted, one stands amazed. An amusing exception is, however, made in favour of Dr. Gilbert Murray, whose honesty the authors admit to be above reproach ! One imagines he must be deeply sensible of the compliment which singles him out from among so many eminent investigators on account of his moral probity !

The fly-blown trick of slate-writing is revived, coupled with the story of a Persian gentleman named ' Boorzu,' who insisted on recognizing himself under the title of ' Books ' ! And there is an incident concerning Miss Rebecca West, who became ' emotional ' at a sitting with some unspecified medium, because ' Grandfather West ' appeared on the scene, and she had to suppress her enjoyment of the knowledge that ' West ' was only her pen-name ! Much of the chapter, too, is decorated with unpleasant pictures of ' materializations ' ; but *nowhere* is the slightest hint given that a serious mass of evidence exists, which it is the duty of any man of science who broaches the subject to reveal.

The psychical researcher, who reads this account of ' Borderland Science,' is amazed when he realizes that it is offered as a *scientific* description of psychical facts. The reflection occurs that the book is written with the avowed intention of instructing the public in science, and that the public will take it seriously on account of the eminence and authority of its authors ; and, further, that there is no red lamp at the beginning of the chapter marked ' Borderland Science.' This is the point of view from which it is serious.

Scientific method has been abandoned for a piece of literary brush-work, which is thoroughly tendentious. It is not science : it is special pleading. But this does not mean that either the integrity or the scientific ability of its authors is thereby impugned. The important point is that Messrs. Wells and Huxley have succumbed, in the particular subject of psychical research alone, to a *subconscious* resistance against

its facts and their implications, which is in no wise peculiar
to themselves, but is quite general amongst scientists and philosophers and other cultured people, who are men of the highest
ability and repute.   We are not here witnessing a lapse on
the part of individuals, whether moral or intellectual : we are
witnessing the manifestation of a powerful subconscious
instinct, which is incorporated in the structure of human
personality.   It is probable also that there are reasons for their
attitude of a more deliberated kind.   For one thing, scientific
men feel it to be their duty to protect science against an influx
of superstition.   As M'Dougall has said : ' Men of science are
afraid lest, if they give an inch in this matter, the public will
take an ell, and more.' [1]   For another, the climate of opinion still
sets fairly strongly against psychical things, and professional
men have to defer to it for the sake of their reputations.   But I
think that the root-cause, which goes deeper than these, is the
one we have already been considering, and that the key to it is
given us by certain passages in the chapter from which I have
quoted.   The authors say that they believe that telepathy, if a
fact, would not be at variance with the ' general scientific
ideology.'   This, though I think a mistaken conclusion, introduces an illuminating phrase.   They go on to say : ' We have
attempted no philosophical nor metaphysical " explanations."
We have dealt with the facts, and our picture is a presentation
of fact,' [2] and this, I think, gives us the key-position.   It is not
a ' will to disbelieve ' in psychical phenomena as such which
lies at the root of the scientific man's attitude towards them,
so much as a ' will to believe ' in a ' scientific ideology '
which is incompatible with them.   This scientific ideology
is grounded on the assumption that scientific fact is to be
interpreted literally.   It is, in fact, a *philosophy* of science, or
a metaphysics of interpretation, despite Messrs. Wells' and
Huxley's denial.   In Chapter IX, we referred to the relativity
of scientific fact, showing how the meaning of biological facts
in particular depends upon our conception of the nature of
Time, and in the last chapter we showed that this scientific

[1] See Chapter XXIII, p. 341.
[2] *The Science of Life*, p. 839.

ideology is based on a literal interpretation of sense-perception. The ' Scientific ideology ' wishes to interpret biological, as well as other facts, in terms of notions of process, causality and becoming taken over in the raw from common sense.   And the scientist is imbued with the belief that, on the integrity of this philosophy, the fate of science depends.   He is therefore out to defend it.   The bias against psychical research and its findings rests, I think, primarily on the belief that they are incompatible with this philosophy of science, and it seems to me that the belief is well founded.   The scientist takes his last stand on his ' facts.'   What will happen, he wonders, if, owing to the incidence of other facts of an irreconcilable nature, these facts become ' sicklied o'er with the pale cast of thought,' and lose their uncompromising clarity, and deprive him of his accustomed right of interpreting them literally ?

We are back again, therefore, on the old ground of the absence of coherence between psychical facts and the facts of common experience.   Scientists think, or perhaps half unconsciously feel, that if psychical phenomena are admitted, the whole structure of science will be endangered.   If by the ' structure of science ' they mean the ' scientific ideology,' it seems to me that they are right.   But if by the ' structure of science ' they mean scientific *fact*, they are surely wrong. Nature may safely be left to see to it that her facts do not contradict one another.   The important thing is not the facts, considered as bare observations, but the *interpretation* which, inevitably, we put upon them before we can reason about them.

Compare Messrs. Wells' & Huxley's stand on scientific fact with the following passage from A. N. Whitehead :

' The old foundations of scientific thought,' he says, ' are becoming unintelligible.   Time, space, matter, material, ether, electricity, mechanism, organism, configuration, structure, pattern, function, all require reinterpretation.   What is the sense of talking about a mechanical explanation when you do not know what you mean by mechanics ? ' [1]

The whole issue is a philosophical one.

Professor Whitehead's pertinent question has a more

[1] *Science and the Modern World*, p. 21.   (London, 1928.)

general application. What is the sense of talking about evolution when you do not know what you mean by Time ? What is the sense of talking about the causal functions of a gene as explanatory of an organism when you do not know what you mean by a physical object ? If the scientist replies that metaphysics are not his business, the answer is that he is steeped up to the neck in metaphysics already. It is precisely a metaphysical belief which determines his present attitude. Science does not bring us knowledge of the intrinsic nature of reality : it only shows us various forms of *appearance*, and this is the source of the antinomy between orthodox science and psychical research. The faculties we call ' supernormal ' bring us into relation with reality in quite a different way, and present it to us in quite a different guise. Once this is grasped, the way to the reconciliation of the irreconcilables becomes intelligible, at least in principle. But it remains entirely unintelligible so long as we accept scientific fact at its face value and take it for a literal and ultimate account of the nature of things.

If physics cannot tell us the intrinsic nature of a physical object, it is not likely that biology can tell us the intrinsic nature of a living organism, or that psychology can tell us the intrinsic nature of a mind. This is the root fact which we stumble against whenever we try to understand the significance of psychical phenomena. We have assumed that science can tell us these things, and expect everything to fall in with our assumption. It would surely clarify scientific work a good deal if it were clearly stated in treatises and text-books that the author does not know the intrinsic nature of the entities he is writing about, and, so far as science is concerned, never will. Authors do not always seem to be quite clearly aware of this. We should then know much better where we stood. As it is, the world is full of specialists who take their subjects too literally, because they believe their knowledge to be final. Each working in his own groove, appears to be sublimely oblivious of all the others, and to regard his own subject as providing the key to the universe. One man will base his life's work on beliefs which another will not regard as worth five minutes' consideration : but the two never meet to thresh the matter out.   How much more interesting the world would be if this mutual exclusiveness were dissolved —if, say, Catholic and Anglican bishops (or possibly cardinals and philosophically minded deans, if bishops were disqualified on the ground of being specialists in finance) were to meet for a frank discussion of the claims of Buddhism, or perhaps to hold a mediumistic séance.   If biologists sat with philosophers to receive enlightenment on the nature of Time from Kant, McTaggart, Whitehead, and Bergson.   If philosophers, in their turn, were instructed in the latest experimental results of the psychological laboratories.   But specialists are all too busy to have time for one another, with the result that there is increasing scepticism among the few who look from one to another of these disparate lines of thought, trying to form a general view of the whole.

Is it not possible that the growing evidence for psychical phenomena will bring the matter to a head ?   There is a limit to the ' escapist ' methods of looking the other way and ' waiting for more evidence ' to turn up.   It will soon be necessary to come out into the open and either to declare oneself on the side of von Helmhotz or else to revise one's ' scientific ideology.' The fence, if sat upon too long, may give way.   To side with von Helmhotz might involve rather drastic measures.   It would, perhaps, be necessary to establish a totalitarian scientific state, with psychical facts placed on an ' Index,' and a ban of excommunication from the scientific fold for all who ask awkward questions !   But the other course will need considerable mental elasticity and will be bitterly opposed by materialists, positivists, and naïve realists.   In fact, if psychical research continues, the intellectual future for the next few decades promises to be scarcely less turbulent than the political future.

We shall now leave these theoretical considerations to resume our study of the evidence.   In Part IV we shall turn to the mediumistic trance, and shall try to estimate the value of the material which it has produced.   We shall take some actual examples, and shall examine the methods which have been used to check and assess the evidence, as well as other lines of research which have arisen out of it.

Part IV

THE MEDIUMISTIC TRANCE

'If you have had your attention directed to the novelties in thought in your own lifetime, you will have observed that almost all really new ideas have a certain aspect of foolishness when they are first produced.'

Whitehead : 'Science and the Modern World'

Chapter XII

THE PIPER CASE

CONDITIONS UNDER WHICH TRANCE - COMMUNICATIONS ARE OBTAINED.—The most widely known group of psychical phenomena is that relating to the Mediumistic Trance, since it is through this that communications are received which ostensibly proceed from the dead. There are three main conditions under which such communications are obtained : (1) The condition in which the sensitive or medium passes into the type of trance in which normal consciousness disappears and a secondary entity or state of consciousness takes its place and operates the motor and sensory mechanism of the body. Messages given in this way may be either in speech or writing, and they usually purport to emanate from a deceased person. When the secondary entity or state of consciousness is habitual, it is called the medium's ' control ' ; and we shall refer to this type of trance as ' control-trance.' Those who attend the trance for the purpose of obtaining information are called the ' sitters,' and the occasion is called a ' sitting.' The control does not, as a rule, claim to originate the information given, but to act as an intermediary, who passes on messages from deceased human beings remaining in the background. The latter are called the ' communicators.' (2) Sometimes one of the communicators assumes direct control, displacing the habitual control, and operating the bodily mechanism of the medium direct. This condition we will call ' directly controlled trance.' (3) There is a rare, though important, form of trance which arises as a development of automatism. In this, the sensitive retains his or her own consciousness throughout the proceedings, giving messages in speech or writing, much as in the automatic state. The state of dissociation, always to some extent present in automatism, becomes more pronounced with certain of these individuals, until it develops into a kind of trance of its own. We shall refer to this as ' autonomous trance.'

Types of trance (1) and (2) will be illustrated from the records of Mrs. Piper and Mrs. Osborne Leonard. Type (3) will be illustrated from the records of Mrs. Willett (pseudonym).

The case of Mrs. Piper will be briefly dealt with in an introductory sketch, while the main sample of trance-evidence will be taken from Mrs. Leonard's material. Possible explanations, alternative to that of supernormality, will be considered, and in Part V a summing up of the balance of probabilities will be attempted, in addition to a statement of the evidential facts.

The case of Mrs. Willett will be reviewed from a rather different point of view, since the evidence it presents is of a more indirect nature than in the other cases. Its chief function is to throw light on the *modus operandi* of the trance-processes, and it is from that point of view that it will be considered.

In the final chapters of this Section, the question will be considered, supposing the supernormality of the phenomena to have been granted, to what type of supernormal explanation the evidence points as a whole. The theory of communications from the dead will be balanced against the theory of telepathy from the living.

First, let us glance briefly at the history of the Piper phenomena.

Mode of Reference to the Trance-Personalities.—To facilitate reference to the communicators who appear at trance-sittings with various mediums, a simple convention is commonly used. The medium through whom the ostensible communicator appears is indicated by a letter-suffix. Thus, the Myers communicator appearing through Mrs. Piper's trance is indicated by $Myers_P$, or through Mrs. Holland's automatic writing by $Myers_H$. The Hodgson communicator through Mrs. Piper is $Hodgson_P$. The Gurney communicator through Mrs. Willett is $Gurney_W$, and so on. This is not to be taken as indicating any theory as to the identity of the communicators, but merely as a convenient abbreviation.

The Piper Trance.—Mrs. Piper, one of the most widely known of trance-mediums, practised between 1884 and 1911. She was an American woman of moderate education, and most of her work was done in America. She first went into trance when visiting a medium, Mr. J. R. Cocke, for medical advice in June 1884. Phinuit, an early control of hers, seems to have been taken from Mr. Cocke's control, Finny, who, it was claimed, was originally a Frenchman named Finnett. Other controls of hers were called ' Chlorine,' Mrs. Siddons, John Sebastian Bach, Longfellow, Commodore Vanderbilt, and Loretta Ponchina—the latter alleged to have been an Italian girl ; but Phinuit soon became the chief control.[1]

Professor William James first came across Mrs. Piper in 1885, and introduced her to Dr. Richard Hodgson in 1887, the latter being at that time Secretary of the American Society for Psychical Research. From that time onwards she was almost constantly in touch with the English and American Societies for Psychical Research, and worked under their supervision. Her trance activities divide themselves naturally into four periods : (i) from 1886 to 1892. This is covered by reports made by Hodgson and William James. (ii) From 1892 to 1897, during which a leading part was played by a new control, ' G. P.,' who purported to be a gentleman who had recently died. This was reported on by Hodgson and Professor Newbold. (iii) From 1897 to 1905, when a new group of controls, called the ' Imperator Band,' formerly controls of Stainton Moses, took command. Under them, the process of going into trance, which had hitherto been accompanied by convulsive movements, became quiet and placid. A long report on this period was made by Professor James Hyslop.[2] (iv) From 1905 to 1911, when there appeared, in consequence of Dr. Hodgson's death in 1905, a Hodgson communicator and control.

[1] See Mrs. Henry Sidgwick, ' The Psychology of Mrs. Piper's Trance,' *Proc. S.P.R.*, vol. xxviii.
[2] *Proc. S.P.R.*, vol. xvi.

Supernormality of the Piper Trance-Material.—Space does not permit of much quotation to be made from the lengthy records of the actual Piper sittings ; nor is it possible in a few words to discuss on its merits the question whether the Piper material shows supernormality or whether it can be explained by fraud, fishing, and other normal means.   It must be sufficient to refer to the fact that all the investigators who made a study of the case agree that the evidence for supernormality is incontestable.   Dr. Hodgson, one of the chief investigators, says : ' I need hardly say that in estimating the value of my own, as of other sittings, I was compelled to assume, in the first instance, that Mrs. Piper was fraudulent and obtained her information previously by ordinary means, such as inquiries by confederates, etc.'   But he continues, ' There is, I think, in the reports which follow, enough evidence to show that fraud on the part of Mrs. Piper is very far from being an adequate explanation, though it is, of course, conceivable that in some cases Mrs. Piper, had she been fraudulent, might have acquired by ordinary means such information as Phinuit gave the sitter.' [1]   This was written in 1892 ; but during the twenty-five years of the Piper case, none of the expert investigators who conducted the sittings believed that fraud or normal means of obtaining the information given by the trance-personalities could account for the facts as a whole. I shall therefore assume that its supernormal character is established and that the onus of proof is thrown on those who maintain the opposite view.

Although supernormal activity seems to have been clearly at work, there is plenty of evidence against taking the trance-personalities at their face values.   Thus, in discussing Phinuit, the leading control during the earlier period, Dr. Hodgson says in the report above quoted :

' Is there sufficient ground for concluding that Phinuit is in direct communication with " deceased persons," and that he is a " deceased " person himself as he alleges ?   I think that the evidence here presented, together with that previously published, is very far

[1] *Proc. S.P.R.*, vol. viii. p. 6.

from sufficient to establish any such conclusions, and indeed the failures in answering test-questions, and the apparent ignorance displayed in other ways by the alleged " communicators " . . . constitute almost insuperable objections to the supposition that the deceased persons concerned were in direct communication with Phinuit, at least in anything like the fullness, so to speak, of their personalities.' [1]

'*G. P.' and other Communicators.*—The most convincing communicator through Mrs. Piper was George Pelham (pseudonym), usually referred to in the reports as ' G. P.' He was a lawyer, living first in Boston and then in New York, had been an Associate of the American Society for Psychical Research and had taken an open-minded interest in its work. In 1892, at the age of thirty-two, he was killed by a fall. Previously to this he had had one sitting with Mrs. Piper in 1888, but Hodgson says that he believes that Mrs. Piper never knew until some time later that she had ever seen him in life. Four or five weeks after G. P.'s death, a G. P. communicator appeared in Mrs. Piper's trance, and for the next four years gave striking communications.[2] The evidence is far too voluminous to be quoted here, but it had a powerful effect on the mind of Richard Hodgson as well as on the minds of other sitters, and caused a modification of his opinion.

' In my previous report,' he says, ' on Mrs. Piper's trance (*Proceedings*, vol. viii.) in discussing the claims of Phinuit to be a " spirit," and to be in communication with the " deceased " friends of sitters, I urged that there were almost insuperable objections to the supposition that such " deceased " persons were in direct communication with Phinuit *at least in anything like the fullness of their personality* ; but it seemed to me a hypothesis that should be continually borne in mind that there might be some actual communication, even if it was only partial and fragmentary. . . . I am now fully convinced that there has been such actual communication through Mrs. Piper's trance, but that the communication has been subject to certain unavoidable limitations. . . .' [3]

[1] *Proc. S.P.R.*, vol. viii. p. 57.
[2] Ibid. vol. xiii. p. 295.   [3] Ibid. p. 357.

Again, he writes in 1898 :

' It may be that further experiment in the lines of investigation before us may lead me to change my view ; but at the present time I cannot profess to have any doubt but that the chief " communicators," to whom I have referred in the foregoing pages, are veritably the personalities that they claim to be, that they have survived the change we call death, and that they have directly communicated with us whom we call living, through Mrs. Piper's entranced organism. There are doubtless many incidents which seem inexplicable in accordance with the hypothesis which my experience has compelled me to adopt. I also hold the general doctrine of Evolution, but unless my memory deceives me, there are many biological incidents which have not yet been fully explained on that theory.' [1]

Professor Hyslop, writing in 1901, says :

' When I look over the whole field of the phenomena and consider the suppositions that must be made to escape spiritism, which not only one aspect of the case, but every incidental feature of it strengthens, such as the dramatic interplay of different personalities, the personal traits of the communicator, the emotional tone that was natural to the same, the proper appreciation of a situation or a question, and the unity of consciousness displayed throughout, I see no reason except the suspicions of my neighbours for withholding assent. But when I am asked to admit the telepathy required to meet the case, the amazing feats of memory involved in the medium's subliminal, the staggering amount of deception demanded, and the perfect play of personality presented, as capable of explaining the phenomena without spirits, I may say, yes, if you choose to believe this against all scientific precedents.' [2]

Sir Oliver Lodge, in concluding a report on Piper sittings in 1909, writes as follows :

' On the whole, they [the Piper sittings] tend to render certain the existence of some outside intelligence or control, distinct from the consciousness, and as far as I can judge, from the subconsciousness also, of Mrs. Piper or other medium. And they tend to render

[1] *Proc. S.P.R.*, vol. xiii. pp. 405–6.
[2] Ibid. vol. xvi. p. 293.

probable the working hypothesis, on which I choose to proceed, that that version of the nature of the intelligences which they themselves present and favour is something like the truth.   In other words, I feel that we are in secondary or tertiary touch—at least occasionally—with some stratum of the surviving personality of the individuals who are represented as sending messages.'

He means by secondary or tertiary that communication is through the medium or medium and control.   He continues :

' Very well then, I feel bound to say that in the old days when conversing with the Gurney control through Mrs. Piper, as reported in Chapter II, I felt very much as if I were conversing under difficulties with Edmund Gurney.   And he appeared to be in real " control " for the time—so that lapses and uncertainties and occasional confusions, in his case, were rather rare.   But when the Myers and Hodgson controls now send messages through Mrs. Piper, as reported above, I have very little feeling of that kind. They seemed in my case rather shadowy and, so to speak, uninteresting, communicators.   It is true I did not give them much chance of encouragement, and under better treatment they flourished and blossomed as reported by Mr. Piddington ; but if my opinion had to depend on my own Piper sittings alone, I should not be strongly impressed by these personalities.' [1]

In spite of communications whose cumulative effect was impressive, there was much in the Piper phenomena which weighed the scales of evidence against the theory that the communicators were literally the surviving persons they claimed to be.   Mrs. Henry Sidgwick, whose clear-sighted judgement and instinct for the balance of evidence were second to none, weighed these claims in an admirable report on the Piper trance, which every student of the subject should read. First, however, the following note by Mrs. Sidgwick and Mr. J. G. Piddington with regard to the Hodgson control is instructive.

' From what we have said it is clear that our attempt, by introducing Hodgson's friends, to obtain evidence of continuity of memory between Hodgson $_P$ and Hodgson must be regarded as a

[1] *Proc. S.P.R.*, vol. xxiii. pp. 282–3.

failure. The same, it may be remarked, is true of the similar experiments we made in connexion with Henry Sidgwick. His communications in the trance were much rarer than Hodgson's, and they did not occur at all when friends were introduced whom it was hoped he would recognize. What the inference to be drawn from these negative results should be—whether the failure is to be attributed to the absence of continuous memory or to the absence of conditions essential to its manifestation—it is not possible in our present state of ignorance about the whole subject to decide.' [1]

In a footnote is added :

' Since 1901 a control calling itself Henry Sidgwick has put in occasional appearances in Mrs. Piper's trance. The personation has been, however, of the feeblest description ; a fact all the more strange because Mrs. Piper was personally acquainted with Dr. Sidgwick.'

This should be borne in mind in view of the fact that a Sidgwick communicator appeared through Mrs. Willett of a very different description, as will be seen later.

In the concluding summary of a long and exhaustive report on the *Psychology of Mrs. Piper's Trance*,[2] Mrs. Henry Sidgwick writes :

' The principal questions to which we want answers are : (1) Is there reason to think, as was maintained by Hodgson in his second report, that any spirit independent of Mrs. Piper exercises at any time direct control over any part of Mrs. Piper's organism ? (2) If not, or indeed in any case, what kind of divided consciousness is manifested in Mrs. Piper ? Are the controls secondary personalities and in what sense ? To the first question my answer is probably already plain to the reader, even if it has not been explicitly stated. The intelligence in direct communication with the sitter, whom we have called the control, is not, as it professes to be, an independent spirit using Mrs. Piper's organism, but some phase or element of Mrs. Piper's own consciousness. . . . I do not see how on any other hypothesis we are to account for absurd personations like, e.g. Julius Caesar, which, it will be observed, is in no way

[1] *Proc. S.P.R.*, vol. xxiii. p. 126.
[2] Ibid. vol. xxviii. pp. 315 ff.

distinguished by other controls as different in nature from themselves. Nor on any other hypothesis can we easily account for the absurd statements made and the ignorance exhibited by these other controls. We cannot, for instance, reasonably suppose that the limitations of Mrs. Piper's organism not only inhibit the getting through of scientific information, but alter what does come through into nonsensical statements dressed up in pseudo-scientific jargon. Even if we ought not to expect Rector and Imperator, who profess to have lived on earth in more or less remote times, to be acquainted with modern science—any more than we can expect it of Mrs. Piper—we should still less expect these exalted spirits to use scientific nomenclature in a way that shows total want of understanding of what they are talking about. And the ignorance is not confined to science. Mrs. Piper might easily have given little attention to Old Testament history or the history of Christianity, but that Imperator, if the great spirit he professes to be, should undertake to instruct Hodgson in the true inwardness of these things, and contrive, even while confining himself to vague generalities, to talk so much nonsense about them, is difficult to conceive. Again, Mrs. Piper might well have erroneous notions concerning Adam Bede and imagine him to be a real person whom she might meet in the other world, but it is hardly possible that George Eliot should make a similar mistake and report having met him without expressing any surprise. G. P.'s philosophical talk . . . is another case in point. But I need not multiply instances which in the trance utterances are natural enough as coming from Mrs. Piper, but not as coming from the supposed control, even if allowance be made for confusion and difficulty.'

In a footnote Mrs. Sidgwick adds :

' It must be allowed, however, that some of the nonsense talked (e.g. monkeys in the sun, p. 86) is not what we should expect the normal Mrs. Piper to utter, and must, if a centre of consciousness of Mrs. Piper is responsible, be attributed to a dream-like abeyance of the inhibitory faculty. . . .' [1]

A curious passage which would seem to be confirmatory of the view that Mrs. Piper's controls were phases of her own personality occurred at a sitting on April 10, 1907, at which

[1] *Proc. S.P.R.*, vol. xxviii. pp. 315–17.

Mrs. Sidgwick was the recorder. In the stage of waking from the trance, Mrs. Piper said confidentially to Mrs. Sidgwick : ' People in the body never tell me anything [I think this was in contrast to the spirit people.—E. M. S.]. They seem to expect me to find out things and I don't [know how they expect me to do it.] ' [1] The last words in square brackets were inserted afterwards because Mrs. Sidgwick caught the meaning but did not write down Mrs. Piper's actual words at the moment. Mrs. Piper, in the waking stage, thus identifies *herself* with the personages of the trance proper. But it is *they* who are expected to find out things. Mrs. Sidgwick says further :

' The hypnotic self, or some element of it, successively personates a number of different characters—Phinuit, G. P., Stainton Moses, Rector, George Eliot, etc., but I think there is no divided-off part of Mrs. Piper which has assumed and permanently retains the character of, say, Rector, and is in that sense a secondary personality. Rector has no more persistent existence than Hamlet has.' [2]

This view, if correct, would definitely mark off controls from secondary personalities of the type known to abnormal psychology, which often appear to have a continuous existence and sometimes to be co-conscious with the primary self.

Again, Mrs. Sidgwick says that :

' Mrs. Piper in a state of self-induced hypnosis may sometimes deliberately and consciously personate the control, and at others believe herself to be Rector or Phinuit, while at still other times something between the two may occur and she may have a more or less hazy consciousness of being Rector, but also of being Mrs. Piper. That such mixed states of consciousness are possible we all know from dreams ; and we may also observe them in children in a normal waking state. Children may, e.g., be genuinely frightened by a wolf, knowing all the time that it is not a wolf, but their own father assuming the character at their own request.' [3]

[1] *Proc. S.P.R.*, vol. xxviii. p. 323.
[2] Ibid. p. 324.   [3] Ibid. pp. 326–7.

Professor William James, writing about the Piper controls in 1909, and referring to the large amount of nonsense talked by them, says :

' Dramatically, most of this " bosh " is more suggestive to me of dreaminess and mind-wandering than it is of humbug. Why should a " will to deceive " prefer to give incorrect names so often, if it can give true ones to which the incorrect ones so frequently approximate as to suggest that they are meant ? True names impress the sitter vastly more. . . . It looks to me more like aiming at something definite and failing of the goal.'

The Piper Communicators.—One curious point about the communicators was that they were more impressive in the respective countries to which each belonged. ' Gurney p was a much more interesting communicator in England than in America, while with Hodgson p the reverse was the case, and the importance of Myers p as a communicator was greatly enhanced when Mrs. Piper came to England in 1906.'[1] This would seem to suggest that the sitters contribute in one way or another to the result, the best condition being when friends of the deceased are present.

Hodgson p was a most vivid and impressive communicator in the United States for the first few months after Hodgson's death ; but he failed to recognize intimate friends of Hodgson's in England.

' The case of Gurney is still more curious. Gurney died in the summer of 1888, and a Gurney control made its appearance through Mrs. Piper in America on several occasions in March 1889, when Professor William James was present. He gives some account of it in *Proceedings*, vol. vi. pp. 655–6, which was published in 1890, calling the control " E," and says " neither then, nor at any other time, was there to my mind the slightest verisimilitude in the personation." '

Hodgson, who was present at least at one of these sittings, also describes this control in vol. viii. pp. 44–5, agreeing that it was not like Gurney. He adds :

' If we assume that this control was the " make-up " of Mrs. Piper's secondary personality, it apparently involved some very

[1] *Proc. S.P.R.*, vol. xxviii. p. 300.

subtle use of information drawn telepathically from at least the minds of the sitters, and at the same time the most extravagant ignorance and confusion concerning other facts, some of which were known to the sitters, and which we should expect to be vivid in the remembrance of " E." ' [1]

Thus, reasons for regarding the communicators, as well as the controls in the Piper case, as being hypnotically constructed pseudo-personalities, appear to be very strong. Mrs. Sidgwick says of them :

' . . . I may as well say here that, in the case of what I have called the dramatic communicators—communicators as manifested at the sittings . . . there are much the same arguments for refusing to regard them as entities independent of Mrs. Piper as there are in the case of the controls. Dramatic communicators, like controls, are sometimes clearly false, and no criterion is offered in the representation itself, or in its relation to the control, by which a false communicator may be distinguished from a true one. The existence of false communicators is not admitted at all.' [2]

One must not, however, be in too great a hurry to jump to the conclusion that the whole phenomenon of the mediumistic trance can be explained as a rather elaborate piece of auto-hypnosis. Indeed, the more one learns about psychical research, the more distrustful one becomes of any neatly cut-and-dried solution to its problems. Professor William James, in the course of his report on the Hodgson-Control before quoted, suggests that a more complicated hypothesis is required. He says :

' Extraneous " wills to communicate " may contribute to the results as well as a " will to personate," and the two kinds of will may be distinct in entity, though capable of helping each other out. The will to communicate, in our present instance, would be, on a *prima facie* view of it, the will of Hodgson's surviving spirit ; and a natural way of representing the process would be to suppose the spirit to have found that by pressing, so to speak, against " the light," it can make fragmentary gleams and flashes of what it wishes to say mix with the rubbish of the trance-talk on this side. The

[1] *Proc. S.P.R.*, vol. xxviii. pp. 301–2.   [2] Ibid. p. 317.

two wills might thus strike up a sort of partnership and reinforce each other. It might even be that the " will to personate " would be comparatively inert unless it were aroused to activity by the other will. We might imagine the relation to be analagous to that of two physical bodies, from neither of which, when alone, mechanical, electrical, or thermal activity can proceed. But, if the other body be present, and show a difference of " potential," action starts up and goes on apace.'[1]

It is because the trance phenomena as a whole give him the feeling that a will to communicate of some sort is there, that he suggests this hypothesis. He says almost at the end of his report :

' I myself feel as if an external will to communicate were probably there—that is, I find myself doubting, in consequence of my whole acquaintance with that sphere of phenomena, that Mrs. Piper's dream-life, even equipped with telepathic powers, accounts for all the results found. But if asked whether the will to communicate be Hodgson's, or be some mere spirit counterfeit of Hodgson, I remain uncertain and await more facts, facts which may not point clearly to a conclusion for fifty or a hundred years.'[2]

The important idea here suggested by William James is that the trance-phenomena contain *depth* : the surface explanation may not be the whole explanation. It may not be a question of a flat alternative—either the deceased person is simply *there*, speaking through the medium as through a kind of psychic telephone ; or else no deceased person is there at all, but the medium has merely fallen into a hypnoidal state and the communicators are the result of auto-suggestion. That suspiciously over-simplifies the situation. There *are* these hypnotic or hypnoidal states with their suggestible and impersonating tendencies. But there is evidence also of another factor in the background, as we shall see with greater clearness as we proceed with further evidence. As Mrs. Sidgwick says : ' . . . If the whole dramatic form were play-acting, it might still be the framework in which veridical communications come to us. In fact, the question of what is the nature of the

[1] *Proc. S.P.R.*, vol. xxviii. p. 117.   [2] Ibid. p. 121.

12

communicator as dramatically presented to us, is distinct from the question whether there is any real communicator in the background.'[1]

The Piper Waking Stage.—There was always an interesting phase of the Piper Trance, which took place just as the trance proper was coming to an end. In this, Mrs. Piper, while re-entering on her normal state of consciousness, still continued to be aware of the personages who had manifested during the trance. The only point about this which will now be mentioned is the evidence it affords of the genuine reality for the partially entranced personality of the medium of the sense-imagery with which it is surrounded. This question of sense-imagery was mentioned in Chapter II, where it arose in connexion with the spontaneous cases there dealt with. It will arise again in connexion with the mediumistic trance. Here, before leaving the Piper case, I will make one last quotation on the point from Mrs. Sidgwick's report. She says :

'The externalized quality of the waking-stage visions is, as will be seen in the next chapter, so manifest that it gives us a useful standard of comparison. I think it hardly possible that any one should read records of waking-stage visions without realizing that to the seer they are entirely objective—that she really believes herself to be seeing and hearing, as outside herself, what she describes. I am quite sure that no one could be present during a waking-stage of any importance without realizing it. There is no acting about it any more than there is in the hallucinations of delirium, or, for that matter, than there is in our ordinary dreams.'[2]

The Piper case suggests, then, that in trance-mediumship we are dealing with certain states of consciousness which bear an analogy to hypnosis or auto-hypnosis ; that these are full of dream-like associations leading to much nonsensical material ; that impersonations of the dead take place, sometimes unconvincingly, sometimes presenting false communicators, sometimes more convincingly, but that behind all this there is evidence of a will to communicate which, when conditions are at their best, gives a strong impression of a genuine deceased

[1] *Proc. S.P.R.*, vol. xxviii. p. 180.   [2] Ibid. p. 180.

communicator somewhere in the background. In the next chapter we shall deal, in as much detail as space permits, with a case of communications given by a single ostensible communicator through the mediumship of Mrs. Osborne Leonard. We shall see what further light this case can throw on the will to communicate, which William James and others have felt to be dimly present behind the Piper phenomena.

Chapter XIII

THE ' A. V. B.' CASE

PRELIMINARIES.—This case has been chosen as an example of ostensible communication from the dead through the mediumistic trance because the sittings comprising it form a clear and connected whole, free from complications and confined for the most part to the two sitters concerned ; also because these two sitters and investigators conducted the whole research with admirable care and scientific caution. The medium through whom the results were obtained, Mrs. Osborne Leonard, is in the forefront of those practising mediumistic trance in this country, and has for years enjoyed an excellent reputation with her many sitters for candour and caution and for a desire to assist the scientific precautions taken by investigators.

The evidence as presented here has, perforce, been greatly abridged. It is all taken from the report referred to below,[1] and therefore when quotations are made, no further references will be given. The reader should understand that the evidential value of trance-sittings depends so much on detail that no abridged account of them can be altogether satisfactory, and he is urged to study the actual record.

Prior to the time when these sittings took place, the two sitters and investigators, Miss Radcliffe Hall and (Una) Lady Troubridge, were living with their friend, A. V. B., at the White Cottage, Malvern Wells, and none of them took any interest in psychical research. On May 25, 1916, A. V. B. died as the result of a ' stroke ' ; and the following July or August Miss Radcliffe Hall first heard of Mrs. Leonard through a lady who asked her to test the latter both on her

---

[1] ' On a Series of Sittings with Mrs. Osborne Leonard,' by Miss Radcliffe Hall and (Una) Lady Troubridge (*Proc. S.P.R.*, vol. xxx. pp. 339–547).

behalf and her own. (In what follows I shall refer to Miss Radcliffe Hall, as in the report, by the initials M. R. H., and to Lady Troubridge by the initials U. V. T.) M. R. H. says :

' I therefore went to Mrs. Leonard's flat to arrange for a sitting. Mrs. Leonard was away, and a friend of hers who was taking charge of the flat, told me that it would be necessary for her to write to Mrs. Leonard, and requested me to leave my name and address. This I refused to do, promising to call again in three days' time for my answer. In three days' time I did so, and an appointment was given me for August 16, 1916, at 3 p.m. On leaving Mrs. Leonard's flat I went directly to the station, and thence to the country, not returning to London till the day of the sitting. I addressed no conversation to Mrs. Leonard prior to my sitting, beyond thanking her for the appointment, and she went quietly into trance. Her control, Feda, began by describing a young soldier ; I did not recognize him, and said so, asking if there were no other communicators wishing to speak. It seemed that there were, for I very soon got the description of a great friend of mine who had died some months previously. [This was A. V. B.] . . . The description was brief, but unmistakable ; except my friend, whom it fitted exactly, I had lost no one to whom it corresponded in the very least. After Mrs. Leonard had been in trance for what I think must have been a little over half an hour, Feda complained that my friend was an inexperienced communicator, and would probably get on much better if I had a table sitting. Feda therefore withdrew, and the medium woke suddenly. I told Mrs. Leonard what had happened, and we had a table sitting. Mrs. Leonard had both her hands on the table, but for the best part of the time only one of my hands rested on the table, as I was taking notes with the other. My friend immediately gave her full name through the table, though I should have preferred her not to do so. She also gave the name of a place to which we had been together. When the table spelt out " Do you remember a place we went to called —— " I instantly thought of Orotava, a town that had been visited by my friend and myself. For some reason I felt almost certain that this name would come, but, curiously enough, instead of getting it I got the name " Watergate." I recognized the name and asked if it had another name as well, to which the table replied, " Yes, Bay." Now Watergate Bay was the last place visited by myself and my friend prior to her death.'

It must be remembered that the ' table sitting ' provided a mode of motor automatism in which M. R. H. took part, so that her own latent knowledge might have externalized itself.

On October 2, 1916, M. R. H. and U. V. T. went together to visit Mrs. Leonard, introducing themselves as anonymous sitters recommended by Sir Oliver Lodge ; and after this they went together, one always acting as note-taker while the other conducted the sitting. ' The recorder bore specially in mind the importance of taking down everything said by the sitter, and equally careful notes were made of any conversations held with the medium in the normal state, before and after the sittings, which conversations were invariably brief.' It is therefore possible to judge from the record of any sitting what possibility there was (if any) for the medium to have gathered information from hints dropped by the sitter. The student who reads the records of these sittings carefully will be impressed by the absence of such hints or suggestions throughout, and by the admirable care exercised by these two experimenters.

The first four sittings were held on August 16, October 2, October 9, 1916, and on June 6, 1917, and were concerned chiefly with a personal description of A. V. B. given by Feda, Mrs. Leonard's control, speaking through Mrs. Leonard's vocal organs. Feda, it may be remarked, like most controls, claims once to have lived on earth. She says she was an Indian girl (or perhaps *is* an Indian girl) and accordingly speaks in childish language. It will be sufficient here, in order to indicate the nature of a sitting, to give in full that of August 16, which was very short. After that, a summary of the points descriptive of A. V. B. given in all these four sittings will be placed side by side with the sitter's comments, so that the reader may be presented with the gist of the evidence.

August 16, 1916 :
Feda introduces the soldier before mentioned.
M. R. H. I do not know him ; is there no one else ?
F. Yes, there's a lady of about sixty years old, perhaps.

M. R. H. Please describe her, she interests me more. (Feda
did not take the hint, however, but continued to describe
the soldier, who appeared to be very insistent.)

M. R. H. Please leave him ; as I do not know him I am afraid
I cannot help, though I would do anything I could. Will
you describe the lady of about sixty ?

F. The lady is of medium height, has rather a good figure but
is inclined to be too fat, Feda thinks ; she has a straight
nose, a well-shaped face, but the face is inclined to lose its
outline a little. The eyebrows are slightly arched ; her
hair is not done fashionably.

M. R. H. Is it worn on the neck ?

F. No, it's done on the crown of the head. She has passed
over quite recently. She had not been well for some time
prior to passing ; she was sometimes conscious of this,
but put it behind her. Feda doesn't mean to say that she
worried over it much, or that she suffered much ; she didn't.
Feda thinks she didn't know how ill she really was. She
went about doing things just as usual ; she gives Feda
the impression of internal weakness. You were much
with her in her earth life ; you gave her vitality. . . . The
lady's eyes look to Feda to be dark, perhaps grey.'

It will be noticed that there is no nonsense about this, of
the kind frequently occurring in the Piper trance. The points
given, if not particularly striking, were in fact true. M. R. H.
says about them :

' A. V. B. was fifty-seven when she died, had had a fine figure,
but latterly became too stout ; she had a straight nose, which was
very slightly tip-tilted ; she wore her hair dressed high on her head,
and at the time of this sitting she had only been dead two months,
three weeks, and a day. For some time prior to her death she had
not been strong, partly owing to the effects of a bad motor accident.
She must often have put her ailments behind her, however, and we
do not think for a moment that she had any idea of how ill she was ;
I can only say that I had none. She went about doing things as
usual up to the very day of her last illness, which came on without
the slightest warning. She did suffer from internal weakness,

though this had nothing to do with her death.   A. V. B. and I were the closest friends for eight years, and lived together for a great part of that time.   She would sometimes say to me that she believed that my vitality kept her up and helped her ; we used to discuss this together.   A. V. B.'s eyes were of a dark blue ; some people might have called them of a dark bluey-grey colour.'

Personal Characteristics of A. V. B.—If we take all the statements made about A. V. B. by Feda during these four sittings and make a table of them we get the following :

Feda's Statement.	*Sitter's Comment.*
(1) Age about sixty.	Right, age fifty-seven.
(2) Medium height.	No comment.
(3) Good figure.	Right.
(4) But got too fat.	Right.
(5) Straight nose.	Right.
(6) Well-shaped face.	No comment.
(7) Face inclined to lose outline.	No comment.
(8) Eyebrows slightly arched.	No comment.
(9) Hair done on crown of head.	Right.
(10) Not well for some time before death.	Right.
(11) Put her ailments behind her.	Right.
(12) Did not know how ill she was.	Right.
(13) Suffered from internal weakness.	Right.
(14) M. R. H. gave her vitality.	Right.
(15) Grey eyes.	Partly right ; eyes bluey-grey.
(16) Legs numb in last illness.	Right.
(17) Had a humorous look.	Right.
(18) Had a young soul.	Right.
(19) Latterly found her body a nuisance.	Right.
(20) Mouth medium size ; not very red.	No comment.
(21) Has a way of looking sideways.	Right.

Feda's Statement.	Sitter's Comment.
(22) Clot on the brain which stopped her feeling.	Right.
(23) ' Old Lady ; Oh, Ladye ! '	Right.
(24) Choking in the throat.	Right.
(25) Hair brown, like the medium's.	Partly right ; wrong shade indicated.
(26) Nothing could have been done for her illness.	Right.
(27) Nice complexion, smooth.	No comment.
(28) Mouth drawn down at *left* side during last illness.	Right.
(29) Pretty, rounded chin.	No comment.
(30) Particularly hollow back.	Right.
(31) Sudden determination.	Right.
(32) Smooth walk.	Right.
(33) Characteristic pose.	Right.

Of these 33 points, 7 are not directly commented on by the sitter ; 2 are partly wrong ; and 24 are right. It may be said that many of these remarks are of such a character as to be fairly safe guesses, but we have to remember that where we have a string of successful guesses, the odds against their all being produced by chance becomes enormous, even though the odds against each one separately being produced by chance are small.

Item (23). A. V. B. was habitually known by the nickname of ' Ladye.' Feda had said *sotto voce* ' Old Lady, old Lady, oh, Lady ? ' and then added : ' She says you said : " Oh ! Ladye. Oh ! Ladye, it's all right." ' M. R. H. comments on this, ' During her illness, when speaking to her, I most certainly said, " Oh, Ladye," on several occasions ; I never called A. V. B. " old lady " in my life, and this indecision on Feda's part as to whether the words used were " Oh, Ladye," or " old lady " is rather enlightening, as showing, it appears to us, the bias occasionally given to certain messages owing to preconceived ideas on the

part of the control. " Ladye," being an unusual nickname, Feda cannot quite believe, apparently, that she has
heard correctly.'

It is obvious that the odds against guessing that some
one's nickname is ' Ladye ' at the first shot are very large.

Item (28). Feda had said : ' Before she passed on her cheeks
fell in a little bit and, do you know, her mouth had got
drawn down a little at the left corner, like this ? (Feda
draws down one side of her mouth a little.) She's showing
that ; it was straight at the other corner, but the left side
is drawn down, and in a bit, but not very much.'

M. R. H. says with regard to this :

' Now this slight drawing down of the mouth on one side was a
consequence of A. V. B.'s stroke ; it was the only visible blemish
caused by the stroke. Only those few people who were with her
during her last illness can have seen this blemish, as it disappeared
a short time after her death. Our impression had been that this
drawing down of the mouth was on the right side, not the left, and
we accordingly contradicted Feda on this point. It appears, however, that she was right, and we were wrong ; for the paralysis was
right-sided, and we now learn from our medical friends that right-
sided paralysis affecting the face would cause the mouth to be drawn
down on the left side.'

Item (33). Feda described a characteristic pose of A. V. B.'s
which included several points—a looking from under
drooped eyelids, which, as Feda stated correctly, were
very prettily cut ; a protruding of the lip, which gave her
a cheeky look as well as throwing the head well back—
a pose which Feda imitates. This, says M. R. H., ' is an
exact description of a characteristic attitude of A. V. B.'s—
a pose so familiar as to have become second nature.'

Again, with regard to Item (30), M. R. H. says that
A. V. B.'s back was so pronouncedly arched that it often gave
her backaches, so much so that when ill in bed for any length
of time, she had to have her back supported by pillows.

The odds against guessing these four items right alone by pure chance would be enormous, apart from the string of minor items. Chance, as an explanation of the personal description of A. V. B. is evidently out of the question.

Could the sitters have given away by their remarks hints from which the information could have been gathered ? All remarks were recorded by the note-taker, and, on examination, one finds that no information whatever has been given away. After an exact description of A. V. B.'s face has been given by Feda, U. V. T. once remarks, ' Excellent ! ' but that is the nearest one can find to a hint. But it may be said that even if nothing was given away verbally, the sitters involuntarily showed by their facial expressions when the control was on the right track and so encouraged her to proceed. There is probably some truth in this, and I think that a definite, though not a large, allowance should be made for it. But no one could possibly communicate a nickname like ' Ladye ' by simply looking pleased or the reverse.

The next question which arises is whether Mrs. Leonard could have acquired the information by the use of detectives or inquiry agents. Before discussing this point, however, we will consider some further sittings.

The White Cottage.—During the sittings held on October 9 and 25, 1916, Feda gave a description, purporting to come from A. V. B., of the house in which the three ladies had lived at Malvern Wells, called the White Cottage. Feda's descriptions are often lengthy, and there is no space to quote them in full. There are also certain points of confusion ; but an unmistakable description of the house is given. The chief points are summarized below (in linear form to save space), with the abridged comments of the sitters in parentheses after each item. (1) There were vestibule, doors, hall, and staircase on entering. (Right.) (2) Light came down the stairs from a ' skylight or something.' (Yes. From a glass door.) (3) There were pictures on the stairs. (Right.) (4) There was a half-landing. (Wrong.) (5) There was a carved chest at the top of the stairs. (Wrong.) (6) There was a different staircase leading to another floor. (Right.) (7) Reference to standing on the roof without using a ladder. (Not understood.) (8) Reference to repairs to the roof—laughing. (Repairs to the roof were a standing joke.) (9) A straggly house : long passages and staircases. (Right.) (10) A Persian rug in one room ; light ground and on brown floor-cover. (Right of M. R. H.'s room.) (11) Walls dark ; a little ledge ; lighter at the top. (Wrong. The walls were cream ; but they had discussed panelling them in oak.) (12) The garden a funny shape ; in three parts. (Right.) (13) Three entrances to the house. (Right.) (14) A. V. B. was most interested in the back one. (Right ; she always used it because it was on a higher level.) (15) There was a comfy room cut off from the house, with something wicker in it and pink cushions. (Right ; describes the servant's cottage, which stood alone.) (16) ' Guilty ' in connexion with this room. (Not understood.) (17) A leading question was deliberately put here by M. R. H. ' Ask her, does she remember that the place she speaks of has been sold ? ' Feda replies : ' She didn't seem to remember until you said it.' M. R. H. asks : ' Does she remember it now ? ' Feda replies : ' She says she really hadn't thought of the place as having been sold or not, only as a test.' This reception of a question conveying a suggestion is interesting. There is no tendency here, as in some of the Piper phenomena, to seize on hints dropped by the sitter and afterwards proffer them as pieces of genuine information. Feda, on the contrary, is usually most pertinacious, sticking to her points even in face of denials from the sitters. (18) A reference to a tree which came down. (Right.) (19) A church, with farther on steam from a steam-engine. (Right. Beyond the church were traction-engines in a stone quarry.) (20) ' She loved that place. . . . Happy times.' (True ; but neighbours did not know it.) (21) ' Feda doesn't know why she is interested in telegraph poles and wires.' (The telegraph officials had cut down some fine thorn trees to make room for their poles and wires, not long before A. V. B.'s death, which had raised much discussion.) Feda made some entirely wrong statements about basement rooms which she represented as belonging to the White Cottage. But another house, Highfield House, which had belonged to M. R. H. previously, and in which A. V. B. had stayed, had basement rooms more or less corresponding to the description.

Here, then, in spite of two or three wrong statements and a confusion at one point between rooms belonging to two real houses, Feda gave a description of the White Cottage, not only easily recognizable but specifically true in many details. The report itself brings this out more clearly. Could Mrs. Leonard have obtained these details about the White Cottage, as well as about A. V. B., through inquiries ?

The sitters came to her anonymously. M. R. H. refused to give her name and address when asked to do so on her first visit to Mrs. Leonard's flat, Mrs. Leonard herself being absent ; and information about A. V. B. began to arrive at the first sitting, that is to say when Mrs. Leonard saw M. R. H. for the first time. On what grounds would Mrs. Leonard have got up the details about these ladies to such an extent as to have them all at her finger-tips, ready to give out the moment she saw one of them, whose face, we must suppose, she had memorized from a photograph ? They were not public characters ; they were not members of the Society for Psychical Research or of any other body interested in psychical research ; they had previously taken no interest in the subject ; they were not differentiated from any other three ladies living in the country. In order to be ready for such an emergency as this, Mrs. Leonard would have to know the most intimate details about every one in the United Kingdom who might come to her for a sitting—that is about every one who could afford to pay her fees. If it is maintained by critics that this is what in fact all mediums do, then it follows that they must have intelligence departments which any government might envy ! Where, in Mrs. Leonard's modest London flat, one wonders, were the filing cabinets stored, and the multiple telephone lines, and the clerical staff which she would have to employ ? But Miss Radcliffe Hall and Lady Troubridge, in spite of their interest in psychical research, had not what Lord Kelvin called ' innocent, trusting minds.' To make sure they employed a detective. The detective was instructed to find out at Malvern

Wells whether any inquiries about M. R. H. or A. V. B. had been made since the latter's death, and he reported that none had been made.   He was also instructed to make inquiries in London, but failed to find anything suspicious.   One may reasonably suppose that, if Mrs. Leonard possessed anything in the nature of an inquiry agency of her own, the professional detective would have come across some traces of it.   However, M. R. H. was not satisfied with the detective's report, but wrote to the lady who had taken possession of the White Cottage directly she left it.   She says :

> ' I fear I descended to subterfuge in order to avoid creating a bias.   I worded my letter as expressing the hope that a person from the Colonies, known to my deceased friend and myself, and who had expressed a wish to see over the house, had been permitted to do so. It struck me at the time that some pretext of this sort would probably be used by a fraudulent person wishing to gain admittance to the house.   From the lady I obtained a reply to the effect that no friend had called at the White Cottage requesting to see over it.'

One interesting point was disclosed by the detective's investigations at Malvern Wells.   He ascertained ' that there was an almost universal impression current to the effect that A. V. B. disliked the White Cottage, Malvern Wells, and the neighbourhood thereof intensely.'   Several people thought that it was A. V. B.'s fault that the house had been sold ; but in reality A. V. B. loved the White Cottage and surrounding country, and deeply felt the necessity of having to sell it on account of the war.   Feda's statement in item (20) above, ' She loved that place. . . . Happy times,' was therefore true.   But had the information been gleaned from inquiries, the opposite statement would have been made.

It may be said here that there was never the slightest reason for doubting Mrs. Leonard's honesty, and that since the date when these sittings were held, Mrs. Leonard's reputation for complete sincerity has become widely known ; but these precautions taken by Miss Ratcliffe Hall cannot but enhance the value of the case.   When, in fact, at a later time, Mrs. Leonard was informed that a detective had been employed, she fully realized that this provided a valuable testimony to the genuineness of her powers.

In view of the knowledge manifested by Feda about A. V. B.'s last illness, M. R. H. also instructed the detective to go to the Registrar of Deaths for the district in which A. V. B. had died, and to ascertain whether any person had made inquiries there as to the nature of the illness from which A. V. B. had died. The detective was told that no inquiries had been made, and that if they had been, they would not have been answered. Lady Troubridge then visited the hotel where A. V. B. had died, and interviewed the proprietress, under the pretext that some hypothetical friend of A. V. B.'s might have come to inquire for her. The proprietress assured Lady Troubridge that she had received no inquiries, and that had any been made of any of the hotel employees, they would have been at once referred to herself. There seems, therefore, to be no possible loophole for the theory that the information given had been obtained by Mrs. Leonard by normal means. But if any critic feels still inclined to hold it, knowledge was later shown of details of events occurring when the three ladies were abroad on holidays, which it would have been impossible for any eavesdropper to have discovered.

Teneriffe.—The sittings of November 22, 1916, and January 3 and 17, and May 23, 1917, repeatedly recurred to one topic. Feda described a scene, evidently referring to a place abroad, in which there were precipices and some one leading a mule along a ledge, saying : ' Oh, they *are* nasty places.' A valley and ' half of a great big sun sticking up over one of the banks,' and a powdery road, which felt, as Feda said, ' like walking *on cinders.*' There was a good deal more description, all of which corresponded to a scene in Teneriffe, to which place A. V. B. and M. R. H. were much devoted. The place described was apparently the Baranco del Anävingo, a rock-strewn valley traversed by a lava road. ' I have no doubt,' says M. R. H., ' that if Feda was made to sense walking on this road, it *did* feel to her like walking on cinders, since that is precisely what the road is composed of.' ' When A. V. B. and I,' she says, ' started on our homeward journey after our visit to the Baranco, the sun was setting, making a fine red glow across the lava road. This made a deep impression on us both at the time. . . .'

There are some lengthy descriptions of the hotel they stayed at and the people they met, but some of the most interesting things in this section are the emergence of names. Names appear to present a peculiar difficulty to the mechanism of expression used in the trance. Often a complete and unmistakable description of a thing will be given, but the name cannot be uttered. When names do emerge, they are as a rule groped after with great difficulty, use being made of trains of associations. Thus :

Feda. . . . Wait—this is a place called Cruz—Cruz—Cruth —Cruz.

M. R. H. Is she trying to give you something, Feda ?

F. Feda is afraid that is only part of the word.

M. R. H. It is only part of it.

F. (*sotto voce :* Cruth—Vera—Vera. Now, Ladye, don't mix it up). . . .

The attempt goes on for some time, but is not further successful. Evidently Santa Cruz in Teneriffe is the name being aimed at. ' Vera ' gets tacked on instead of ' Santa ' by a wrong train of association. Feda recognizes the fault, but cannot set it right. It is noteworthy that A. V. B. used to pronounce it Santa Cru*th*.

Again, it is interesting to watch Feda working towards two more names. She speaks of an island : ' It's a piece of land standing in water.'

M. R. H. What is ?

F. That place is, she says. The place is an island.

M. R. H. Yes, it is an island.

F. She says that place is called Ter—ter—terra—— Oh ! Feda can't quite get it, but she wants to say that it's a place called Ter—Te——No, Feda can't get it, but it starts Te. It's Tener—Tener—Ten—Ten—— What, Ladye ? Tener——

M. R. H. Tener is right.

F. Teneri—Teneri—ee—ee—ff—ffe—iffe—teneri—fer. She says she doesn't agree with the ' fer '; she says Tener is right, she says cut off the last ' er ' and it's right.

M. R. H. (to *U. V. T.*). Is it right ?

U. V. T. Quite right.

F. (*sotto voce :* Teneriffe, it's Teneriffe !). She keeps on saying an island, it's an island she says, and she says it's a nice place, she says : ' Teneriffe ' ! Do you know, she pushed that through suddenly ? She pretended that she was exasperated at your not understanding. She thought that Feda would get hold of it if she pretended to be cross. Now she's saying there's that place called M. again—Masagar—Masagar—Madaga—Maza.

M. R. H. Maza is right, Feda.

F. Mazaga—Mazager—Mazagi—Mazagon——

    (We here omit several other efforts on Feda's part to pronounce the name, which efforts end with *Mazagal.*)

M. R. H. No, not quite Mazagal, Feda.

F. Mazagan !

M. R. H. That's right, Feda. . . .

It will be seen that, although the sitters have admitted when anything said by Feda was right, they have not prompted any positive information. Mazagan was a port in Morocco which A. V. B. and M. R. H. had visited *en route* to Teneriffe.

In some subsequent sittings Feda described with a good deal of expressive pantomime and in considerable detail the injuries which A. V. B. had received in a motor accident which happened at Burford ; but in her efforts to give the name of the place, she never got further than ' Bur——' Of course all these names were consciously known to the sitters.

I shall omit the memories shown of certain photographs ; of riding and bathing, and of M. R. H.'s method of composing. But an interesting pseudo-word, which had been invented by M. R. H. and A. V. B., was got through by Feda after the usual struggles. What, A. V. B. was asked, was the antithesis

13

to ' Poon ' ?   After trying in two sittings Feda suddenly shouted the word, SPORKISH ! very loud.   This was right.   These invented words had been used to classify people in a light-hearted way into attractive and unattractive varieties.

In several sittings, evidence was given of knowledge by the A. V. B. communicator (or by Feda) of contemporary events which were happening to M. R. H. and U. V. T. as well as to others.   With these we shall not deal.

One sitting was devoted to a description of A. V. B.'s playing on a guitar, on which she had, during life, been an expert performer.   It is very curious that, although Feda imitates the guitar-notes exactly ; describes an instrument with a rounded end and a waist ; says that A. V. B. used to turn a peg, screw it up and then go ' tum ' ; tells the sitters that she is not trying to imitate a cornet or a trombone, yet throughout the whole performance is not able to say the word ' guitar ' !

Personal Touches and the A. V. B. Control.—Although personal touches cannot have the same evidential value for strangers that they have for friends of a communicator, they yet form an important branch of the evidence.   On January 19, 1917, A. V. B. appeared to oust Feda and take over the direct control herself, much to Feda's surprise.   After the medium had remained perfectly still for a minute or two, a voice said in an almost inaudible whisper : ' Where are you ? Pull me forward.'   Some emotion was shown, but speech appeared very difficult at first.   Gradually, however, the A. V. B. control gained in power and evidential value, until it was at last able to control in some ways as well as Feda.   It was mainly under these conditions that personal touches, characteristic of A. V. B., made their appearance.   Such mental characteristics as a marked tolerance, balance and moderation, together with a sense of humour which was never unkindly ; a quiet, almost stubborn determination ; a childish love of being appreciated in little things—these, which were characteristic of the living A. V. B. made their appearance in the trance A. V. B. during the direct control.

At first the A. V. B. control complained that she could not make the medium laugh.   When she succeeded, ' what ensued

was extraordinarily reminiscent of A. V. B.'s own laugh.'
M. R. H. records : ' On several occasions the timbre of Mrs.
Leonard's voice has changed and has become very like
A. V. B.'s voice ; startlingly so once or twice.' Once A. V. B.
said : ' Oh ! now the power is going ; can't you hear my
voice getting Mrs. Leonardy again ? ' which statement was
correct. Both the sitters agreed about this.

Sometimes the A. V. B. control was dissatisfied with the
pronunciation of certain words as they came from the medium's
mouth. This was particularly the case with the word ' often,'
which Mrs. Leonard habitually pronounces as ' off-ten,' but
which A. V. B. always used to pronounce as ' orfen.' ' She
only once succeeded in saying " orfen," repeating " off-ten,"
and then " orferten, orferten," several times in a rather
bewildered manner.'

On the second occasion on which the direct A. V. B. control
occurred, ' she began almost immediately to feel Mrs. Leonard's
face with apparent curiosity ; then she remarked : " What's
the matter with my face ? It feels thinner and bonier than it
used to be." ' In fact, Mrs. Leonard's face was of a thinner and
bonier construction than A. V. B.'s had been. Further
instances of these personal touches will be found in the report.

Matters entirely unknown to the Sitters.—So far all the
evidence given referred to matters known to the sitters. It is
a noticeable fact that things which are *consciously* in the minds
of the sitters, seem, as a general rule, though not always, to be
inaccessible to the trance-intelligences. For example, in the
first sitting of this series, the question occurred : ' Do you
remember a place we went to . . . ? ' and M. R. H. thought
of, and fully expected, ' Orotava ' to follow, but got instead
' Watergate Bay.' But there is every reason to suppose that
knowledge subconsciously possessed by the sitters is frequently,
if not always, accessible to the communicating intelligence. It
is possible to take the view, then, that all the information so
far given proceeded from the minds of the sitters. In that case
it forms a piece of evidence for telepathy which appears to be
irrefutable ; for to put it down to chance is absurd, and the
precautions taken by the investigators have rendered the theory

that Mrs. Leonard normally acquired the information untenable. No one has, in fact, attempted to show that the information given in this series of sittings was acquired by normal means; yet we should be greatly mistaken if we imagined that every one admitted it as incontestable evidence for telepathy. We have only to recall Messrs. Wells and Huxley's statement that the evidence for telepathy can be imitated by a conjurer. But no conjurer has offered to imitate the A. V. B. sittings with Mrs. Leonard under the same conditions, or is ever likely to.

At the end of the A. V. B. report, three cases are given in which the information supplied in the trance was not all known to the sitters. Owing to considerations of space, these can only be very briefly referred to.

The Dog Billy.—' Billy ' was a white-haired terrier belonging to Lady Troubridge, but pensioned with some ladies at Boscombe, so that at the time of these sittings, Lady Troubridge had not seen him for eleven years. In sittings in December 1916, and January and March 1917, statements were made by Feda as follows :

(1) That Billy had died suddenly. (This was known to U. V. T.)

(2) That Billy had an injury under his ' arm ' which had nothing to do with his death. (Also known to U. V. T.)

(3) That Billy died suddenly ; was *not* in good health when he died ; but had not been unhealthy long.

(4) That Billy had a knobbly thing sticking out of one of his hind legs.

(5) That Billy had something wrong under the ' arm,' i.e. where the fore-leg joins the body.

(6) That Billy's feet were turned up and examined between the toes.

Items (3), (4), (5), and (6) were unknown to the sitters, and were subsequently found by them to be true. Item (6) was at first thought to be incorrect, as the people with whom Billy was boarded knew nothing about it. But it was subsequently discovered that the canine specialist to whom Billy was sent prior to his death did turn up his feet and examine them, and found pustules between the toes, and that the dog did not like the process, as Feda had said. A signed statement was obtained from Miss G. C. Dutton, the canine specialist, who was the only person aware of item (6).

' *Burnham.*'—During her lifetime, A. V. B. had known a certain ' Sir Richard Rogers ' (pseudonym), and had stayed at his house, ' Burnham ' (pseudonym). Both the house and owner were unknown to M. R. H. and U. T. V., except that M. R. H. had met him on two occasions some years previously. In the course of a sitting on December 20, 1916, a good general description of Sir Richard's house, surroundings, and interests was given.

Daisy's Second Father.—A lady known to M. R. H., here called ' Daisy Armstrong ' (pseudonym), who had lost her husband during the war, asked M. R. H. to hold a sitting with Mrs. Leonard on her behalf, she herself being in the Near East. Feda states, in a sitting on February 21, 1917, that ' There were two of us that stood in the same relation to Daisy, but in a slightly different way,' the message ostensibly coming from a person who makes it clear from personal and other descriptions that he is Daisy Armstrong's father, who had died some years previously. When the father died, his great friend, the Rev. Bertram Wilson (pseudonym), assumed practically the relation of father to Daisy, who came to call him ' Daddy,' so that the statement made in the sitting of two who stood in nearly the same relation to Daisy was true. A curious point is that the message as given by Feda is rather conspicuously in the past tense : ' There *were* two of us that *stood*,' and again, ' two of us *did* stand.' Now, at the time when the sitting was held (February 21, 1917), Daisy Armstrong, then in the Near East, believed her ' Second Father ' to be still alive, but actually he had died on February 18, 1917, three days before the sitting was held ; so that, if the past tense is taken to indicate knowledge that the Second Father was already dead, and if that knowledge came from the minds of living people, these people must have been perfect strangers to the group concerned.

Possibly it came from the mind of the ' Vicar of Wickham,' who supplied information of the date of the Second Father's death. The case contains many complicated and interesting points which must be read in detail to be appreciated.

These three last cases show that the theory that the information given by trance-personalities is necessarily obtained telepathically from the subconscious minds of the sitters, needs at least considerable expansion ; for items of information appeared in these cases which were only known to complete strangers. This necessitates a much wider field of telepathic operation—a field not limited by the interest and affection of the supposed agents. In fact, one can scarcely suppose that the unconscious stranger from whom this wider information comes is playing the part of an active agent in the affair. It looks as if the telepathic theory would have to be augmented by what, in Chapter I, we defined as ' Telaesthesia'—that is to say, by a reaching out on the part of the trance-personality to prehend the information it needs in whatever mind happens to contain it. This is a very different thing from ' Telepathy,' which, as a term, originated from simple experiments in so-called ' thought-transference.'

A good deal of the recent evidence obtained in trance-sittings confirms the fact that the information given in the trance does not, or does not necessarily, emanate from the minds of the sitters.

Absent or Proxy Sittings.—This evidence occurs in what are known as ' Proxy ' sittings, in which some experienced person is asked to hold the sitting on behalf of a bereaved person or family who remain absent. He may or may not have some acquaintance with the family, but in any case he is not, as a general rule, acquainted with the deceased person who is expected to communicate, so that he does not know whether the information which is being given is veridical or not. These proxy sittings take experiment forward in two ways : (1) They prevent the possibility of help being given to the communicating personality by unconscious hints or leading questions by the sitters (although all experienced sitters are well on their guard in these matters). (2) They eliminate telepathy from the sitter as a possible source of information. Cases of proxy sittings are now fairly numerous, and it may be said at once that the results of a good proxy sitting are comparable with the results of a good ordinary sitting. It is unnecessary to give a detailed example of one here, since the procedure is exactly the same as that of any other sitting. The student who wishes to compare proxy with ordinary sittings in detail will find plenty of material.

The Rev. C. Drayton Thomas has published an account of twenty-four sittings.[1] As a check on possible overvaluation of true evidence by the relatives of the communicators, these cases were valued and classified by an independent committee of judges. The results vary from 4 correct items in the worst class of case to 50 correct items in the best. In 21 out of the 24 cases, the deceased was unknown to the sitter.

A long, but interesting, proxy case, extending over eleven Leonard sittings, was that of ' Bobby Newlove,'[2] in which pipes of infected water, with which Bobby had played not long before his death, and without his parents' knowledge, were discovered from information given in the sittings.

Two excellent books by Miss Nea Walker, *The Bridge* and *Through a Stranger's Hands*, contain a collection of proxy cases well worthy of study.

A recent American investigator and writer on psychical research, Mr. John F. Thomas, gives an account of two proxy sittings held with Mrs. Leonard in 1928 and 1929 in his book, *Beyond Normal Cognition*.[3] Mr. Thomas had previously had personal sittings with Mrs. Leonard in 1927, at which he introduced himself anonymously. After his return to America he arranged that Mrs. M. Hankey, Secretary of the British College of Psychic Science, should hold two proxy sittings on his behalf, sitting alone with Mrs. Leonard, and taking a stenographic record of all that passed. Since Mrs. Leonard at that time was only giving sittings to previous clients, this

---

[1] ' A Consideration of a Series of Proxy Sittings,' *Proc. S.P.R.*, vol. xli. p. 139.

[2] *Proc. S.P.R.*, vol. xliii. p. 439.

[3] Boston Society for Psychic Research, 1937.

appointment was made for ' the American who sat with her in 1927.' This was all the information she had. Mr. Thomas conducts his work with every care and, in reporting his results, summarizes these in the form of a table after the record of each sitting. In that of October 29, 1928, 87 points were given, of which 73 were verifiable, and the percentage of correct verifiable statements was 95·8. In that of May 20, 1929, 104 points were given, of which 72 were verifiable, and the percentage of correct verifiable statements was 97·2.

In June 1929, Mrs. Lydia W. Allison held four proxy sittings with Mrs. Leonard on behalf of Mr. John F. Thomas. Mrs. Allison is an American lady and an active member of the Boston Society for Psychic Research, and is also a very experienced and scientifically cautious investigator. She is an old sitter with Mrs. Leonard. At the time of these sittings she had only a slight acquaintance with Mr. Thomas, who, she says in her report, ' was almost a complete stranger to me, and I knew hardly anything about his family or his affairs.' [1] The three first sittings were not very striking, but the fourth contained several points of considerable interest. The communicator was E. L. T.—that is to say, Mr. Thomas's wife, who died in 1926. Besides personal details about Mr. Thomas's family, which were unknown to Mrs. Allison, an instructive point is Feda's answer to Mrs. Allison's question : ' Where did they live ? ' Feda gives a dramatic description of busy workshops—metal, cutting, noises, stamping, fitting, circles, wheels, hundreds of men working, hammering, ringing noises. ' They runs along, like this (imitating whirring noises) enormous cases, and at last " Detra—Detra—Detroi——" ' Mr. and Mrs. Thomas had lived in Detroit ; but it is apparently easier for Feda to give a description of the enormous Ford Car industry there than to give the name of the place, although she gets it in the end, except for the final ' t.' There are several other true facts about Mr. and Mrs. Thomas of an interesting kind, including the mention of a special light railway, on which they used to travel twice a year, but it is

[1] ' Proxy Sittings with Mrs. Leonard,' by Mrs. Lydia Allison (*Proc. S.P.R.*, vol. xlii. p. 104).

unnecessary to occupy space with a description of what the reader, who is interested, can study for himself at length. Enough has been said to indicate that veridical matter can be obtained through a good medium of facts unknown to the sitter about people who are hundreds of miles away, and are not even aware that the sitting is going on. And this after every precaution has been taken to eliminate possible leakage of information to the medium by normal means, and when the identity of those concerned has been concealed.

Many, no doubt, will incline to attribute the veridical knowledge shown to chance in the form of ' lucky shots ' on the part of the mediums. In the next chapter we will consider a numerical method of estimating the likelihood that chance could account for mediumistic material.

Chapter XIV

THE EVALUATION OF CHANCE IN MEDIUMISTIC MATERIAL

THE SALTMARSH-SOAL-PRATT METHOD OF EVALUATING MEDIUM-ISTIC MATERIAL.—Mr. H. F. Saltmarsh published in 1929 a highly interesting report on a series of sittings with a trance-medium, Mrs. Warren Elliott,[1] part of which he devoted to the development of a new method of estimating the probability that the statements made by the medium (or control) could have been true by chance. Since many mediumistic statements are of a rather vague character, and would apply to a good many people, it is desirable to make some estimate of the likelihood of their being correct by chance. The method used is described by the author as follows :

' Copies of the records of certain selected sittings were sent to persons totally unconnected with the real sitters. These persons were asked to imagine that the sittings referred to themselves, and to annotate accordingly. Any coincidences which might occur would, therefore, be attributable to chance alone. A system of scoring or marking was devised, and the chance sittings were scored in exactly the same way as the real. It was argued that if the score for the real sittings was considerably in excess of that for chance, when taken over a fair number of cases, it might be claimed that chance as a possible explanation was excluded. The figure for the ratio by which real should exceed chance in order to afford complete proof was fixed at eight times.'

In the first experiment the communicator was ostensibly a young flying officer who had been killed in the war, and six chance-annotators were selected, each of whom had sustained the loss of a young relative, so that, in general, they would be

---

[1] ' Report on the Investigation of some Sittings with Mrs. Warren Elliott,' *Proc. S.P.R.*, vol. xxxix. pp. 47 ff.

in much the same situation as the relatives of the actual communicator. The results were :

Total Possible Score.	Real Score.	Chance Score.
5,642	4,107 = 72·8%	452 = 8%

The last figure gives the average of the six chance-score results. The real score is thus nine times as great as the chance score. In two individual instances, however, chance scorers came considerably nearer to the real score than did the chance average. In one of these, the real score was 3·8 times the chance score, and in the other 4·6 times.

In the second experiment, there were eighty-five sittings in all. The result was :

Total Possible Score.	Real Score.	Chance Score.
5,554	3,226 = 58·1%	487 = 8·75%

Here the real score is 6·6 times the chance score. In three individual cases of five sittings each, the chance scores were, however, considerably higher than the average, namely :

	Real Score.	Chance Score.
(1)	52%	23%
(2)	59%	28%
(3)	46%	33%

But, in a large number of sittings, some individual chance scores would be certain to be above the average, if chance alone were operating. The preponderence of scores in real sittings over scores in chance sittings seems to be very clearly marked.

The method of scoring was to divide the statements made at the sittings into three classes : (i) Vague (V), (ii) Definite (D), and (iii) Characteristic (C). ' V ' statements were given a score of 1 ; ' D ' statements of 5 ; ' C ' statements of 20. The total possible and actual scores were computed by addition, and the percentage worked out. The marking, of course, left great latitude for the individual judgement. ' The closest analogy,' says the author, ' seems to be the marking of examination papers on some literary subject where differences of opinion, individual idiosyncracy, nuances of meaning, all complicate the matter. It is impossible to eliminate the personal factor in both the annotator and the scorer.' Also, the method creates a bias in favour of a chance explanation. It is, for example, quite possible for a wrong statement, which would send the score down, to be made in a way which is peculiarly characteristic of the communicator, and so, if taken qualitatively, to count the other way. But, if a quantitative method of scoring such as this shows considerable odds against chance, it creates an important piece of evidence on the chance question.

That the method is rough is indicated by an ideal example which the author gives. He says :

' The total possible and the actual scores are computed by addition. This is, of course, not strictly correct. An example will make this clear. If out of 100 statements, 99 V and 1 D, 49 of the V statements and the D statement are found to be veridical, this would give a score of 54 out of a possible 104, or 51·9%.

' But if, out of these 50 veridical statements, 5 were D statements and 45 were V, this would give a score of 70 out of a possible 120, or 58·3%.

' It is clear that the addition of four more definite statements add far more to the real value than is indicated by the increase of 6·4%.'

This is an extreme case, but it shows that when one is dealing with statements of a qualitative kind it is impossible to cite figures which will at all strictly represent the probabilities that chance, acting alone, would have verified them. This is only possible when dealing with circumscribed choices as in guessing cards, etc.

The method of evaluating the probability that chance could account for the veridical statements given at a sitting with a trance-medium, given the raw data obtained in the way explained above, was improved in later work which Mr. Saltmarsh carried out in conjunction with a mathematician, Mr. S. G. Soal.[1] The formula used (see report cited) was supplied by Mr. Soal, after having been submitted to Professor

[1] ' A Method of Estimating the Supernormal Content of Mediumistic Communications,' *Proc. S.P.R.*, vol. xxix. pp. 266 ff.

R. A. Fisher for his opinion.   Applied to the results of an actual sitting with Mrs. Warren Elliott, the calculations showed that the likelihood that pure chance, acting alone, would have produced these actual results was of the order of one in a thousand million.

Since then, the method has undergone still further development at the hands of Mr. J. G. Pratt in the Psychological Laboratory of Duke University, North Carolina.[1]

As in all statistical methods applied to psychical research, the crucial point lies in the assumptions made when the mathematical formulæ are applied to the experimental data. The mathematician assumes that figures are available stating correctly the probability that chance could account for each veridical statement.   Granted that, there is very little doubt that the formula will give a reliable result.   But these figures, which form the data of the whole process, have been arrived at by marking or scoring statements in a manner involving qualitative judgements.   So long as we remember this and are not misled into thinking that a mathematical formula of imposing appearance can *add* anything to the accuracy of these qualitative judgements, all is well.   In deciding the marking estimates, the experimenters are doing just what any one does who is making a qualitative judgement of any case with respect to chance.

The difference is that, having made his judgement, the investigator now puts a figure to it.   Thus we see that this ' quantitative ' method rests upon a qualitative basis.   Nevertheless, as a check on the qualitative judgement of common sense, such a method of estimation as this is very useful.   As has been said, it is not likely to favour the supernormal as against the chance explanation, so that, if the results pass this test, one may feel confident that chance as a possible explanation is entirely ruled out.

A much more exhaustive application of the methods of statistics to the phenomena of the mediumistic trance will be dealt with in the next chapter.

---

[1] ' Towards a Method of Evaluating Mediumistic Material,' by J. C. Pratt (*Bulletin* xxiii., Boston Society for Psychic Research).

Chapter XV

THE QUANTITATIVE STUDY OF
TRANCE-PERSONALITIES

THE APPLICATION OF A METRICAL TEST TO TRANCE-PERSONALITIES.—The object of introducing the quantitative method described in the last chapter was to test the possibility that results such as those obtained could have been attributable to chance. Mr. Whately Carington, the author of the present method, has boldly carried quantitative analysis beyond this point and has applied it to a scheme for testing the independence of trance-personalities. He has embodied the results of this most interesting and original piece of work, up to the stage so far reached, in three reports, published in the *Proceedings* of the Society for Psychical Research,[1] and further work is still in progress. Mr. Carington has had to contend with all the difficulties inherent in a pioneer scheme, and circumstances have necessitated certain changes of method *en route*. But, whatever differences of opinion may exist as to the significance borne by the results, there is no doubt that the work reflects the greatest credit on its author.

In introducing his novel method, Mr. Carington says : ' The object of the researches here described has been to explore the possibilities of substituting anthropometrical for legal methods, and of bringing the personalities concerned out of the witness-box and into the laboratory.' It is ' measure and calculation,' he says, ' which alone characterize the transition from speculative inquiry to exact science.' He sets out to solve three main problems. ' First, to devise a quantitative method of experimenting on trance-personalities. Secondly, to use this method to find out whether it could provide evidence

[1] *Proc. S.P.R.*, vol. xlii. p. 173 ; vol. xliii. p. 319 ; vol. xliv. p. 189.

for or against the autonomy of spirit communicators. Thirdly, to find out as much as possible about the psychology of the trance state.'

As the reports which Mr. Carington has issued are full of mathematical processes of a difficult kind, far from easy for any to follow who have not made a special study of the mathematics of statistics, I shall take the following description from a remarkably able and lucid review of these reports written by Professor R. H. Thouless.[1]

To give the reader a general idea of the principle, I may perhaps say that Mr. Carington was looking for some test psychically analagous to the finger-print. If the trance-personalities communicating through mediums could be got to manifest some mental trait as unique and characteristic of the individual mind as the finger-print is of the body, the problem of their autonomy might be solved. The test which presented itself to Mr. Carington's mind as being possibly adaptable for this purpose, was one devised by Jung in order to investigate the emotional complexes of his patients. The method consists in this : A series of words is called out to the subject, who is required to respond as quickly as possible with the first word which comes into his mind. The time taken for the response to each word is measured by means of a stop-watch, and this is called the ' reaction-time.' At the end of the experiment, the same list of words may be called out again and the subject asked to try to respond with the same words as before. This is called the ' reproduction test.' If any word in the list has a hidden emotional significance for the subject, this fact is revealed by an unusually long reaction-time, and also by a strong tendency to fail in reproduction and to substitute a different word on the second reading. The whole experiment is called the ' word-association test.' The emotional responses may be registered in another way, namely, by connecting the subject with suitable electrical apparatus and noting the change in his electrical resistance during the response to each word. High emotional significance is shown by a large

[1] ' Review of Mr. Whately Carington's work on Trance Personalities,' *Proc. S.P.R.*, vol. xliv. pp. 223 ff.

drop in resistance. This method is called the 'psycho-galvanic reflex.' It was, however, found unsuitable in these experiments and was abandoned. Most of the work was carried out by measuring reaction-times.

The Besterman-Gatty Experiment.—Mr. Carington set out with the idea that if two personalities, say the medium and the communicator, possess a common subconscious, ' they could not, apart from deliberate cheating, produce significantly different sets of reaction-times or disturbances in reproduction ; with the corollary that where such differences are observed they constitute strong evidence of the autonomy of the personalities concerned.' In order to test this assumption, he carried out a trial experiment. The subject, Mr. Oliver Gatty, who kindly presented himself for the experiment, was selected because he had led a ' double life,' in the innocent sense that he had devoted part of his time to scientific work at Oxford, and part of his time to sporting and country pursuits in his home in Hampshire. For the purpose of this test, Mr. Gatty was first asked to think of himself as immersed in his Oxford life, and in this pose (referred to as Gatty (O)) was tested for responses to a list of words. He was then asked to think of himself as immersed in his Hampshire life, and in this pose (referred to as Gatty (H)) was tested with the same list of words over again. The result was that both the reaction-times and reproductions showed significant differences in the two states, thus proving that a mere voluntary change in attitude of mind is sufficient to alter word-association responses. Mr. Gatty, who clearly possessed the same subconscious in both his poses, nevertheless gave different responses in each. Mr. Carington was therefore obliged to abandon his initial assumption and to seek a new way of applying the quantitative method.

He next sought to measure two things : (*a*) the Similarity between the personalities to be tested, as shown by their responses to the word-association test, and (*b*) the Difference between them, as shown by the same method—the term ' Difference,' however, being understood to mean, not merely the converse of Similarity, but *Consistency* of Difference. The numerical measurements of Similarity and Difference were deducible from the experimental data by the use of the mathematical method of the Analysis of Variance, a statistical technique developed by the well-known statistician, Professor R. A. Fisher.

The Method.—The application of the method is as follows : Suppose it is desired to measure the degree of Similarity between two personalities A and B (A might be a trance-medium, and B her control), the same list of words would be read out to each in turn, and responses given with the first word which presented itself. The reaction-times to these responses would be measured with a stop-watch. For the purpose of comparing the two personalities, it is not the actual times which are wanted, but the *differences* between A's and B's reaction-times in each case. This list of differences forms the raw material from which Similarity and Difference are calculated.

The criterion for comparison taken is the *pattern* of the responses, not the actual time-periods. Thus, if all the responses of one personality were exactly half a second longer than those of the other, they would be regarded as completely correlated.

The measurement of ' similarity ' is, in effect, a measurement of correlation. ' The average size of the response of one personality A to the first word in the list, his average response to the second, to the third, and so on, form one series. The other series is formed by the average responses to these same words given by the second personality B. The amount of correlation between the two series is a measure of the similarity of the two personalities. . . .'

Unfortunately, the test cannot be considered as at all comparable with the finger-print test as a mark of identity, because of its low degree of self-consistency. Two people with identical thumb-prints would not be found once in a billion times ; but two people with word-association responses resembling one another as closely as the same person's responses resemble one another on different occasions would not be hard to find. This is one of the difficulties of the method. To a certain extent it may be said that all human beings tend

14

to respond to words alike, and this general human similarity has to be eliminated before specific similarities can be detected. The faces of any two boys, for example, may be said to be very much alike when compared with the face of a chimpanzee. But that degree of likeness is not sufficient to prove that they are twins.

Let us suppose that a list of words is read out to two personalities, A and B, in turn, and that their reaction-times are taken ; and, further, that this experiment is repeated on several different occasions. The results would be tabulated as follows :

Occasions :

Words.	I	II	III	IV	V	VI	Average.
1.	(A_1-B_1)	(A_1-B_1)	(A_1-B_1)	(A_1-B_1)	(A_1-B_1)	(A_1-B_1)	a_1
2.	(A_2-B_2)	(A_2-B_2)	(A_2-B_2)	(A_2-B_2)	(A_2-B_2)	(A_2-B_2)	a_2
3.	(A_3-B_3)	(A_3-B_3)	(A_3-B_3)	and so on.			a_3

(A-B) anywhere in the table represents the *difference* between the reaction-times of the two personalities to the same word on any occasion. The different occasions are tabulated horizontally ; the different words vertically. The average values of the respective rows are a_1, a_2, a_3, etc. If the pattern of the A-responses, and the B-responses to all the words were nearly the same, the (A-B)s would tend to be constant, and a_1, a_2, etc., would tend to be equal. There would be complete correlation or similarity. But that in practice is not the case, for the responses differ on different occasions, so that a_1, a_2, etc., are different. The problem is to find out whether the differences contained in the column of averages is greater than could be accounted for by the differences occurring between the (A-B)s.

Briefly, the principle of the method employed to solve this problem is (*a*) to measure the amount of ' scatter ' which exists amongst all the (A-B) entries, (*b*) to calculate how much scatter this would account for in the column of averages, (*c*) to measure the amount of scatter which actually exists in the column of averages. If this latter does not differ significantly from that which has been found in (*b*), similarity between the response-patterns of A and B is indicated.

The question of what constitutes *significant* differences is dealt with on the same principle as that explained in Chapter VII.

Besides ' similarity ' there is ' difference ' to be considered. The same value of the measure of correlation (indicated by the letter *z*), given by a certain *similarity* of responses might, however, be given if there were no similarity, as a result of lack of consistency in the responses on different occasions. This raises a further complication. Professor Thouless says : ' Thus, both difference between the reactions of A and B, and consistency between these differences are necessary for a significant value of *z*, and this measure would be more correctly described as one of " consistency of difference " than simply as one of " difference." '

As has been said before, Mr. Carington has been obliged to change his methods and his opinions concerning the results from time to time in the light of experience as the work progressed, and this experimental phase is not yet over. Consequently, such conclusions as can be drawn at the present time are of a tentative nature, and the result of a long chain of reasoning and counter-reasoning. One may say, however, that one conclusion, reached earlier in the work, still stands, namely, the ' countersimilarity ' of the controls.

Countersimilarity of Controls.—By ' countersimilarity ' is meant ' negative correlation,' an example of which is the relation existing between a face and its plaster cast. Where the features project, the cast is indented and *vice versa*. That kind of relation seems to be shown, so far as reaction-time results are concerned, between Mrs. Leonard and her control Feda, and between Mrs. Garratt and her control Uvani. But it was confined to reaction-time experiments and was not borne out in the reproduction tests. Further, all except one of the figures showing this countersimilarity were insignificantly small when taken alone ; it was only when taken all together that they showed significance. Still another point is that the evidence for countersimilarity in Mrs. Leonard's case rests upon a single experiment. In spite of this, Professor Thouless thinks that both in Mrs. Leonard's and Mrs. Garrett's cases we may conclude that the relation of countersimilarity with their controls exists, but he adds, ' It is a pity that this important conclusion could not have been established in a more convincing way from data freer from inconsistencies.' The same test, when applied to a third medium, Mrs. Sharplin, gave no evidence of countersimilarity between her and her control, Silver. The reader is left, therefore, without any feeling of strong conviction on the point. If the evidence for counter-similarity be accepted, it points to the controls as being dissociated ' fragments ' of the medium's personalities. Perhaps it would be more cautious to say that it points to some dissociated constituent of the medium's personality as forming an *element* in the control, for we must not lose sight of the possibility that all trance-personalities may be compound entities.

Intermedium Work.—The trance-personalities who were not controls but communicators, purporting to be deceased persons, gave no evidence of countersimilarity with the mediums. A different method was applied in the hope of testing their identity. This method consisted in applying the word-association test to the same ostensible communicators when manifesting through two different mediums. The communicators known as ' John ' and ' Etta,' well established as direct controls with Mrs. Leonard through the work of Mr. Drayton Thomas, were tested with the word-list, first through Mrs. Leonard and then again at separate sittings through Mrs. Sharplin. It was thought that if evidence of similarity could be found between the Leonard John and the Sharplin John, and also between the Leonard Etta and the Sharplin Etta, a ground for believing in their autonomy would have been provided. One difficulty was that, if similarity were found, it might be due to similarity in the response-patterns of the two mediums, and it was sought to eliminate this by applying the method of partial correlation. This work also passed through many vicissitudes. A correction in the method of combining probabilities reversed the first tentative conclusion. Then the method of partial correlation was rejected as a result of criticism from Professor R. A. Fisher, and a new method, not open to the previous objections, was devised by Mr. Carington.

The problem which this method was designed to solve is thus stated by Professor Thouless : ' We must prove not merely that a given communicator is like himself but that he is more like himself than he would be if he were not himself. More exactly, we must be able to show whether or not X_A (communicator X communicating through medium A) is more like X_B than he would be if the two Xs were not the same personality in the two cases.' He illustrates the problem by giving the following imaginary case :

' Let us suppose that I received two years ago a letter from some one who knew me in the past and now needs my help. Let us further suppose that he is an illiterate man who has not composed the letter himself, but has given a secretary the general idea of what he wanted to write and has left her the task of expressing it in her own words. Let us suppose further that I received yesterday a letter ostensibly from the same man but composed by a different secretary. I have some reason for suspecting that the writer of the second letter is an imposter, and is not really the same person as the writer of two years ago. How am I to establish whether or not the two letters have identical originators ?

' Naturally, the two letters will not be identical ; they may not even be closely similar. Each of them has many individual peculiarities which reflect the personality of the secretary and not of the originator. On the other hand, they are not likely to be wholly dissimilar. Any two human beings in similar circumstances may give somewhat similar instructions to the person who is writing a letter for them, and any two secretaries writing letters under similar circumstances may be expected to compose somewhat similar letters. With this amount of data, indeed, the problem will be insoluble. Even though I can measure how much the two letters resemble each other, I cannot draw any conclusion as to the identity or non-identity of the originators, since I do not know how much the two letters might differ although the originator of both was one and the same person, nor do I know how much the two letters might be expected to resemble each other although the originators of them were different.

' If, however, I were so fortunate as to have, written by the same two secretaries, two more letters written in similar circumstances, but not written by the alleged individual of whose self-identity I am in doubt, I should have the data for the solution of the problem. In order that the problem may be as closely as possible analogous to that of W. W. C.'s research, we may suppose that the second letter of each secretary was written at the same time as the first, and that I am as doubtful about the common authorship of this pair of letters as I am about the common authorship of the other pair.

' Let us call the two secretaries A and B, and the two alleged authors (who may prove to be four), X and Y. I want to know whether X_A is the same individual as X_B, and whether Y_A is the same as Y_B. Comparison of X_A with Y_B and of X_B with Y_A will tell me both how much the style of the two secretaries has in common and how much two letters written by two individuals in the same circumstances have in common. This knowledge will enable me to allow both for the factor of resemblance of secretaries and for the common human factor. If now I find that the letter of X_A resembles that of X_B strikingly more than the pair of comparisons I made previously, I may conclude that X_A and X_B are one and the same person ; similarly for Y_A and Y_B.'

We have only to substitute the ' John ' communicator through Mrs. Leonard for X_A and through Mrs. Sharplin for X_B, and the ' Etta ' communicator through Mrs. Leonard for Y_A and through Mrs. Sharplin for Y_B to understand the Intermedium method. Also, instead of the qualitative comparison of letters, we have the quantitative comparison of word-association responses, estimated and expressed in figures by the mathematical device of the Method of Variance.[1]

The result, so far as these experiments have gone, is that no significant evidence is shown for the autonomy of the

[1] For details of the application of this method, the reader is referred to Mr. Carington's and Professor Thouless's Reports, above quoted.

communicators.   Professor Thouless ends his statement by saying :

' Even, however, if the procedure is shown to give a sufficiently sensitive test of the autonomy of personalities [living] tested directly by the word-association test, it might be the case that the necessity for communicators to respond through a medium prevented the responses from adequately characterizing the communicator. This possibility appears to be more difficult to investigate, and unless it can be eliminated, it seems that W. W. C.'s results may provide no evidence for autonomous communicators, but also no very strong evidence against autonomous communicators.'

Criticism of the Quantitative Method.—The crux of the word-association method really lies in Professor Thouless's last remark. In other words, can we assume that, even if the surviving self of the communicator does lie behind the communications, it will make a characteristic contribution to a word-association test ? It seems far from obvious. Is the illustration of the letter-writers a true analogy ? How do we know that the pattern of a word-association response, given by a communicating trance-personality, is not something *sui generis*, characterizing a psychological organization temporarily formed for the purpose of communicating and informed by the self-principle of the communicator ? There are plenty of analagous instances of qualities which characterize a grouped complex but do not characterize the elements of the complex taken alone. The taste of salt, for example, is uniquely characteristic of the compound sodium chloride ; it is not a compound of the taste of sodium with the taste of chlorine, and it would be quite fallacious to argue that any compound into which sodium entered must have at least a trace of salty taste about it. It must be remembered that we only meet with word-association responses in the compound personalities of living people. We have no evidence that the elements of such personalities, if isolated and recombined differently, would each bring with it its proportional contribution from the old word-association test into another one. They might conceivably do so ; but it is a pure assumption, which I, for one, should regard as unlikely. For one thing, to speak of a personality as a quantitative thing, consisting of an association of numerically distinct units, seems to me to be to speak in symbols.

Mr. Kenneth Richmond [1] has, I think, put us on the right lines for thinking about trance-communicators. Speaking of the belief that the communicator ' is ' the deceased person, he says :

' If we substitute " is partly " for " is," we are making assumptions about the nature and behaviour of personality-elements, which are very likely to be misleading. It is here that we can keep closer to justifiable assumptions by thinking in terms of communicator-impulse rather than communicator-personality. I think we can argue, with a minimum of fantasy, the existence of an impulse to dramatize on the part of the medium (a natural and respectable impulse when the mediumship is of high grade), combined in greater or less degree with an impulse to co-operate with and assist the dramatization on the part of the discarnate person. Essentially, we are in touch, at a sitting with a subliminal actor in the medium (there is plenty of evidence to be gathered from hypnotic experiments for the existence of a subliminal actor in the human mind), who in turn is in more or less close telepathic touch with the original of the rôle.'

Would such a communicator-impulse, informing in turn two such communicator-vehicles as would be the case in the intermedium tests, carry over with it a characteristic contribution from one complex to the other ? One cannot tell without experiment in a known case ; and such experiment is, from the nature of the case, impossible. The Gatty experiment, as far as it goes, seems to me to point against it. Professor Thouless says : ' It is an advantage of a quantitative statistical inquiry that the method of proving the self-identity of bags of manure is the same as that of proving self-identity of spirits.' Personally, I cannot see that it follows that what is true of quantitative things like bags of manure is necessarily true of non-quantitative things, or quasi-quantitative things, like

[1] *Proc. S.P.R.*, vol. xliv. p. 22.

psychical entities. What do we know about the characteristics which necessarily accompany identity of selfhood ? A very interesting and significant incident occurred with that rare sensitive, Mrs. Willett (see Chapter XIX, p. 272) when she was in a state not far removed from normal consciousness. She seemed to herself to enter into a reconstructed scene from Plato's *Symposium*, and whilst in the midst of it and enjoying it, she described it, speaking in the first person, as a scene she loved and often saw. An hour afterwards she had no recollection at all of the scene which she had described and did not know what any of it meant when the record of her own words was shown to her. If we admit, as I think we must, that the experient of this scene was Mrs. Willett herself, we have to face the fact that a complete break in memory and continuity of experience, as well as a profound change in the content of knowledge, do not impair the identity of selfhood. On what, then, does this identity depend ? What is the criterion of selfhood ? If a self can change its memories, its experience and its knowledge without sacrificing its autonomy, why should it not also change its mode of response to a string of words ? Word-responses are merely the result of certain subconscious associations ; they are not different from other emotional traits and characteristics, and we know from the Gatty experiment that an imaginative change of mental pose is sufficient to alter them. Is there any reason why the more profound change undergone by Mrs. Willett on the occasion quoted above should have had no effect on her word-association responses ? And what about the still more profound change involved in death and re-synthesis in temporary mediumistic communicating personalities ? The assumption made in these experiments is that, if there is autonomy of the self-principle of a communicator entering into two mediumistic trance-complexes, this principle must necessarily carry with it a similarity of word-responses. But on what evidence does this assumption rest ? Apparently on none ; yet on this assumption the whole value of this quantitative experiment depends.

But if lack of evidence for similarity would not justify us

in drawing any conclusion, would positive evidence of similarity tell us any more ? Suppose that ' John ' through Mrs. Leonard showed definite similarity with ' John ' through Mrs. Sharplin, would that contribute more towards the proof of an autonomous John than does the qualitative evidence we have already ? It does not seem at all certain that it would. We already have in the Willett trance (see Part V) communicators of a remarkably life-like type, with mental and emotional characteristics appropriate to the deceased persons they purport to be. If we do not accept these as evidence of autonomy, why should we accept word-association responses ? For example, Myers $_W$ and Myers $_H$ both showed the passionate desire to prove survival which animated the living Myers. They might conceivably, had they been tested, have given similar responses to a word-association test. But, if they had, how would this trait have been a more convincing proof of autonomy than the former ? I suspect that at the root of the matter lies the superstition that, if an emotion can have a number attached to it, it becomes, *ipso facto*, more informative than an emotion without a number ! It is the legacy of physics, which makes us worship the stop-watch. Psychical characteristics are all intrinsically *qualitative* things, and by trying in ingenious ways to tack numbers on to them, we run a grave risk of merely confusing ourselves. The upshot, then, of this brief review of the quantitative method of studying trance-personalities, is that, although the method is interesting and ingenious and, as a piece of pioneer exploring, reflects great credit on its author, and although it might in time bring to light useful facts, it would be unsafe in the light of our present knowledge to draw any conclusions from the results, whether they are positive or negative.

The Merits of Qualitative and Quantitative Methods.—The foregoing experiments suggest some reflections on the comparative merits of qualitative and quantitative methods. Are quantitative methods necessarily superior to qualitative in psychical research ? There seems to be no doubt that, where chance is a possible explanation of any phenomenon, it is much better to be able to say that the odds that pure chance, acting alone, would have produced this result are just so much in figures, rather than to say it is extremely unlikely that chance would have produced this result. Figures with regard to chance undoubtedly lend definiteness in connexion with experiments with cards or machines, and in all cases where the chance-probability is at all near the point of significance. But it is a very different matter to import mathematical statistics into psychical research as a main method of investigation. The weak point lies in the uncertainty of the assumptions which are made, and which must be made, before any meaning can be attached to the numerical results. We are very apt to overlook the fact that, if these fundamental assumptions are unsound, no greater accuracy or certainty can be infused into them by dealing in figures afterwards. There is a great tendency to think that figures and formulæ render a method accurate and certain, and increase its reliability, because science is still dominated by the tradition of Physics and physical methods are thought to confer prestige. But psychology is an entirely different subject from physics, and metrical methods are often quite unsuited to it. Mathematics is, of course, merely a tool, and is in itself perfectly neutral as regards truth. Sir Arthur Eddington illustrates this amusingly in a quotation he makes from Bertrand Russell. Mathematics is, he says : ' The subject in which we never know what we are talking about, nor whether what we are saying is true.' [1] This at first sounds as if it were intended to be a slur on the pure mathematician, but it is quite literally a fact. All that the pure mathematician is concerned with is to make statements of the form : *If* such and such a proposition is true of *anything*, then such and such another proposition is true of that thing. But *whether* the first proposition is true, and if so *what* it is true about, are no concerns of his. The truth of the results in experimental science, given by any mathematical or quantitative method, depend entirely on the truth of the initial assumptions which link the mathematical data with empirical fact. If these are false, no amount of mathematical reasoning will make them any truer. Hence the first thing

[1] *Space, Time, and Gravitation*, p. 14.

to inquire into when a mathematical method is broached, is the soundness of the postulates which translate the numerical results into meaningful conclusions. In the present instance, these postulates seem to have received too little attention.

It is often argued that a sounder judgement can be based on quantitative than on qualitative data. In physics, where we are dealing with things which lend themselves to quantitative methods, this is undoubtedly true. But in psychology it does not necessarily follow. Traits of character may be far better grasped qualitatively than quantitatively. Suppose, for example, that a general is required to select an officer for some unusual and exacting kind of duty. What would be thought of him if he demanded the Intelligence Quotients of all his staff, saying that he could not rely on a mere qualitative judgement, but must select his man ' by numbers ? ' Every one would say that he was a fool who did not know his own men ; the point being, not that a quantitative ' measurement ' of intelligence is in such a case *unnecessary*, but that it is *not good enough*. Such tests or ' measurements ' are much too clumsy and uninformative. They let everything that matters slip through their meshes. Every age has its superstitions, and that of the present age seems to be the illusion that figures constitute a highway to truth.

We shall now turn to another subject and shall have little more to say about numerical methods. In the next chapter we shall come to the first example of an experiment which was not planned by the investigators, but which was discovered by them to be in progress.

Chapter XVI

BOOK-TESTS

THE NATURE OF BOOK-TESTS.—The kind of evidence for the supernormal, contained in Book-tests, is still connected with the mediumistic trance. Instances began to appear about the year 1917, in which attempts were made by Mrs. Leonard's control, Feda, to indicate passages on specified pages of closed books as they stood in the library shelves. This was not an experiment devised by the investigators ; the initiative for it rested with the communicating intelligences. The books used in these tests had never been seen by Mrs. Leonard, and were usually, at the time of the sittings, unknown to the sitter. There are at least 130 cases of book-tests on record, varying greatly in degree of clarity and success.

Feda professes that the communicators are interested in book-tests because they exclude the explanation of telepathy from the sitter. She will say : ' He (the communicator) wants to give you one of the book-tests . . . tests that prevent people thinking it is telepathy.' She does not generally profess to be able to read the contents of the closed books herself, which is, perhaps, a fact of some interest ; [1] she claims that the communicator does this, and that she passes on the information to the sitter. It would certainly seem as if, in cases of book-tests where the results cannot reasonably be attributed to chance, either Feda or the communicator must be able to exercise the power of pure clairvoyance, or else a very omniscient kind of telepathy must be postulated, by means of which the information can be gained from the mind of any person who has read the book in question.

[1] Mr. Kenneth Richmond (*Proc. S.P.R.*, vol. xliv. p. 19) says : ' Good examples of clairvoyance by Feda when apparently operating alone seem to be all in unpublished material.'

This would have to extend to the reading of another copy of the same edition, as sometimes the particular volume indicated has been unread and the pages are still uncut.

A typical example of a hypothetical book-test would be as follows :

> ' Feda might tell the sitter that the communicator wants him to go to the bookcase between the fireplace and the window in his study, and on the third shelf from the bottom to take the seventh book from the left and open it at the forty-eighth page, where, about one-third of the way down, he will find a passage which may be regarded as an appropriate message from the communicator to him.' [1]

There are two unsatisfactory points, which introduce some vagueness into many of these tests. (1) The sitter is usually referred to a particular page in the book where it is said that he will find a ' message ' which will be significant for him, and little or no indication is given of the substance which the message actually contains. (2) There is often ambiguity about the number of the page intended, whether the number printed on the page is to be taken, or whether the number is to be found by counting the pages from the beginning of the book. There are, of course, usually certain unnumbered pages at the beginning and often certain prefatory pages numbered in Roman numerals before the serial pages of the book begin. As far as the first point is concerned, it actually turns out to be by no means the case that a ' message ' which could be construed as appropriate as from the communicator to the sitter can be found on almost any page of the book indicated.

Interesting cases of book-tests which illustrate these various points will be found in the *Proceedings of the Society for Psychical Research*, particularly in the report entitled, ' An Examination of Book-Tests obtained in Sittings with Mrs. Leonard,' already referred to : also in the Society's *Journal*. It appears from these book-tests that Feda, or the com-

[1] Mrs. Sidgwick, ' An Examination of Book-Tests,' *Proc. S.P.R.*, vol. xxxi. p. 242.

municator, seems sometimes to sense the actual *words* on the page, and sometimes only to get hold of the *meaning* of the passage. In one instance, Feda said that in the fifth book from left to right on a shelf that she clearly indicated, there was, on p. 14, about half-way down, something that ' gave her a feeling of heat,' but that she had better explain that it might come from two sources, ' it might come from a mention of heat, like a hot sun, or a hot fire, or it might come from a mention of great anger, but spoken of as heat ; in fact she'd be obliged if you'd tell her which it is next time you come.' The book proved to be *Larkmeadow*, by Marmaduke Pickthall, and had not been read or opened by the sitters. On the sixteenth line (there were 33 lines to the page) of page 14 occurred the words ' ardent patriot,' while on the fifteenth line of page 15, facing it, occurred the word ' bonfire.' When the book was closed, as it stood in the shelf, the words ' ardent,' and ' bonfire,' almost touched one another. This illustrates a curious point about these book-tests. Feda frequently makes a mistake about the page, indicating the page which is actually opposite to the one evidently intended, so that when the book is closed, the passage she means to indicate is pressing against the one she actually does indicate. There should be in this fact some clue as to the *modus operandi* of the clairvoyant faculty if only we knew how to follow it up. On one occasion Lady Troubridge (U. V. T.) accused Feda of making this mistake, and pointed out that she had made it two or three times. F. ' She knows she does that, she says it's most awfully difficult. She says she is not apt to get the other side of the leaf. It's when the power lies in between the pages that it's difficult, she says if the page were open it would be all right, the trouble is sensing it in a closed book. She says she just had to gauge, the way you gauge the height of a certain building, she wonders sometimes that she can find the page at all.' U. V. T. ' The sentence was very clear, but on the opposite page.' F. ' Very likely, and some- times it will be in the right position on the page.' U. V. T. ' Yes, it was.' F. ' She says it is so difficult when the pages are touching each other.'[1]

[1] Ibid. pp. 349–50.

There were certain cases in which the room in which the book was situated was unknown to the sitter ; and there were three cases in which the pages of the books were uncut. But these cases were none of them very good, whether on account of these facts or merely by chance.

Another experiment, again suggested, not by the investigators, but by the A. V. B. communicator, mentioned in Chapter XIII, was that books should be tried in a language unknown to Mrs. Leonard and to the sitters. A shelf of Greek books was put at Feda's disposal, and as a result of 14 cases given from these, 4 seemed definitely right, 4 perhaps right, 4 very dubious, 1 probably wrong, and 1 certainly wrong.

Mrs. Sidgwick, in summing up her conclusions about book-tests, says :

' I have endeavoured to tabulate roughly the number of successes and failures in the cases before us. Roughly speaking, out of about 532 items, rather over a third were completely or approximately successful. But I do not think this really tells us very much ; first, because the classification is difficult and uncertain, and secondly, because the evidential importance of successes, as unlikely to occur by chance, varies enormously.'

When one is considering the possibility that a book-test may have been fulfilled by chance, in a case where the passage is stated to have been selected as having significance for the sitter, it is not easy to put a figure to the probability of chance-fulfilment. Often the message has more significance for the sitter than is apparent to an outsider.

An Actual Book-Test.—The following is an abridgement of a book-test which illustrates several characteristic points ; also the items of this test have been subjected to an assessment of chance-probability.[1]

The book-test occurred during a sitting with Mrs. Leonard on January 27, 1931, the sitter being the Rev. W. S. Irving and the recorder Mr. Theodore Besterman. In Mr. Irving's sittings, the communicator, Dora, is ostensibly his deceased wife.

[1] *Journal S.P.R.*, vol. xxvii. pp. 59–69.

(i) Feda opened the sitting by talking of a red book, and asked whether the sitter had been doing anything with a book ' with a rather particularly vivid shade of red on the cover or covers.'

(i) Mr. Besterman had, on the previous evening, at the sitter's request, taken a book at random from his shelves and put it in an attaché-case, where it had remained in his flat. This was with a view to a book-test. The book had vivid red covers. After selecting it, Mr. Besterman noted that it was a copy of *The Poetical Works of Alexander Pope.*

(ii) Feda said : ' It's about a medium size. I should say it might have two hundred and fifty to three hundred pages, which I s'pose you'd call medium size.'

(ii) The book was of medium size, measuring $4\frac{1}{4}$ in. $\times 7$ in., and had in all 330 pages.

(iii) Feda said that the sitter was going to see this book ; that he had not used it, and that he was going to take it from some one else's hand.

(iii) These points were true. Mr. Irving had not then seen the book ; he was going to see it and did eventually take it from Mr. Besterman's hand.

(iv) Feda said that the book was not a treatise on psychical matters, but that it touched on them.

(iv) The book was a volume of poetry, but did frequently touch on psychical matters, e.g., ' What beckoning ghost along the moon-light shade, invites my steps . . .' and in the ' Ode on St. Cecilia's Day ' there are references to ' tortured ghosts,' and ' See, shady forms advance ! And the pale spectres dance ! ' etc.

(v) Feda said : ' You are going to see the book at once, at once, during the next two or three days.'

(v) Mr. Besterman handed Mr. Irving the book the morning after the sitting.

(vi) Feda described a ' funny sign ' on the book, saying that it was ' rather shaped like a star,' but has ' got more like a curve '—' more like what Feda thinks the petals of a flower,' and mentioned ' scallops round the edge,' saying also that it was ' not just a little ordinary design.' She added, ' I feel it's

15

a sign, or symbol specially suited to the book,' and she made a rough drawing of it.

(vi) This was a very good description of the mark of Messrs. Bell, the publishers, which appeared on the spine of the book, and which includes a bell in the design and is therefore a sign or symbol, and is particularly suited to the book.

(vii) Feda said that the book contained a great many references to the mind.

(vii) This volume included the ' Essay on Man ' and ' Moral Essays,' which are full of reflections on the mental faculties ; and it may, perhaps, be said that Pope is a poet who is particularly concerned with the mental processes and the intellect.

(viii) Feda said that on page eighteen (repeated and stressed) there were ' rather beautiful words ' about ' bars '—' bars like barriers,' and that these were to a certain extent applicable to the sitter.

(viii) The page *numbered* eighteen in the book was found to be blank ; but if the pages were *counted* from the beginning, in the way which Mr. Irving thought had recently been adopted by the communicator, since this method seemed to have applied to recent tests, the eighteenth page was that numbered eleven, and on this was part of the story of two parted lovers (lines 187 to 217 of ' Eloisa to Abelard '). This poem turns on the idea of bars or barriers preventing the reunion of the lovers, although ' bars ' are not specifically mentioned. Mr. Irving fully agreed that it was to a certain extent applicable to himself as parted from his wife by death. But, as Feda said, only to a certain extent, as the separating ' bars ' in the poem are not those of death. The vagueness in indicating the page as well as the habit of giving a passage of personal significance to the sitter are both illustrated by this case.

(ix) Feda said that the sitter would see the book in a rather dark or shaded room.

(ix) Mr. Besterman actually handed him the book on a dull morning in the back room of the Society's Library, ' always a rather dark room.'

Mr. Besterman next made an estimate, as well as this could

be done by common-sense judgement, of the probabilities that Feda's statements could be verified by chance.

(i) The only point here that can be judged is the vivid red cover. Mr. Besterman estimated that one book in five has vivid red covers, but adds that an examination of average book-shelves will show that the proportion is actually much smaller.

(ii) No value was attached to this because the estimate given was not literally correct.

(iii) Most of the books from which book-tests are given are standing on shelves and only a few would have the recent touch of a hand on them, so that the odds against this statement being correct would be considerable. But in case the medium had inferred that a special kind of test was involved, this statement is given only a value of 1 in 2.

(iv) Mr. Besterman says : ' A vast majority of books are not treatises on psychical matters and very few of them have touches of a psychical kind in them. Let us say, to be moderate, 1 in 10.'

(v) ' No value ; being a forecast, it would be impossible to prove that it had been confirmed quite spontaneously.'

(vi) Many publishers have no mark, and no publisher puts his mark on all his books. A bookcase in the Library of the S.P.R., chosen as containing miscellaneous books, contained only eight books with some kind of symbol on their covers out of 234 volumes, and this would be a higher proportion than the average, since novels hardly ever bear signs, and there are no novels in the S.P.R. Library. Mr. Besterman gives this statement a value of 1 in 25.

Feda's drawing and description could only apply to the ' bell ' mark of Messrs. Bell's books, and Mr. Besterman thinks that the proportion of books having this mark would be very greatly overestimated at 1 in 100. The probability of the statements in this paragraph being fulfilled by chance would therefore be 1 in 2500, an extremely conservative estimate.

(vii) Since only a few books contain ' a great many refer-ences to the mind, mentality,' as Feda said, the value given to the statement is 1 in 10.

(viii) Mr. Besterman estimates that the proportion of books

which would contain a passage as relevant as this one was to the sitter would be ludicrously overestimated at 1 in 100. The doubt as to the page should reduce this to 1 in 50, but, to be on the safe side, he reduces it to 1 in 10.

(ix) This is given no value.

Multiplying these values together to give the combined probability of the series gives the odds against all these statements in succession being verified by chance as 1 in 25,000,000 ; but the scales here have been heavily weighted in favour of chance, and this figure is quite ridiculously low. Worked out by a mathematician, the figures were shown to be ' astronomical.'

This case differed from the ordinary book-test in that Mr. Besterman knew certain points, such as the colour, size, and title of the book selected and the publisher's mark (presumably), and these things could therefore have been obtained from his mind by telepathy. The element of book-test proper is contained in paragraph (viii). As a rule, Feda describes a book as it stands on the shelves and not one which has been picked out beforehand. But the case contains several instructive points, and has therefore been selected for illustration.

The Element of Chance in Book-Tests.—In spite of the high anti-chance figures given by the better examples of book-tests, such as the one just quoted, it was felt desirable that control experiments should be tried and compared with the actual results given by real cases. It is no easy thing to carry out such experiments, since only the roughest quantitative estimate can be made of the likelihood that the kind of statements made in book-tests will be fulfilled by chance. Mr. Besterman pursued the following method.[1] There were 26 full shelves of books in his flat, and he sent a list of the numbers from 1 to 26 to each of three members of the Society, and, without telling them the reason for the request, asked them to place against each number a figure not higher than 20, followed by an R or an L. In this way he obtained references to 78 books, selected by a purely chance method. For example, if against the number 26 was placed the reference 9L, then the 9th book from the left on shelf 26 would be indicated.

[1] See *Proc. S.P.R.*, vol. xl. p. 59.

Meanwhile, three actual book-tests had been selected by another member of the Society, and the page-references given in these actual tests were taken and applied to the books selected by chance. Tables were now made in which each actual book-test was compared with the 78 passages occurring on the corresponding pages in the chance-selected books, to see how many corresponded by chance. Faced by these tables, which contain 234 entries, one can do nothing towards summarizing them. All that one can do is to quote Mr. Besterman's cautiously worded concluding paragraph : ' I think we may reasonably sum up by saying that all the control experiments in book-tests so far devised strongly indicate the presence of some extra-chance factor in the book-tests given by Mrs. Leonard.' In fact, book-tests, like every other experiment that has been tried, show that, on the balance, there is unmistakable evidence of supernormal faculty at work when one is dealing with a good sensitive or medium, after every care has been taken to test the alternative possibilities.

This concludes the bird's-eye survey we have made of the control type of trance from the point of view of evidence for its supernormality. When we refer to it again, it will be from the point of view of the *modus operandi* of its processes, and not from the point of view of whether or not its material is explicable by normal means. We now go on to consider a different class of phenomena, namely, those arising out of Automatism.

Chapter XVII

CROSS-CORRESPONDENCES

AUTOMATISM.—In Chapter I we defined an Automatist as a person who is able to write without consciously controlling the process. But the scope of automatism is in reality wider than this ; it applies to the sensory as well as to the motor functions. Automatism may, perhaps, be best thought of as a mode of signalling from the subliminal to the supraliminal element of the self. When considering spontaneous cases of telepathy, we laid stress on the scenes, created in terms of sense-imagery, which the telepathic message made use of in order to bring itself before the normal consciousness of the percipient ; and we noted that the messages embodied themselves in imagery belonging to all the senses—visual, auditory, tactual, olfactory, and even gustatory. These were all cases of Sensory Auto-matism,[1] which formed the end-process of the telepathic phenomenon, and signalled the message, after ' reception ' by the subliminal, to the supraliminal of the percipient.

But sensory automatism does not only form part of the process of telepathy. It plays other parts, as, for example, in one case in which the hallucinatory figure of a man standing in the doorway prevented a woman from stepping down the well of a lift. And it can be used experimentally, notably in the art of ' scrying ' or crystal-gazing, which is only a device for ' shunting ' the normal consciousness, as it were, off the main line of its habitual activities, and allowing the subliminal to present to it its created pictures of visual sense-imagery. It would seem that the subliminal self has knowledge (whether in the case of a few individuals only or in the case of all)

[1] See Myers' *Human Personality* for information about Sensory and Motor Automatism.

which it can communicate to the supraliminal in no other way than by some kind of automatism. The art of scrying is, of course, very ancient—in fact, it is world-wide in space and time, having been practised by almost every race. Often the scryer looks into a clear pool of water ; sometimes into ink ; sometimes into blood ; but the usual modern practice is to look into a crystal ball.[1]

The other form of automatism is that in which the motor functions, instead of the sensory functions, are made use of to convey the message. Table-tilting, planchette, and automatic writing are forms of this. The normal consciousness being slightly displaced from its habitual position of control of the bodily muscular system, the subliminal takes charge of it instead, and transmits its message to consciousness by causing the muscular system to perform the act of writing. Table-tilting and planchette are merely clumsy forms of writing. The only advantage they possess over the simple plan of holding a pencil is that more than one person can participate in them at once.

Dowsing.—Another form of motor automatism, which has attained notoriety since early times, is that of ' Dowsing ' or Water-divining, in which the subject walks about holding a forked twig or some such indicator. When he passes over water, the forked twig is deflected by unconscious muscular action, just as the planchette moves or the table tilts or the pencil writes, and conveys the message of the subliminal's knowledge of the presence of the water to the conscious mind. Not only water, but metals or oil, or, indeed, anything can be ' dowsed ' for.[2] When the practice was introduced into England in the sixteenth century, it was for metals and not for water that it was used. It is interesting to observe that practical dowsers often hold the theory that the twig or rod is deflected by some physical influence proceeding from the object dowsed for. This belief, though almost certainly erroneous, probably

[1] See the experiences of ' Miss X ' (Miss Goodrich Freer), *Essays in Psychical Research*. (Redway, 1899.)

[2] There are even some who use this method for making a medical diagnosis.

has a beneficial effect on the dowsing process, because there is no better way of preventing the supraliminal from interfering in the automatic process with its logical expectations and deductions than by persuading it that the whole thing is occurring according to some normal, causal plan. This leaves the subliminal a clear field in which to get its messages through. Dowsing has an enormous literature, not because it is in any way different from other forms of motor automatism, but because it has a cash value in practical life. The reader who is interested in it will find plenty of material for study.

As there can be automatic writing, so also there can be automatic speech ; and we will now go on to consider examples of the evidence for the supernormal which has been acquired through these two channels, particularly through the former.

Cross-Correspondences—The Personalities Concerned.—What cross-correspondences are will be explained directly. They arose amongst a particular group of people all personally known to one another, and linked through early friendships with F. W. H. Myers and those who founded the Society for Psychical Research. In view of their common interests, it was not surprising that communications should arrive ostensibly from those members of the group who had died ; but, as events turned out, these communications took an unexpectedly interesting form.

The principal members of the ' other-side ' group were : (1) F. W. H. Myers, a classical scholar and minor poet, whose intense interest in psychical research led to the foundation of the Society in 1882, and whose work, *Human Personality, and its Survival of Bodily Death*, has long been a classic. He died on January 17, 1901. (2) Edmund Gurney, his friend and collaborator, who carried out much early experimental work in the subject and wrote a comprehensive book entitled, *Phantasms of the Living*. He died on June 22, 1888. (3) Henry Sidgwick, well-known as a philosopher, having conspicuously occupied the Chair of Moral Philosophy at Cambridge. He was a strong champion of psychical research against the incredulity of the nineteenth century, and was the first President of the S.P.R. in 1882. He died in August 1900.

(4) A. W. Verrall, a celebrated classical scholar and Fellow of Trinity College, Cambridge, who became interested in psychical work through his wife's participation in it. He died in June 1912. (5) Henry Butcher, also a Cambridge scholar of high distinction and a friend of Dr. Verrall's, who later occupied the Chair of Greek at Edinburgh University. He died in December 1910.

Prominent members of the ' this-side ' group were four ladies who possessed the power of automatic writing, namely, Mrs. Verrall, wife of Dr. A. W. Verrall, and Lecturer in Classics at Newnham, of whom Frederick Myers had said that she is ' among our best observers ' ; Mrs. Holland (a pseudonym), a lady who had lived for some time in India, and whose interest in the work of the S.P.R. developed out of her own natural faculty for automatic writing ; Mrs. Willett (also a pseudonym), an automatist of remarkable power, introduced to the experimenting group and, apparently, in a way sponsored, by Mrs. Verrall in 1910 ; Miss Verrall (afterwards Mrs. Salter), the daughter of Mrs. Verrall. In addition to these, contributions to the cross-correspondences were made in some of the sittings of Mrs. Piper, the American medium whose work was dealt with in Chapter XII. Mrs. ' King ' (Dame Edith Lyttelton) also produced automatic writings which entered into the cross-correspondences, though to a lesser extent ; also a lady known as Miss ' Mac ' ; Mrs. ' Forbes ' and Mrs. Thompson.

Besides the group producing these writings, there were those who supervised the experiments and collated the results. Mr. J. G. Piddington, also a classical scholar, took the foremost part in the arduous task of unravelling the literary problems which the cross-correspondences contain ; and it was through his skill and perseverance that much of the most striking evidence was brought to light. Miss Alice Johnson, of Newnham College, Cambridge, who became Research Officer to the S.P.R., also did much of the ' headquarters ' work. There were also the present Lord Balfour, his sister, Mrs. Henry Sidgwick, Sir Oliver Lodge, and Mrs. Verrall—the latter acting in the double capacity of automatist and investigator.

The cross-correspondences, therefore, were conducted by a group of able and distinguished men and women, in whom the highest confidence can be placed. It is, perhaps, to be regretted that certain of them felt constrained, for personal reasons, to publish their work under pseudonyms, but it must be remembered that the prejudice against psychical inquiry was greater some years ago than it is to-day.

What Cross-Correspondences Are.—About the years 1906–7 it was first noticed that there were straightforward correspondences between the productions of certain automatists belonging to this group. Some attempts were then made experimentally to obtain correspondences between the writings of the group and Mrs. Piper, the American trance-medium. Meanwhile the Research Officer of the S.P.R., Miss Alice Johnson, had discovered that correspondences, had begun to show themselves between the automatic scripts of Mrs. Verrall and Mrs. Holland, and she was led by a study of these to propound the theory that something more was taking place than simple references to the same topic in more than one script, and that a plan was in existence of a complex character, giving evidence of selection and design. Further, Mr. Piddington, when examining the experiment with Mrs. Piper, said that in some cases the subjects treated of ' were, so to speak, links in a concatination, or cubes in a mosaic of ideas which had been distributed among several automatists.' [1] As time went on, and the volume of automatic material grew, the interlinked character of the scripts became plainer ; the existence of separate cross-correspondences was recognized and their method of correlation studied. But only very gradually did it become apparent that all these cross-correspondences were items in one interrelated whole. Again, to quote Mr. Piddington : ' They are not clear-cut, isolated things, with a definite beginning, and complete in themselves. They are tiny bits of very complex patterns.'

The plan behind the cross-correspondences is as follows : If a communicator were to show knowledge of some incident which happened to him during his lifetime, and were to offer

[1] *Proc. S.P.R.*, vol. xxii. p. 242.

this as proof of his continued identity, the explanation given by the living would be that the medium had acquired this knowledge telepathically from the minds of his surviving friends. But, if a kind of jig-saw puzzle were devised in which various automatists took part, each producing a separate piece of the puzzle which conveyed no meaning to them when taken alone—and if, when these separate pieces were put together, they made a coherent whole, then the evidence for some constructive mind behind the whole design would be greatly strengthened, and the explanation of telepathy from the living made correspondingly difficult. If none of the automatists knew the meaning of the messages they had received, they could not very well influence other automatists telepathically to produce messages complementary to them. This is the theory of the cross-correspondence ; needless to say, nearly all the actual cases are imperfect and, in one way or another, fall short of the ideal.

Another advantage accruing from the automatist's ignorance of what she is producing is that conscious associations are not so likely to influence and deflect the thought while it is being transmitted. This, according to the communicators, is a source of considerable difficulty. Thus, the Gurney communicator through Mrs. Willett (Gurney$_W$) explaining, as an example, how he would get the idea of ' fire ' transmitted through an automatist under a slightly veiled form, says that he might give the automatist the idea of ' phœnix,' but he adds that her subliminal might quite well (to use his own words) ' go one better and shove in Salamander.' Salamander, being in the right line of association, would not matter ; but the automatist's contribution might equally well be an associated idea which could lead away from the desired subject altogether.

Cross-correspondences are particularly difficult to present in a compact form, because they consist of references to recondite points in classical literature, rendered purposively obscure and allusive by the intelligences which construct them, so that they tend to spread out and ramify instead of converging towards a neat conclusion, a feature which is apt to be distressing to the tidy type of scientific mind. The threads of which they are composed intertwine with one another in a most complex manner, and a single cross-correspondence often spreads out over a long period of time. Also they are so much the work of a particular group of investigators, that they have something of the air of being a family affair, and this makes judgements on the points at issue a difficult matter for the outsider. It is, no doubt, true generally of all psychical evidence that those who stand nearest to it have the best chance of coming to a true conclusion ; but this is particularly the case where cross-correspondences are concerned. The uninitiated will often see less point in a literary allusion than will the expert, and may underrate it accordingly. I suppose that if a foreigner were to come across the words : ' I shall softly and silently vanish away,' he would undertake an elaborate research to trace them to their origin, and it would be difficult to persuade him that they might not refer to various passages in the works of different authors. Exactly why every Englishman would at once assign them to Lewis Carroll would not be an easy thing to explain to a foreigner. In the same way, just why classical scholars, who have known Frederick Myers and A. W. Verrall in the flesh, give such and such a value to a literary reference which purports to come from one of them, would not be easy to explain to a stranger. The reader of these experiments is thus to a considerable extent in the hands of commentators who are in the know, yet a certain suspicion will probably remain at the back of his mind that the commentator *may* sometimes be reading meanings into the text which are not there. This suspicion he will find it difficult to check. Yet it may well be that the commentator has formed the truer judgement and he would be wise to defer to him.

Here, to begin with, is a very simple and straightforward example of a cross-correspondence.

A Simple Cross-Correspondence—' *Thanatos.*'—In 1907 Mrs. Piper held some sittings in England, under the auspices of the Society for Psychical Research.

April 17, 1907.—In the course of this sitting, the words ' Sanatos ' and ' Tanatos ' occurred.

April 23, 1907.—In the course of this sitting the word
' Thanatos ' occurred.

April 30, 1907.—In the course of the waking stage, after
this sitting, the word ' Thanatos ' occurred three times.

Thus Mrs. Piper, between these dates, had repeated several times the Greek word for ' death,' and it was interjected
into the rest of the matter in a disconnected way.

Meanwhile, Mrs. Holland was writing automatic script
in India.

April 16, 1907.—' Maurice. Morris. Mors.
> And with that the shadow of death fell upon him
> and his soul departed out of his limbs.'

The prefacing of Maurice, Morris to the word ' Mors ' is
quite characteristic of the way in which words are felt after
in all psychic utterances, by way of other words having more or
less similar sounds. Thus, we see Mrs. Holland brought out
the Latin word for ' death ' the day before Mrs. Piper brought
out, or nearly brought out, the Greek word for it ; and the
words about the ' shadow of death ' reinforce the meaning.

April 29, 1907.—Mrs. Verrall (in England) produced the
following script :
> ' Warmed both hands before the Fire of Life.
> It fails and I am ready to depart.'
> (Then occurs a large Greek delta and some less relevant
> matter.)
> Manibus date lilia plenis [give lilies with full hands].
> ' Come away. Come away.
> Pallida mors æquo pede pauperum
> tabernas regumque turres
> (put in)   pulsat
> Tu beate Sesti.
> [Pale death with equal foot the huts of the poor and
> the towers of the rich   (put in) ' strikes.'
> Thou happy Sestius.]
> Another time will help
> Good-bye.
> But you have got the word plainly written all along in
> your own writing. Look back.'

The Greek letter delta was always personally associated by Mrs. Verrall with the idea of death. ' Give lilies with full hands ' is a quotation from the *Aeneid* connected with the prediction of the death of Marcellus. ' Come away,' of course, refers to ' Come away, death ' in *Twelfth Night*.

Here, then, several references to death appear in Mrs. Verrall's script the day before Mrs. Piper utters ' Thanatos ' three times.

In this cross-correspondence, the idea of distributing the theme amongst different automatists has been carried out ; but the differentiation of the idea does not go beyond the expression of the same thought in three different languages. One may suppose that Mrs. Piper, knowing no Greek, was selected to give the Greek version, while Mrs. Verrall, the classical scholar of the three, was chosen to express the idea by means of quotations.

This case, though not without interest, does not illustrate the complexity and ingenuity which characterises the majority of the cross-correspondences. The next case will illustrate this, though it is defective in that the material is conveyed mainly through one automatist. It may be noticed that if we regard the ' Thanatos ' case as merely due to telepathy between three automatists, we have a good illustration of telepathy taking place over a long distance, since one of the participants was in India, while the other two were in England. It is, in fact, a good case for the consideration of those who uphold a physical theory of telepathy.

For a case which is both complex, and also distributed among automatists, the reader is referred to the cross-correspondence entitled, ' *Autos Ouranos Akumon*,'[1] as an example, but the case is too complex for reproduction here, even in an abridged form.

The following is an attempted summary of the main points contained in the cross-correspondence called *The Ear of Dionysius*. It came almost entirely through the scripts of Mrs. Willett, though there were also apparently some allusions to it in the scripts of Mrs. ' King.' It was reported by Lord

[1] *Proc. S.P.R.*, vol. xxii. pp. 107 ff.

Balfour.[1] It is made clear, as Lord Balfour points out, by internal evidence, such as personal references and characteristic personal touches, that this literary puzzle *purports* to have been planned and transmitted by the two friends, who were both distinguished Cambridge scholars, Dr. A. W. Verrall (A. W. V.), and Professor S. H. Butcher (S. H.). The former had died in 1912, and the latter in 1910. Present at the reception of one or other of the scripts were Lord Balfour, Sir Oliver Lodge, and Mrs. Verrall. The scripts are here abridged and the points numbered for ease of reference.

January 10, 1914 :

    (1) Do you remember you did not know and I complained of your classical ignorance IGNORANCE
        [It had been already indicated that this sentence was intended to be addressed by A. W. V. to his wife, who was not then present.]

    (2) It concerned a place where slaves were kept—and Audition belongs, also Acoustics.

    (3) Think of the Whispering Gallery

    (4) To toil, a slave, the Tyrant—and it was called Orecchio—that's near

    (5) One ear, a one-eared place, not a one-horsed dawn (Here the automatist laughed slightly),[2] a one-eared place—You did not know (or remember) about it when it came up in conversation, and I said, Well, what is the use of a classical education—

    (6) Where were the fields of Enna
        (Drawing of an ear)
        an ear ly pipe could be heard

    (7) to sail for Syracuse

    (8) Who beat the loud-sounding wave, who smote the moving furrows.

    (9) The heel of the Boot

[1] See *Proc. S.P.R.*, vol. xxix. pp. 197–243.
[2] The ' One Horsed Dawn ' was a telepathic experiment which A. W. V. had tried with Mrs. Verrall during his lifetime.

(10) Dy Dy and then you think of Diana Dimorphism [1]
(11) To fly to find Euripides
(12) not the Pauline Philemon
This sort of thing is more difficult to do than it looked.

The reader will probably agree that the originators of this script have succeeded in making it sufficiently cryptic. Now to attempt to explain these points.

Items (2) and (3) and the word ' Orecchio ' in (4) are best explained in Lord Balfour's own words :

' The Ear of Dionysius,' he says, ' is a kind of grotto hewn in the solid rock at Syracuse and opening on to one of the stone quarries which served as a place of captivity for the Athenian prisoners who fell into the hands of the victorious Syracusans after the failure of the famous siege so graphically described by Thucydides. A few years later these quarries were used again as prisons by the elder Dionysius, Tyrant of Syracuse. The grotto of which I have spoken has the peculiar acoustic properties of a whispering gallery, and is traditionally believed to have been constructed or utilized by the Tyrant in order to overhear, himself unseen, the conversations of his prisoners. Partly for this reason, and partly from the fancied resemblance to the interior of a donkey's ear, it came to be called *L'Orecchio di Dionisio*, or the Ear of Dionysius ; but the name only dates from the sixteenth century.'

Items (1) and (5) are explained by the fact that, during Dr. Verrall's lifetime, Mrs. Willett had spoken automatically the words, ' Dionysius' Ear the Lobe,' and Mrs. Verrall had asked her husband what the words meant. He had told her, remarking humorously on her ignorance of the subject, since she, too, was a classical scholar.

In Item (10), Dy Dy are most probably attempts to write Dionysius, but mental associations of the sensitive's own lead off on to wrong tracks, as the communicator is aware.

In Item (6) the object seems to be to stress further the theme of Sicily, where the Ear of Dionysius was situated. The meadows of Enna, a town in Sicily, were famous in antiquity as the scene of the Rape of Proserpine. The punning

---

[1] Note the automatist's train of association going off on the wrong line.

reference to the ear ly pipe is not clear. Possibly some reference is intended which the commentators have missed.

Items (8) and (9) refer to the ill-fated Athenian expedition against Syracuse, which ' smote the moving furrows ' (these words are used in Tennyson's *Ulysses*) on their voyage to Sicily round the heel of Italy.

Items (11) and (12) were traced by the investigators to Browning's *Aristophenes Apology*, in which Philemon (certainly *not* the Pauline Philemon) is mentioned in connexion with Dionysius, the Tyrant of Sicily, and in which Philemon says :

> ' I'd hang myself—to see Euripides.'

The disjointed topics of this first script are intended, then, to concentrate attention on Dionysius, the Tyrant of Syracuse ; on the stone-quarries which were his prisons and which contained the whispering gallery, called the ' Ear of Dionysius.'

February 28, 1914.—This script opens with something like an apology from the communicators for the confused mixture of topics which is to follow. It says :

> ' Some confusion may appear in the matter transmitted, but there is now being started an experiment not a new experiment but a new subject and not exactly that but a new line which joins with a subject already got through.'

The script also says :

> ' It may take some considerable time to get the necessary references through,' and adds that ' this is something good and worth doing.'

In various ways the topics of the previous script are referred to again, and amongst these, references to new topics are strewn about anyhow. The new points are as follows :

(1) We are told to join one ear to one eye.
' 1 eyed ' is a topic ; and through many different references,
16

including a cave, a flaming torch, Homer, Poseidon and his trident (the Greek sea-god), Noah and the grapes, it is made clear that the story of Polyphemus and Ulysses is being aimed at.

(2) ' A Fountain on the Hill Side ' is mentioned, together with a rough drawing of a volcano. Then, near the end of the script, there comes :

> ' He was turned into a fountain that sort of Stephen man, he was turned into a fountain, WHY ? that's the point : WHY ? . . .'

(1) The story is told by Homer of how Ulysses is driven by a storm to the country of the Lotus Eaters, and then reaches the land of the Cyclopes, a race of one-eyed giants. How Ulysses and his companions enter the cave of one of them, by name Polyphemus, the son of Poseidon. How Polyphemus proceeds to devour the Greeks, but Ulysses plunges a flaming torch into his single eye, and effects his escape and that of his companions. All the references in (1) lead up to this single idea of Polyphemus.

(2) The allusions here are intended to introduce the story of Acis and Galatea. Acis, a shepherd dwelling at the foot of Mount Etna, and Galatea the sea nymph, were lovers. But the ' monster Polyphemus,' again playing the villain of the piece, loved Galatea, who rejected him. Mad with jealousy, he hurled a rock at Acis and crushed him to death. Galatea conferred upon her lover a kind of immortality by changing him into a stream, which issued from beneath the rock which overwhelmed him. Acis is called the ' sort of Stephen man ' because Stephen, the first Christian martyr, was stoned to death. And the insistent ' WHY ? ' is to bring out the point that Acis was killed through *jealousy*—the jealousy of a rejected lover.

Note that these stories are both introduced without any mention of the principal characters by name. The two new points are, then, (1) Polyphemus, and (2) the jealousy of a rejected lover.

March 2, 1914.—It is unnecessary to quote much from this script. The points hitherto given are stressed again and the following new points are added :

> Music and the sound of a musical instrument.
> Something to be found in Aristotle's *Poetics*.
> Satire.

Gurney $_W$ also says :

> ' Until the effort is completed the portions as they come are not to be seen by any other AUTOMATIST.'

A curious blank of a year and a half now occurs, during which time the subject of the cross-correspondence was dropped in the scripts. Either some kind of misunderstanding seems to have occurred or else there was a curious lapse of memory on the part of the communicators. The investigators had been given to understand that more was coming and had simply waited for it. At the same time, the communicators appear to have been waiting to be told when the allusions already given had been traced.

August 2, 1915.—In the script of this date, Mrs. Verrall being present, S. H. Butcher $_W$ asks whether *Satire* has been identified, thus reopening the subject of the cross-corre-spondence, and seems surprised to learn that it has not been. The script then reiterates some of the former points, and adds a final clue.

It says that Polyphemus is to be conjoined with Cythera and the Ear-man, and then :

> ' Cyclopean Philox   He laboured in the stone quarries and drew upon the earlier writer for material for his Satire   Jealousy.'

Supplied with these new clues, the ingenious investigators got to work again. Lord Balfour gives us the final explanation as follows : Philoxenus of Cythera was identified as a writer of dithyrambs, a species of lyric poetry generally accompanied on the zither. (Music and the zither had been specifically mentioned.) He had been a poet of some note in antiquity, and at the height of his reputation had spent some time in Sicily at the Court of Dionysius the Tyrant of Syracuse. ' He ultimately quarrelled with his patron and was sent to prison in one of the stone-quarries. Most writers, according to Smith's *Dictionary of Greek and Roman Biography and Mythology*, ascribe the oppressive action of Dionysius to the wounded vanity of the tyrant, whose poems Philoxenus not only refused to praise, but, on being asked to revise one of them, said the best way of correcting it would be to draw a black line through the whole paper.' This version of the quarrel is also followed by the writer in the *Encyclopedia Britannica*, and by Grote in his *History of Greece*. There was, however, another account mentioned in the *Dictionary of Biography and Mythology* only to be rejected, which ascribed the disgrace of the poet ' to too close an intimacy with the tyrant's mistress Galateia.'

I now come to the heart of the mystery which has hitherto baffled us. The most famous of the dithyrambic poems of Philoxenus was a piece entitled ' Cyclops ' or ' Galatea.' This was written as a burlesque on Dionysius, who was blind in one eye, according to the *Encyclopedia Britannica*. But still there was not much foundation for the stories of Ulysses and Polyphemus and of Acis and Galatea. After exhaustive search, a story comprising all the points of the scripts was unearthed. Here it was said that Philoxenus was banished to the stone-quarries partly on account of his passion for Galatea, a beautiful flute-player, who was the mistress of Dionysius. ' In his confinement he revenged himself by composing his famous dithyramb entitled either ' Kyklops ' or ' Galateia,' in which the poet represented himself as Odysseus, who, to take vengeance on Polyphemus (Dionysius), estranged the affections of the nymph Galateia, of whom the Kyklops was enamoured.'

This story occurs in a work of a specialist nature, intended for scholars, entitled *Greek Melic Poets*, by Dr. H. Weir Smyth, Professor of Greek at Bryn Mawr College, Pennsylvania, a copy of which Dr. Verrall was known to have possessed and to have used as a text-book in connexion with some of his lectures.

Lord Balfour says : ' Here evidently is the literary unity of which we were in search. . . .'

An ingenious scheme, capable of being originated only by scholars of ripe knowledge, and far beyond the classical ability of the automatist, was thus gradually unfolded. It contained many touches which were, in a rather subtle way, characteristic of the two authors who purported to have constructed it, and it was so given as to be, and to remain to the end, a mystery which required all the perseverance and ingenuity of the investigators to solve. And, finally, its scattered topics came together in a book of a rare and specialist nature, which Dr. Verrall was known to have possessed and used. It must be admitted, I think, that in cases such as this, there is strong evidence that *some* mind is exhibiting purpose and design, which is foreign to the personality of the automatist.

August 19, 1915.—In this final script, Gurney$_W$ is told that all the allusions are now understood. He says, ' Good, at last.' Then in reply to Lord Balfour's remark that the combination was extremely ingenious and successful, he says : ' And A. W.-ish ; also S. H.-ish '—that is to say, characteristic of A. W. Verrall and of S. H. Butcher. That, if the account be read in full, the reader will probably agree that it was.

With regard to the theory that Mrs. Willett could have concocted the whole scheme out of her own reading, Lord Balfour says that she is ' in no sense a " learned " lady. She has a taste for poetry, and a good knowledge of certain English poets ; but with classical subjects she is as little familiar as the average of educated women. This I can affirm with confidence, and I have had good opportunity for judging.' He does, however, give details as to the previous scripts, etc., which she had read. For these, the reader is referred to the full report.

One very interesting feature of the cross-correspondences in Mrs. Willett's case, is that in the partially dissociated state in which she writes or speaks (for both methods are used), she shows a strong repugnance to the material she is producing. She has to be coaxed by the communicators, rather like a child. Gurney$_W$ says in one place to her, ' Powder first and jam afterwards,' and she retorts that is it a long time since she was with the communicators, and she wants to talk to them and enjoy herself.   Again she says : ' Oh, this old *bothersome rubbish* is so *tiresome* ! ' and the reader who has attempted to wade through several cross-correspondences will quite possibly feel considerable sympathy with her !

But why, one is tempted to ask, did not A. W. V. give to one automatist the words : Dionysius ; the Ear and the stone-quarries of Syracuse.   To another, the stories of Ulysses and Polyphemus and Acis and Galatea.   To another, the words Jealousy and Satire.   Then to a fourth, the message : ' You will find the whole in a book by an American author which was known to me.'   Probably, for one thing, it is very difficult to carry out a programme like that.   Mrs. Willett is an exceptionally good automatist, and it seems to be about as difficult to get the right words through, even in her case, without false associations as it is to drive a pig into a sty.   Whatever we may think about the identity of the communicators, it is very hard to doubt that these difficulties of communication, which they describe, are genuine.   Indeed, they are shown to be, also, by the remarks and behaviour of Mrs. Willett *in propria persona*.

A Criticism of the Ear of Dionysius.—The main question is, of course, where do all these ingenious puzzles (for the cross-correspondences, of which this is one sample, are many) really come from ?   In a criticism by Miss F. Melian Stawell,[1] the idea is suggested that Mrs. Verrall possessed all the knowledge necessary to supply the material for the case, although she had forgotten it, and had forgotten that she had ever possessed it. But it remained in her subliminal or subconscious mind, and ' her subconscious self could weave the associations together, much as it might in a fairly coherent dream.'   When, after nearly a year and a half of inactivity, the subject of the cross-correspondence was suddenly revived at the sitting of August 2, 1915, Mrs. Verrall was present.   This circumstance, thinks Miss Stawell, points to the view that it was not Dr. Verrall but Mrs. Verrall who was the author of the scheme.   The topics in question, she suggests, ' leak through, in an obscure and fragmentary fashion, from Mrs. Verrall's mind into Mrs.

[1] *Proc. S.P.R.*, vol. xxix. p. 260.

Willett's.' And further, she says : ' I suggest therefore that the effect of purposive design is accidental. . . .'

Lord Balfour, in a reply to this criticism,[1] points out among other things, that if Mrs. Verrall had ever read all the details necessary for her to originate the case, it is very strange that even a study of the reference books in August 1915, after the case was over, ' failed to recall to her that she had ever heard of Philoxenus.' Secondly, it is not at all clear how ' telepathic leakage ' could be so thoughtful as to arrange all the topics in such an ingenious way. It seems a little like ' explaining ' the working of a motor-car by saying that it goes because petrol leaks out of a tank into its front end ! Somewhere, at least, one very ingenious mind must have been at work. We want to ask questions about the active processes of the mind which are not in any way answered by the word ' leakage.'

Lord Balfour also asks how it was that Mrs. Verrall's own automatic writings at the time showed no trace of these ' Dionysius ' topics if her subconscious mind was so full of them that they were ' leaking over ' into Mrs. Willett's mind.

This brief sketch must suffice to convey to the reader the general idea of cross-correspondences, but it is quite insufficient to bring out in its varying degrees of subtlety the evidence for intention which they contain. For a number of years they formed the main item in the work of the Society for Psychical Research ; the records fill several hundred pages, and no abridgement can do them full justice. Nevertheless, an excellent book on them has been published by Mr. H. F. Saltmarsh,[2] in which summaries of several cases will be found.

One more aspect of cross-correspondences must be touched upon in the concluding section of this chapter.

Pseudo-Cross-Correspondences.—In order to test as far as possible the communicator's claim that the cross-correspondences proceed from discarnate minds, some control experiments were devised and carried out by Mr. W. H. Salter. It had been said by some critics that the appearance

---

[1] *Proc. S.P.R.*, vol. xxix. p. 270.
[2] *Evidence for Personal Survival from Cross-Correspondences.* One of a series entitled ' Psychical Experiences.' (Bell.)

of design in the scripts was illusory, ' produced by the arbitrary selection and grouping of detached fragments, eked out by an unfair straining of literary allusions.' [1] Therefore, in March 1927, fourteen members of the S.P.R., entirely separate from the group of investigators who carried out the real cross-correspondences, were chosen as a team for an experiment in blank or pseudo cross-correspondences.   Five explanations of the real cross-correspondences seemed to be logically possible, namely, (1) chance, (2) collusion, (3) common association of ideas, (4) telepathy, and (5) the influence of discarnate minds. Although surprising chance-coincidences do occasionally occur, chance, as an explanation of cross-correspondences as a whole, is obviously out of the question.   Collusion, that is to say deliberate fraud, is fantastic in view of the character of the experimenting group.   Apart from discarnate intelligence, then, the two possible explanations would seem to be, (a) common association of ideas, and (b) telepathy.   Mr. Salter's experiment was designed, as far as possible, to test both these theories.

The names of the fourteen pseudo-automatists were known only to four persons, Mr. and Mrs. Salter, the Secretary of the S.P.R., and a clerk temporarily engaged by the Society to do typing work.   The constitution of the pseudo-group was more homogeneous than that of the real automatists, so that one would expect common associations of ideas to have a better chance of showing themselves in the pseudo-scripts.

A paper containing twelve phrases, taken respectively from Shakespeare, Milton, Shelley, Rostand, Virgil, Words-worth, Coleridge, and Homer, was circulated to the fourteen pseudo-automatists, the phrases being previously known only to the above-mentioned four people.   Each was asked to select a phrase, or group of phrases, and to write any words or phrases which these suggested, whether they made coherent sense or not.   From 200 to 300 words were to be written and sent to Mr. Salter within ten days.

Meanwhile, in order to test the telepathic theory, two experiments on that line were being tried.   (1) Mr. Salter

[1] ' An Experiment in Pseudo-Scripts,' by W. H. Salter (*Proc. S.P.R.*, vol. xxxvi. p. 526).

kept his mind fixed on two literary topics more or less continuously during the experiment. One topic (suggested by the two books, Statius' *Thebais* and Æschylus' *Seven Against Thebes*) was the latter part of the Theban legend concerned with the events succeeding the fall of Œdipus from the kingship, and in particular with the fate of three of the Seven Argive Champions. The second topic was the fall of Hephaestus on Lemnos, a story related in the *Iliad*. The last quotation in the paper of phrases, which was circulated to the pseudo-automatists, was from Homer, and referred indirectly to this second topic. The last seven of the phrases in this list were chosen as referring obscurely to the subject of the first topic. Here, therefore, was an artificially arranged opportunity for telepathic leakage to occur from a living mind. (2) Meanwhile, Mr. J. G. Piddington, who may perhaps be called the official unraveller of cross-correspondences, selected a literary topic, which he copied out and sent in a sealed envelope to the Secretary of the Society, to remain unopened until he gave the word, so that it was unknown to any one but himself. He said that he did not let a day pass while the experiment was in progress without deliberately thinking of this passage. It was an extract from Anatole France's *Putois*.

The result was quite unlike the real cross-correspondences. Mr. Salter says :

' To sum up both parts of the experiment, the considerable mass of pseudo-scripts received shows no point of contact with any of the three test topics chosen independently by Mr. Piddington and myself in Part I, or with the script selected by him for Part II, unless J's reference to Elphenor be a very distant approach to the fall of Hephaestus or the other falls referred to in Mr. Piddington's paper. [The pseudo-automatist known by the letter " J," had written " Elphenor," remarking on it, " Homer, but I don't see the connexion."] Of the correspondences between the different pseudo-scripts, if we take into account the strictly limited choice of starting-points allowed to the writers, nothing seems clearly to pass the limits of the obvious, except, again, J's contribution, his allusion to Tennyson's " touch of a vanished hand," which he arrives at *via* Elphenor. One may in fact say that if some unaccountable impulse had not resurrected the dead Elphenor in J's mind, the experiment would have been notably barren of results in any way resembling the cross-correspondences of the real scripts of the " S.P.R. group," although, for reasons already stated, the conditions of the experiment were far more favourable to the production of correspondences by common association of ideas than the conditions under which the " S.P.R. group " function.'

Mr. Salter points out :

' (1) that none of the pseudo-automatists, singly or jointly, produce any allusion outside the range of their normal literary knowledge, in the way that members of the " S.P.R. group " frequently do ; and (2) that such correspondences as were produced were of the simplest possible kind ; there is momentary contact, after which the streams of association diverge without the tendency characteristic of the real scripts to come back again and again to a common point of meeting. Nor are the pseudo-scripts, with a few exceptions, in the least like the real article in general appearance. They are, to take a single point of difference, obviously much more influenced by the writer's own personal doings and experiences : when confronted with a church spire, the clerical members of the team think of churches with which they have personal associations, such of the lay members as served in the War think of their training on Salisbury Plain or the shattered churches of the War zone.'

Finally he says :

' What the experiment seems strongly to indicate is that the hypothesis of telepathy and common association of ideas must not be rashly invoked as obvious, complete, satisfactory explanations of the phenomena of the real scripts.'

This concludes our review of the different branches of psychical research treated from the point of view of the evidence they show for the existence of the supernormal. We will now look again at the evidence, but from a different point of view, endeavouring this time to discover what we can of the *modus operandi* of the trance-processes. This will bring us in the end to a consideration of the two main explanations of the trance-phenomena, namely, extra-sensory perception between living minds on the one hand, and the action of discarnate intelligences on the other.

Part V

THEORETICAL ASPECT OF THE MEDIUMISTIC TRANCE

' That is a doubtful tale from faery land,
Hard for the non-elect to understand.'

Keats : ' Lamia '

Chapter XVIII

THE *MODUS OPERANDI* OF THE MEDIUMISTIC TRANCE

AUTONOMOUS TRANCE.—At the beginning of Chapter XII, we pointed out that trance-communications were obtained under three different conditions : (1) Through the habitual Control, which the majority of mediums possess. This we called ' control trance.' (2) From a Communicator, who has temporarily assumed the position of the habitual control. This we called ' directly controlled trance.' (3) Through a type of trance in which there are no controls, but in which the sensitive herself remains always in control of her own organism. This we called ' autonomous trance.' The bulk of the directly assessable evidence for the instrumentality of discarnate minds comes through the first two types ; but the third type contains much important indirect evidence, and is also full of interest from the point of view of the *modus operandi*. It is here exemplified by the case of Mrs. Willett, and we will now consider a report on her case published by Lord Balfour.[1]

Mrs. Willett has been mentioned in the last chapter as one of the ' S.P.R. group ' of cross-correspondence automatists. It seems scarcely necessary to speak of the bona fides of any member of this group, but it may be worth while to quote the following paragraph in which Sir Oliver Lodge speaks of Mrs. Willett.

' For my own part,' he says, ' I am assured not only of Mrs. Willett's good faith, and complete absence of anything that can be called even elementary classical knowledge, but also of the scrupulous

[1] ' A Study of the Psychological Aspects of Mrs. Willett's Mediumship, and of the Statements of the Communicators concerning Process,' by Gerald William, Earl of Balfour, P.C., LL.D. (*Proc. S.P.R.*, vol. xliii. p. 41).

care and fidelity with which she records her impressions, and reports every trace of normal knowledge which seems to her to have any possible bearing on the script. We are able, in fact, to regard her as a colleague in the research, in the same sort of way that we are able to regard Mrs. Holland.' [1]

This was written in 1911, soon after Mrs. Willett had joined the investigators. After this, she worked for years in close collaboration with Lord Balfour and other members of the group.

It is often said that automatic writing is done in the normal state of consciousness, and it is true that automatists are, as a rule, aware of their surroundings, and even of the words as they come, but I do not think that it is true to say that the state in which automatism occurs is quite normal. There is a certain degree of mental dissociation or departure from conscious attention which enables that portion of the mind which initiates the script to obtain control of the motor mechanisms of the body, and so to effect the externalization of the message. This slight degree of dissociation may increase, and, if it does so with the ordinary type of trance medium, the normal consciousness disappears and the control takes its place. But with a rarer type of sensitive, the normal consciousness still retains control of the body, as in automatic writing, although it has receded in some sense more into the background and there begins to undergo experiences of a non-physical kind. In Mrs. Willett's case, the communicators who appeared in her automatic script deliberately fostered this kind of trance, being very insistent that it should not be allowed to lapse into the control-trance variety. Put into crude words, they aimed at drawing the real Mrs. Willett just so far out of her normal position that they could hold intercourse with her and give her messages, yet not so far that she would be incapable of passing these messages on to the experimenters through her own processes of speech and writing. They seem to have considered that this type of trance would have advantages over the control kind, and, to judge from results, they were entirely justified.

[1] *Proc. S.P.R.*, vol. xxv. p. 115.

To read the record of the communications which came through Mrs. Willett is to enter at once into a different atmosphere. The communicators are strong, intelligent, natural, and give one the impression of being human beings engaged in a difficult task, hampered by certain natural impediments, and explaining their difficulties and what they are doing as they go along. Listen to Myers w explaining the difference between the Piper and the Willett trance :

Script of April 16, 1911

' Myers   Let me again emphasize the difference that exists between Piper and Willett phenomena   the former is possession the complete · all but complete   withdrawal of the spirit the other is the blending of incarnate and excarnate spirits   there is nothing telergic   it is a form of telepathy   the point we have to study is to find the line where the incarnate spirit is sufficiently over the border to be in a state to receive   and yet sufficiently controlling by its own power its own supraliminal and therefore able to transmit. . . .'

In his book, *Human Personality*, Myers had used the word ' telergy ' to mean the direct operation of the motor centres of the brain by a mind other than the one habitually controlling them. Myers w is using the word in the same sense here. In the control type of trance, he means, the control *telergically* operates the medium's brain. In the autonomous trance, the sensitive receives her messages from the communicators *telepathically* and herself transmits them by operating her own bodily motor-mechanisms in the ordinary way. The process may actually be much more complicated than that, but this embodies the main idea.

Mrs. Willett remarks on the process as seen from her end in a little aside passage in the Ear of Dionysius. In the script of March 2, 1914, she says : ' Do you know, it's an odd thing, I can see Edmund as if he were working something ; and the thing he is working is me. It isn't really me, you know ; it's only a sort of asleep me that I can look at.' By ' Edmund ' is meant Gurney w.

Mrs. Willett's automatic trance-work extended approximately over the period from 1909 to 1928. She began in girlhood to discover that she possessed the power of automatic writing, but only took it up seriously when in contact with Mrs. Verrall in 1908; so that she, in common with the other members of this group of automatists, developed her faculty within the ideological framework of the Society for Psychical Research. There is importance in this fact, because it means that the underlying assumptions of Spiritualism, which are early rooted in the subconscious of many trance-mediums, were here absent. The atmosphere was one of balance and criticism.

The Myers and Gurney communicators early took her in hand. Apart from her automatic writing, she began to *feel* them. In January 1909, for example, she says: ' I was at dinner, when I felt a strong impression of F. W. H. M. [Myers w] scolding me. . . . I had the impression that he was conveying to me that if I doubted the impression I was receiving I was to try for script after dinner. I was quite *normal. . . .*'

Soon after Gurney w said through the script ' . . . try and set down thoughts can't you hear me speak it saves trouble I want to say something Gurney yes'; and Mrs. Willett notes, ' Here I left off writing and held a sort of imaginary conversation with E. G. . . . I was perfectly normal.'

A fortnight later, Myers w writes through the script:

' . . . I am trying experiments with you to make you hear without writing therefore it is I Myers who do this deliberately do not fear or wince when words enter your consciousness or subsequently when such words are in the script . . . do not analyse whence these impressions which I shall in future refer to as Daylight Impressions—come from, they are parts of a psychic education framed by me for you. . . .'

After this, the Daylight Impressions became habitual. Lord Balfour abbreviates them to ' D. I.s ' for convenience, and divides them into *Silent D. I.s* (those which were written down after being mentally received) and *Spoken D. I.s* (those which were spoken in the presence of the sitter after being mentally received).

The attempts of the communicator to establish direct mental communication with Mrs. Willett were evidently successful, for in a letter describing her experiences, she said :

' Last night . . . I was sitting idly wondering at it all . . . when I became aware so suddenly and strangely of F. W. H. M.'s presence that I said " Oh ! " as if I had run into some one unexpectedly. During what followed I was absolutely normal. I heard nothing with my ears, but the words came from outside into my mind as they do when one is reading a book to oneself. I do not remember the exact words, but the first sentence was, " Can you hear what I am saying ? "—I replied in my mind, " Yes." '

One may compare with this Mrs. Willett's introduction to S. H. Butcher w, one of the collaborators referred to in the Ear of Dionysius, which took place in January 1911.

' Last night after I had blown out my candle and was just going to sleep I became aware of the presence of a man, a stranger, and— almost at the same moment—knew it was Henry Butcher. I felt his personality, very living, clear, strong, sweetness and strength combined. A piercing glance. He made no introduction but said nothing. So I said to him, " Are you Henry Butcher ? " He said, " No, I am Henry Butcher's ghost." I was rather shocked at his saying this, and said, " Oh, very well, I am not at all afraid of ghosts or of the dead." He said, " Ask Verrall . . . if he remembers our last conversation (or meeting) and say the word to him—Ék e tée." He said it several times. I said " Very well." He seemed only to want to give that message and then he went in a hurry. . . .'

Here, again, there is something very natural and sane about the ' ghostly ' visitor, and his humorous way of introducing himself. Mrs. Willett had no notion what Ék e tée meant. It was ' Hecate,' and Lord Balfour believes it referred to a paper by Dr. Verrall in the *Classical Review*, which Dr. Butcher had almost certainly read.

Direct Evidence through Mrs. Willett's Trance.—The reader will probably wonder why, since the communications through the Willett trance are of such a clear and coherent kind, no evidence is quoted from it which tends, as in the Leonard trance, to prove directly the identity of the communicators. The answer is that such evidence exists but cannot be divulged. Lord Balfour says in this report, ' It would be impossible to do justice to the argument in favour of spirit communication on the basis of the Willett phenomena without violating confidences which I am bound to respect.' [1]   Again, on the first page of the report we read, ' The bulk of Mrs. Willett's automatic output is too private for publication.'   That the material withheld from publication is of a very strong and convincing kind is apparent from the following declaration of opinion, which Lord Balfour makes on a later page of his report :

' If I had before me only those Willett scripts to which I have been referring, I frankly admit that I should have been at a loss whether to attribute them to subliminal activity or to a source entirely outside the personality of the medium.   Probably, like Dr. Walter Prince, I should be content to suspend judgement.   But having before me the whole of the Willett scripts, and being in a position to compare them with the scripts of other automatists of our group and with facts known to me, but not known to Mrs. Willett herself, I am personally of opinion that they contain evidence of supernormally acquired knowledge which no mere subliminal mentation will suffice to account for.   My readers are not in this position, and for reasons stated in the introduction to this paper I cannot put them in possession of the considerations that have chiefly weighed with me.' [2]

It is indeed very greatly to be deplored that such supremely important evidence must be withheld from publication in the interests of privacy.

Owing to the exigencies of space, it will only be possible to touch on a few points of the Willett trance, taken from the many with which this report deals—a report which is second to none in importance for the student of psychical phenomena.

Mode of Emergence of Trance and Automatic Material : Difficulty in Transmitting Names.—The circumlocutory methods

---

[1] *Proc. S.P.R.*, vol. xxv. p. 45.
[2] Ibid. pp. 155–6.

of the control type of trance are well known. The control will often occupy a whole page in describing something rather than give its name, and the critic who is unused to these phenomena is at once sceptical. ' That cannot be so-and-so communicating,' he says. ' Why, he has forgotten his wife's name,' or whatever it may be. Even in the trance of the best mediums it is evidently a matter of the greatest difficulty to get a specific name through, or to answer a point-blank question. There seems to be a kind of law of deflected effort, which is reminiscent of the mechanical law of the revolution of spins. The thing directly aimed at is the thing which eludes you. Something similar occurs in ordinary memory. The most familiar names may be forgotten for a moment, and when they are, direct efforts to revive them are useless. We have to *describe* the thing or person we mean.

In the A. V. B. sittings dealt with in Chapter XIII, Feda described a guitar, imitated its notes, showed how it was tuned, but could not say its name. On another occasion it takes her more than a page of description to arrive at the word ' Sporkish.' She begins by hissing ; goes on to ' Spor ' ; says a ' long letter ' comes next—a long letter ' above the line ' ; tentatively tries ' Sporti ' and ' Sporbi ' ; then tries drawing the letters on Lady Troubridge's hand, and arrives at H as the final letter of the word. Then, just as she is apparently about to give it up, she ejaculates very loudly the right word, ' Sporkish.'

In the Willett scripts, although we do not get the same round-about descriptions, the same difficulty in the transmission of words occurs. In a script of August 25, 1912, the name Deucalion emerges in this way :

' Now another thought
                                Doocalon
    No no try again
                                Dewacorn
(this word ended in a scribble)
                                Dewacorn
    NO DEUCALION
    the sound is DEW

                        K
                    LION not Lion

Write it slowly
                    Deucalion
I want that said   It has a meaning
The stones of the earth shall praise thee
that is what I want said   it is I who say it and the word is
                    Deucalion
that was well caught
Good Child
That sort of thing makes one feel out of breath doesn't it
on both sides——'

Lord Balfour adds in a note that Mrs. Willett is hardly ever able to reproduce Greek or Latin words correctly. The way in which she tends to get off the rails and slip away from the communicators' intention is, indeed, very obvious. In a D.I. of October 8, 1911, the following occurs :

' Oh he says, back of that again lies something I dimly reach after and you would call, he says, the Absolom—*not* Absalom—I'll spell it to you he says : A B S O L and then he says O M and rubs O M out and puts instead U T E. Oh he says—Edmund, when you laugh I can't help laughing too—and he says the ascending scale bound by gold chains round the feet of God.'

The interjection, ' Edmund, when you laugh, etc.,' is of course addressed by Mrs. Willett to the communicator.

Many instances could be quoted showing the difficulties which trance-material evidently encounters in its emergence. They teach us to be careful in making judgements about what ' ought ' to happen. Mr. Kenneth Richmond, in the course of his valuable notes on the study of the Leonard material,[1] says :

' When the psychic phenomenon to be tested is reduced to the simplest type . . . the organization involved is found to be none too simple or easy to understand ; when we come to the very complicated structure of the Leonard organizations it is most difficult to experiment with any knowledge of what we are about. What is useless is to form judgements of this type : " If he (a given com-

[1] 'Preliminary Studies of the Recorded Leonard Material,' *Proc. S.P.R.*, vol. xliv. p. 25.

municator) can do this, he should be able to do that." " He " is likely to involve an assumption that the communicator " is " the deceased person, not a complex representation ; and " should " assumes that we know how the representation can and cannot operate, when in fact we know very little about it.'

This means that, if we are to approach the problems of the trance in a fruitful and scientific spirit, we must not assume that there are only two alternatives, either (i) that a communicator, substantially the same as the deceased person in question was when alive, is standing at the other end of a psychic telephone, or (ii) that some hypnotic stratum in the medium is playing a part, eked out by telepathy from the living. It is pretty clear that both these theories are too crude and too simple. We must patiently try to form new ideas about the depths of human selfhood, by studying the phenomena intelligently and as far as possible without prejudice, in a fruitful and scientific spirit.

Telaesthesia.—It will be remembered that in Chapter I, telaesthesia was defined as a kind of telepathic perception of the contents of one mind by another, in distinction to telepathy, which was thought of as the definite transmission of the thought of one mind to another. Myers, in his book, *Human Personality*, did not use the word ' telaesthesia ' in this sense. He made it the equivalent of what we have here called Clairvoyance. But Gurney_w uses the word ' telaesthesia ' in practically the same sense in the Willett scripts as that which we have here adopted. It is important to know for our explanation of trance-phenomena, whether telaesthesia exists or not.

The positive evidence for telaesthesia, as distinct from telepathy, resides in those cases of trance-communications in which knowledge is shown of things or events which are unknown to the sitters—such cases as *The Dog Billy*, *Burnham*, and *Daisy's Second Father*, mentioned in Chapter XIII ; and also those proxy sittings in which the information given was unknown to the sitter, and must have come from distant minds, of which, as has been said, there are many examples. If the information is not derived from the mind of the discarnate communicator in these cases, it must be obtained from whatever mind happens to contain it. And that would seem to entail telaesthesia, or the reaching out by the trance-personality to gather the fact it needs from wherever the knowledge of it is to be obtained.

The faculty of telaesthesia, if it exists in this unrestricted form, would seem to represent a range of extra-sensory power of quite extraordinary universality and extent, and evidently if mediums possess it, the theory that communications are due to telaesthesia among the living rather than telepathy from the dead would be greatly strengthened. It is interesting, therefore, to notice that Gurney w enthusiastically endorses it. In a long D. I. on October 8, 1911, the following occurs :

' He says, I want to suggest something which, while not contradicting your question, will open another window. Oh if I could only not drop like that. Oh hold me tight. And he says, she can select—he says a word to me—telaesthesia—oh he says, you none of you make enough allowance for what that implies, and the results of that can be shepherded and guided up to the threshold of normal consciousness.

' Oh he says, telaesthesia is a bed-rock truth, a power of acquiring knowledge direct without the intervention of the discarnate mind.

' Oh he says, telepathy's one thing—that's thought communication ; telaesthesia is knowledge, not thought, acquired by the subliminal when operating normally in the metetherial.' [1]

' Oh he says, Here comes in our work again. Oh he says, What I'm saying may be used to cut at the spiritualistic hypothesis, but it doesn't. Again, who selects what of the total telaesthetically acquired knowledge shall externalize itself—shall blend itself with those elements received by direct telepathic impact ? Oh he says, Supposing I take her into a room, and I screen off any action of my own mind on hers : her subliminal with its useful copious pinch of Eve's curiosity takes stock of the contents of the room. Normal consciousness is later regained, and lying in the subliminal is knowledge of certain objects perceived, not as a result of the action of my mind, but as the result of telaesthetic faculty. Oh he says, Here come I on script intent. Here be arrows for my quiver. Who selected which of the—— Have patience with me, oh, Edmund, I am

[1] *Willett Report*, p. 293.

trying, oh, I'm such a great way away.   Oh, Edmund,—Oh he says, Who applies the stimulus under which certain ideas—use that word, not what I wanted—emerge, blended, which upon study will be found to be relevant to the total aim of that particular piece of automatism ?   Oh he says, of all the contents of that mythical room say she carries back a rough and partial knowledge— . . . in the process of externalization, there is where the loss occurs.   Oh he says, of those ten say two emerge—to me how interesting.   I see the work of my hand, the double process.

' Say I wrote of horses.   I get telepathically the idea of sound, clatter of the horses' gallop.   I get the idea in a Verrall channel, for instance, of Pegasus ;   I get the idea perhaps of chariot races—equus, or something like that, he says—and I select and push up into its place where it will be grasped and externalized two trump cards telaesthetically acquired—call it horseshoe, or, he says, the steeds of Dawn.   The point is, I didn't place them there ;   I found and selected them ;   and the eight other elements—or objects—seen in the room remain dormant and never externalize themselves perhaps. The spiritistic agency decides what element appropriate to its own activity shall emerge alongside and intertwined with matter placed in position by direct telepathic impact.'

There is much food for thought in this interesting script. It is part of a description given by Gurney$_W$ of the process involved in getting cross-correspondences through, as he is describing it from his end.   Another script, too long to quote here, describes the process of externalizing selected topics through different levels of the automatist's self.   Telaesthesia takes place in a deep stratum of the automatist's mind and in that of the communicator's, where some kind of mutual agreement takes place as to what is to be selected.   It seems that Gurney$_W$ is referring, in this telaesthesia, to a faculty of cognition, natural to a very deep level of the self, which Gurney$_W$ calls the ' H-self,' but far removed from anything of which, in our supraliminal state of consciousness, we have experience. This telaesthetically acquired material is put into the ' uprushable ' self, ' just the grade below the uprushable.'   ' But in putting it into the uprushable focus, as it were, it will know that a sort of crystallization, often through symbolism, must be arrived at : and we will imagine, if you like, that that having been foreseen both by me and the H-self, we determined upon what sort of crystals to aim at, so that the uprushable self has, as it were, presented to it what I called a " room," the knowledge which the H-self is informing to the point where it becomes uprushable.' After that, Gurney$_W$ explains, there comes a moment of ' binding ' and finally the material emerges as written or spoken word or dream or precognition, etc.

According to this, as I read it, the emergence of so-called ' automatic ' material is a very complex process, the ideas rising, under guidance, through level above level of the self and finally crystallizing into the clear-cut and discrete ideas with which we do our normal thinking, and in which form alone they can attain verbal expression. But they originate as thought of some more universal and less atomic character in the depths of the personality. Telaesthesia may be called a deep-level faculty of cognition, and the question which of course arises is : If this faculty can work between the sensitive and the communicator, why not between the sensitive and a living person ? Gurney$_W$ evidently realizes that the argument can be used to tell against the spiritualistic theory, for he points out that the telaesthetic faculty does not explain the communicator away, since the communicator is needed to select and to control, guide and shepherd the material into the right channels for externalization.

There are many points of the greatest interest which are dealt with in this report of Lord Balfour's on Mrs. Willett, which cannot possibly be condensed into an outline summary, and it is hoped that readers of the present volume will turn to the report and study it for themselves. The question of the nature of the Subliminal Self and its relation to the Supra-liminal occupies much question and answer between Lord Balfour and Gurney$_W$; and the latter gives his description of the nature of the persistible self, saying that it consists to a large extent of the subliminal element together with ' an admixture—and a very vital admixture—of the supraliminal.'

We will now consider, in connexion with the Willett material, a subject we have touched on more than once before, namely, the subject of sense-imagery.

Chapter XIX

SENSE-IMAGERY

PERCEPTION WITH AND WITHOUT THE IMAGERY OF SENSE.—In Chapter II we noted that spontaneous cases of telepathy frequently reach the consciousness of the percipient in the form of hallucinatory sense-pictures, which *represent* the gist of a telepathic message in more or less symbolical form. The ' pillow ' case [1] was an example, where the telepathic intimation of the death of a friend reached the percipient in the form of a message apparently written on half a sheet of notepaper, and lying on the pillow. The notepaper and its message were *created*, visual sense-imagery, for which some stratum of the percipient's personality must have been responsible. At the same time, it was pointed out that all the five senses could be subject to similar hallucinatory treatment, creation of such imagery being evidently possible on demand. Further illustrative cases were quoted.

In his book, *Phantasms of the Living*, Gurney had long ago given a discussion to this question, saying that, ' all that is veridical in it [the telepathic apparition] is packed into the telepathic impulse in the form of " a nucleus of a deferred impression " ; the embodiment is the percipient's own creation.' These are Lord Balfour's words, and he adds, ' In the main I do not dissent from this view.'

In Chapter X we saw that the creation of sense-imagery was by no means confined to states of the self which might be described as ' supernormal,' but that in normal and everyday perception, what appear to be the qualities of physical objects are really the qualities of our own private ' sense-data,' causally linked with an independent world in some obscure

[1] p. 24.

265

and roundabout fashion which we do not understand, and
not simply and directly as we invariably believe. Moreover,
many self-suggested illusions produce sense-imagery indistinguishable from that which we call ' normal,' and believe
to be simply veridical, and these blend with the latter with
perfect ease. There was also the curious example, mentioned
in Chapter X, of Mrs. Verrall's attempt to recognize playing-
cards by the sense of touch. When the attempt began to be
successful, the *fact* of contact gave direct rise to visual imagery.
Again, in the phenomenon of eidetic imagery, the normal act
of perception was, as it were, prolonged after the perceived
object had been removed. All these facts go to show that
experiences which we believe to be descriptive of an outer
world originate within ourselves to a far greater extent than
we are wont to believe.

When we turn to the states of consciousness associated with
trance, we find that an extraordinary wealth of sense-imagery
accompanies it. It will be remembered that, in the account of
the A. V. B. case given in Chapter XIII, Feda gave a description of Daisy's father, the purporting communicator, as
follows : [1]

M. R. H.—Would he like to give any message to Daisy ?

F.—He wants to give a description first ; he's got a square
forehead, and it looks to Feda as though the hair receded
on the temples, or else that he brushes it back very much.
He wears a soft sort of hat ; Feda doesn't think it's a cap
with a peak, it looks like a hat with a brim, and the brim
seems to be turned up more on one side than the other.
He's showing a suit that he thinks Daisy would recognize ;
it's a sort of browny coloured suit, and has what looks like
a check pattern, but it's a mixed-up pattern, not a decided
check, and there seem to be other shades in it as well as
brown.

Actually, Daisy did recognize the ' soft sort of hat,' which
had been known as ' the old hat,' and the browny-coloured
suit as well. But the point is that, after the communicator is
stated to be going to give a description of *himself*, Feda describes

[1] *Proc. S.P.R.*, vol. xxx. pp. 526–7.

a figure which is evidently the communicator as present to her visual sense. And this figure is altered to exhibit any feature desired, first the square forehead and receding hair ; then the old hat, evidently being worn. Then the brown suit. The communicator must therefore have the power of transmitting *ideas* to Feda which take on the form for her of something very like visual perception. At other times the sense-imagery is auditory, as in the reception of names, for example, in Feda's attempts to get hold of the word ' Sporkish.' Also in Mrs. Willett's struggle with the word ' Deucalion ' above, when the communicator says to her, ' The sound is DEW.' Or the imagery may be tactual, as in Feda's description of the Baranca del Anăvingo, where she said that the lava road *felt* like ' walking on cinders.' Feda also said on at least one occasion that the communicators could make her feel a thing as hot or cold ' exactly as if she felt it with her fingers,' and added, ' you know how hypnotized people can be made to feel like that.'

This comparison with hypnosis is, I think, highly significant. It brings home to us the fact that in all trance and supernormal experiences we are dealing with sense-situations which have been *created within*, wherever the influence to create may have come from. The Willett trance further confirms this.

In a D. I. on March 5, 1912, Gurney_W says :

' . . . Inspiration may be from within, but it may be from without. Oh, he says, Every moment I gave to the study of hypnotic states and post-hypnotic states I feel was among the best spent of all my time.

' (*G. W. B.* Yes, Gurney, those were splendid papers of yours.)

' Oh, he says, It's not only what I learnt then, but what I've been able to apply here. For instance : Say, using the words in their rough way, that a mutual selection is made—mutually from her mind and mine. It's possible for me to suggest to her subliminal that at a given time such and such an idea shall, as it were, be recovered out of the sediment—and come to the top. . . .'

Gurney had, actually, during his lifetime done a good deal of work on hypnotism and written much about it.

During some sittings with Mrs. Leonard in 1917, Mrs.

Salter obtained from Feda a very good description of her father, Dr. A. W. Verrall, who died in 1912. In the first sitting he was described as having a beard. In the second sitting Feda says : ' The mouth is a bit large, the lips are pink, not red. The chin is more rounded '—statements which are inconsistent with a description of a bearded face. Mrs. Salter says :

' Now this description, in which the communicator's face is apparently viewed sometimes from the front, sometimes in profile . . . is on the whole distinctly good, but it contains details which seem to imply that the man described is beardless, the size and colour of the mouth, the shape of the chin. It is impossible to suppose that any one who was describing in detail a man visibly present could be mistaken as to whether or no he had a beard. Against the interpretation that Feda is seeing my father as a quite young man, clean shaven, is first her own statement that he is " towards middle life, hardly that," and secondly the fact that at the sitting of January 29, 1917, the man afterwards identified with my father is stated to be bearded. My own interpretation of what occurred is that Feda was not really " seeing " anything, but that on this, as on other occasions, she was receiving a series of mental impressions which she translated into visual terms. Her statements that my father had a rather large mouth and a face not rounded but too broad to be oval, are in fact correct, as early photographs show.'

In fact, the sense-imagery is *private* to Feda, created in or by her, in correspondence with ideas which she receives in non-sensuous terms.

At a sitting on January 29, 1917, Mrs. Salter received from Feda a description of her mother, Mrs. Verrall, who had died in the preceding year, in which several of the features described were correct as witnessed by a photograph. But Feda added several details which were not true, such as that Mrs. Verrall wore ' a made bodice,' ' bands at the wrists,' and an ' oval brooch with a gold rim.' Mrs. Salter comments :

' The general inference which I should draw from the above extract is that a certain amount of veridical information about my mother was woven by Feda into an imaginary picture of an elderly widow, based on preconceived ideas of the appearance such a picture might be expected to present. The " bands at the wrist " are presumably widow's bands, which my mother never wore. She was, in fact, a widow at the time the photograph was taken.' [1]

There is no doubt that Feda ' gags ' to a certain extent when doubtful, sometimes adding points which are really inferences drawn by herself. But in view of the curious way in which her information takes sensuous shape, she may not always be aware that she is doing so. It is interesting to reflect that, in such a case as this, recorded by Mrs. Salter, some of the correct constituent features in the picture which Feda drew of Mrs. Verrall evidently came from a source external to Feda, while others came from Feda's own imagination. Yet the items from the two sources, when translated into sense-imagery, blend into a single picture in such a way as to be indistinguishable from one another. This would seem to go far to show that *all* the sense-imagery, including that which is veridical and expresses true information coming from an external source, is of Feda's own creation. The imagined idea and the telepathically received idea would seem to set in operation the same sensory mechanism, so that sense-items from the two sources arise in the same manner and blend into an indistinguishable whole.

Statements by Feda about Life in Another World.—In the control type of trance, though not in the Willett trance, the communicators are usually reported as representing the scenes and events of the so-called ' spirit ' world in terms which are almost the exact equivalents of scenes and events in this world. It is certainly startling when such a communicator as A. V. B., having correctly described through Feda the things she used to do in this world, goes on to state that she does them still.

In the sitting of October 2, 1916, Feda describes A. V. B. as with a brown, sleek horse looking over her shoulder.[2] At a

---

[1] ' Some Incidents occurring at Sittings with Mrs. Leonard which may throw Light on their *Modus Operandi*,' by Mrs. W. H. Salter, *Proc. S.P.R.*, vol. xxxix. pp. 306 ff.

[2] ' On a Series of Sittings with Mrs. Osborne Leonard,' *Proc. S.P.R.*, vol. xxx. pp. 361–2.

later sitting, she says that A. V. B. has her arm round his neck, that A. V. B. is keeping the horse for M. R. H., that she has been learning to ride in her present state of existence, that there are plenty of horses that love to be exercised, and that the ground is so springy. Miss Radcliffe Hall quotes these passages as evidence of A. V. B.'s memory of the incidents of her earthly life, for they were true in that respect—A. V. B. was a poor horse-woman ; M. R. H. possessed a hunter, and so on. But obviously they constitute a puzzle, in that they are interspersed with very good veridical material, which the communicator shows intelligence in selecting, and are proffered without any suggestion that either the control or the communicator expect the sitters to find them surprising.

Another passage of a similar kind occurs when Feda is describing A. V. B.'s fondness for playing and singing to her guitar. (A. V. B. in life had actually been an extremely expert performer on the guitar.)

' Feda says : " And now she's showing Feda something that you can pull strings to, she's going tum, tum, tum." (Here Feda gives an exact imitation of the sound of notes picked on a guitar, imitating with her hand the plucking of the strings.) " Mrs. Twonnie " (Feda's name for M. R. H.) " she's plucking them." M. R. H. answers : " That's splendid, you are making the exact noise." Feda says : " She's making the noise, and Feda can always imitate what she can do, she says it does make your fingers sore too. . . . She says, do you know, she sees them in the spirit world plucking those string things and singing softly to them." '

At six separate sittings, Feda represents A. V. B. as enjoying bathing, of which she used to be very fond. Feda states that she now has a bathing-pool in her garden, and that she had had a bathe just before one of the sittings. She also states through Feda that the dog Billy, before referred to, is with her now.

Feda's descriptions of happenings, which, she states, are now taking place in the other world, are indistinguishable from her descriptions of what are evidently (like the brown suit) the ideas or memories of the communicators, thrown into perceptual form. There is nothing to suggest that what is

happening is in any way different in the two cases. When Feda
states that she sees them in the ' spirit-world ' plucking guitars
and singing softly to them, is not this A. V. B.'s memory
decked out in Feda's sense-imagery with some embellishments ?

On the other hand, if Feda is entirely responsible for the
transference of earthly scenes and occupations to the other
world, why does not such a clear communicator as A. V. B.
correct Feda's statements when she assumes control herself,
as Dr. Verrall afterwards corrected Feda's mis-description of
him as being without a beard ? [1] On the contrary, Feda
purports to be quoting A. V. B.'s own words when she says :
' Then I bathe ; you know, don't you, that I always loved
that part of it.' These things strongly suggest that A. V. B.,
at least while communicating, is subject to sense-experiences
of the same kind as Feda's, and accepts them as veridical.

Perhaps we do not realize how copious and compelling this
sense-imagery must be for minds in states other than that
which we regard as ' normal.' The following extract from a
sitting held on February 24, 1922, with Mrs. Brittain by Mrs.
and Miss Dawson-Smith is worth quoting.[2] The communicator was ostensibly Mrs. Dawson-Smith's son, Frank, who
had been killed in the War. As the medium was beginning to
come out of trance, she suddenly interjected : ' Have you
a St. Bernard dog ? There's a big one standing by you. It
died of distemper. It is with Frank, he found it waiting for
him.' The sitter's note on this is as follows :

' That is a brief paragraph and not written entire because we
thought the sitting was over and Belle had gone. We had put our
pencils and notebooks away and sat quietly waiting for the medium
to wake. What followed was this : Mrs. Brittain opened her eyes
and suddenly stared over my shoulder, looking startled and alarmed.
I was sitting in a low chair facing her. She said with a gasp, " Oh !
don't growl like that—oh, how dreadful ! " Then she grew calmer
and said, " Have you a St. Bernard dog ? It is a big one. He died of
distemper." My daughter at once said, " No, we haven't a St.
Bernard. Our dog is an Airedale." Mrs. Brittain instantly said,
" You never saw him ; it was long before you were born. The dog

---

[1] p. 268.   [2] *Proc. S.P.R.*, vol. xxxvi. pp. 307–8.

is standing by your mother—he loves her and is very jealous of everybody who goes near her."

'This was all perfectly correct. We had a St. Bernard, and he died of distemper when my boy was four months old. The dog was devoted to me and to my baby (Frank) but would not allow anybody to come near us.

'KATIE DAWSON-SMITH.'

Here information must have been telepathically acquired, either from the sitters or from the communicator, about the existence of the St. Bernard, about his having died of distemper before Miss Dawson-Smith was born, and about his fondness for her mother and his jealousy. But some element in Mrs. Brittain's personality embodies these facts, or most of them, in the form of a sense-image of the dog—one might almost call it a cinematograph 'talkie' of the dog—growling in so vivid and life-like a way, that the awakening Mrs. Brittain is for a moment almost terrified by it. The idea suggested by incidents such as these is that somewhere below the conscious level of the personality, there is a mechanism which is capable of producing all kinds of sense-imagery with such pervasiveness and completeness as to persuade the experient of the literal reality of the persons or objects which it represents. A striking instance is recorded in Mrs. Willett's case, which is worth quoting in full :

Perception and Sense-Imagery in the Willett Phenomena.—On December 17, 1913, Mrs. Willett, in a state more or less akin to her customary trance, but which Lord Balfour considers to have presented some differences from the ordinary D. I., dictated a contemporary experience : [1]

'It's a picture—a picture that I love and often see. Marble pillars everywhere—a most heavenly scene. A company of men—small company, discussing everything in heaven and earth, and really reaching the heights of reason—almost unconscious of their visible surroundings. It is a sort of parable of life.

'There was such intercourse of the human mind going on in that room, and I know it so well I almost fancy I must have been there, though it happened a long time ago.

[1] *Proc. S.P.R.*, vol. xliii. p. 69.

'Fred uses the expression somewhere—a small company of like-minded men. That's how those men were ; and, you know, they never die. (*Here I asked for the dictation to be a little slower.*) Oh, I wish I could say it quickly, because it's all floating past me.

'There's a poem of Matthew Arnold's about Christ, that whenever the feet of mercy move up and down where poverty is, Christ is actually present in them now.

'Oh, how I wish I could tell what I know. You know, to ordinary people those men who sat talking there long ago are just historical figures, interesting from a hundred points of view, but dead men. Do you know, there's nothing dead in greatness, because there can't be, because all greatness is an emanation from the changeless Absolute. That's why I know these people as if they were alive to-day. I know them much better than many of the people I live with—especially the older man, the Master. He had disciples, you know, and whenever—— What I said about that Matthew Arnold poem was because I wanted to say that what was true of Christ is true of the man I'm speaking about.

'Oh, do you know that Knowledge isn't the greatest faculty of the human mind. There's a deeper faculty, deriving its—something or other, I missed that—through a more central zone. It's Intuition. It's in Intuition that the Soul acts most freely, and it's by Intuition that it best demonstrates its freedom. There's something about that in Paracelsus. Paracelsus is a *great* allegory.

'What a long way I've got from my picture that I like to look at, or rather from my room where I choose to walk. The meal is for the most part over, and there's a sort of hush of the spirit ; because in that quick interchange of thought new ideas have arisen, and the man that they all look up to, he's borne very far aloft on the wings of the Spirit. And suddenly on the quiet of it all there bursts the sound of revelling coming nearer and nearer—flute-players ! (*ecstatically*). Oh, is it Bacchus and his crew ? Anyhow there's something rather Bacchanalian about it. They're getting nearer and nearer, and they're hammering on the door, and then in they come. *My* people are all disturbed, and there's great toasting. They take it all in very good part, and they revel away. There are wreaths of flowers, and cups passing, loud jokes. And then, do you know, by degrees some of the crowd melt away, and some of the people go to sleep. And then the whole thing ends up with such a majestic thing, I think ; just that one figure, when the interruption

18

is over, he stays there, like some great beacon shining out above the clouds, walking on the heights of thought ; and the absolute silence reigns, and there he sits.

' Do you know that man's as real to me as if I could touch him ! He's an ugly man, only I feel he's sublimely great. You know I've not got to be tied up always to myself. I can get up and walk about in other worlds ; and I very often like to walk through the room where that scene took place.

' Have you ever seen the shadow of the Parthenon ? Oh ! (*Pause.*) It's all very beautiful there. Do you know Edmund would have been very happy in that world. It was the sort of world he wanted, and he strayed into such a hideous age.

> (*A disturbing noise occurred, which upset Mrs. Willet.*)

' Oh !—oh !—oh ! (*Pause.*)

' I've quite lost the thread, I've quite lost the thread.

> (*A further noise occurred, and Mrs. Willett resumed in writing.*)

I've lost the thread. It's all gone. I was so happy I was seeing visions and I did not ever want to leave. Fred was with me, F. W. H. M. I also saw Henry Sidgwick, he had a white beard.

' Do you know who the young man was I only just caught sight of him for a moment.

' How NOTHING time is

' All human experience is *One*. We are no shadows nor do we pursue shadows. Pilgrims in Eternity

' We few we few we happy band of BROTHERS.'

On this Lord Balfour notes :

' During the greater part of this sitting Mrs. Willett, although not in a condition of trance, was certainly further removed than usual from a normal state of consciousness. On my showing her, about an hour later, the part which I had taken down from dictation, she said, " I haven't the faintest recollection of all this, nor do I know what it means." I then told her that it described a famous scene in Plato's *Symposium*, to which allusion had already been made in another script of hers, nearly three years ago. . . . The word *Symposium*, however, seemed to convey no meaning to her, though I reminded her that she must have seen it in Mrs. Verrall's account . . . of the attempt to reproduce Myers's posthumous message.'

It is a remarkable fact that states of consciousness, which, to outward appearance, are not so very far removed from the normal, may yet be completely amnesic. Whether we choose to say that Mrs. Willett was here in trance, or even whether she is in trance during her D. I.'s seems to be a matter of choice in terminology. What we call 'normal' consciousness is really a fluctuation about a mean condition with every one, and with a few individuals the extremes of fluctuation are greater. It is these extreme fluctuations which open the door to the study of so-called 'psychical' phenomena.

In the above passage there are several literary allusions, as for example, 'Bacchus and his crew,' which appears to refer to a verse in Keats's *Endymion* ; 'What shadows we are and what shadows we pursue,' occurred in a famous speech of Burke's ; and the final quotation, of course, is from *Henry V*.

It cannot be said in this case, that we are taking the un-verified word of a trance-personality. Mrs. Willett *herself* experiences the *Symposium* scene. She has not even undergone a very profound mental readjustment, yet her new world is extremely real to her. 'Do you know that man's as real to me as if I could touch him !' And again, 'I know them much better than many of the people I live with.' The idea, there-fore, suggests itself that in the A. V. B. case quoted above, the communicator may be living in a world of self-created sense-imagery, something like this of the *Symposium* scene, but which contains horses, bathing-pools, and guitars. If we feel inclined to say : How can any sane, well-balanced, and critically-minded individual live in such a state of illusion without being aware of it ? let us reflect for a moment on our own condition in this present world. We, also, are living in a world of sense-imagery. Of course we feel inclined to say that *we* live in a world of real objects ; not in a world of illusions. But let us reflect on the very important considerations touched on in Chapter X, where several reasons were given for supposing that the world of normal sense-perception is in reality a world of *appearance*, though correlated in some way which we do not understand with a reality which is not ourselves. Not a world of subjective illusion, but still, in a very real sense, more a human construct than a presentation of the intrinsic character of reality. Suppose that the sense-imagery of trance-communicators (self-created like our own), were correlated with independent reality in some looser and more flexible fashion than is the case with us ; would not this give us some inkling into the possibility of life in other finite worlds ? The world of experience would be a function of the percipient's personality. But is not this true of our own present world ? We might further suppose that in temporary or unstable states of personality (as in the somewhat arbitrary complex which constitutes a communicator), the sense-imagery would tend to be unstable and wild : and that in proportion as the personal complex became more stable the sense-imagery would become more self-consistent, and its appearance of independence more convincing.

Mrs. Willett's sense-experiences are by no means confined to the visual and auditory senses. In deep trance, D. I., on February 28, 1914, the following passage occurred :

'. . . Somebody said something about Father Cam walking arm in arm with the Canongate. What does that mean ? Oh ! (*Sniffs.*) What a delicious scent ! No rosebud yet by dew empearled. . . .'

' " Father Cam," and " The Canongate," walking arm in arm symbolizes the co-operation of the two friends Verrall and Butcher (Cambridge and Edinburgh). The automatist is wondering what the meaning can possibly be, when suddenly she stops and sniffs. She is smelling something, declares it to be delicious, and finally recognizes it as the scent of roses.' The rose, for a personal reason, was symbolical of S. H. Butcher, and this was readily understood by his friends, but Mrs. Willett was quite ignorant of it. But the point is here the hallucination of the sense of smell.

Physical feelings and pain, telepathically transmitted to Mrs. Willett, also invoke in her the appropriate imagery. In the stage of awakening from trance on May 11, 1912, Mrs. Willett had been speaking of a communicator, known as The Dark Young man ; then she said :

' Oh ! I fell down, I fell down. Oh ! my head, my head, my head. Oh, oh, oh. (*Groans.*) Oh, oh, oh, I bumped my head. Oh, it's all here (*putting her hands to her head below and behind the ears*).

' (*Pause : heavy breathing.*) Oh, I wish my head would get empty.'

Lord Balfour notes : ' All this was so dramatically uttered that for the moment I thought Mrs. Willett had really hurt her head. Apparently, however, it was only the idea of the Dark Young Man's fall and consequent injury passing into a sympathetic feeling so strong that the automatist imagines it to have happened to herself.

Is There Such a Thing as Supernormal Sense-Imagery ?— The most obvious criticism of the idea here suggested, that in abnormal or supernormal states of consciousness, self-created sense-imagery could form a realistic world linked in some more or less distant way with an external reality, is that in all these states the imagery described is of our own normal type. It might be said that we are here dealing with hallucinations, which clothe different types of fantasy, but that all are drawn from a remembered stock of sense-imagery, ultimately derived from the normal senses of this present world. This is very likely true, especially in intermediate and unstable states of consciousness, and certainly true in dreams. But is it always true ? Are the descriptions of scenes given by trance-personalities sometimes *translations* made for our benefit into *our* sense-imagery from imagery of a very different kind ? I will quote some further examples from Mrs. Willett, relevant to this point :

' In the D. I. of February 18, 1909, occurs the following :

' About 11.30 to-day . . . I began to feel that very restless feeling. . . . At 11.45 I sat down, close to a cheerful window, with a feeling of " heavy " impression that F. was waiting. I felt as if it were somebody else's impatience.

' The first words that came to my mind were : " Myers yes now take a sheet of paper—only for notes no script but make notes of what I say " I enclose the notes I made. . . .

' The whole conversation ended by F. saying he did not want to tire me, and so " farewell." I just got a flash of an impression of

E. G. wanting to make a joke and F. not letting him—but it is all *very* dim *that*, I am clear up to " farewell." '

On February 1, 1910, occurs :

' Gurney   it is quite a short script I want to write   Myers says a note made re D. I. of Friday may give rise to . . . inaccurate deductions. . . . Myers wishes the record AMMENDED (*sic*) by a note

' Myers   yes   let me go on. . . .

' *Mrs. Willett notes :* " During all this script I felt very muddled and confused. The writing came in bits. Just before the [name Myers] I got a sense of F. *being there* and then of his brushing E. G. away and starting off the script himself with great impatience and in a very peremptory mood." '

Note the dual aspect of these passages : (i) Mrs. Willett *herself* feels restless, impatient, etc., but (ii) she also *refers* these emotions to their sources. In other words, her experiences are in some way *cognitive*. The suggestion is, I think, that something akin to sense-imagery enters into these cases, but imagery of a *different kind* from anything which we experience in normal life—imagery which cannot be directly turned into terms of normal thought—imagery which *immediately* conveys knowledge of somebody in the state of wanting to make a joke, of being in a peremptory mood, etc.

Mrs. Willett wrote in a letter to Mrs. Verrall on September 27, 1909 :

' I got no impression of *appearance*, only character, and in some way voice or pronunciation (though this doesn't mean that my *ears* hear, you know !). That is always so in D. I. [i.e. in silent D. I.] I don't feel a sense of " seeing," but an intense sense of personality, like a blind person perhaps might have—and of inflections, such as amusement or emotion on the part of the speaker. If you asked me *how* I know when E. G. is speaking and not F. W. H. M., I can't exactly define, except that to me it would be impossible to be in doubt one instant—and with E. G. I often know he is there a second or two before he speaks. . . . I then sometimes speak first. . . . To me, by now, there isn't anything strange in D. I.'s except when I try to explain anything about them ; then I realize suddenly they are unusual ! But otherwise it gives me no more sense of oddness to be talking to these invisible people than it does to be talking to my son, for instance. But I don't think I mentally visualize any sort of " appearance " with regard to them—it is as " minds " and " characters " that they are to me, and yet *not at all* intangible or non-solid realities. . . .'

This subjective light thrown on the nature of the trance-processes by the experient herself is of the very highest value. Another most interesting example occurred when the communicator, Gurney $_W$, [E. G.], attempted to throw his memory of himself as he was when living on to the sensitive's mind, so that she might pass on the description of it to Sir Oliver Lodge. It seems to be intended to illustrate the process for his benefit. The date was September 24, 1910 :

' [*Mrs. W.*] E. G. is talking.

E. G. Don't feel oppressed. You're going to do well. (*To O. J. L.*) I want you to see the passage of thought, not ocular or aural. Mediums. (*To Mrs. W.*) Now come, how does it seem to you now ? Answer out loud. What he says, do you often say ? Well, say it to Lodge.

Mrs. W. I see what he wants. I'm to tell you what I feel, my thoughts. He's very very near. I feel him just there (*in front near face*). I can only think of those words, they come running in my head : ' Nearer he is than breathing, closer than hands and feet.' I'm all as if I was in the light. I'm not seeing with my eyes (*eyes closed all the time*), but it feels as if he was holding both my hands and looking down at me. I'm not seeing his face by—I'm feeling it there. It's always got that look of having known pain. And he says to me, go over it just as it strikes you. I think it's the eyes, the lids are so——

E.G. Stop a moment, and tell Lodge the thought . . . I'm throwing in the recollection of what I took my bodily semblance to be, incarnate ; see how she catches it. How dangerous analogies are, and yet you could get something by thinking of a magic-lantern slide. Dependence on the vividness of my recollection ; it's a calling up on my part, a conscious effort, not involuntary. Lodge, are you seeing ?

O. J. L. Yes.

E. G. Go on.

Mrs. W. I see the lids drooping over the eyes, and how very restful
   they are to see, like something strong, something that makes
   me not afraid. Very sad, and yet at the back of that sadness
   something else ; strength and something else. Next thing I
   think about, it seems, the delicate backward sweep of the
   nostrils and the mouth, not quite straight, but oh, how
   humorous it can look. Not with the eyes, this sight.

E. G. Go on, go down.

Mrs. W. And it's a, yes, how thin his face is ; then the ears rather
   low on the head, and how the chin balances all the face, and
   such——

E. G. Yes, it was my chiefest attitude to life, that compassion.

Mrs. W. And then——

E. G. Yes, say it out loud, that's what I want Lodge to know.

Mrs. W. It's what I feel, I feel it's good to be here.'

Lord Balfour says :

' Evidently what we have here is an attempt to illustrate the
telepathic transmission of a memory-image from the communicator
to the percipient. The impression is without doubt meant to be
understood as a deliberately communicated impression involving
not only intention on the part of the agent but effort.'

Again, when Dr. Butcher introduced himself to Mrs.
Willett as ' Henry Butcher's ghost,' [1] she *felt* his personality,
including his ' piercing glance,' with no suggestion that there
was sense-imagery of the normal kind. Take this in conjunction with, ' Not with the eyes, this sight,' just mentioned,
and it looks very much as though Mrs. Willett, in her non-
normal states of consciousness, experiences an entirely unfamiliar kind of sense-imagery which conveys, not only features
of character, such as ' sweetness and strength,' but also those
features we call ' physical.' I suggest that in this direct
way she was acquiring knowledge of Gurney's appearance
and that she was *translating* this knowledge into visual sense-
imagery in her description. It does not follow that sensitives
in non-normal states experience only normal sense-imagery ;
but it does follow that they must translate their experiences
into such normal imagery if we are to understand them.

[1] p. 257.

Telepathic Possession.—In connexion with the theory of telepathy, it has been pointed out that there is no need to suppose that the *actual experience* of the agent is ever *shared* by the percipient.[1]   In cases of thought-transference it may always be supposed that the mechanism of telepathic action is such as to cause the percipient to undergo an experience of his own which is *similar* to the agent's but not *identical* with it. In this way the privacy of experiences would be maintained. It might be said that to share an experience with another mind is an impossibility, because it would dissolve the distinction between one mind and another.

I will conclude the present chapter by quoting three cases which have a significant bearing on this question and which Lord Balfour classes as instances of ' Telepathic Possession,' or of telepathy leading up to it.

In the waking stage of a D. I. on February 7, 1915, Mrs. Willett said :

' I've seen this room before, but I can't remember where it is. (*Points to a water-colour picture representing the Firth of Forth and the coast of East Lothian, seen from some point in Fife.*)   I'm not accustomed to the view from that side, I generally see it from the other side.   Why has that man painted it from behind to fore, so to speak ?   Do you see what I mean ?   He's stood in the wrong place— stupid idiot !   You see, why I like my view best is because I'm accustomed to it, and I've seen it all my life from the other side.   It makes me quite giddy seeing it the wrong way about.   You can't reverse pictures so that they stay right, can you ?   I'm looking at it where I generally stand ;   and that's what's bothering me, you see. (*Gets up and goes to the fireplace.*)   That's where I used to stand—just about there.   (*Points with finger to the spot.*) '

The Dark Young Man had been the communicator who, ostensibly, had just departed as the waking stage came on, and a footnote is here added, saying : ' The point indicated was on the southern side of the Firth of Forth, and might quite well represent the position of the Dark Young Man's Scottish home. The automatist herself had no personal knowledge of the

[1] *Proc. S.P.R.*, vol. xliii. pp. 397–438.

neighbourhood.'   In his remarks about this incident, Lord
Balfour remarks :

'The personality of the automatist appears to merge so completely into that of the communicator as to lead one to suspect the
latter of a desire to give a practical illustration of that reciprocal
interweaving of two minds which he had described earlier in the
D. I., and which, without being " possession " in full sense of the
term, may yet reproduce some of the characteristics of " possession."
I regard it, in fact, as an illustration of what I call telepathic
possession.'

One sees, too, how difficult it is to discuss telepathy on the
assumption that it is a mode of communication between two
atomically distinct selves.   The nature of the self is the central
problem in psychical research, bound up with which is the
nature of telepathy, and it is evident that we have to learn to
form ideas which will fit the facts, and not to force the facts
into our preconceived ideas.   For instance, in a further portion
of the script dealing with the transferred pain of the Dark
Young Man's fall, occurs the following :

'Oh, I feel so giddy, I'm tumbling down. (*Rests her head on the
table.*) I can't remember who I am. I know I'm somebody ; and
I'm coming together, you know, and the bits don't fit.'

And on October 31, 1908, the day after Myers$_W$ had claimed
to have succeeded in getting into Mrs. Willett's mentality,
the latter notes to her script :

'I had had other confused dreams the previous night, as well
as an intensely vivid impression of Fred's presence. I can only
describe it by saying I felt myself so blending with him as almost to
seem to become him.'

Note also the script above referred to in which Mrs. Willett
says : 'It was as if barriers were swept away and I and they
became one.'

In the waking stage of the trance-script of April 19, 1918,
Mrs. Willett said :

'Oh ! (*pause*) Fred, Fred. So strange to be somebody else. To
feel somebody's heart beating inside, and some one else's mind

inside your mind. And there isn't any time or place, and either you're loosed or they're entered, and you all of a sudden know everything that ever was. You understand everything. It's like every single thing and time and thought and everything brought down to one point. . . .'

Compare above also ' How *nothing* time is.'

It is clear that if this is telepathy, it is a very different kind of thing from the simple thought-transference of the early experiments. The evidence leads us on to cases like these which suggest a sharing of experience, and even a sharing of selfhood, which we cannot understand. It is reminiscent of religious mystical experience. The same thing inspired Tennyson's poem, ' In Memoriam,' and particularly the verse beginning with the words, ' The living soul was flashed on mine.' Theories of telepathy must take these facts into account, as well as the simpler ones.

In the next chapter we will go on to consider briefly the light which these trance-phenomena throw on the nature of personality.

Chapter XX

TRANCE-PERSONALITIES

SECONDARY PERSONALITIES.—The natural tendency of the scientific student of psychical phenomena, and particularly of the psychological student, will be to explain trance-personalities as instances of the dual and multiple personalities met with in abnormal psychology. But (as always in psychical research) there is need for caution. It is possible that such a view may be true up to a point, and yet not cover the whole field. Dr. William Brown [1] speaks of ' " Feda," who is apparently of a childish nature, and may psychologically be regarded as a regression in relation to Mrs. Leonard's adult consciousness.' But he goes on to say, ' If I speak there as though I agreed with this theory, I hasten to add that it is only a very superficial way of describing and envisaging the facts, and what we have to consider is the possibility that this relationship is not anything like so close as those who have not made much direct study of mediums are ready to believe.'

The subjects of ' split ' personalities are advanced hysterics ; but Dr. Brown says, after a study of Mrs. Osborne Leonard, that he is inclined to think that a case of successful mediumship shows very little evidence of hysteria.

There seems to be some evidence, however, for the view that controls such as Feda are secondary personalities of a kind. Mr. Whately Carington, as we saw in Chapter XV, produced evidence by his word-association method tending to show that Feda is ' countersimilar ' in her responses to Mrs. Leonard herself.

Control- and Communicator-Vehicles.—Mr. Kenneth Richmond, in his notes on Mrs. Leonard, above quoted, intro-

[1] ' Psychology and Psychical Research,' *Proc. S.P.R.*, vol. xli. p. 78.

duces the idea that there may be psychological mechanisms in the medium's subconscious which act as *vehicles* through which there operates a purposive will to communicate. He adopts provisionally the view that ' we are dealing with two chief psychological mechanisms : one an organized and habitual secondary personality, which is usually (I do not say always) the vehicle for the Feda control ; and the other, a dramatizing function of the trance-mind, which adapts itself to become the vehicle for the different communicators. In saying " vehicle " I free myself from any suspicion of thinking that " secondary personality " or " dramatic pose " (to adopt Mr. Carington's useful phrase) can explain or characterize the impulses that operate through these mechanisms.'

This conception is, I think, a valuable step towards the understanding of trance-phenomena, because it recognizes that the problem contains *depth*. ' Flat ' explanations, such as that the deceased communicator, substantially as he was before his decease, is speaking through a kind of psychic telephone, or that mediumistic phenomena are merely the result of auto-hypnosis, simply will not do. The problem contains vistas ; there is a receding and uncomprehended background. The fruitful idea is that there are psychological organizations acting as ' vehicles,' which are being used by some will or intention behind them. And there seems to be mutual adaptation, each in the process conditioning, and being conditioned by the other. Further, in these control- and communicator-vehicles, Mr. Richmond sees alternative paths of free association, which are utilized by the communicating impulses. Sometimes, he observes, these alternate, ' Sometimes Feda seems to be speaking, sometimes the communicator, sometimes you cannot be grammatically sure which. . . .'

The importance of maintaining fluent lines of association is clearly brought out again and again in the trance-sittings. In fact, the possibilities of communication seem to be hedged about by available association-trains. Mr. Drayton Thomas records that a controlling communicator, Etta, once says : ' Feda often takes some important thought from a communicator without his desire and she will use it to fill up and keep things moving ;

for a long spell of silence would make Feda lose hold of the medium. This accounts for trivial matters being brought in disconnectedly at times.' [1]

Again, in some book-tests with Miss Radcliffe Hall, occurs the sentence (referring to the books), ' You may have to dislodge some of them in order to see the title . . .' after which the flow of speech was diverted into a new channel and the words, ' Lodge, Lodge, Raymond,' etc., followed. The word, ' dislodge,' slightly unusual in this context, had been inserted by the communicator as a switch-word to lead to the topic of Raymond Lodge. Feda follows this up with :

' You know, Ladye says it's so extraordinary, but she has to act upon Feda sometimes in a way Feda don't understand when she's in the medium, and she was afraid Feda wouldn't take up the reference to Raymond, so she had to worry to get a word that would suggest Raymond to Feda ; she says she's done that often and she's wondered if you had guessed she was doing that, and how carefully she has to lead Feda to a new idea. Feda knows that, 'cos when Feda's in the medium she's only got like half of Feda's own sense, she's not half so clever as when she's out of the medium.'

One might have thought that the systems of association belonging to these ' vehicles ' would take charge of the communicated material and mould it according to their own natural trends, but this proves actually to be not the case, at any rate where good or fairly good sittings are concerned with a first-class medium. ' *Clichés* ' are surprisingly few.

' Organized routes,' says Mr. Richmond, ' for leading up to a favourite type of subject are certainly present, such as one can observe in the conversational habits of one's friends (these are easier to observe than one's own habits) ; but I find on careful examination that these stock openings have a remarkable way of leading each to a different track of association which is appropriate to the given communicator. I have tried to interpret this as a process in which the motivation arises in the trance-mind alone, and the deflection towards evidential fact is due to telepathic impacts from the living ; but the difficulty of accounting for selection among such impacts is very great. . . .'

[1] *Proc. S.P.R.*, vol. xxxviii. p. 58.

Again he says :

' Given a wish on the part of the medium to produce evidence of survival, and long experience in trance, with a multitude of sitters, of the lines of suggestion which are most likely to produce vivid personal associations, it is very possible for systems of safe guesses to be automatically organized, which become endowed with a great appearance of authenticity and individual quality when they are enriched by striking annotations. The intentions manifested at a sitting might be types of intention in the trance-mind alone which have been found to be readily supplemented by the associations of sitters and annotators. I think this machinery certainly exists, though much less pervasively than I imagined when I started the investigation ; but I think the most interesting thing about it is the regularity with which it defeats its apparent object. In the best sittings, it is the allusions which the communicator-impulse appears to have forced away from the expected rut that arrive at something specific in the mind of the annotator.'

And :

' The vague forms of organized intention that seem attributable to the trance-mind alone, with its past experience, appear as being quite distinctly manipulated, deflected, and sometimes negatived by another form of intention.'

So that we find that, when trance-material of good quality is carefully analyzed, the psychological organizations in the medium turn out to be by no means dominating the situation ; their inherent tendencies and trains of association are being utilized by intelligent effort, which is acting on them from without.

Fictitious Communicators.—The fact that entirely fictitious communicators occasionally appear in the trance shows clearly that secondary organizations of some kind exist in the medium. I think that such false communicators are a sign of bad conditions and seldom occur with the best mediums ; but Mrs. Sidgwick, in her thorough examination of Mrs. Piper's trance,[1] refers to such cases.

[1] ' The Psychology of Mrs. Piper's Trance Phenomena,' *Proc. S.P.R.*, vol. xxviii. p. 176.

A Mrs. E., who had had three sittings with Mrs. Piper in 1902, received the impression that ' some intelligence was impersonating, deliberately and with considerable ingenuity, and yet on the whole doing it so ill that the deception is proved beyond a peradventure.' ' On the third sitting,' she says, ' I asked leading questions which were calculated to mislead ; and in every case the communicator fell into the trap, with a result that would have been ludicrous had it not been so disgusting.'

The point is best dealt with by making a rather long quotation from Mrs. Sidgwick's report. She says that the dissatisfaction expressed by Mrs. E. was borne out by the full record of her sittings, and expresses well the impression produced on herself by a good many sittings. She gives the record of one such sitting at which she was present, at which Hodgson p was the communicator and apparently failed to recognize the sitter, an intimate friend of his in life, or to understand the clues she gave him, thus making it very difficult to suppose that his claim to be Hodgson was justified. Yet, in the midst of the confusion supernormal matter occurred in the shape of part of a cross-correspondence. But, she continues, ' We are not . . . limited to inference from the failure of communicators for evidence that they are sometimes not what they profess to be, for Dr. Stanley Hall in 1909 took a short cut to positive evidence by deceiving the control Hodgson p,[1] and asking for a niece, Bessie Beals, who had never existed, but who was nevertheless produced at several sittings.' The sitting went as follows :

' *Dr. Hall.* Well, what do you say to this, Hodgson. I asked you to call Bessie Beals, and there is no such person. How do you explain that ?

' *Hodgson* p. Bessie Beals is here, and not the——
(Note by Miss Tanner.)
[At this point we laughed and I made some remark to the effect that that was just what we had said Hodgson would do, and the hand continued thus,]

[1] Dr. Stanley Hall, *Studies in Spiritism*, p. 254.

' *Hodgson p.* I know a Bessie Beals. Her mother asked about her
    before. Mother asked about her before.
' *Dr. Hall.* I don't know about that, Hodgson. Bessie Beals is a pure
    fiction.
' *Hodgson p.* I refer to a lady who asked me the same thing and the
    same name.
' *Dr. Hall.* Guess you are wrong about that, Hodgson.
' *Hodgson p.* Yes, I am mistaken in her. I am mistaken. Her name
    was not Bessie but Jessie Beals.

   ' We can only say about this explanation that it is not plausible.
. . . Dr. Hall might accidentally have hit on the name of a previous
communicator, but it is very unlikely that this communicator would
have had memories appropriate to Dr. Hall's fictions and have
admitted him as her uncle.

   ' It must then be admitted that some communicators are not
genuine, while other communicators offer evidence of identity
which, if it does not necessarily come from the spirits they claim to
be, at least shows knowledge of those spirits which cannot have
reached Mrs. Piper's mind by normal means. This being so, is it
possible to find a formula which will express the relation to the
control of all communicators—both successful and unsuccessful ?
Are they or are they not essentially different ? Is the unsuccessful
communicator a figment of the control's imagination, while the
successful communicator is an independent entity ? If so, can we
draw a definite line between them ? Are we to judge a communicator representing himself as the same, to be on some days a figment
and on others an independent centre of consciousness, according as
he is unsuccessful or successful in producing a plausible semblance
of the figure he professes to be ? And if the communicator is a
figment, is the control conscious of it, or is he himself deceived ?
In other words, what is the degree of independence of control from
communicator ? Are two more or less independent centres of
consciousness involved ; whether consciousnesses of separate individuals or different centres of consciousness of Mrs. Piper ? Or is
the communicator a dream or hallucination of the control ? Or is
the dramatic presentation of him pure play-acting by the control ? ' [1]

Mrs. Sidgwick's conclusion, so far as the Piper phenomena
are concerned, has been referred to in Chapter XI. Although

---

[1] *Proc. S.P.R.*, vol. xxviii. pp. 178–9.

she recognizes in the trance personalities a greater capacity in some directions than the normal Mrs. Piper possessed, particularly in the ' G. P.' case, some of whose friends found it easier to suppose that he was not an impersonation but G. P. himself, yet she thinks that these are ' quite as compatible with the hypothesis that the trance-personalities are phases or elements of Mrs. Piper as with any other.' One must not, however, suppose that this was Mrs. Sidgwick's opinion about all trance-phenomena. She allowed it, in fact to be known at a later date, that she accepted the identity of the Willett communicators.

Three cases of a very extraordinary kind are reported by Mr. S. G. Soal,[1] in one of which, the case of James Miles, the information supplied by the communicator at the sittings seems to have been derived in some way or other almost wholly from newspaper reports. In another, the case of Gordon Davis, the communicator, purporting to be deceased, was afterwards found to be alive ; while in a third, the communicator, John Ferguson, was entirely fictitious. This remarkable trio of spurious cases lacks, however, customary corroboration.

On April 5, 1918, Dr. L. P. Jacks had a sitting with Mrs. Leonard in which a young man was described by Feda, his appearance being given in considerable detail.[2] The sitter notes : ' I cannot identify him. I thought at first it was my son, Captain S. Jacks, at the front, as the description tallies at several points. I was afraid he might have been killed. I now know he was alive at the time of the sitting.' Mrs. Salter notes, writing in 1921, ' He was, and is, still alive.' Part of the general note on the sitting made by the sitter runs as follows :

' The total impression left on my mind is similar to that left by many common dreams. There is the same muddle and incoher-

[1] ' A Report on some Communications received through Mrs. Blanche Cooper,' *Proc. S.P.R.*, vol. xxxv. p. 471.
[2] ' A Further Report on Sittings with Mrs. Leonard,' by Mrs. W. H. Salter (*Proc. S.P.R.*, vol. xxxii. p. 133).

ency at first, in which definite personalities seem to appear for a
moment and then change into somebody else, the facts getting
hopelessly mixed up, the action of one person shading off into that
of another. And then towards the end the dream becomes more
coherent and interesting, keeping up a definite character for a time,
with a sudden return to nonsense (the Archdeacon, etc.) and a
momentary reappearance of the people first on the scene.'

This seems to have been an instance of a Leonard sitting
of poor quality. In the A. V. B. series, quoted above, it will be
remembered that Feda was, on the whole, remarkably clear and
definite.

Mr. John F. Thomas, in his recently published book,
Beyond Normal Cognition, also gives an instance of a living
person being represented as being deceased. He says :

' In my own records there is a case that shows similarity to the
one just described. A trance-personality purported to communicate in an experiment with Mrs. Soule,[1] when I was present. The
points from this trance-personality were sufficiently applicable to
establish the impression that he was presented as the father of
E. L. T. So far as I knew, the father of E. L. T. was living at the
time, but his physical condition was such that his death would not
have been unexpected. I thought that possibly he was deceased
without my knowledge, and I telegraphed a daughter as to the time
of his death. He proved, however, to be still living, and he survived
until about a year and a half after the date of the " communication." '
(pp. 206-7.)

In 1923, Dr. F. C. S. Schiller reported a curious case [2]
of a lady who had taken up *oui-ja* board writing, obtaining
messages which she believed to come from her stepfather,
to whom she had been devoted. She had a nervous breakdown
and was warned to give up the writing. In the sequel she
became insane and had to be put in a sanatorium. The
diagnosis of the doctors was, however, that she was suffering
from senile dementia, due to arterio-sclerosis, and that this
was wholly the result of her age. The interesting point was

---

[1] Mrs. Soule is a celebrated American medium.
[2] *Journal S.P.R.*, vol. xxi. p. 87.

that messages came through Mrs. Piper in which the insane woman appeared to communicate as a deceased person. Moreover, the controls stated that she believed that she had already died, and gave a correct diagnosis of the illness from which she was actually suffering, agreeing with that given by the doctors.

Such examples show that there can be ostensible communicators, which cannot be regarded as genuine and which accept any suggestion of the sitter's, use ' fishing ' methods to gain information, make unplausible evasions when brought to book, and seem, in fact, to be hypnoidal dramatizations within the medium's self. Their performances are not sufficiently intelligent to support the belief, held in some quarters, that they are of diabolical origin. If they are, the demons would not appear to be very formidable. But it is interesting to note that certain cases tend to show that sick or insane persons can, through telepathic action, appear falsely as communicators. This fact reminds one of the ' One Horsed Dawn ' experiment,[1] tried by Dr. Verrall, and referred to in Chapter XVII, which showed telepathic action from the living appearing in dramatic form in the percipient.

But these cases form the lower end of the scale of trance-phenomena. At the other end appear such forceful, clear, and natural communicators as those of the Willett scripts ; while between the two are communicators of varying degrees of plausibility and veridicality. Communicators, also, can vary in quality with the medium and with the occasion, all of which tends to support the view that the communicators are variable entities of a compound nature.

We will now go on to consider certain points in the psychology of the Willett phenomena.

The Willett Trance and Allied States.—To give anything like a full account of the states or phases of the self involved in the Willett phenomena from the scripts and comments in Lord Balfour's report would be an exceedingly difficult task. The Willett trance has been called ' autonomous,' and it is true that, during the scripts and D. I.s, it is Mrs. Willett herself, and no other entity, who controls the motor mechanisms

---

[1] See *Proc. S.P.R.*, vol. xx. pp. 156–67.

of her body : but that changes of some sort occur in the personality is obvious. Besides the fact that there is as a rule no recollection in the normal state of what was said in the D. I.'s, there are two distinct types of script, the disjointed or allusive type and the connected type, and the change from reporting in the third to reporting in the first person, which marks the transition from one to the other, would seem to indicate some change in the sensitive's personality. In the allusive type of script we seem to see Mrs. Willett herself struggling with the matter she is being given to externalize. Almost every sentence begins, ' Oh, he says,' and the distaste of the automatist for many of the words and the topics is very marked. For example :

' . . . But, he says, the subliminal—he says the supraliminal has access to—he says to me, You've got the analogies all wrong, try again. Begin the other end, he says. The transcendental self—he says something about a point of release—oh, Edmund, you *do bore me so*—the passing of itself into stratas [sic] of subliminality, etc.'

On the other hand, the D. I. can be extremely smooth and connected. On January 21, 1912,[1] G. W. B. asks Gurney w a question about telaesthesia, and about the mythical ' room ' into which the sensitive was said to be taken, and the reply came in this way :

' " I'll throw something at you, and you must make what you can of it. I'll take that portion of her which can emerge in uprush, and I, as it were, link it on with that deeper subliminal which can be in touch with what I want to get known . . . " and so on.'

Here the script is in the first person, as if Gurney w himself were speaking, and Mrs. Willett is referred to as ' her.' There are no breaks or protests from Mrs. Willett : the whole runs smoothly. G. W. B. comments :

' The writing stage that preceded the D. I. had been comparatively short, but the sitting as a whole was an unusually long one, lasting nearly two hours. The passage we are now considering

[1] *Proc. S.P.R.*, vol. xliii. p. 243.

came at the very end of it, and was preceded by discussions of a decidedly abstruse character which seem to have bewildered the sensitive and put a severe strain upon her attention. The record of these discussions abounds in the familiar interjected phrases, " He says," " Oh, he says," whereas the long answer to my question about the " room " is uniquely free from them. Just before I asked it, Gurney had addressed a word of encouragement to the sensitive : " He says, you've got it now, and he says, No bones broken—and he says to me, You know, dear, I feel sometimes I must appear to you like the Devil when he said, Cast thyself down, but he says if only you'll go blindly there'll be no pieces to pick up." I suggest that the advice to " go blindly " was acted upon by the sensitive, and that the almost complete absence of the usual interjections was due to her simply repeating each word and not attempting to grasp the meaning sentence by sentence.'

But clearly there is a change in personality, or in what Mr. Richmond would call the ' communicator vehicle,' of such a kind that the sensitive has become in some way more identified with it.

In everything they say, the Willett communciators describe the transmission of matter from their end as a difficult and complex process traversing *layers* or *strata* of the sensitive's personality which lie beneath the level of the normal, conscious self. On one occasion Gurney $_W$ says :

'. . . I want to make a shot at a partial definition of what constitutes mediumship. That organization in which the capacity for—what an odd word—oh, Edmund, say it slowly—*excursus* is allied to the capacity for definite selection. Then finally the possession of as it were a vent, through which the knowledge can emerge . . .'

A good deal more explanation follows, which is rather obscure and interrupted, but the ' excursus,' which Gurney$_W$ is trying to explain, is evidently something which takes place in a very deep level of the self, and has an affinity with mystical experience. It is, in fact, reminiscent of the idea of *contemplation*, as it occurs in the philosophy of Plotinus. It is an *act* of entering into relationship with the spiritual environment.

' The passing into it, which is the effect of the excursus, is variously described in the scripts as " the crossing of a border," " the freeing of that which is capable of intuitional visions of far-distant worlds," " the falling of barriers," " the delocalization of the soul testifying to the existence of a whole," " the escape from the limits of self," " the escape of the smaller into the larger." '

And again :

' The Myers of the scripts tells us . . . that, " Ecstasy springs from meditation " ; and he draws an emphatic distinction between meditation and lethargy or torpor.   The very term " excursus " suggests an active process ; and the language employed by the sensitive herself, in such phrases as " I want to get out of myself, I'm so tired of myself, I want to be enlarged," carries a similar implication.' [1]

It is by this faculty of excursus, according to the Willett communicators, that the ideas for transmission are acquired ; then there comes a shepherding of them up through levels of the sensitive's personality, a final selection and then a crystalliza-tion in terms of supraliminally objectified ideas—a translation, as it were, into the kind of thinking we call ' normal.' So that phases or levels or strata of the self are involved in the passage of these ideas, but in what manner these are separated from one another, and in what manner united, remains a mystery.

Again, in speaking of the visions which Mrs. Willett has in the lighter stages of her trance, which she can to some extent afterwards remember, Lord Balfour says : ' They are pseudo-hallucinations, not hallucinations. And the difference is of kind, not merely of degree. Like presences, these visions have an objectivity of their own, but not exactly the objectivity associated with sense-perception.' [2] This latter sentence suggests that the *perceptual consciousness* in which these trance-visions are experienced is not identical with the consciousness of normal perception : consequently, the quality of objectivity belonging to the imagery which occurs in them is not the same

[1] *Proc. S.P.R.* ,vol. xliii. p. 221.
[2] Ibid. p. 86. Here again the idea of non-normal sense-imagery is suggested.

as the quality of objectivity which belongs to the imagery of normal perception. It is as if the kind of ' real-seemingness ' (if one may coin such a term) is a function of the kind of consciousness accompanying the particular kind of perception. Yet, all the time, in some real sense, both are the consciousness of the same Mrs. Willett. There is, in these phases of selfhood, a unity in difference which refuses to accommodate itself to our habitual modes of thought. The lesson we should learn from it is, I think, that we must expand our categories of thought to take in the facts ; not try to force the facts into our existing categories.

Remarks of the Willett Communicators.—The degree of independence between the Willett communicators and Mrs. Willett's trance-self is throughout very striking ; and certain statements and remarks made by them, which illustrate this, may be interesting. For instance, the limitation which makes them unable to know telepathically what is going on in the mind of the sitter. In a D. I. of June 4, 1911,[1] Gurney $_W$ is giving a difficult passage, which he fears may be misunderstood :

' Oh, he says, Gerald—oh, he says like that. He's calling some one. Nobody answers—he keeps on calling some one. He says Gerald. Oh, he keeps on calling. Oh ! He says where is Gerald ?
(*G. W. B.* I'm here.)
' Oh, he says, does he hear ? How can I know that he hears ?
(*G. W. B.* All right, I'm hearing perfectly.)
' Oh, he says, the waste of material when we keep on hammering at one point—approaching it from every—can't read that word—of the compass—only to find that the point had been grasped and that we might have passed on to new matter.
' Oh, he says, I can't see your mind, Gerald, but I can feel you in some dim way through her. He says, it's a sort of lucky-bag, her mind to me—when I'm not shut out from it.'

It seems to be a general rule in all trance-phenomena (with occasional possible exceptions) that what is in the *conscious* minds of the sitters is inaccessible to the trance-personalities.

State of the Communicator when Communicating.—There

[1] *Proc. S.P.R.*, vol. xliii. p. 234.

seems to be a concensus of opinion among communicators that they are not in their natural state while communicating. Mr. Drayton Thomas, for example, quotes statements from his communicators at Leonard sittings, in the paper above referred to, in which they testify to their deficiencies when in the communicating state : ' I am not at my best even when conditions are at their best . . . I do not see, remember, and feel with the same lucidity as I do when not communicating.' ' I feel that I am not complete during a sitting. I have not my whole mental power of memory and consciousness.' ' Etta has, on occasion, gone away to get remembrance of what we required, but on returning forgot again before she could tell me.' That this is not peculiar to the control type of trance would seem to be indicated by the words with which Gurney w ends the D. I. of June 16, 1911 :

' He says, I must let her go away, G. Oh, he says, When I'm not trying to transmit, I'd write script the very Gods might envy, and I go over and over the things that would be of priceless value to transmit. . . .'[1]

Myers h, communicating through Mrs. Holland's automatic script, once said :

' The nearest simile I can find to express the difficulties of sending a message—is that I appear to be standing behind a sheet of frosted glass—which blurs sight and deadens sound—and dictating feebly—to a reluctant and somewhat obtuse secretary.'[2]

It seems as though these difficulties might probably be due, in part at least, to the compound nature of the communicator himself *as* communicator at the time of the communication. If we consider the communicator with whom we are in actual contact during these trance-sittings to be in some sense a compound resulting from Mr. Richmond's suggested ' communicator-vehicle ' acting jointly with the entity which provides the will to communicate, we have an explanation of the sense of imperfection to which all com-

[1] *Proc. S.P.R.*, vol. xliii. p. 234.   [2] Ibid. vol. xxi. p. 230.

municators testify. We can also see how there may be various grades of communicators. We can think of the compound communicating entity as being composed of two constituents in varying proportions (although a quantitative way of viewing the communicator is almost certainly misleading)—partly ' vehicle ' and partly ' communicator-impulse.' The vehicle may be of good or poor quality. The amount of influence which the will to communicate has over the vehicle will depend on the extent of its own contribution to the compound. There could, therefore, be a range of communicators varying from those as vigorous, lifelike, and highly intelligent as Gurney w to the poor and unconvincing communicators, which appear at seances with bad mediums. There could even be spurious communicators, which one imagines would consist of a vehicle, mainly a secondary personality out of touch with any genuine will to communicate.

The communicators sometimes speak interestingly of their own limitations of knowledge, for example :

' . . . Much is unknown to us even, and you are all far behind us in knowledge. . . .'

' . . . I cannot explain half the mysteries of Life yet, but I see more than you do. . . .'

' . . . Much and more than you suspect is absolutely hidden from me, Myers, the small amount in one way of accretion of knowledge which succeeds Myers bodily dissolution is a surprise to every spirit that crosses the Rubicon. . . .'

(This frequent interjection of the communicator's name was characteristic of Mrs. Willett's early scripts. It is not clear what the object of it was. It afterwards ceased.)

A Comparison of the Myers Communicators.—That the same communicating personality should show differences in its appearance in the scripts of different automatists is not surprising on any theory of the nature of the communicator ; but some observations made by Miss Alice Johnson on this point are worth quoting here, since she had ample opportunity for noting and comparing characteristics of the script-person-

alities.   There is,' she says,[1] ' an emotional tone and a note of
personal appeal in the utterances of Myers$_H$ which shows in
contrast with the calmer and more impersonal, matter-of-fact
tone of Myers$_V$.' And, she continues,

' *If* Mr. Myers really knew what was going on and *if* he was
really concerned in the production of the scripts, it would be natural
and appropriate that he should attempt to impress the two automatists in these different ways. Mrs. Verrall, a personal friend and
trained investigator, was already familiar with scientific methods
and in close touch with other investigators. She did not require
urging to go on with her writing, from which some important
evidence had already resulted. Mrs. Holland, on the other hand,
was in an isolated position ; she was conscious of the superficially
trivial and incoherent nature of her script, and could not tell whether
there was anything in it beyond a dream-like *réchauffé* of her own
thoughts. She would naturally shrink from exposing this to
strangers and thereby appearing to attach an unreasonable degree of
importance to it. We may suppose then that the control realizes
her situation and tries to impress on her a vivid realization of his
own—his intense desire to provide evidence for survival.'

This was in the early days of Mrs. Holland's scripts.

' In a letter dated Feb. 25, 1905, she says : " I cannot tell you
how glad I should be to know if the longing for recognition (it is
such a passionate craving sometimes that I find myself crying out :
' If I could help you. Oh ! if I could only help you ! ' while I
write) is a real influence from beyond or only my own imaginings.
But why should my imagination take that form ? I have been
singularly free from bereavements thus far in my life, and therefore
my thoughts have been very seldom in the Valley of the Shadow. . . .

' " In Nov. 1905, when I had asked her to read through the early
script and send me any comments that occurred to her, she notes
among other things : ' This sloping writing [that of the Myers
control] often brings a very sad impression of great depression with
it—a feeling that some one, somewhere, urgently and passionately
desires to be understood, or reported even without understanding,
and that no mental strain on my part can adequately respond to this

[1] ' The Automatic Writing of Mrs. Holland,' *Proc. S.P.R.*, vol. xxi.
pp. 239 ff.

demand. This feeling has been strong enough to make me cry and to make me speak aloud. I frequently control it, for it seems to me perilously akin to hysteria ; but it is a very real part of the automatic script.'"'

It is noteworthy, I think, that Miss Alice Johnson, as long ago as 1905, was also led by the evidence to the conclusion that the actual communicator we are dealing with is Compound. She gives an analogy :

' It is hardly possible to discuss the subject without the use of material analogies, which are constantly liable to be mistaken for real similarities. The best method perhaps is to vary the analogies as much as possible, so as to avoid confining ourselves to fixed grooves of thought. In particular, any analogy referring to a process—such as the comparison of telepathy to wireless telegraphy —is to be deprecated, as it inevitably suggests the inference that the processes referred to are essentially similar. It is better to confine ourselves to analogies which relate simply to the facts before us and suggest nothing as to the causes that produce them.

' I will then compare the scripts to chemical compounds of two or more elements, which are found in different proportions in the various compounds. Thus, if we call the automatists P and V and the hypothetical external intelligence X, we may get in the one script such compounds as PX or P_2X, or PX_2, and in the other VX, etc. ; or we may get in either of them such compounds as PVX, P_2V_3X, etc. We may also get such compounds as PV or PV_2 ; or we may get the elements P and V by themselves. The one element that we never get alone is X.

' If this be so, the Piper-Myers is not, and never could be, identical with the Verrall-Myers. The utmost that can happen will be that the same element is found in both scripts. The burden of proof must lie with those who maintain that it is there to be found ; but our methods of analysis are not yet so far perfected that we can assert positively either its presence or absence.'

This analogy with chemical compounds is helpful to the mind in its attempts to picture what is going on ; but it is very necessary to bear in mind the warning that Miss Johnson gives us, namely, that we are dealing with mind, and that our materialistically inclined thought suggests conceptions of it couched in terms of matter, so that, as she says, material analogies are constantly liable to be mistaken for real similarities. This warning is particularly needful when attempts are made to apply statistical methods to psychical research, as in Mr. Whately Carington's work referred to in Chapter XV.

We will now consider some theories as to the nature of communicators and the explanation of trance-material, and will afterwards go on to consider some arguments for and against survival, based on general grounds.

Chapter XXI

NATURE OF THE COMMUNICATORS—
ANTECEDENT PROBABILITY OF SURVIVAL

THE THEORY OF THE COMPOUND FACTOR.—Besides the fact that
the evidence for intention contained in the cross-correspondences and automatic scripts could have been presented
more forcibly and succinctly by the living Myers and Gurney
than it has been by the Myers and Gurney communicators,
there are other criticisms which might be brought against the
view that these communicators are identical with the persons
they claim to be. Why, one may ask, do they appear to have
undergone so little change since their deaths ? Why do they
quote Tennyson and Browning in a way which has now quite
gone out of vogue ? Are we to suppose that their characters
became ' frozen ' at the moment of death, and have remained
fixed ever since ? And why do the communicators who appear
through Mrs. Leonard speak as if they were still surrounded by a
terrestrial environment, and still engaged in terrestrial occupations, while the communicators through Mrs. Willett do not
mention these things, and are strangely reticent about their
present state ? Does it not seem as if we were here getting
merely a reflection of the educational influences which have
operated on Mrs. Leonard on the one hand, and on Mrs.
Willett on the other ? All these points, it might be said,
suggest that an explanation of trance-phenomena should be
sought on non-survivalist lines.

Professor Broad has put forward such a theory under the
title of the ' Compound Theory.' Let us consider it.

' I do not think,' he says, ' that there is anything in the
normal phenomena which requires us to suppose that a mind
depends for its existence and functioning on anything but the

body and its processes.' [1]   But the evidence of abnormal and supernormal phenomena inclines him to adopt a Compound instead of an Epiphenomenal theory of Mind, in which the latter is the resultant of the union of the Body with a ' Psychic Factor.'

' Might not what we know as a mind,' he says, ' be a compound of two factors, neither of which separately has the characteristic properties of a mind, just as salt is a compound of two substances, neither of which by itself has the characteristic properties of salt ? Let us call one of these constituents the " psychic factor " and the other the " bodily factor." The psychic factor would be like some chemical element which has never been isolated ; and the characteristics of a mind would depend jointly on those of the psychic factor and on those of the material organism with which it is united.' [2]

So far as the application of this theory to psychical phenomena is concerned, the psychic element would be something which ' persists ' rather than ' survives ' the death of the body. It would not be a person, capable of thinking and willing, but a repository of some sort of mnemic traces. ' This psychic factor is not itself a mind, but it may carry modifications due to experiences which happened to (the former owner) while he was alive. And it may become temporarily united with the organism of an entranced medium. If so, a little temporary " mind " (a " mindkin," if I may use that expression) will be formed. Since this mindkin will contain the same psychic factor as the mind of John Jones, it will not be surprising if it displays some traits characteristic of John Jones, and some memories of events in his earthly life.' ' When the medium is entranced the psychic factor which was a constituent of John Jones' mind forms with the medium's body a mindkin which lasts just as long as the medium remains in trance. At intermediate times, on this view, all that exists is this psychic factor ; and this by itself is no more a mind than John Jones' corpse is a mind.' [3]

This is the theory. Professor Broad says : ' Now the

[1] *The Mind and its Place in Nature*, p. 538.
[2] Ibid. pp. 535–6.   [3] Ibid. p. 541.

Compound Theory has at least this merit. It is compatible with all the facts which every one admits ; it has nothing against it except a superstitious objection to dualism ; and it leaves open the possibility that these debatable phenomena are genuine.' [1]

But he does not put forward this theory alone to explain all the evidence for mediumistic phenomena. Where the concordant automatisms and cross-correspondences are concerned, he suggests that these may have been derived telepathically from sources in Mrs. Verrall's subconscious mind, or in the minds of other members of the group concerned in them. He thus suggests two distinct theories to account for the phenomena of trance-mediumship and automatic script, (1) the Compound Theory, and (2) the Telepathic Theory. Of the latter, he says :

' There is another remark to be made on the Cross-Correspondences. Suppose that they rendered it practically certain that *some* other mind than the conscious mind of the automatists is controlling the experiments, can we feel any confidence that it is the mind of a certain deceased person who professes to be communicating ? Is it not at least equally probable that it might be the unconscious part of the mind of one of the Officers of the Society for Psychical Research ? It would certainly be true to say that some of the automatists (in particular Mrs. Verrall) were well aware of the problem of getting evidence for survival which could not be explained away by the hypothesis of telepathy between the living ; that it must have occupied their thoughts a great deal ; and that they must have had a permanent desire to devise some means of solving it. It is also true that the alleged communicators in the Cross-Correspondences had been well known in life to Mrs. Verrall and to many prominent and active members of the Society who were not themselves automatists. Now I think we may take the following propositions as reasonably well established : (*a*) That when a person is greatly interested in a problem this problem is often worked upon and solved by processes which are unconscious relatively to the part of the mind which is normally in control of his body. I need only mention in support of this the quite common experience of solving a problem while asleep, or the post-hypnotic calculations which I

[1] *The Mind and its Place in Nature*, p. 550.

spoke of in an earlier chapter. (*b*) That it is extremely probable that telepathy can and does take place between the unconscious parts of living minds. In sittings with Mrs. Leonard and other mediums I have met with clear cases of telepathy between myself and the medium when entranced. But I have noticed that these almost invariably involved past events of which I was not consciously thinking at the time. Thus, the telepathic influence must have been due to mere " traces," or at most to processes of thought going on in my mind without my being aware of them, i.e. processes which were unconscious relatively to the part of my mind which normally controls my body. (*c*) That the unconscious part of the mind is often extremely willing to " oblige " the conscious part by providing " evidence " for what the conscious part wishes to believe.

' Now if these propositions be admitted, it is not unplausible to suggest that the unconscious part of the mind of one of the automatists worked out the problem of providing " satisfactory evidence " for survival and telepathically conveyed the fragmentary messages, which were to constitute the " evidence " to the other automatists. Personally, I strongly suspect the unconscious part of Mrs. Verrall's mind to have accomplished this feat. I am, of course, quite well aware that such a theory goes far beyond anything for which we have direct evidence ; for it seems to imply that the unconscious part of Mrs. Verrall's mind was capable of a kind of selective telepathy conveying so much and no more to one automatist and so much and no more to another automatist. But I must point out, that, if we do not ascribe this power to any embodied mind, we have to ascribe it to the disembodied mind of the supposed communicator. So this much must be assumed in any case if we accept the interpretation which the investigators have put on the Cross-Correspondences. And except on the principle of *Omne ignotum pro magnifico*, I do not see why we should think it more likely that the disembodied mind of a dead man should be able to exercise selective telepathy than that the unconscious part of the embodied mind of a living member of the Society for Psychical Research should be able to do so.' [1]

1. *The Compound Theory.*—First with regard to the Compound Theory, the psychic factor, which was once a constitutive element of the living person, becomes ' temporarily united

[1] *The Mind and its Place in Nature*, pp. 545–6.

with the organism of the entranced medium,' and in so doing produces an evanescent ' mindkin,' which betrays some of the memories and characteristics of the dead person.   As has been previously pointed out, messages ostensibly proceeding from deceased persons are received under three conditions, two belonging to the control type of trance and one belonging to the autonomous type of trance exemplified by Mrs. Willett. The latter sensitive was certainly largely occupied with the cross-correspondences, for which Dr. Broad has suggested an alternative theory ; but many messages from communicators were also received through her when in her particular form of trance, which formed no part of the cross-correspondences, and these naturally fall into the class of mediumistic communications.   Lord Balfour's report on Mrs. Willett,[1] quoted above, supplies many instances of these communications.   The three conditions, then, are : (i) the condition in which messages are given by the medium's habitual control, who passes them on from an ostensible communicator in the background ; (ii) the condition in which the communicator himself directly controls the medium's organism ; (iii) the condition in which the medium retains control of her own organism throughout and passes on messages which have been telepathically received from an ostensible communicator.   This is the case of the Willett trance.   Clearly these conditions are very different from one another.   In (i) and (iii) the ' mindkin,' which is formed by the uniting of the psychic factor with the medium's organism, does not occupy the centre of the field.   In (i) the medium's habitual control is in charge of the medium's organism and in (iii) Mrs. Willett herself is in control of her own body.   The psychic factor in these cases can only unite with the medium's organism in a peripheral manner, since the central positions are occupied. The condition is not at all analagous to that in which the psychic factor is, on this theory, united to its own organism in the case of a living person.   The ' mindkin ' formed in these cases can only be the result of the entry of the psychic factor into the

[1] This Report was not published at the time when Dr. Broad suggested the theories we are now discussing.

fringe of influence of the medium's body. Case (ii), however, is different. Here the communicator is in direct control. The psychic factor has a chance to get into a central position and to unite with the medium's organism in a thoroughgoing manner. One would expect a far more satisfactory ' mindkin ' to be formed in Case (ii) than in Cases (i) and (iii), and therefore a far more convincing communicator to appear. But, in fact, this is not the case. The best and clearest communicators are those manifesting in Mrs. Willett's trance, that is in Case (iii) ; while the communicators in Cases (i) and (ii) are not markedly different from one another.

It might be said that Cases (i) and (ii) are fundamentally the same, the communicator in direct control being really the habitual control in another guise. But the consistent character of the controls renders it scarcely plausible that they sometimes ' act ' the communicator. In any case, Mrs. Willett controls her own organs of writing and speech all the while that a vigorous and life-like communicator is giving his messages. For this reason it appears to me that the Compound Theory of communicators must be rejected.

Professor Dodds urges another point.[1] Communicators often show knowledge of events which have occurred since their death. This knowledge could not have been acquired in the interim by the psychic factor in its presumed state of isolation, since alone it is not a mind. If we say that this knowledge was acquired by the subliminal of the medium, why not say that *all* the knowledge manifested by communicators was similarly acquired and so dispense with the need for a psychic factor ? We must bear in mind, however, that what has to be accounted for is not merely the information given but the existence of a personality manifesting will, intention, and design appropriate to the deceased person. These characteristics must be obtained from some model if the communicating personality is not identical with the deceased person.

But in stressing the compound or synthetic nature of both the normal, living personality and the trance-communicator,

[1] *Proc. S.P.R.*, vol. xlii. p. 155.

Dr. Broad is, I think, stating a valuable truth. The communicator we are dealing with, as he is at the moment of communication, seems to be a temporary synthesis, whether he is in direct control of the medium's organism or not ; and somewhat less a synthetic construct, it seems to me, in the Willett trance, where he is at his best, than in the Leonard type of trance, where he is poorer and more variable. Similarly, the normal, living personality appears to behave more like a synthesis of elements than like a simple conjunction of body and mind ; and it is valuable to regard both as exhibiting the characteristics of a group of related constituents.

2. *The Telepathic Theory.*—To account for the clear evidence of planning shown in the automatic scripts which form the cross-correspondences, Dr. Broad suggested that they might be due to the minds of living members of the group concerned and particularly to the mind of Mrs. Verrall, a view which had, indeed, been discussed a long time previously. He pointed out that there is evidence to show (*a*) that urgent problems tend to work themselves out in the subliminal self ; (*b*) that telepathy takes place between the subconscious portions of living minds ; (*c*) that the unconscious part of the mind is very likely to ' oblige ' the conscious part by producing evidence for what the latter wishes to believe. Hence the plan of cross-correspondences might be an elaborate hoax, planned by the subliminal for the ' benefit ' of the supraliminal.

If this sort of thing is indeed going on, there are certainly circumstances pointing to Mrs. Verrall as the probable ' culprit.' She was, for one thing, the pioneer of the group of automatists and began to produce her script before any of the others ; and a good many, though not all, the cross-correspondences seem to have begun with her. I say *seem* to have begun, because recent research has shown that there are links connecting the whole series of automatisms in complicated chains, making it very difficult to define the exact starting-point of any one of them. As long ago as 1911, Miss Alice Johnson, who discovered that the complex type of cross-correspondence was in being, wrote : [1]

[1] ' Third Report on Mrs. Holland's Script,' *Proc. S.P.R.*, vol. xxv. p. 291.

' The reason why the plan of the cross-correspondences might with some show of plausibility be attributed to Mrs. Verrall was that hints of it appeared in her script (though they passed undetected by herself) some time before there were any discoverable allusions to the subject in the scripts of other automatists. This did not, of course, prove that the plan originated in Mrs. Verrall's mind, because it might have been transmitted to her telepathically by its originator ; but it did tend to show that if any one of the automatists had originated it, she was probably the one. Further, many of the cross-correspondences started in her scripts, so that it might be supposed in these cases that she was the telepathic agent from whom the others derived them.'

This theory confronts us with two main questions : (i) How does the information, if telepathically transmitted, succeed in assuming the organized form in which it appears ? (ii) What is the nature of the personalities who deliver it through the speech or writing of the automatists ?

(i) *The Organization of the Communicated Material.*—It will be remembered that in Chapter XVII a criticism of the *Ear of Dionysius* by Miss Stawell was quoted, in which she suggested that the cross-correspondence given out by Mrs. Willett might have ' leaked ' to her telepathically from the unconscious mind of Mrs. Verrall ; and that Lord Balfour, in reply, asked how ' telepathic leakage ' could be so thoughtful as to arrange all the topics in such an ingenious way. Surely, if it had been due to anything at all analogous to what we understand by ' leakage,' the topics would have emerged in a haphazard manner. It must be remembered that the cross-correspondence emerges in a form which simulates its inception and delivery by a person whom Mrs. Willett herself never knew. How and where does the material assume this dramatic form ? Not the items of information only but the organization of them has to be given to Mrs. Willett, and to other automatists when others are involved. Nothing in the nature of ' leakage ' can do this. There must be something resembling a subliminal committee-meeting amongst the group, and, although we are not able to say, in our ignorance, that such a thing is impossible, it gives a very big stretch indeed to the meaning of ' telepathy.'

If I may quote Mr. Richmond once again, he says on this point that if the material

' proceeds from other incarnate minds, these minds, to produce the observed phenomena, must be able to collaborate telepathically to form an integrated system of memories and characteristics, not only conveying this as a whole to the medium, but conveying, also by telepathy, a characteristic personal drive and manner of self-expression.'

Miss Alice Johnson says almost the same thing in the report above referred to :

' It has never been maintained, then, that the whole scheme of cross-correspondences, and many individual cases among them, were beyond the inventive capacity of Mrs. Verrall's subliminal self. The difficulty lies in *the execution of the plan* ; in the approximate distribution of the parts among the different automatists, who *ex hypothesi* are not in communication with each other except telepathically ; for to carry out such a plan would seem, as already said, to involve much greater powers of telepathy than the experimental evidence so far obtained would warrant us in assuming.' [1]

Very much the same problem, we may note, arises in connexion with the absent-sitter or proxy sittings.

(ii) *The Existential Status of the Communicating Personalities.*—What do we mean when we advance the theory that the communicator is a ' dramatic pose ' of the medium's subliminal ? We know well enough what dramatic posing or acting is. It means *consciously* pretending to be what one is not. That is certainly what acting means on the stage ;. and when Mr. Gatty, in the Whately Carington experiment (Chapter XV) assumed the rôle of ' Oxford-Gatty ' and then of ' Hampshire-Gatty,' he was literally and consciously adopting dramatic poses. But is there any evidence of conscious acting of this sort on the part of any portion of the medium's self in trance-phenomena ? Whether we look at the controls or the communicators, there seems to be very little evidence of intentional posing. They are, I think, quite obviously being

[1] ' Third Report on Mrs. Holland's Script,' *Proc. S.P.R.*, vol. xxv. p. 292.

themselves and struggling with real difficulties. It is inconceivable that, if Feda were really a portion of Mrs. Leonard's
personality, consciously and deliberately playing a part, this
portion could possibly keep up the part without ever for a
moment making a slip and revealing its true nature. Similarly with the communicators, it is inconceivable that they are
somebody, or something, *consciously pretending* to be what
they are not. I do not think that this point needs elaboration.
We must surely admit that the trance-personalities, whatever
they are, are behaving in a perfectly naïve and natural manner
and are simply being their natural selves. They are in no way
comparable with stage characters or with the conscious poses
adopted by Mr. Gatty. In fact, I see next to no evidence of
dramatizing or posing on the part of trance-personalities in the
literal and conscious sense. Does this mean, then, that no
dramatization occurs ? I do not think it does. There is a more
subtle thing. There is such a thing as ' unconscious posing ' :
it frequently happens in ordinary life. If a person is given a
character by his friends for possessing some quality, as, for
example, for being always cool and collected, he will begin
to adopt that pose. It may be a conscious pose at first ; but
soon he believes that his friends are right and that he really *is*
a very cool person, and he comes to act in a cool way towards
events because he really believes coolness to be inherent
in his character. Gradually the conscious pose becomes an
unconscious reaction.

A child may be frightened by some one who is pretending to
be a bear. The child may even have asked the person to
pretend to be a bear ; yet he has a feeling of real fear. This
fear is real, yet, at the same time, he laughs, which shows that,
in some deep but real sense the fear is being acted. In some
such way, it seems to me, trance-personalities may be acting
without knowing it. But posing of this kind involves some
duality of personality. The great puzzle in these cases is :
Who is the acted character and who is the actor ?

If posing of this subtle kind is carried as far as is necessary
to account for the appearance of a good communicator, the
following difficulty arises. This communicator *exists*. It

may be that he exists only as a secondary personality or segregated portion of the medium's self ; but if he possesses in sufficiently full degree individual and characteristic memories, peculiarities of thought, speech and action, moral and mental qualities, has belief in himself and possesses his own will and intention, in what way is he to be distinguished from a real autonomous personality ?   We may call him a ' pseudo-personality ' ; say that he is evanescent and that he is a ' part of the medium's mind.'   Very well, but in spite of all this, for the time being at least, he *is* a real and autonomous person as much as we are ourselves.   And, what do we mean, if all his qualities are independent of those of the medium, by saying that he *is* part of the medium ?   He happens to manifest through the medium's organism, but that, most people would admit, is consistent with autonomy and independence.   It would be difficult to define autonomy on the contrary view. All that we can say is that he is formed of the *substance* of the medium's self ; but what do we mean by such ' substance ' ? How do we define it ?   Lord Haldane mentions that when Berkeley asked what Locke meant by substance, he was told ' that it was a mere name significant of nothing with an assignable meaning.' [1]   In any case, and apart from metaphysical definitions, there the communicator *is*, and it is nonsense to talk about him as a product of ' telepathic leakage.'   If we maintain that he *is* the medium in ' fancy dress,' we shall have to give some satisfactory definition of what we mean by this.   What it amounts to is that we are compelled to admit that, in the case of good communicators such as Myers$_W$ and Gurney$_W$ at any rate, personalities can be literally *duplicated* in the medium's subconscious and the deceased person re-created, possibly in a temporary, but still in a quite genuine fashion.   This is surely a very staggering suggestion.   It was all very well for Sir James Barrie, in *Dear Brutus*, to bring into existence the lovable character of Alice Dearth, and, when the magic wood vanished with the dawn, to send her wailing into oblivion because she was only a ' might-have-been.'   It was a charming exercise of the legitimate right of the creative

[1] *The Pathway to Reality*, p. 23.

artist. But now we are asked to believe that this sort of thing goes on in real life. When the medium's consciousness lapses into a trance-state (or barely that) there occurs the re-creation of the ' once-was.' And if we try to comfort ourselves with the reflection that these trance-communicators are only evanescent beings, appearing when the medium is entranced for a short-lived period and disappearing again as soon as the medium is awake, we receive another shock when we remember that that is just what we are ourselves ! We are our true selves only as long as we keep awake. Every night we go into a kind of psychic storage, just as we are supposing the trance-personalities to do between sittings. It is, indeed, conceivable that beings existing in some other sphere might refuse to regard us as more than psychisms enjoying a semi-spurious and intermittent life. Gurney$_W$ makes a curious remark in one place. He says that, although we might not think it, there is a great deal of scepticism in his world. Can he be suggesting that there exist beings who refuse to take *us* seriously !

It has to be remembered that there is a great difference between the so-called ' splitting ' of a personality in pathological cases and the formation of trance-communicators. The pathological sub-personalities are complementary to one another, but there is nothing of this kind about communicator-personalities, which do not appear to be elements abstracted from the medium's self. In abnormal cases it is very rare to find as many as half a dozen sub-personalities ; but Mrs. Leonard's communicators must run into hundreds. Also they are created instantly on demand, appearing at once with each new sitter. They may certainly improve as time goes on by gaining skill in communicating ; but often the first appearances are as veridical and as striking as any. In the A. V. B. case it will be remembered that, although Miss Radcliffe Hall introduced herself to Mrs. Leonard anonymously and with every precaution to hide her identity, the A. V. B. communicator appeared at once and showed a character consistent with that of the deceased original, which she has maintained ever since. If the communicator is a dramatic pose on the part of some stratum of the medium's personality, what are we to suppose is happening in such a case ? We can suppose that information *about* the deceased is obtained telepathically by the mind of the medium from the sitters or from other living minds which possess it. But that will not account for the appearance of a characteristic communicator-personality. A *model* of the deceased's personality, complete with mental and physical traits, must also have been telepathically acquired by the medium, and some phase of the medium's subconscious mind must have dressed itself up according to the model. What is extraordinary is that this simulation in the case of a good medium is extremely consistent. The medium must be able to create these modelled personalities in unlimited quantities and at a moment's notice, as though out of a kind of psychic plasticine, and store them away when not wanted. And yet, during the time when they are wanted, they seem to be, for all practical purposes, re-creations of the originals.

The telepathic-and-dramatic-pose theory of the communicators becomes, therefore, not so much an *alternative* to the theory of survival as another version of the survival theory of a very weird and bizarre kind. If the friends of a deceased person happen to go to a medium, and if the sittings are successful, then that person regains an intermittent and sporadic life of a parasitic kind, dependent on the medium's states of trance. It is not at all unlike the idea that Alice was part of the Red King's dream. It also demands an extra-sensory perception swelled into a faculty of an amazing kind, bordering on omniscience.

One strong objection to the theory that Mrs. Verrall's subconscious mind was the originator of the cross-correspondences and of the Holland and Willett communicators, is, to my mind, the fact that she died in July 1916, and neither the cross-correspondences nor the communicators ceased with her death. Mrs. Salter (daughter of Mrs. Verrall), who has had long experience of cross-correspondences, says with regard to them : ' What I think may fairly be said . . . is that, taking the scripts as a whole, neither their general trend nor their evidential value was affected to any considerable extent by my mother's death. The idea that she, as a living agent, was at the back of the scripts simply will not work.' Mr. Piddington, who has had more experience than any one else in the matter of cross-correspondences, says, in a letter which he allows me to quote : ' I don't believe for one moment in the theory that Mrs. Verrall, when alive, was the unconscious author of cross-correspondences. . . . My opinion in this matter is not grounded upon my belief that the scripts of the S.P.R. group of automatists are influenced by the discarnate.'

It is necessary, I think, in order to explain the cross-correspondences by the theory of telepathy from the living, to suppose that whatever mind was responsible for planning them was acting on the minds of the automatists producing them *continually* and, not only distributing the constituent parts among members of the group, but also maintaining the supposed pseudo-personalities of the communicators in being, each with his characteristic manner of expression. Gurney, for example, still continued, after Mrs. Verrall's death, in Mrs. Willett's scripts to be his characteristic self, and I do not think it is plausible to suggest that Mrs. Verrall could have created him during her lifetime as a secondary personality of Mrs. Willett's, after which he ' carried on ' by himself.

Of course it may be said that, if Mrs. Verrall was not the author of the cross-correspondences, it may have been some other interested member of the group who is still living. There is no way of testing this suggestion, but certain reasons have been given for thinking that, if any living mind was the source of the cross-correspondences, Mrs. Verrall's was the most likely. I do not know whether it would be plausible to suggest that some sort of group mind among the living might have initiated the plan and carried it out. The suggestion seems to be rather vague. A consideration which weighs very strongly with me personally is, that some of those who stand closest to the evidence and have made the profoundest study of it, extending over some thirty years, say that they have been convinced of the genuineness of the communicators ; and they include some of the most critical and well-balanced minds which have been devoted to the subject.

We will now consider some general arguments which have a bearing on the question of survival.

Antecedent Probability of Survival.—This title opens a vast subject. In a book of this kind it is not possible to deal with the question of survival from the points of view of general philosophy, ethics, or religion, although some remarks on the relation of psychical phenomena to religion will be made in Chapter XXIV. It is only possible here to summarize certain arguments which have been presented in brief form in papers published in the *Proceedings of the Society for Psychical Research*, and which therefore lie within the scope of the present volume.

In 1924, Professor Charles Richet made some observations on the question of survival in a discussion with Sir Oliver Lodge.[1] His main point is given by the following three quotations :

' To what then is the spiritistic hypothesis in opposition ? First of all, very briefly, there is Physiology, that is to say, a very precise science, rich in demonstrations, which have established by innumerable proofs a narrow, rigorous parallelism between intellectual functions—otherwise called memory—and the brain.' ' Consciousness, mobility, sensitiveness, are functions of the nervous system.' . . . ' For myself, without being able to give a firm demonstration (for one cannot prove a negative), I cannot believe that memory can exist without the anatomical and physiological integrity of the brain. Whenever there is no more oxygen, whenever the temperature is either too low or too high, when there are a few drops of atrophine or morphine or chloroform introduced into the blood, whenever the course of cerebral irrigation is stopped— memory alters and disappears. Spiritists cannot deny these facts.'

Richet has dealt, of course, much more fully with these questions in his book, *Traité de Métapsychique*, but these quotations seem to represent the kernel of his argument. I must confess that I find it difficult to believe that he can be seriously putting forward such an argument as this as bearing decisively on the question of whether or not mind can exist

[1] ' Difficulty of Survival from the Scientific Point of View,' *Proc. S.P.R.*, vol. xxxiv. p. 107.

or function apart from a living body. All the ' innumerable proofs ' by which physiologists establish the rigorous parallelism between mental and physiological processes have, obviously, been made under one particular set of conditions. The mental processes going on in the subject under observation have caused certain movements in that subject's organism, which have in turn brought about certain changes in the external world, and these again have affected the observer's organs of sense, and so have been observed. These are the only conditions under which the ' proofs ' of psycho-physical parallelism are possible. But the question is : Do any mental processes go on in the subject without any of these physical accompaniments ? Obviously if they do, the observer, placed as he is, will not be able to observe them ; and the fact that he always fails to observe the unobservable proves nothing either way. The ' innumerable proofs ' count for nothing. We have only Professor Richet's statement that he finds it extremely difficult to believe that memory can exist without the integrity of the brain. As far as the *argument* goes, one might just as well say that because we, who live in England, never meet our cousins who, we have reason to believe, live in Australia, therefore it is extremely unlikely that we should find them in Australia if we went there !

It is interesting to ask whether extra-sensory perception does not, perhaps, provide an instance of mental processes which do go on without physical correlates. May it not be that it is only the final process, in which telepathically acquired knowledge becomes consciously apprehended, that has its physiological counterpart ? Any one who has closely observed a sensitive cannot fail to have been struck by the two different types of awareness which frequently co-exist, (*a*) knowledge or belief which has arisen as the result of sense-perception, or rational inference in the ordinary way, and (*b*) knowledge which has been supernormally acquired. One can see clearly that the two stand in different relations to the motor mechanisms of the brain, and that the latter cannot, or can only with great difficulty, initiate bodily actions. But when the event to which the supernormal knowledge referred is past, the sensitive is able to describe the experience of having had two different beliefs simultaneously present in two departments of the mind. It looks very much as if here there were two kinds of mental events, standing in different relations to the brain. How can we be sure—how does the physiologist know—that the latter kind may not be without physical correlates at all ?

It is interesting to note that Richet was firmly convinced of extra-sensory perception in all its phases, speaking of precognition as an ' undeniable fact.' Yet he regarded the theory of survival as only the revival of a very ancient superstition.

In an interesting paper,[1] Professor E. R. Dodds has dealt with certain *a priori* arguments concerning survival. A good deal of this paper is devoted to a discussion of survivalist and anti-survivalist interpretations of the psychical evidence. But the earlier part of it deals with antecedent arguments against survival of a more general kind. Professor Dodds puts forward his views as representative of a member of the class of ' educated people who are neither scientists nor professional philosophers,' and says that his arguments are only applicable to those who share the general framework of his presuppositions.

' The presuppositions I have referred to,' he says, ' are two in number. The first is that our sole means of reaching a conclusion on this question consist of observation and experiment together with the exercise of reason. This excludes the view that we have divine authority for the belief in survival. A complete statement of the case against survival would have to take account of this view, and investigate its claim to historical truth. I do not share the curious opinion that such investigation is bad form, nor the alternative opinion that it has been rendered unnecessary by the conclusion of a treaty of peace between science in the person of Professor Jeans and religion in the person of Bishop Barnes. But it is evident that to attempt in the present paper any statement of my reasons for rejecting this view would carry the discussion too far from the immediate question at issue.

' My second presupposition is that the validity of our apparent experience of mind and matter as two distinct modes of reality is accepted as a working hypothesis on the empirical level, without

---

[1] ' Why I do not Believe in Survival,' *Proc. S.P.R.*, vol. xlii. pp. 147 ff.

excluding the possibility that either may prove in the last analysis to be a mere appearance of the other. Both idealism (or mentalism) and materialism seem to me to be *possible* ways of interpreting our experience ; neither seems to be *required*.'

Leaving on one side the metaphysical and ethical arguments which Professor Dodds discusses, and considering only antecedent arguments of a general kind, the first is one which arises out of the metaphysical argument :

'. . . If we accept the metaphysical argument as a valid proof of survival, we must accept it also as a valid proof of pre-existence. This for me is unfortunate. For the doctrine of pre-existence is open to several objections which I do not know how to meet. Until these have been resolved for me, I feel constrained to reject the theory of pre-existence, and with it the metaphysical argument for survival.'

The objections to pre-existence are given as follows :

' (*a*) If the doctrine means anything, it means that in addition to the recognized factors of heredity and environment a third, presumably far stronger factor, is operative in the formation of human character : is it not strange that no certain trace of the activity of this factor has been detected by psychologists ? (*b*) It means, again, that the new-born infant possesses, or rather is, a mature and experienced mind : is it not strange that all the manifestations of that mind are precisely what we should expect them to be if it were neither mature nor experienced but were, in fact, what it appears to be, an infant mind in an infant body ? (*c*) The doctrine involves the assumption of an act of incarnation whose mechanism it is exceedingly difficult to picture and which lacks even the remotest analogue in our biological knowledge.'

These arguments all, it seems to me, proceed on the assumption that human personality is such that the *whole* of it shows on the surface. But psychology has shown that this is not the case. Its method of analysis could not have been developed and have become successful unless a large region of the self had existed hidden from view. And now it appears that psycho-analysis enters only one small part of the hidden region : the facts discussed in the present volume show that further vistas open on every hand the farther we push our inquiry.   Human individuality, like everything else in our present world, *appears* to present all its characteristics openly to view.   But the moment we look closer, we find this appearance to be delusive.   Our present personalities look uncommonly like specialized constructs abstracted from larger modes of being, and I am not at all convinced that, if a preexisting or surviving element were there behind the scenes, it would show itself in such an abstraction or proclaim its character.   And, as far as the third argument goes, we have already seen that there is good reason for believing that neither biological nor any other kind of scientific knowledge ever gets to the bottom of anything ; owing to the nature of things, it is prevented from doing so *in principle*.

Professor Dodds puts forward two further considerations which, he says, renders survival improbable.   (i) The first is the argument from silence.   He says :

' All spiritualists believe that the dead have both the will and the means to communicate with the living, either by controlling the hand or vocal organs of the medium or by influencing her mind telepathically.'

He goes on to mention other supposed means of communication, and then continues :

' Now if the dead are really endowed with powers so varied and so remarkable ; and if it is true as they themselves tell us, that they are much occupied with the problem of comforting and assisting their surviving relatives ; on these assumptions is it not a matter for surprise that they refrained so long from exercising their powers and making their existence known ?   During two and a half millenia of which we have fairly full written records—say from 650 B.C. to 1850—they failed so far as I know to produce satisfactory experimental evidence of their identity.   Why ? '

Why ?   This sounds a very sensible argument so long as one allows it to filter into one's mind without thinking about it. But the moment one *does* think about it the obvious rejoinder occurs that it takes two to make a conversation. The quality of mediumistic communications depends upon the conditions supplied at this end. That is undoubtedly true : all the experimental work bears it out. The best communications have always been obtained when the most intelligent investigators were working with the highest type of medium. The clear, sane, and intelligent Willett communicators resulted from the formation of a ' cell ' of highly intelligent workers, co-operating with a sensitive of very high quality, which made possible the development of the autonomous trance. The reason why the dead (supposing that they are the dead) refrained so long from making their existence known is, therefore, as easy to explain as the fact that railway trains refrain from going to places where there is no railway.

(ii) The second argument runs as follows :

' The two groups of pre-nineteenth century mediums about whom we have most information, the κάτοχοι of the late Greco-Roman period, and the witches of the sixteenth and seventeenth centuries, while performing a number of the feats performed by modern mediums perversely attributed them in the one case to the agency of non-human gods or demons, in the other to the agency of the devil. Once again, why ? A satisfactory answer may one day be forthcoming ; but until it is, I cannot but feel some doubt about the correctness of the spiritualist interpretation of the contemporary phenomena.'

There is plenty of evidence to-day pointing to the view that trance-personalities are sometimes auto-suggested secondaries of the medium's and are possibly always that to some extent. We have been through that evidence and have found that it does not account for the whole of the phenomena, which are not so simply explained. The evidence points to a compound type of communicator. The poorer the mediumship, the more the auto-suggested element is to the fore, and these cases are, of course, always in the majority. Anything in the nature of an auto-suggested secondary personality of the medium's would be imbued with the beliefs current in the country and age in which the medium lived. The question,

21

once more, is not merely what is taking place on the surface, but also what is happening in the background.

(iii) The third argument is the fact of the biological cycle of life, from birth to old age and death.

' Any one who has lived much in the society of the aged,' says Professor Dodds, ' and has observed them closely, will I think agree, whatever interpretation they may put upon the facts, that not only the human organism but the human mind, or that portion of it which expresses itself in thought, feeling, and action, does appear to grow old.   I am thinking here not merely of the grosser effects of time, those which a physician would classify as symptoms of senile decay ; but also the subtler psychological changes which come with advancing years, the gradually increasing imperviousness to new ideas, the gradually diminishing response to emotional stimuli, above all, the growing sense of finality, of fulfilment, of a destiny accomplished and accepted—in a word, the progressive encroachment upon the will to live of a new will to cease from living.'

Professor Dodds suggests two possible answers to these observed facts as telling against the survival of the self.   (a) The apparent ageing of the mind may, in reality, be due to the toxins secreted by the ageing organism, or (b) there may be a remoter, ageless self—a noumenal self—which does not die because it does not grow old.   His counter-answer to (a) is that, if the mind is really so much under the influence of the body, it is scarcely likely that it will survive it ; and to (b) that anything so remote as a noumenal self would be ' an unlikely carrier for the collection of small personal reminiscences which are the stock-in-trade of the average ' communicator.'

Arguments of type (iii) well illustrate the contention which it has been one of the main aims of this book to develop, namely, that, when regarding psychical matters, we fail to get our minds away from the outlook in which they are set by reason of their adaptation to the world in which we live.   The outlook underlying this kind of argument assumes that, if there is another life than this, it must be *this* life projected into another sphere. Time (and time-like processes) are assumed to go on in it as they do here.   The personal complex, after its break-up or readjustment, is nevertheless supposed to be, somehow, back again as it was before. These are the assumptions on which the argument depends. An old person, who says that he is tired and wishes to expire, really means that he (i.e. the personality he now is) does not want to go on growing any older, or even to remain, in some way, fixed at his present age. He projects the conditions of his present life into any imaginable other life. But we already know that the biological life-cycle is a thing belonging to this present world : no one expects it to be prolonged into any other ; nor is it at all certain that our familiar time need be taken out of this world for it to be prolonged in. That would be to assume that we know all the conditions in which life is possible. The problem is : What happens to the complicated synthesis of psychic elements which form our present personalities at death ? All we can say is that something very like entry into another world (albeit an unstable and self-generated world) does occur in states of ecstasy and in the higher forms of trance, even although the internal rearrangement of the personality is not very profound, and although its condition is unstable. What would happen if these states of trance (which are really incipient phases in a dissociation which leads towards death) were carried so far that they passed the elastic power of recovery ? The many who agree with Professor Dodds would, I suppose, say that instantly all the constituents of the personality would vanish and that it would disappear as a whole, like a soap-bubble which has been blown too big. I do not think myself that this is what the facts point to. For one thing, this view places the personality too literally *within* a world which must, on any count, be to some extent its own world of appearance. It is too naïve—too childishly trusting of common-sense views of nature and time. It seems far more likely that a re-synthesis of the elements of the personality would take place, and that it would reach a new state of stability; and this, on the present view, would be accompanied by some kind of stable world of appearance, which would be exactly adjusted to it. The arguments on which Professor Dodds bases the antecedent improbability of survival seem to me to rest on a misapprehension of the actual situation ; and meanwhile the empirical evidence of psychical research points towards some kind of transcendence or independence, even here and now, of the essential self over its environment.

It is necessary now to make a digression, in this compressed account of the psychical field, in order to refer very briefly to certain phenomena which lie technically within the field of psychical research, though outside the main field of interest comprising the mental phenomena. After that we shall glance at the relation of our subject to Spiritualism, and shall then touch on certain aspects of its relation to Religion before finally summing up.

Chapter XXII

THE PHYSICAL TYPE OF MEDIUMSHIP

THE PHYSICAL PHENOMENA OF MEDIUMSHIP.—As is well known, in the presence of a certain type of trance-medium, various kinds of physical phenomena are alleged to occur, brought about by supernormal means. These phenomena include rappings, movements of objects without apparent contact, the appearance of lights and shadowy forms, touches coming from nowhere, cold breezes and so forth. If they happen, these things possess an undoubted interest, for they indicate that the physiology of the living organism is far from exhaustively understood, and that here, as in the mental sphere, there is a great deal going on behind the scenes. Unfortunately the existence of these things is even harder to establish than that of the mental phenomena, for they lie within the province of the conjurer and the charlatan, and, unless one has personally attended all the relevant sittings and is, in addition, conversant with the conjurer's art, it is very difficult to arrive at any definite conclusion. For this reason, little space has been devoted to this branch of the subject in the present volume. The verdict of those who have made a careful study of it is by no means unanimous ; the evidence is conflicting, and the honesty of most of the mediums so far tested is at least doubtful.

It might naturally be thought that there should be little difficulty in establishing the occurrence of a physical event with the aid of scientific method and apparatus, but the fact is that the investigators are not given a free hand in the control of the conditions. If they were, they would arrange for the same phenomenon to be repeated over and over again, while they eliminated a fresh possibility on each occasion. But the medium, or the medium's control, either does not or cannot permit this, and produces instead a continual stream of fresh phenomena, making it very difficult for investigators to eliminate all possibility of fraud. Most physical mediums have either been discovered in fraud at one time or another, or else the conditions have been strongly suggestive of it. It must not, however, be thought that this is an adequate reason for discarding the medium or for assuming that none of his or her phenomena can be genuine, since it is quite possible that genuine and fraudulent phenomena may be mixed. The system by which mediums are paid by the sitting tends to encourage fraud. If it were the case that genuine phenomena existed but were sporadic and unreliable, the medium would be greatly tempted to produce spurious phenomena at times when the genuine failed, in order to sustain the interest of the sitters and provide a *quid pro quo*. And this, very possibly, is what often occurs.

In any case, judgement on the results of sittings for physical phenomena has to be left very much to the sitters. The third party who reads the records can do little in the way of checking this judgement, or of forming an independent judgement of his own, since he has to rely on the accuracy of the sitter's observations for all the details.

The following is a *résumé* of a few points of interest taken from the *séances* of a few of the best known physical mediums.

Cases of Physical Mediumship—D. D. Home.[1]—The series of sittings recounted by the Earl of Dunraven with this celebrated nineteenth-century medium, took place between 1867 and 1869, and there were present on different occasions fifty different witnesses. The phenomena included raps, the playing of an accordion, apparently without contact, the movement of objects, the fire-test or holding of hot coals in the hand, the appearance of lights and luminous objects and of hands and forms, the apparent elongation of Home on several occasions, and also his levitation. These culminated on one occasion in the alleged passage of Home through the air, out of one window and in at another. The record of this incident says : ' We heard Home

---

[1] See ' Experiences in Spiritualism with D. D. Home,' by the Earl of Dunraven (*Proc. S.P.R.*, vol. xxxv. pp. 1–284).

go into the next room, heard the window thrown up, and presently Home appeared standing upright outside our window ; he opened the window and walked in quite coolly.'[1] Home then gave the writer a demonstration of how he had gone out of the window, which it is stated ' was not raised a foot.' The writer says : ' . . . he told me to stand a little distance off ; he then went through the open space, head first, quite rapidly, his body being nearly horizontal and apparently rigid. He came in again, feet foremost, and we returned to the other room. It was so dark I could not see clearly how he was supported out-side. He did not appear to grasp, or rest upon, the balustrade, but rather to be swung out and in.'[1]

There are not, in these old cases, the safeguards or the minuteness of record used in the investigation of these matters nowadays. The case of D. D. Home has been severely criticized, and it is difficult for those who can only read the record to form an opinion about them.

Eusapia Palladino.—This Italian medium attracted a great deal of attention about the beginning of the century. She was an uneducated peasant woman, whose phenomena were brought to the notice of Professor Lombroso. He experimented with her in 1890, and was favourably impressed. A group of prominent scientists, including Schiaparelli the astronomer and Richet the French physiologist, took up her case in 1892 and witnessed levitations of the table in full light, which they were convinced could not have been produced by trickery. Sir Oliver Lodge and Myers sat with her in 1894, both giving a favourable report, which, however, was criticized by Dr. Hodgson, on the ground that the control of the medium's hands had been inadequate. In 1895, Eusapia gave a series of twenty-one sittings at Cambridge. These showed that certain methods of trickery, already suspected, were resorted to when opportunity was given, particularly the substitution of hands or feet in the dark. Many sittings were held on the Continent, and the case accumulated a large literature, Professor Morselli, of Genoa, contributing a work in two volumes, in which the genuineness of the phenomena were upheld.

[1] *Proc. S.P.R.*, vol. xxxv. p. 156.

In 1908 the English Society for Psychical Research sent out three investigators to sit with Eusapia at Naples. These were Mr. Hereward Carrington, Mr. W. W. Baggally, and the late Hon. Everard Fielding, the two former being amateur experts in the art of conjuring. They issued their report in 1909.[1] They arranged a room in their hotel with great care, providing the usual ' cabinet,' made by hanging black curtains across the corner of the room, behind which was placed a small table bearing some musical toys. A group of variable electric lights was hung overhead, and the medium was controlled by one investigator on each side of her, whose foot rested on or under her foot while each held one of her hands. Substitution, when practised by the medium, was done by moving the hand or foot restlessly about, until, for a moment, it was freed from control, and then substituting a single hand or foot for both the controllers to touch. In front of the medium, and end on to her, stood a light table.

The phenomena observed during the eleven sittings of this series included levitations of the table, raps and noises, movements of the curtain, bulgings of the medium's dress, touches, the appearance of objects like hands and heads from the cabinet, the plucking of a guitar-string in the cabinet, lights, etc. In most cases there was a greater or less degree of light from the arrangement of electric lamps overhead. Cool breezes were sometimes felt.

All the investigators agreed that some of the phenomena, at least, which they had witnessed were genuine, and that some of the best had occurred when the control was strictest.

Meanwhile, an unfavourable report of the medium had been issued by an American investigator, and a further series of five sittings was held with Eusapia to confirm one or other of these two conclusions. This led to a declaration by the sitters that almost all the phenomena in this series were fraudulent. In this unsatisfactory state the case of Eusapia Palladino closed.

[1] ' Report on Sittings with Eusapia Palladino,' *Proc. S.P.R.*, vol. xxiii. p. 309.

The Crawford Experiments.[1]—In 1918, and subsequently, experiments were carried out by Dr. W. J. Crawford, Lecturer in Mechanical Engineering at the Municipal Technical Institute, Belfast, with a physical medium, Miss Kathleen Goligher. There was a circle, consisting of Miss Goligher and the six other members of her family, and the experiments were concentrated for the most part on the investigation of levitations of the table. Different tables were used, varying in weight from about three to eleven pounds, and the levitations were sufficiently prolonged and frequent for measurements to be made on the forces of reaction acting on the medium. The latter was placed on a weighing machine, and it was verified that when the table left the floor the medium's weight increased by approximately the weight of the table. This fact incidentally negatives the possibility that the other members of the circle might have been lifting the table. A red light of varying intensity was used, and, on at any rate one occasion, the experimenter says : ' I put my arm right underneath the table from end to end near the floor, moving it gently to and fro, but I experienced, as before, no sense of pressure anywhere.'[2] It is hard to believe, under these circumstances, that Dr. Crawford would not have noticed if the medium had been lifting the table with her leg. His own theory was that a cantilever, composed of some kind of invisible substance emanating from the medium's body, was raising the table. He says that occasionally he felt, immediately below the under surface of the table,

' something that appears to be matter. It has a cold, clammy, reptilian feeling, impossible adequately to describe in words, but which, once felt, the experimenter always recognizes again. . . . The matter under the table felt quite still and at rest, and, in fact, when I moved my hand to and fro amongst it, the table soon dropped showing that it was essential to levitation. Indeed, the operators were always very chary about letting me work in amongst it, the only thing in that connexion they did not object

[1] See W. J. Crawford, *The Reality of Psychic Phenomena, Experiments in Psychical Science*, and *The Psychic Structures in the Goligher Circle*.
[2] *The Reality of Psychic Phenomena*, p. 86.

to greatly being the moving of a *thin* rod across the space occupied by it.' [1]

A little further on he says :

' During the levitation of the table I have never interrupted the line of stress from medium to table with my hand, but I have placed a delicate pressure-recording apparatus in that line, with the result that it was shown that there was mechanical pressure close to the body of the medium . . . acting outwards from her to the levitated table ; and furthermore, the placing of the apparatus in the stress-line caused the table to drop.'

These statements are decidedly interesting. If there was an invisible substance, reaching from the medium's body to the under surface of the table, capable of supporting ten or more pounds' weight, how could it have transmitted the mechanical stress and yet be insubstantial enough to admit of a thin rod being moved across the space occupied by it ? If the substance is so insubstantial as to admit freely of motion *across* and through it, can it be substantial enough to transmit force *along* it at the same time ? The two properties seem to be physically inconsistent with one another. Looking more closely at Crawford's observations, however, I am not sure that we are bound to assume these inconsistent properties. He remarks that, from his observations, the substance has varying degrees of density and keeps on changing its nature. He says it only reaches its maximum force on the table five or six seconds after it begins to act, and that the rigidity of the rod producing raps varies with the strength of the red light, the raps becoming softish when the light is too bright. It might be that in immediate contact with ordinary matter the substance softens, so that when a *thin* rod (the word ' thin ' is underlined) is passed through it, the substance softens ahead of the rod and rigidifies again behind it. Thus a rigid column of the substance, capable of supporting a weight, might allow the rod to pass through it and yet remain intact. There is a well-known experiment in physics analogous to this. If a block of ice be placed on two supports and a wire hung across it with a weight at each end,

[1] *The Reality of Psychic Phenomena*, pp. 224–5.

the wire will cut its way right through the ice, while the block remains all the time strong and solid. The ice melts under the wire, owing to the pressure, and freezes again above it. If we imagine that something of this kind happens when the rod is passed through this ' ectoplasmic ' substance, only very much more quickly, we shall have an explanation of the phenomenon. It is not easy to see otherwise why stress is laid on a *thin* rod. Perhaps if the rod were moved quickly, it would meet with resistance. Light seemed to have a disintegrating effect on the substance, and yet in later experiments, flash-light photographs were obtained of it.

After Dr. Crawford's death in 1920, Dr. E. E. Fournier d'Albe made an investigation of Miss Goligher and stated that he found evidence of fraud : and this threw doubt on Crawford's results. In particular, photographs obtained of what seemed to be the substance extruded by the medium, showed graining like that of muslin, which seemed a suspicious circumstance. But the doubt thrown by Fournier d'Albe was of rather a vague kind, and it does not appear that Fournier d'Albe gave any convincing alternative explanations of Dr. Crawford's detailed observations.

The Schneider Brothers.—Willi and Rudi Schneider were the sons of an Austrian printer, and both possessed remarkable powers of physical mediumship. Willi, the elder, developed them first and came under the patronage of Baron von Schrenck Notzing, first attaining notoriety as a medium in 1922. The phenomena were of the same general character as those of Eusapia Palladino and, indeed, of most physical mediums ; but the technique of controlling the subject had by this time improved. The medium was specially examined prior to a sitting, sewn up in a tight garment, with luminous bracelets and luminous pins affixed to it at various points, so that movements could be checked in the dark, while three observers controlled his hands and feet. Positive results are said to have been obtained with him.

Meanwhile, the brother, Rudi, was coming to the fore, and was holding sittings with various people, though under some suspicion of fraud. In 1929 and 1930, Mr. Harry Price, in his own laboratory, had a series of sittings with Rudi, using a special chair, which recorded the movements of the medium by means of indicator-lights worked by a series of special contacts. The usual phenomena were repeated, and were witnessed by several prominent men of science. They seemed to be convincing at the time ; but subsequent allegations of fraud again clouded the issue.

The most interesting experiments were those conducted by Dr. Eugène Osty,[1] Director of the Institut Métapsychique International of Paris in 1930. They consisted of a long series of 77 sittings, conducted in an extremely scientific and thorough manner. Dr. Osty felt that physical phenomena could not become really interesting until arrangements had been made to record the effects photographically and auto-matically, and so to eliminate reliance on human observations. Accordingly, in addition to the usual hand-and-foot control, luminous patches, etc., he employed a beam of infra-red light as a detector. There was already reason to suppose that the ' ectoplasmic ' substance extruded from the medium when in trance, though invisible in ordinary light, was to some extent opaque to the infra-red. The arrangement of the infra-red beam was similar to that used for burglar-alarms. The beam was focused on a photo-electric cell, placed at a certain distance from it. When interrupted by an opaque body, its intensity diminished or it was completely obscured, the resistance of the cell changed, altering the current, which produced the ringing of an alarm-bell.

Dr. Osty arranged not merely for the interruption to ring a bell. There was also a continuous record of the state of the beam made by a reflecting galvanometer, recording on a moving band of photographic paper. Actually, two infra-red beams were employed, so that it could be inferred from which direction the obscuring body was approaching. On the same strip as the record of the state of the beam, the rate of breathing of the medium was recorded by means of a Marey drum attached to the medium's chest and connected to the recording instrument by a long rubber tube. Along the edge of the record a chrono-

[1] See *La Revue Métapsychique* for 1932.

meter marked the time in seconds. All the apparatus was firmly fixed to a table which was separated from the medium by a fine-mesh screen. Not only were the movements of the instruments continuously recorded on the photographic strip, but they could be, and were, in addition watched all the time either by Dr. Osty or his son. A very important addition to all this was the following device. As soon as anything obscured the infra-red beam, a shutter was automatically opened which flooded the laboratory with ultra-violet light for a tenth of a second, and simultaneously exposed a camera provided with a quartz lens. This took a complete picture of the scene, showing the position of every one in the room at the moment when the beam was being obscured.

What the photographs disclosed was that an *invisible* substance was setting off the apparatus. An interesting point about it was that the infra-red beam was *partially*, but not wholly interrupted, as it would have been if an arm or other physical object had been interposed in it. Moreover, the absorption varied rhythmically, as if the interposed substance were continually changing its density.

One startling phenomenon was the ' hyperpnoea,' or very rapid breathing, of the medium when in trance. The rate of breathing rose from the normal of 15 per minute before trance to something between 120 and 300 per minute, and was usually over 200 throughout the duration of the trance. Nor did this have any injurious effect on the medium, whose pulse and arterial tension were normal at the end. But a very remarkable fact was discovered in connexion with this rapid breathing. By using a quick-period galvanometer or oscillograph to record the fluctuations of absorption of the infra-red beam, it was discovered that the strength of this beam was pulsating in synchronism with Rudi's breathing. The galvanometer oscillated twice for each respiratory cycle, thus corresponding with the two muscular efforts of inspiration and expiration. It was further observed that the major obscurations of the beam seemed to be under the control of Rudi's will, or rather of the will of the trance-control. They usually occurred when he said they were going to.

The radiation used for the beam had a wave-length of about 1 μ, that is to say one-thousandth of a millimeter.

An attempt made by the Society for Psychical Research to repeat these experiments in London in 1933–4, yielded very little result ; but there is some reason to suppose that Rudi's powers were then on the wane.

Other Physical Mediums—There have, of course, been many other physical mediums, including ' Eva C ' ; George Valiantine, a celebrated ' direct-voice ' medium ; Mrs. Crandon, an American medium famous for the production of thumb-prints in paraffin-wax ; and so on ; but little is to be gained by giving abbreviated accounts of these. In all cases it is upon a study of *details* that judgement must depend, and details can only be studied by reading the first-hand accounts of those who were present at the sittings. It is to these accounts, therefore, that the reader is referred.

Reliability of Testimony.—It has been suggested that physical mediums do not in reality produce objective pheno-mena, but that they hallucinate their audience after the manner of a hypnotist. It may be that some witnesses suffer minor hallucinations, but this can scarcely be the explanation of the phenomena as a whole. In many cases the camera has shown that, whether fraudulently produced or not, something objective is there. But an interesting experiment was made by the Society for Psychical Research in 1928, and again in 1931,[1] to test the reliability of the observations made by those present at a *séance*. The latter of these experiments was the most elaborate and on the largest scale. A dummy *séance* was held in a room arranged exactly as for a real one, the medium being represented by a member of the Society who sat on a chair with the usual curtained ' cabinet ' behind her, and a table of musical toys, etc., in front. Forty-two volunteer sitters occupied the seats and observed what took place, while the Research Officer raised and lowered the lights, played the gramophone at intervals, walked to the door in response to a knock from outside, opened it, went out and returned, putting

[1] ' The Psychology of Testimony in Relation to Paraphysical Phenomena,' by Theodore Besterman (*Proc. S.P.R.*, vol. xl. pp. 365 ff.).

a white card in his pocket as he did so, while simultaneously the ' medium ' moved a bell from one end of the table to the other. Other detailed movements took place, including a pretence flash-light photograph, during which sitters were expected to observe the scene. After the *séance*, the sitters adjourned to answer test-papers on what they had seen and to receive marks for their answers as in an examination. The maximum marks, obtained by the best sitter, were 61 per cent. of the possible total ; the lowest 5·9 per cent., and the average for all was 33·9 per cent. There were some remarkable omissions in the testimony, 11 sitters giving no account of the ' knock-on-the-door ' incident, 5 not mentioning the fact that Mr. Besterman went to the door, and 13 saying nothing about the opening of the door, and 21 failing to mention that he went out of it. Only 4 reported the important fact that he put something in his pocket on returning. In answer to what object the medium had touched early in the sitting, 21 sitters gave wrong or no replies. It was the bell, which had been moved in good light from one end of the table to the other. So the experiment showed to what a large extent the observation and memory of a sitter at a *séance* of this kind is untrustworthy. But the importance of this is not so great now as it was formerly, since it is becoming increasingly evident that the solution of the problem of physical mediumship must depend on the use of automatic recording apparatus.

Although there is a great deal of undoubted fraud mingled with these physical phenomena, and in spite of the fact that many carefully carried out experiments have ended inconclusively, it is hard to doubt such results as those of Dr. Eugène Osty, mentioned above. These make it appear as if there must be some emanation of a quasi-physical kind, which issues from the organisms of the mediums when in trance, obeys their volition and absorbs certain kinds of radiation. This fact, if confirmed, should be of great interest to physiologists. Looking at the subject from a general point of view, it is perhaps, also, unlikely that identically the same kind of phenomena should have been repeated over and over again in many different countries, unless there had been a nucleus of supernormal fact for the accretion of fraud to grow upon.

In the next chapter we will speak of the relation of the scientific branch of the subject, with which, in this volume, we are dealing, to the general domain of occultism out of which it has grown.

Chapter XXIII

PSYCHICAL RESEARCH AND SPIRITUALISM

THE DOMAIN OF THE OCCULT.—Perhaps some reader who has followed me so far will say : This is all very well, but you have picked out the plums of sense and ignored the mass of super-stition and the absurdities which you know abound in the main body of this subject. The ' Occult,' as a whole, is a farrago of nonsense. Even if this were true, I should reply that it is the plums of sense which count, and that their evidence is in no wise invalidated by seas of spurious evidence. A nebulous region of the ' occult,' out of which psychical research has grown, nevertheless exists.

The belief in occultism and magic is as old as mankind ; primitive man, as evidenced in the caves of the Auvergne and elsewhere, drew animals on the walls for purposes of magic. Magic blended with early religious cults ; and in classical times there was Delphic Apollo, the Dionysiac frenzy ; and terrifying beliefs in occult powers were massed behind the religions of antiquity. Dr. Edwyn Bevan [1] speaks of :

' the greatest collection of ostensibly authentic ghost-stories which has come down to us in ancient literature, the stories in the *Dialogues* of St. Gregory the Great—Gregory I in the roll of the Popes, whose pontificate goes from A.D. 590–604. Many of the stories concern the appearances of persons after their death, who announce that they are suffering purgatorial pains or that they have been relieved by the prayers of the faithful and Masses said on their behalf. . . . It is interesting to find an explanation offered why the dead are now appearing in such numbers, a thing which had been unknown before. The explanation is that the present world is so near its end. The spirit-world, so soon to break upon mankind in overwhelming

[1] *Sibyls and Seers*, p. 95.

manifestation, is already shimmering through. . . . Thirteen hundred years ago ! '

As the author adds :

' One thing which these stories make quite plain, when we compare them with the teachings attributed to departed spirits in our own time, is that, whether there is or is not a nucleus of reality in such communication, they largely take their shape from the ideas already current in the minds of the recipients.'

There seem to be two possible explanations of this fact.

Either the communications come entirely through secondary personalities of the mediums or sensitives concerned, which act as a reflector of current ideas ; or else the communicators are genuine and have in some way, in their new state of existence, created a world of vivid perceptions in conformity with the beliefs which imbued them at the time of their death. They would, then, really seem to themselves to be undergoing the experiences which they describe. A similar thing happens with modern trance-communications ; communicators describe themselves as living the kind of life which filled their thoughts when they died. Neither explanation, however, seems to fit very well with the whole of the evidence ; and perhaps the truth is more likely to consist in a combination of both. On the one hand, the entranced medium, constructing plastic psychological organizations, which act easily as vehicles for current types of thought. On the other, the essence of the communicator ' descending into generation ' and compounding itself in some way with these vehicles, thus producing a kind of abstracted phase of itself by being drawn into the sphere of terrestial thought and memories. Thus the communicators, *as such*, would be temporary constructions only, though including the principle of selfhood of the genuine communicator. In any case, communications through mediums and sensitives never appear to have transcended the climate of terrestial thought which dominated the age in which they occurred. It is difficult to see how, with the means at their disposal, they could have done so ; nor is there evidence to show that human beings would have understood them if they had.

An interesting sentence quoted by Dr. Bevan from Cicero reads like an ancient version of the ' Angels of Mons.' ' Often have Fauns been heard speaking in battles, and in troublous times voices are said to have come forth from the unseen and to have proved true.' Was there in the Daimon, a recognition of something akin to Myers' Subliminal Self ? The author, for instance, speaks of the *daimonion* of Socrates, ' not the diminutive of *daimon*, but the neuter of *daimoninos*, a ' divine something.' There was the Bath-qol of the Hebrews, not the voice of God which came to the prophets, but, literally, the ' daughter of the voice.'

Incidentally, we see, much as to-day, that side by side with continuous beliefs in the occult, there was as far back as Plato's time an attitude of toleration and respect for authoritative religious orthodoxy among intellectual non-adherents when it had been separated from the ' occult,' and received the respectability of custom. This would seem to be indicated by a sentence quoted from Plato's *Laws* ; ' . . . no sensible man will try to disturb the directions delivered from Delphi or Dodona or Ammon or the way marked out by some ancient utterance or other. . .' Interesting, too, is the following indication of the recognition of precognition : ' In slumber the eye of the soul waxes bright, but in daytime man's doom goes unforseen.' [1]

In mediaeval times, astrology and witchcraft carried on the tradition of the occult, until at last it began to assume a new aspect with the coming of the scientific age. With Mesmer, a ' magnetic fluid,' began to be talked about. Andrew Jackson Davis in 1847, and the Fox Sisters in 1848, mark the beginning of modern spiritualism in America, and thereafter followed the epoch of ' Mr. Sludge, the medium ' ; spiritualism became a quasi-religious cult. The reaction of the scientists towards the whole of this movement was one of supreme contempt. The first serious attack on the ' occult ' by rigorously scientific methods was made when the Society for Psychical Research was formed in 1882 by a group of Cambridge men, of whom Frederick Myers and Edmund Gurney were the leading

[1] Æschylus, *Eumenides*, 104–5.

spirits, and the protagonist in the face of a hostile world was Professor Henry Sidgwick. It met with intense opposition. To the temper of the time it seemed an absurdity to regard psychical phenomena as a fit subject for serious or scientific investigation. But the rise of the medical branch of psychology due to the work of Freud, Jung, and Adler, has assisted in more recent times in modifying somewhat the materialistic outlook, since it fostered a view of mind in its various manifestations as something existing in its own right, and not to be dealt with always as an epiphenomenon or derivative of matter. Also the Hormic idea and Holistic principles have tended to carry certain schools of psychologists further away from a psychology of the old associationism, modelled too strictly on physics.

The climate of opinion has thus changed towards the whole group of phenomena with which psychical research is concerned, but the need for scientific caution has in no wise diminished. Throughout the spiritualistic movement there is widespread fraud and credulity—a public which allows itself to be pathetically duped by a particularly repulsive type of parasite. A good living can be made by producing faked phenomena, and with very little risk. Fraudulent mediums have been shown up again and again, caught red-handed in their trickery, yet they have only had to make some paltry excuse, and a group of believers rallies round them again and enables them to carry on their trade as before. Meanwhile, outside the small circle of rigorously scientific work, it is probably true to say that vagueness, ambiguity, and banality characterize psychic manifestations as a whole, and to this is usually added a religious flavour and more than a dash of sentiment. As Professor Broad has put it, the average spiritualistic seance is ' very much like what I believe is called a " Pleasant Sunday Afternoon " at a Non-conformist Chapel, enlivened by occasional bump-suppers.' [1] It is little wonder, then, if thinking people, reviewing the ' occult ' movement as a whole, are repelled by it ; it undoubtedly creates a strong impulse to reject the whole subject and to return to sanity

[1] *The Mind and its Place in Nature*, p. 518.

and common sense. Probably the majority of people are wise if they acquiesce in these feelings. It is Nature's recall to the world for which she has fitted them and in which it is their business to live. Psychical research demands a very robust faculty of criticism and a strong self-control, and, unless these qualities are brought to it, it is better left alone. But for scientists and philosophers and for all those who have graduated in that course of stern discipline which makes people capable of thinking for themselves, the case is different. To reject specific phenomena because the atmosphere in which they are set is repellent, is far from a scientific attitude and betrays a woeful lack of discrimination. What should we think of physiologists and surgeons who abandoned their subject on the ground that it was ' nasty ' ? The reason why thinking and scientific people reject psychical phenomena is not because they lack the power of discrimination, but because, as has been repeatedly said, of the innate pull of nature back towards the sensible world. They intuitively feel that the facts of psychical research will no more mix with the beliefs of common sense than will oil with water.

But if there is no case for rejecting or ignoring these facts, there is, on the other hand, a sound reason why scientists and leaders of thought should be careful in expressing their views about them. As Professor McDougall has put it :

' Men of science are afraid lest, if they give an inch in this matter the public will take an ell, and more. They are afraid that the least display of interest or acquiescence on their part may promote a great outburst of superstition on the part of the public, a relapse into a belief in witchcraft, necromancy, and the black arts generally, with all the moral evils which must accompany the prevalence of such beliefs. For they know that it is only through the faithful work of men of science through very recent centuries that these debasing beliefs have been in a large measure banished from a small part of the world. . . .' [1]

Psychologists, perhaps, feeling that they have to protect the reputation of a comparatively new and growing science, are more on their guard than physicists, whose science is too

[1] Presidential Address, *Proc. S.P.R.*, vol. xxxi. p. 107.

firmly established for its reputation to be in doubt. Biologists, incidentally, seem to have based their science on the non-philosophical physics of the old school, which has meanwhile passed out of existence.

The spiritualistic movement has, in addition, rendered a great disservice to psychical research by blurring the outline which separates rigorous from non-rigorous experiment and critical from non-critical deduction. It has misapplied the title of psychical research so as to make it cover both fields. Also its literature, being of a more popular kind than the annals of scientific experiment, is read by a much larger public, and so creates a general impression that psychical research is quite a different thing from what it is. It is a matter for some regret that the English Society for Psychical Research, pursuing its admirable policy of scrupulously collecting facts and expressing no collective opinions, has not in the past conceived it to be part of its duty to bring its immense store of carefully recorded observations to the knowledge of the public or to stimulate interest in their significance by the issue of readable summaries.

Meanwhile, it is quite a mistake to suppose that scientific psychical research tends to reopen the pathway to superstition : it is, on the contrary, the best safeguard against it. To quote once more from Professor McDougall's stimulating address :

' But that work,' he says, ' does not really add to the risk of relapse into barbaric superstition ; rather it is our best defence against it. For Pandora's box has been opened, the lid has been slightly lifted, and we are bound to go on and to explore its remotest corner and cranny. It is not only or chiefly the work of this Society that has raised the lid a little and exposed us to this danger. The culture of Europe has for a brief period rested upon the twin supports of dogmatic affirmation and dogmatic denial, of orthodox religion and scientific materialism. But both these supports are crumbling, both alike sapped by the tide of free enquiry. And it is the supreme need of our time that these two pillars of dogmatism shall be replaced by a single solid column of knowledge on which our culture may securely rest. It is the policy of sitting on the box that is risky ; a danger and threat to our civilization.' [1]

[1] Presidential Address, *Proc. S.P.R.*, vol. xxxi. pp. 108–9.

In any event the work of this research was well worth doing. Even if it had proved that Pandora's box was empty, that would have been a most valuable fact to have ascertained for certain.

But there is no question of that. The outcome is rather the other way. The positive discoveries of psychical research are too big for us : the human faculties revealed are too far-reaching and ubiquitous. We are frightened and embarrassed by them, and strive to put our heads comfortably back under the sand. But the issue must be faced : its implications for all departments of human thought are too grave and too important to be met by a policy of evasion ; and one of the subjects for which its importance is greatest is that of Religion.

Chapter XXIV

PSYCHICAL RESEARCH AND RELIGION

THE RELATION BETWEEN PSYCHICAL RESEARCH AND RELIGION.— The subject of this book is the scientific aspect of psychical phenomena, and religion, as such, does not fall within its province. But its concern is with the significance of the evidence as well as with the bare facts, so that it would be incomplete without some reference to the points of contact between the two subjects. They have this, at least, in common, that both deal with an influx of experience from beyond the sensible world ; both, also, show an aloofness from common experience and refuse to be assimilated with it. The influx may, indeed, be very different in the two cases ; it may, so to speak, emanate from reality at different levels, so that psychical experiences have nothing necessarily religious about them, and religious experience nothing necessarily psychical about it ; but both types of experience unite in bearing witness to the existence of something outside the sensory world, which does not lend itself to expression in intellectual terms.

In speaking of religion, one must define what one means. The kind of religion which comes as an influx of experience from a supra-sensory source is not what commonly passes by the name. The term is usually identified with belief in a set of intellectual propositions, and with some kind of church or institution. Religion of the latter kind serves really as a form of expression of the former—a representation in terms of thought and sense of that which is supra-intellectual and supra-sensuous. Its importance lies, not in what it is, or in what it states, but in what it *symbolizes*. The great nuclei of religious history have been points of influx of revelation or experience coming from without ; the religions themselves have been accretions clustered round these nuclei. So

344

Jud ism, the sacramental and mystery religions of the Roman Em)ire, and Greek philosophy, were fused together into a single alloy by the dynamic power of primitive Christianity. The life-blood and the mainspring of religion is commonly little heeded ; all attention is devoted to the outward form.

' It is always in terms of concepts and ideas,' says Otto, ' that the subject is pursued, " natural " ones moreover, such as have place in the general sphere of man's ideational life, and are not speci ically " religious." And then, with a cunning which one can hardly help admiring, men shut their eyes to that which is quite uniqu in the religious experience, even in its most primitive manif stations.' [1]

When people speak of the relation of psychical research to religion, they are usually wondering how its discoveries will agree with the dogmas of the latter, or how they will affect its vested interests, thinking of religion as something which stands or falls by these things, and can be upset by scientific discoveries in the sciences of the mind. Dr. David Forsyth in his Presidential Address to the Section of Psychiatry at one of the meetings of the Royal Society of Medicine, said : [2] ' They saw religion plainly decaying all round them, and religious faith had grown cold. Psycho-analysis had severed its very roots by showing that it belonged to the unreal and the fantasmal, and that it carried all the marks of a child-mentality.'

But everything, not religion alone, which is adapted to the general public, shows the marks of a child-mentality. As Dr. Inge says :

' A religion as believed and practised cannot be far in advance of the mental and moral capacity of its adherents. A religion succeeds, not because it is true, but because it suits its worshippers. It may be a superstition which has enslaved a philosophy ; it may be inculcated in the interest of a powerful hierarchy ; or it may have accommodated itself to the political and social movements of the time.' [3]

---

[1] Rudolf Otto, *The Idea of the Holy*, p. 4.
[2] *The Times*, November 14, 1934.
[3] W. R. Inge, *The Platonic Tradition in English Religious Thought*, p. 14.

The more important question seems to be the relation of psychical to religious *experience*. Anything which is beyond the range of the mind cannot be grasped as simple truth, but must be represented by a kind of myth. *Religion* is the unthinkable and the inexpressible—which yet does not lie without the range of experience. *Religions* are calls of attention to *Religion*, not compendiums of universal truth. Dr. Gilbert Murray makes an interesting remark in this connexion : [1]

' I will confess my own private belief, which I do not wish any one to share that, of all the books and of all the famous sayings that have come as a revelation to human beings, not one is strictly true or has any chance of being true. Nor, if you press me, do I really think that it is their business to be strictly true. They are not meant to be statements of fact. They are cries of distress, calls of encouragement, signals flashing in the darkness ; they seem to be statements in the indicative mood, but they are really in the imperative or the optative—the moods of command or prayer or longing ; often they make their effect, not by what they say but by the tone in which they say it or even by the things they leave unsaid.'

It is, then, of the relation of psychical phenomena to Religion in the singular and universal sense that I wish to speak ; and perhaps one may best take as exemplifying the latter the Christian Platonism or Neo-Platonism expounded by Dr. Inge. As is well-known, this author regards psychical research and all that it implies with deep disfavour, as being incompatible with the outlook of religious mysticism.

' Ghost stories have no attraction for the Platonist,' he writes, ' He does not believe them, and would be very sorry to have to believe them. The kind of immortality which " psychical research " endeavours to establish would be for him a negation of the only immortality which he desires or believes in. The difference between the two hopes is fundamental. Some men are so much in love with what Plotinus would call the lower soul-life, the surface-consciousness and surface-experience which make up the content of our sojourn here as known to ourselves, that they wish, if possible, to continue it after their bodies are mouldering in the grave. Others recognize that this lower soul-life is a banishment from the true

[1] *The Stoic Philosophy, Essays and Addresses*, pp. 133–4.

home of the Soul, which is in a supratemporal world, and they have no wish to prolong the conditions of their probation after the probation itself has ended, and we are quit of our " body of humiliation." ' [1]

The immortal and timeless part of us is regarded as now linked with the temporal synthesis of the present personality.

' The Soul which lives Yonder in blessed intercourse with God is not the compound (σύνθετον) which began its existence when we were born. Our true self is a denizen of the eternal world. Its home is in the sphere of the eternal and unchanging activity Yonder, even while it energizes in the execution of finite but Divine purposes here below.' [1]

Again, we read elsewhere : ' Psychical research is trying to prove that eternal values are temporal facts, which they can never be.' [2]

The indictment is, then, that psychical research seeks to substitute a future life of a temporal or mundane kind for the immortality of religious mysticism—an immortality which is a-temporal and external to, rather than successive of, this life. It implies that the ' future ' life, which psychical investigators appear to be getting in touch with, is essentially a temporal prolongation of the life of this world and, as such, excludes the life of immortality. The base, the gross, and the material is being substituted for the transcendental and the spiritual.

I think that this view rests on a misunderstanding, for it confuses psychical research with the religion or quasi-religion of spiritualism. Psychical research has nothing to do with religion, beyond the indirect relation which all the sciences bear to it ; strictly speaking it is a branch of psychology. Whatever it may discover about the human mind belongs to the department of empirical fact and not to that of religious belief. There is no necessity for any conflict between it and any belief which is founded on religious *experience*. Another point is that psychical research can scarcely be said to ' seek '

---

[1] W. R. Inge, *The Philosophy of Plotinus*, vol. ii. pp. 96–7.
[2] *Outspoken Essays* (First Series), p. 269.

to substitute one belief for another ; its aim is not to establish a particular creed but to discover truth by empirical means.

I think that this confusion has been largely fostered by the still powerful, if hidden, influence of an age-long theological tradition. According to this tradition, whatever does not appear in the world of human sense-perception must, *ipso facto*, lie within the province of religion—that for many centuries was regarded as plain and obvious. Even now, when evidence suggests that there may exist a limited life of some kind beyond the sensuous purview, religion is at once dragged into it. One must clearly recognize that a finite life other than our own, if such exists, does not acquire a religious character simply because it lies beyond the range of our physical senses. Such a life need be no more religious than the life we lead now. Religion might bear to it precisely the same relationship which it bears to this life ; it would be only a question of the scope of our senses. There is no reason at all why our present experience should have a monopoly of the finite and the mundane ; nor is there any reason why, if it does not possess such a monopoly, religion should be squeezed out of the picture. No doubt this sounds a very obvious thing to say, but thought is so coloured (largely subconsciously) by the inheritance of mediaevalism, that it is still steeped in the idea of a dualistic universe—' natural ' and ' supernatural '—and sees no further than an antithesis between the ' material ' and the ' spiritual.' The first, the ' secular ' world ; the second, the realm of religion.

This bifurcation of the universe was anthropocentric. The ' natural ' world was nothing but that which happened to enter into the conscious experience of the normal human being through his organs of sense, and the limit of the power of these organs was, for him, the boundary of nature ; in this alone ran the fiat of natural law ; beyond it lay the ' supernatural,' either governed by different laws, or merely subject to the arbitrary will of the Creator. The point was, of course, that the limits of human experience were identified with the limits of the natural world. It was rather as though a savage should look out across the ocean from the shores of his island to the visible horizon and should assume that at that point the world came to an end because *he* could see no farther. What *appears* to be the end of nature must therefore *be* the end of nature.

Incidentally, the phrase ' natural law ' seems to be an unfortunate one, because it suggests an analogy with human law. The law of the state is the arbitrary product of human will, which is usually enforced, but which may, on occasion, be suspended ; and the phrase ' natural law ' seems to have arisen out of the habit of regarding the relation of God to the human world in terms of the relation of a ruler to a state. But, when a scientist discovers a ' law of nature,' he does not discover anything of that kind. All he discovers is that this or that object or class of things possesses such and such a *character*. He discovers what properties the thing has and how it behaves. These properties and this behaviour *constitute* it what it is ; if it suddenly manifested different properties or behaved in a different way, it would simply now be something else. But the term, ' natural law,' grafted onto a theological dualism impregnated with the idea of an arbitrary ruler, has given rise to discussions about ' miracles,' and the ' suspension ' of natural laws by supernatural intervention, all of which appear to rest on a misapprehension and a misnomer.

This is a parenthesis. The theologian filled in the world beyond sense with the ' supernatural,' much as the philosopher fills it in with the ' potential.' The whole position was as anthropocentric as was pre-Copernican cosmogony. But if the only intelligible definition of ' natural ' is that which has a coherent character of some sort, the only meaning of ' supernatural ' must be ' chaotic.'

There is surely a streak of *naïveté* in the egoism which tacitly assumes that nothing of a natural kind can go on unless *we* are aware of it ! It is all of a piece with the pre-Galilean view that our planet must occupy the centre of the universe because *we* happen to live on it.

It seems to me that Dr. Inge's indictment of psychical research has been unable to free itself from the subconscious, and therefore subtle, influence of this ancient philosophy of Christendom. The simple view that psychical research is pushing human knowledge into reality a little way beyond the boundary laid down by the range of the senses, does not seem in the least to conflict with the claims of immortality or with a legitimate trust in religious experience. The clash occurs when religion is forced into the framework of an obsolete theology.

As was said above, *a* religion is an expression in intellectual terms, and a crystallization in institutional form, of *Religion*, a universal experience ; and it is not necessary to quote instances from history in order to show that *a* religion can become thoroughly worldly and materialistic. The point I wish to stress now is that human nature recoils from the contemplation of the supra-sensuous, whether it be on the level of religious or psychical experience, because nature is continually pulling it back into the world of the senses. A religion must be reduced to a this-worldly form before it can become generally acceptable. True, its creeds may appear *as if* they described or defined the supra-sensible, but a close examination will reveal that all the ideas contained in them are thoroughly this-worldly. The mystical element in the Christian Church has always been kept under in favour of rationally held propositions—a wise policy from the point of view of generality of appeal, but a policy with a price to pay. Until a religion has been brought into consonance in this way with ordinary experience, it offends the instinct which is continually pulling humanity back to common sense and to the ' normal.' No one can have failed, incidentally, to notice with what evident relief the Church of England turns from religion proper to philanthropy and social problems, because they represent a field of work which lies entirely in *this* world. It is precisely this instinct which draws people back from psychical phenomena or from the ' occult,' and gives them an uncomfortable feeling that these things are unreal and superstitious and rather foolish. We are pulled back, as if by a magnet, to the ways of common sense because our whole personality has been psychologically constructed to fit into its present world. It may perhaps be said that there are thousands of credulous people who revel in psychical things without showing any signs of a return towards common sense.

But these people have, in reality, made terms with common sense. Their view of psychic matters is as materialistic as it can be. They have brought the supra-sensible down to earth in the psychic sphere as effectively as the mediaeval Christians brought it down in the religious sphere, when they saw heaven over their heads and hell beneath their feet.

It is, I think, very important to grasp that this sense of the unreal and nebulous, which hangs over the supra-sensuous, both in the religious and psychical regions, and which leads to their neglect, is not due to the subject-matter to which they refer being non-existent or unimportant. It is due to the fact that we live in a highly specialized world, insular in the scheme of things, to which the whole of our psychical personality is adapted. This make-up of our personality goes hand in hand with the sensible world, which is itself partly a construct of its own, and works to keep out distractions which would not help life, from nature's pragmatic point of view, by making them appear unimportant if not ridiculous.

So far as the relation of the churches to psychical research is concerned, the question to be asked is, not, What do the churches think about psychical research ? but, What do the churches think about the subject-matter with which psychical research deals ? How do they meet the metaphysical problems which throng about the conception of another world, whether that conception comes from science or religion ?

Psychical and Mystical Experiences.—Although it may be true, as a general statement, to say that religious and psychical phenomena occupy different spheres, or levels, there are nevertheless certain ways in which they appear to merge into one another. Take as an example Mrs. Willett's experience when she entered a room to which she was almost a stranger to try for automatic script. At first she wandered about and looked at the pictures. Then, she said : ' I seemed to pass beyond them, as it were, into the spirit of the room—full of remembered peace and happiness and rest—a strange sense of familiarity and homelikeness. The room seemed full of unseen presences and their blessing ; it was as if barriers were swept away and I and they became one.' There are other experiences of hers of the same type, and they are very suggestive of religious mysticism. There is the same vanishing of the experience from memory, while yet the quality of it lingers ; the same struggle to recapture it ; the same sense of the futility of words ; the same indescribable feeling of fusion. The higher types of psychical experience seem, in fact, to shade off into mystical experience.

There are, of course, in religious literature, many recorded descriptions of the latter. Some of the above points are illustrated in the last canto of Dante's *Paradiso* :

> ' . . . for almost wholly faileth me
> my vision, yet doth the sweetness that was
> born of it still drop within my heart.'

There is also the longing to recapture the vision and to pass it on :

> ' O light supreme who so far doth uplift thee o'er
> mortal thoughts, re-lend unto my mind a little
> of what thou then didst seem
>
> and give my tongue such power that it may leave
> only a single sparkle of thy glory unto the folk
> to come.'

And there is the sense of oneness or fusion :

> ' Within its depths I saw ingathered, bound by
> love in one volume, the scattered leaves of all
> the universe ;
>
> substance and accidents and their relations, as
> though together fused, after such fashion that
> what I tell of is one simple flame.'

Chapter XXV

CONCLUSION

GENERAL SUMMARY.—In the preceding chapters an attempt has been made to pass in review a considerable part of that diverse field of phenomena which is included under the heading of Psychical Research.

In Part I we dealt with the spontaneous evidence and found that it revealed the existence of a cognitive faculty, possessed by at least a small fraction of mankind, and divided into four modes, which were called Telepathy, Clairvoyance, Precognition, and Retrocognition respectively. We examined a few representative examples of each class and considered the precautions taken to ensure the validity of the evidence, and came to the conclusion that the body of evidence for which these examples stood could not be accounted for by chance, fraud, exaggeration, or any other normal cause.

In Part II we saw that the same faculty revealed itself, manifesting the same subdivisions, when tested by experiment, and we passed in rapid review the historical work on the subject, dealing with contemporary work in greater detail. Here we found the explanation of chance eliminated with certainty by mathematical means. We noted the sporadic nature of the faculty when placed under test, its liability to inhibition and its extreme sensitiveness to psychological states. On the other hand, we observed the massive solidity of the character it presented beneath the subdivisions we had assigned to it, and its remarkable indifference to changes in the external conditions.

In Part III we raised the question of whether the extra-sensory faculty was capable of explanation in physical terms, and came to the conclusion that its behaviour was incompatible with any physical explanation. We then turned to the baffling

23

phenomenon of Precognition, noting its vital importance for our conception of the nature of Time, and reflecting further that this conception forms the cardinal hinge, on which depends our interpretation of the facts of science, and in particular the biological facts concerned with Emergence and Evolution. We sketched in brief outline certain theories of Precognition which have been put forward, without finding in any of them a full or convincing solution.

We then cast about for some connecting link with which to bridge the gap between Normal and Supernormal phenomena, and in doing so, turned to the philosophy of normal sense-perception as the nearest parallel with extra-sensory perception. We found it to be full of difficulties, which appear on close examination, but which in ordinary life are skilfully hidden from view ; and it forced us to the conclusion that the visible and tangible world must be far more a construct of our own than common experience had ever led us to dream of.

We then turned to the science of Physics for light on the nature of this common world, and found that its progress was marked by a series of views which were continually changing. Instead of augmenting the world of our senses and filling it in with detail, its succession of pictures moved farther and farther away from it ; nor could we see any reason for regarding one picture as truer than another, or the trend of the whole series as being towards the intrinsic nature of the real. We reflected, further, that all the conclusions of scientists rested on the evidence of their senses and could, therefore, contribute nothing towards an answer to our question, which was : In what sense and to what extent are our senses telling us the truth ? And the testimony of physiologists with regard to the processes of sense-perception was in no better case, for the same reason.

At the end of this survey, we were in a position to realize our peculiar situation. Dependent for our knowledge on the evidence of our five senses, yet entertaining grave suspicions, as the result of philosophical analysis, as to the extent to which these senses are telling us the truth, we began to have an inkling of a possible reason for the complete lack of coherence between psychical and physical phenomena. It might be that the presentations of our normal senses had been ' doctored ' by being sophisticated and adapted in a highly artificial way to our needs as biological individuals. What we thought lay spatially outside us, might, in reality, be being produced by ourselves, and so be representative of independent reality in a symbolical fashion only. The extreme difference between the presentations of the extra-sensory faculty and the normal sensory faculties might thus be due to the fact that the former had not passed through the sophisticated channels of the latter. The antinomy at any rate was there—a gulf with apparently no bridge ; and we found in this fact the main reason why psychical phenomena, despite the paramount importance they evidently possess for human knowledge, are on the whole rejected and treated with contempt. The duality gives rise to the fear that the dissonant facts, if admitted, will disrupt the scheme of the known and the familiar. Hence, those who are mentally committed to the latter try to escape from the necessity for facing the former. This was illustrated by an example of the attitude of contemporary authors of repute.

In Part IV we examined the evidence for the mediumistic trance, first considering it from the point of view of its evidential value, and passing in review the various methods which have been devised for checking this value, and for carrying out control experiments. We also reviewed the Automatisms and Cross-Correspondences.

In Part V we considered the psychology and *modus operandi* of trance phenomena of all the different kinds, and we found that communicators and communications existed in varying grades, ranging from what appeared to be hypnotic sub-personalities of the medium to communicators of a very high degree of intelligence and clarity.

We discussed the prolific sense-imagery that the trance-states reveal, and compared it, from the point of view of its generation by the percipient, with the sense-imagery of normal life ; and we looked into the mechanism of the externalization of mediumistic material.

Then we considered possible explanations of trance and allied phenomena, passing in review the Compound Theory suggested by Professor Broad, which we rejected, and the theory that the concordant automatisms might have been telepathically contrived by the minds of the living, especially by the subconscious mind of Mrs. Verrall. This theory we found improbable.

We then glanced at the physical phenomena of mediumship, noting that the results so far had been mainly inconclusive, but that the way now seemed to be opened to the solution of the problem by the use of automatic recording apparatus.

We next considered the relation of scientific psychical research to the general body of Spiritualism and the Occult. Finally, we touched on certain points of contact between psychical phenomena and Religion.

What has Psychical Research Established?—I do not think that we can point to any fact in psychical research to-day and say that it is universally accepted, unless, indeed, we regard hypnotism as being a psychical phenomenon, as it was once taken to be. At first sight, this seems to be an admission that the evidence for all psychical phenomena must be of poor quality ; but the reader who has followed me so far will realize that there may be other reasons for this. It is true that we know too little about the conditions which govern most of the phenomena to be able to produce them at will, although a certain proportion of the evidence is of an experimental kind. Certain items there are which are obtainable on demand. But some people say that they are waiting for more evidence to appear before they can make up their minds whether or not telepathy exists. These people, if they are really anxious to have their minds made up, have only to attend four or five sittings with a first-class medium, taking adequate precautions to prevent normal leakage of knowledge, and they are fairly sure to get information which cannot reasonably be explained except by telepathy. But do they want to have their minds made up ?

If we ask how many people have seriously examined the

evidence for psychical phenomena, we find that it is the merest handful ; and since the opinion of those who have not examined the evidence is worthless, we have an easy explanation of why nothing in it has been universally accepted. It is not that the evidence is bad ; it is that people are all studiously looking away from it, and are euphoniously disguising the fact by saying that the evidence is ' still in dispute ! '

But, if there is little carefully considered opinion, an increasing number of educated people do, in a loose way, accept telepathy. Interest in the subject is growing, and the climate of opinion is softening.

Under these circumstances, it is impossible to make any definite statement of what psychical research has established in the way of matter of fact. All must be a matter of personal opinion. I should myself regard the following points as established : (1) There is a faculty of extra-sensory perception which manifests itself in the modes of Telepathy, Clairvoyance, and Precognition, and probably in the fourth mode of Retrocognition ; and there is considerable evidence also for the faculty of Telaesthesia. The evidence for the existence of the extra-sensory faculty rests upon the three bases of Spontaneous, Experimental, and Trance Phenomena. (2) This evidence cannot be reasonably explained by means of any normal hypothesis, or by any combination of normal hypotheses. (3) Evidence for the existence and communication of the surviving self-principles of deceased persons is strong. This evidence can be alternatively explained, but not without an equal, if not a greater, draft on the marvellous, and departure from the recognized order.

The Telepathic and the Survivalist Theories.—A superficial reading of the facts of trance-phenomena might suggest that there are two distinct and possible explanations. (1) That they are due to telepathy from the living or, (2) that they proceed from the dead. But our discussion of the *modus operandi* of the trance should have made it clear that these two explanations are by no means clearly separable from one another. Telepathy between living minds undoubtedly exists, whether the survivalist theory is true or no, and we know too little to be able to set a limit to its powers. So that the real question is, whether it is more reasonable to postulate an expansion of telepathic and extra-sensory faculty, sufficient to explain all the facts, or to combine a more moderate theory of extra-sensory perception with the theory of survival. In either case we are carried a long way from the facts of ordinary experience.

The Telepathic Theory.—It has been already pointed out that if we attempt to explain trance-phenomena by the faculty of extra-sensory perception between living minds, the problem is twofold. (1) We have to explain how the medium obtains the information which comes through her, and (2) we have to explain the constitution of the trance-personalities who actually give the information.

(1) So long as the medium is merely supplying information known to sitters who are present with her at the time, there is no great difficulty in attributing this to telepathy from the sitters, even although the information may not have been consciously present in their minds. But in Chapter XXI we saw that the actual facts are more complicated than this. It is not infrequently the case that information is given which is not known to the sitters, but which is afterwards found to be correct. Some instances of this were given in the A. V. B. case in Chapter XIII. Further, a number of ' Proxy ' sittings have been quite successful, when the sitter knew nothing about the information supplied, and those who did know were at a distance, and in ignorance of when the sittings were being held. In addition, there are a few cases in which no one knew the facts stated. Case 8 in Chapter III was one of these, and there are others which have been omitted for lack of space. For example, a man who had been killed in the War,[1] communicating through a medium, described how a receipt was to be found in an old purse of his, and said it was to be particularly preserved. The receipt was looked for and found, and subsequently a claim for the money was made, which would have been a great drain on the mother's resources had not the receipt been there to prove that it had been already paid. In another case, the communicator described an old

[1] *Proc. S.P.R.*, vol. xxxvi. p. 303.

Log Book [1] of his in which, he said, near a table of Arabian languages, and on p. 12 or 13, would be found something very interesting to the sitter after her conversation with him. She did not know of this Log Book, and thought another book was meant, but searched for it, found the table of languages, and on p. 13 there was a curious and unusual account of the experience of passing through death. There are other cases ; and we must not forget some of the spontaneous cases, such as the Chaffin Will case (Chapter II, Case 5), in which a telepathic explanation is very far-fetched, while the survivalist explanation is straightforward and simple. And there are visions of the dying of which the same may be said, as in one case where a dying woman saw two of her relations, who, it seemed to her, had come to meet her ; and one of them was a sister who had died suddenly, and of whose death the sick woman had purposely been kept in ignorance. The telepathic theory, therefore, has difficulties to meet on the score of the source of the information given ; and this difficulty is still further increased when we take into account concordant automatisms, and ask how the pieces of the cross-correspondence jig-saws come to be distributed in such an ingenious way among the automatists.

(2) But that is only one half of the difficulty in the way of the telepathic theory, and I am not sure that it is not the smaller half. What *are* the communicators who give this information during the trance ? We may point to cases of secondary personality, recognized in abnormal psychology, such as Sally Beauchamp and Doris Fischer ; or we may point to the masquerading induced in hypnosis. But in the first of these we are dealing with the ' splitting up ' of a normal personality (although this term is probably only loosely descriptive of the fact) ; and in the second, with some kind of acting in response to suggestion. The problem of the trance-personalities is that they present characters *unknown to the medium.* An actor plays a memorized part ; the hypnotic subject does what he is told to do by the operator ; but the trance-personality, if it is subconsciously acting, *extemporizes* a part without a

[1] *Proc. S.P.R.*, vol. xxxi. p. 253.

model. How does it do it ? It gets its cue telepathically from the minds of living persons who did know the original, we might suppose. But ' telepathic leakage ' could not do that. We should have to suppose that the subconscious mind of the person who had known the communicator in life was sending out to the medium a constant stream of telepathic stage-directions. Or, if we think it more plausible, that the medium was subconsciously reaching out with some telaesthetic faculty and observing a mental model of the communicator in the mind of the other, and basing its excellent characterization on that. In either case we are postulating extra-sensory faculties of extraordinary range and power, and have moved a very long way from the idea of telepathy as ' thought-transference.'

As was pointed out in Chapter XXI, there is little or no evidence of *genuine* conscious acting in these trance-personalities ; and if we assume that they are poses unconsciously adopted by some stratum of the medium's self, we are faced with the difficulty (at least with communicators of a high type) that, while they last, there is nothing to distinguish them from real personalities. We cannot point to anything which prevents us from saying that, at any rate for the duration of the sitting, the deceased person has regained his existence. We cannot define the difference between a stratum of the medium's personality, unconsciously ' posing ' as the deceased person with such completeness as to believe itself to be the deceased person, and to manifest all the essential characteristics of that person on the one hand, and, on the other hand, a temporary but genuine re-creation of the deceased person. And if you cannot define the difference between two things, on what ground are you going to maintain that there *is* a difference ? Furthermore, how do we know that these re-creations *are* temporary ? How do we know that they do not co-exist with the medium between sittings ? And if they are temporary, does that make them less real ? We live in a glass house in this respect, for our own conscious lives are intermittent ; yet we regard ourselves as continuous personalities. So that the telepathic theory turns out to be, not, after all, an alternative to the theory of survival, so much as another, and very odd, version of that theory, namely, the version that a deceased person can survive in the form of a psychic parasite on a medium.

I think, therefore, that the outcome is that mediumistic phenomena *can* be explained by postulating sufficiently comprehensive extra-sensory and mind-creative faculties possessed by the living—faculties which go a long way beyond anything for which there is independent evidence. I would go even further in the direction of admitting it some plausibility by saying that, in my opinion, the evidence increasingly points to the existence of an extra-sensory faculty, becoming wider and more comprehensive the deeper we go beneath the threshold of consciousness. We cannot say what such a faculty might be capable of in depths of the personality far removed from the conscious self. But ' telepathy between the living ' has by this time come to mean something totally different from thought-transference between separate, conscious minds, or even between strata of such minds just below the conscious threshold. And even so, there are many cases in which even this telepathic explanation would seem strained and unnatural ; but I think it must be admitted that it is logically possible.

The real drawback to the telepathic theory is that, in order to make it work, we have to regard the living mind as something different from and immensely wider than what we commonly mean by the term, and we have to endow it with such a range of ' subliminal self ' and with such astonishing extra-sensory powers that the proposition of its survival takes on a new aspect. Having granted that the self is as unlike the human unit of everyday experience as the telepathic theory demands, the arguments which hitherto seemed to make its survival improbable, no longer apply, at least with anything like the same force. And so we find that the object which the telepathic theory was designed to fulfil, the object of providing a ' normal ' explanation, is no longer achieved. It fails to keep psychical phenomena within the orbit of the familiar and the known ; it fails to supply the coherence with ordinary facts which is demanded to give psychical phenomena a definite antecedent probability ; it fails to save the ' scientific ideology.' In these respects, it is no better than the survivalist theory. Indeed, it is worse, for, as has been pointed out, it even fails to escape *being* a survivalist theory of a very fantastic kind. As a method of compromise between psychical and ordinary phenomena, it breaks down : it does not save the naïve realism which the scientist demands ; neither does it save the plain man's ordinary view of the world. The only way to save these is to turn away from psychical phenomena altogether and deny the evidence for them out of hand. But in doing that we shall be landed in another difficulty, for we shall discover that we have denied the principle of empiricism on which the whole body of science rests. We shall have committed ourselves to the course of choosing to admit only those facts which fall in with our pre-established ideas. Here is the dilemma facing us : once psychical evidence is admitted, the battle for ' scientific ideology ' and common-sense philosophy is lost. Yet the belief in the latter is so firmly ingrained, that it is quite certain that people will cling to it with unshakable tenacity. In spite of all arguments, and in spite of palpable facts, they will go back to it again and again.

The Survivalist Theory.—It has already been pointed out that the objections to the survivalist theory are based on the wide departure which this theory involves from the common experience of life and from common notions about the natural and the probable, reinforced by discoveries of science, based ultimately on the data of common experience. We reject what does not square with this, because our inherent sense of self-importance makes us assume that *our* experience must be identical with absolute truth, at any rate in principle. The view most helpful towards overcoming this attitude seems to me to be the conception that human personality is pluralistic or monadic or hierarchical or graded in its character—none of these terms are really satisfactory, but one or other of them has to be used. Leibniz's theory was that the monadic constituents of the personality were atomic and independent, not being in communication with one another. Lord Balfour and Professor M'Dougall [1] have adopted variants of the monadic theory, modified to come more into line with psychical

[1] See his Presidential Address to the *S.P.R. Proc.*, vol. xxxi. p. 105.

facts. According to M'Dougall's view, the monads are organized in a graded hierarchy, like the ranks in an army, the controlling consciousness occupying the position of the general in command, and the psychological elements of the self being ranked as his subordinates. The controlling consciousness issues its orders in ignorance of the detailed life of its inferiors, and bases its commands on condensed reports which it receives from them. Intermonadic communication would be telepathic.

Whatever view of personality one adopts, it is difficult to see how this much truth can be denied to the theory that human personality is of the nature of a synthetic complex, and that it is in some way *graded*. A great moralist once said : ' The good that I would, I do not : but the evil which I would not, that I do.' This sentence is really a study in the reference of pronouns, and implies some sort of complex theory of the self. The dominant ' I ' which wishes to do good, would not have the wish to act contrarily to its own wish, and therefore would not do the evil : that would be to contradict itself. The ' I ' which does the evil is not the ' I ' which wishes to do the good. The former is the ' I ' of that complex synthesis of elements which we call the ' personality.' It is the ' I,' which in Pauline language includes the ' flesh '—that is to say, which includes lower elements of the synthetic self, which are *environmental* to the dominant ' I ' which wishes the good. One can see how this leads inevitably to a view of a self as graded or hierarchical. It is not a case of a mind (' I ') merely conjoined to a body (' it ') ; the body is environmental to one ' I ' and simultaneously constitutive of another, and this is true, not merely of the body, but of a number of psychological intermediaries. The subtlety of the situation lies in the fact that this dominant, and possibly ' noumenal ' ' I,' coexists with an empirical ' I,' into which enters the whole personal complex. A man can wish to do one thing and yet, because of some counter-disposed element in the self, he actually does another ; and this shows clearly that what is merely environmental to the willing ' I ' is intrinsic in the make-up of the doing ' I.' The characteristics of the personality, environmental to the willing ' I,' seem obviously to be graded. There are moments, especially in crises, when one may be surprised to find oneself a spectator of oneself, thinking, speaking, and doing ; and in this case it is the *higher* part of one's personality which the watching ' I ' recognizes as ' other ' than itself.[1]   The animal instincts lie below this again, and are still more ' other ' to the dominant ' I ' ; yet they are such that the empirical ' I ' can *identify* itself with them, and in any case they are unescapably inherent in the total, empirical self and cannot be placed outside it.   Again, the physical organism is so definitely ' other ' than the dominant ' I ' as to partake largely of the character of a thing in the external world.   Yet even the physical organism is ' I ' in some sense, though it is obviously ' it ' in another.   It is more ' I ' than one's clothes or one's possessions, but less ' I ' than one's instincts.   In passing, we might note that the right way to regard the body may be as merely the lowest grade in a continuous personal series, and that the reason why we regard it as *different* from the psychological part of ourselves and call it ' material ' may be only because it happens to fall into the perceptual range of our senses.

The point of importance for our present argument is, that the dominant or noumenal ' I ' is not *numerically* separated from the synthetic or empirical ' I '—though these are two ' I's ' in some sense, there are not two independent ' I's ' in the mathematical sense.   Distinction and unity are *both* present in a sense which we cannot understand.   There is the possibility of disunion and strife without numerical discreteness. In this lies the subtlety of selfhood—the subtlety of the one-in-many—and it transcends our thought.   Yet in it lie hidden some of the deepest implications of religion.   In the language of pietics, it accounts for the possibility of ' sin ' (indeed, the Pauline author seems in some degree to realize this).   And the mystical experience of self-transcendence of the self depends on the rising by the empirical ' I ' in some way to greater identification with the noumenal ' I.'   In this also lies the meaning of the phrase to ' lose one's soul to find it.'

What we are now concerned with is the light which this hierarchical conception of personality throws on the idea of

---

[1] See *Proc. S.P.R.*, vol. xliii. pp. 112-5.

survival. The empirical ' I ' of common Life in this world, together with the personality which it suffuses, is regarded, on the view we have been advancing in these pages, as a highly specialized product—one might almost say an artificially specialized product—adapted to a peculiar form of existence. Now, speaking broadly and generally, most of the anti-survivalist arguments arise from the incongruity of imagining this special kind of personality entering into other surroundings. The personality is a this-world product, the result of evolution in this world in a given environment, with inherited characteristics and fitting this world as hand fits glove. How can it find a place anywhere else ? It pursues its little cycle of life to its natural end, fades away and is gone. These arguments, it seems to me, are true of this specialized personality, but irrelevant to the issue in hand. That personality certainly belongs here and nowhere else ; but it is not a discretely rounded-off unit, like a pebble on the beach. That is the superficial view of common sense and of a science still in its philosophical swaddling-clothes. When we look deeply into the nature of human personality, we find that vistas of the self are hidden behind the scenes, possessing powers and qualities which science is unable to define or bring into line with other knowledge by its superficial methods. That, indeed, is the reason why the deeper research called ' psychical ' is so unpopular. It overturns the complacency of successful science, which has been dealing with the surface-appearance of things based on the findings of the senses. The principle of selfhood and the criterion of being ' I ' are far too subtle to be captured by a net of reason such as ours ; they refuse to be held by our categories of thought ; they transcend and elude every effort we make to grasp them. So do the faculties of extra-sensory cognition and, for that matter, so does the nature of Time and indeed of everything if we enter into it deeply enough. If we try again, and say that this ' self ' beneath the threshold of consciousness is in reality an appearance of a ' cosmic reservoir ' of a pan-psychic kind, we find we are still merely using the language of mechanics, just as we are if we speak of selves as being numerically distinct units. Nothing which we can possibly think of or imagine describes the incomprehensible nature of the ' I.' The point at which we can get enlightenment is where we can see in some way that our present personalities are abstractions from something very much larger, into which the principle of selfhood somehow enters. ' Survival,' therefore, as a term, is something of a misnomer. It implies projection of the *present personality* (with its own kind of Time still clinging about it) into conditions entirely alien to it. Pre-existence in the same way implies the entry of the present personality into this world from an entirely alien state in the past. Neither of these seem to be on the cards. What psychical research suggests is that the complex personality is resolved at death. This resolution is not so much a process of a ' thing ' coming to an end as of a group-complex reshaping or changing its internal relations. It need not destroy the intrinsic character of the constituents ; in particular, it need not destroy the prinicple of the dominant ' I.' Would these elements, or, at least, some of them, be re-integrated in the form of a new and stable complex ? If so, that would, in our view, *ipso facto*, place the new personal complex in a new and stable world of appearance. Thus, we should substitute for ideas of survival and pre-existence the vaguer but wider conception of aggregates or complexes of grades of being, animated by an ' I-principle,' coagulating themselves out of a greater whole and passing in so-called ' death ' into new forms of coagulation. The term ' survival ' would then be seen to be an importation of an idea belonging to the smaller life into the conditions of the larger life, where it has no real application. The idea would be more nearly expressed by saying that selfhood *transcends* the conditions of the present world in some non-temporal way—Time, at any rate as we understand it, being one of the conditions of the present highly special world accompanying one special grouping of the personality.

Let us remember how, in Chapter XIX, Mrs. Willett, in the ' Symposium ' scene, broke off her normal memories and entered into a new field of experience without ceasing to *be* Mrs. Willett. And let us reflect again that this is no isolated case, but is the general tendency of supernormal states of the personality. We shall then realize that there is a tremendous truth behind all this. We think of ourselves, in our earth-adapted personalities, as being the norm of selfhood. But what this little glimpse into psychical phenomena suggests is that there are many possible metamorphoses of the person-ality, which can be integrated under the same ' I-principle,' the latter being characterized by a ' unity ' which is neither the unity of numerical distinctness nor is it dependent on temporal continuity of its qualities nor on anything which our minds are able to grasp. Personality is not the same thing as this ' I-principle '—this inscrutable something which we know only in the unique and unanalysable experience of being ' I.' Personality is a shifting, disruptable, recombinable, adaptable thing ; but the real ' I ' is indefinable and unthinkable and lies behind all this. It is the central mystery round which the whole world of experience revolves.

Conclusion.—The discussion of survival inevitably leads to wide speculation ; but there is this excuse for it, that psychical research has revealed no small thing. Either it is all a fantasy and the evidence we have quoted is valueless ; or, if this is not the case, it is a very big thing indeed. If the evidence is value-less, this fact could, and should, be demonstrated by the many critics who ridicule the subject. They should show, with clear application to detail, what is the true, normal explanation of the leading pieces of evidence, how this normal explanation accounts for the facts better than the supernormal explanation and that it is, on the whole, more reasonable. But that is what the critics never do. Criticism there is in plenty, but, like the Wells-Huxley criticism, it is irrelevant to the serious body of fact and is merely an index of the psychological bias of the critic. Though interesting, it leads nowhere. Why is it that the critic, who is so sure that the supernormal is rubbish that he holds it up to scorn, never has the courage of his convictions when faced with detailed and sober facts ? If the evidence is sound, its significance is enormous precisely because it refuses to fit into the framework of ordinary human experience. It surrounds that experience like a sea of reality encompassing an island world of appearance, which has been carved out of it. The ' supernormal ' is just reality beyond our sensuous ken. This is the view which has been developed above : the hiatus between the physical and the psychical has appeared all through our survey and we have found it unescapable. Explanations which seemed as though they might have bridged this gulf have been considered, such as a physical theory of telepathy and of clairvoyance ; various theories of precognition and a telepathy-among-the-living theory of trance-phenomena ; but all had to be rejected (at least in the form put forward), because they failed to give a convincing explanation. In answer to the question : Why cannot psychical facts be assimilated with the ordinary world which we know and understand ? the answer here suggested has been : Because we do not understand the ordinary world except in a superficial way. It is a system of appearances developed for the purpose of biological utility and that is why deeper reality cannot be explained in terms of it. For example, we try to explain Precognition in terms of Time ; but when we look into the matter we discover that we do not know what we mean by Time or by ' novelty ' or ' change,' nor can we strictly define the meaning of the phrase, ' Might have been.' It is true that the view here suggested leaves countless things unexplained. It does not so much explain as point out the direction in which an explanation lies—if only we could follow the road pointed out.

It may be as well to sum up briefly the view of trance-mediumship to which, I think, the balance of the evidence points. Some kind of psychological organism is built up within the medium of a more or less plastic and suggestible kind (this is Mr. Richmond's ' communicator-vehicle '), comparable in some respects with a secondary personality. It is endowed with extra-sensory faculty, and in poorer types of trance-mediumship there may be little or nothing more than this. Then one gets a masquerading caricature—probably a dressed-up sub-personality of a hypnotic type. But in higher types of mediumship this communicator-vehicle is made use of by an independent entity, which is sometimes, though perhaps not always, an entity animated by the still-existing self-principle of a deceased person. (This is Mr. Richmond's ' communicator-impulse.') Trance-mediumship is also complicated by the fact that there are ' controls ' ; but these may probably be explained on the same general principles as the communicators. A temporary combination is formed between the communicator-impulse and the communicator-vehicle, which constitutes the trance-personality. This latter (in some ways reminiscent of Dr. Broad's Compound Theory) is a variable thing : the stronger the influence of the communicator-impulse, the better it can control and mould the communicator-vehicle to its will, and the more the trance-personality resembles the deceased person it represents. At best, this resemblance may be very strong and lifelike ; but there are all grades down to the most ridiculous travesty. The sense in which it may be true to say that the trance-personality *is* the deceased person may be more or less this. When the deceased person died, the complex synthesis forming his personality underwent a certain amount of disintegration, shedding at any rate its lower elements, and the rest re-integrating into a new, stable complex, with how much or how little change it is impossible to say. On the view above suggested, any stable state of the personality will be accompanied by a stable world of appearance, which is the work of perceptual machinery interwoven in the personality. Unstable states of the personality are accompanied by unstable (' hallucinatory ') worlds of appearance. The inscrutable ' I-principle,' which animated the living person, also animates the new personality. During trance-communications, this new personality undergoes a certain amount of modification in order to join itself in temporary union with the medium's communicator-vehicle. It becomes deranged in the process of helping to form the trance-personality, and harks back to something more or less resembling its former terrestrial self, and while doing so, may even forget a good deal about its other-worldly state of existence. This view is, of course, only a barest outline, but it seems to give a natural and straightforward explanation of the facts as far as it goes, and it makes less demand on the bizarre and the marvellous than does a theory of pseudo-communicators telepathically and wholly constructed

24

by and in the minds of the living.   It involves genuine survival ;
but, as has been pointed out, the objections to survival are
really directed against a different conception from this—the
conception that *this* personality and *this* life are somehow
projected without change into another.   People try to draw
everything *into* their present world in order to explain it,
and are very loth to admit that there is a region in which the
writ of human reason does not run.

The essence of the present point of view is, then, that the
forms of our present knowledge are relative to and contingent
upon the structure of our personality, and when that personality is modified (as in supernormal states it is) the modes of
appearance under which we become cognisant of the independent world are modified with it.   It is the structure of the
self which is the cardinal feature in all these phenomena.   As
Dr. Schiller rightly says : ' The individual man, which science
seemed to abstract from and philosophy despised, is after all
the ultimate principle of unity and order, because it is the only
available agency of selection.   It stands at the core and centre
of the cosmos and occupies the sole point at which the various
sorts of reality intersect, the sole position from which they
can be controlled and unified.' [1]   The further science proceeds,
the more this fact comes to light.   Physics, the oldest and
furthest developed of the experimental sciences, and once the
most independent and objective, now recognizes the relativity
of all its observations to the observer.   At the end of his
exposition of the Theory of Relativity, Sir Arthur Eddington
writes this sentence : ' We have found a strange footprint on
the shores of the unknown.   We have devised theories, one
after another, to account for its origin.   At last we have succeeded in reconstructing the creature that made the footprint.
And lo ! it is our own.' [2]

If this is the conclusion of modern physics, a hundred
times more is it the conclusion of psychical research.   The
world reflects man like a mirror, but nature has skilfully
blinded him to the fact.   Yet this fact is, at the present time,

[1] F. C. S. Schiller, *Must Philosophers Disagree ?* p. 350.
[2] *Space, Time, and Gravitation*, p. 201.

the most important thing to realize, if we wish to make any further advance in knowledge. To penetrate behind the mirror and discover what lies there is, indeed, a very difficult task. Yet, we can penetrate a certain distance—far enough, I think, to see signposts pointing into the unknown ; but whether we shall ever travel far along the roads they indicate is very doubtful. The human mind is a very limited thing, and ' man is not born to solve the problem of the universe, but to find out where the problem begins.'

APPENDIX

THE *Proceedings* of the English Society for Psychical Research may be purchased from the Secretary, 31 Tavistock Square, London, W.C.1, and are also to be found in the following Libraries :

Great Britain

The City Public Libraries, Birmingham 1.
The University, Birmingham.
Public Library, Brighton.
The University, Bristol.
Glasgow Society for Psychical Research, 102 Bath Street, Glasgow.
The University, Glasgow.
Leeds Library, Leeds.
The University, Leeds.
Constitutional Club, London, W.C.2.
Dr. Williams's Library, Gordon Square, London, W.C.1.
Guildhall Library, London, E.C.2.
Theosophical Society, 12 Gloucester Place, London, W.1.
John Rylands Library, Manchester.
Literary and Philosophical Society, Newcastle-upon-Tyne.
Public Library, Newcastle-upon-Tyne.
Public Libraries, Rochdale, Lancs.

United States

Amsterdam Free Library, Amsterdam, N.Y.
Enoch Pratt Free Library, Baltimore.
Boston Athenæum, Boston, Mass.
Bowdoin College Library, Brunswick, Maine.
Grosvenor Library, Buffalo, N.Y.
Harvard College Library, Cambridge, Mass.
Meadville Theological School, Chicago, Ill.
University of Cincinnati, Ohio.
Western Reserve University, Cleveland, Ohio.
Public Library, Cleveland, Ohio.

New Hampshire State Library, Concord, N.H.
Iowa State Library, Des Moines, Iowa.
Pennsylvania State Library, Harrisburg, Pa.
Case Memorial Library, Hartford, Conn.
Haverford College Library, Haverford, Pa.
Public Library, Los Angeles, Cal.
University of Minnesota, Minneapolis, Minn.
Yale University, New Haven, Conn.
Public Library, Jersey City, New Jersey.
Public Library, New York.
Public Library, Omaha, Nebraska.
Leland Stanford Junior University, Palo Alto, Cal.
University of Pennsylvania, Pa.
Public Library of Philadelphia, Pa.
Ambrose Swasey Library, Rochester, N.Y.
Mercantile Library Association, St. Louis, Mo.
James Jerome Hill Reference Library, St. Paul, Minn.
Public Library, Salt Lake City, Utah.
Public Library, Seattle, Washington.
Swarthmore College Library, Swarthmore, Pa.
University of Illinois, Urbana, Ill.
Library of Congress, Washington, D.C.
Wellesley College Library, Wellesley, Mass.

Australia

Public Library, Adelaide.
Commonwealth Parliamentary Library, Canberra.
Public Library, Melbourne.
Public Library of New South Wales, Sydney.

India

Adyar Library, Adyar, Madras.
Jamsetjee Nesserwanjee Petit Institute, Bombay.

Also in Berlin, Munich, Amsterdam, Oslo, Copenhagen, Pietermaritzburg, Natal, and Reykjavik, Iceland.

INDEX

PRINTED BY
MORRISON AND GIBB LTD.,
LONDON AND EDINBURGH

1311